A SKETCH OF SEMITIC ORIGINS

SOCIAL AND RELIGIOUS

A SKETCH

OF

SEMITIC ORIGINS

SOCIAL AND RELIGIOUS

BY

GEORGE AARON BARTON, A.M., Ph.D.
ASSOCIATE PROFESSOR OF BIBLICAL LITERATURE AND
SEMITIC LANGUAGES IN BRYN MAWR COLLEGE

WIPF & STOCK · Eugene, Oregon

Wipf and Stock Publishers
199 W 8th Ave, Suite 3
Eugene, OR 97401

A Sketch of Semitic Origins
Social and Religious
By Barton, George Aaron
Softcover ISBN-13: 978-1-6667-6340-9
Hardcover ISBN-13: 978-1-6667-6341-6
eBook ISBN-13: 978-1-6667-6342-3
Publication date 10/28/2022
Previously published by The Macmillan Company, 1902

This edition is a scanned facsimile of the original edition published in 1902.

TO

My Teachers

CRAWFORD HOWELL TOY, A.M., LL.D.
DAVID GORDON LYON, Ph.D., D.D.
AND
JOSEPH HENRY THAYER, D.D., Litt.D.

Professors in Harvard University

THIS VOLUME IS INSCRIBED
IN GRATITUDE AND AFFECTION

PREFACE

THE studies which have culminated in this volume have occupied much of my attention for the past eleven years, and have previously led to the publication of several articles. In the autumn of 1898, while giving a course of lectures on Semitic religion, the various parts of the subject grouped themselves so coherently in my mind that I could no longer doubt that these studies had led me to the discovery of the path trodden by the Semites in the journey from savagery to civilization, in the course of which the most characteristic features of their social and religious life were created. Since then the details have been worked out with as much care as the complex duties which attach to a very comprehensive chair would permit, and are here submitted to scholars.

The writer is well aware that to many of his fellow workers in Semitic studies, who have been engaged in working different mines in our large territory, any attempt to sketch the course of Semitic evolution will seem premature and impossible. It is the writer's conviction, nevertheless, that he has chanced upon the trail along which the Semites dragged themselves during those weary centuries when they were working their way from savagery to civilization, and that he has had the good fortune in some places to identify their fossil footprints and to perceive the meaning of those identified in many places by others. Here and there an identification of the exact course of the trail is not at present possible, the luxuriant forests, the populous cities, or the overflowing seas of later civilizations have so buried the trail under thick jungles, massive mounds, or strata of rock. Enough of the trail can still be detected to render its general course certain, and to enable us to guess with approximate accuracy where its course must have lain at those points which are hidden from view. Where it is necessary to guess at the direction of this old Semitic pathway, I have endeavored to indicate the course which it seems to me most probable that it followed. In these instances future investigations may show that I have not divined with exactness all its windings and curves, but such knowledge will be welcomed by none more gladly than by myself.

The study of primitive Semitic life necessarily brings to view many unsavory details. Professional students will readily understand the necessity for treating these in the spirit in which it is done. Should this volume chance to fall into the hands of any others, they are reminded that it is a study primarily not of the pure white lily which has sprung from Semitic soil, but of the chemistry of that soil itself. At the conclusion of the book the lily is not only described and appreciated, but a point of view is gained where it can be valued the more highly because we know the blackness of the mire from which it springs. The Power which could bring such purity from such unpromising antecedents impresses us anew, and, when we reflect a little further, the wisdom of the Providence, who prepared in such a soil the very elements which the lily needed for its earthly nourishment, shines out in clearer light. Such a reader is asked to judge the book not from the first impression which its sociological studies may make upon him, but by the vantage ground gained at the end.

In the preparation of this volume I have been greatly helped by my colleague, Professor Lindley M. Keasbey, who first called my attention to the economic importance of the palm tree, who has given me much indispensable information in regard to sociological literature and theories, and has made many valuable criticisms and suggestions concerning the sociological portion of the work. Without his aid this portion of the book must have been far more imperfect than it is. My thanks are also due to my colleague, Miss Florence Bascom, Ph.D., who, in like manner, rendered invaluable aid in those portions of the work which touch upon geological data, and to my friend, Professor W. Max Müller of Philadelphia, who generously loaned me from his library books bearing on the Hamites which were otherwise inaccessible. I am also greatly indebted to my wife, who has drawn the maps for this volume, carefully read all the proofs, and made many valuable criticisms and suggestions. My obligations to other scholars are numerous and great. An endeavor has been made in the foot-notes to acknowledge these, but in some parts of the work, as in the chapter on Yahwe, the names of some of those whose work has indirectly contributed much to my thought could not be made to appear in a definite reference. To all such I thankfully acknowledge my obligation. The articles of Thomas Tyler in the *Jewish Quarterly Review* of July, 1901, and of Hans H. Spoer in *AJSL.* of October, 1901, on the Tetragrammaton reached me too late to be noticed in discussing the origin of the name "Yahwe." I cannot see, however, that they would have materially changed the treatment of the subject. The references to Hilprecht's *OBI.* are to the form in which the work first appeared. Those who have the later reprint should add 214 to the number of the page references in Part II in order to find the references in their edition.

I cease work upon the volume, conscious of its many imperfections, but with the hope that it may contribute a little to the knowledge of its great theme.

BRYN MAWR, PA.,
November, 1901.

CONTENTS

CHAPTER I
THE CRADLE OF THE SEMITES 1

CHAPTER II
PRIMITIVE SEMITIC SOCIAL LIFE 30

CHAPTER III
SEMITIC RELIGIOUS ORIGINS 81

CHAPTER IV
TRANSFORMATIONS AMONG THE SOUTHERN AND WESTERN SEMITES 123

CHAPTER V
TRANSFORMATIONS IN BABYLONIA 155

CHAPTER VI
SURVIVALS 233

CHAPTER VII
YAHWE 269

CHAPTER VIII

PAGE

BRIEF ESTIMATE OF SEMITIC SOCIAL AND RELIGIOUS INFLUENCE ON THE NON-SEMITIC WORLD 309

GENERAL INDEX 323

INDEX OF SCRIPTURE REFERENCES 339

ABBREVIATIONS USED IN THE SUBSEQUENT PAGES

AJSL. *American Journal of Semitic Languages and Literatures.*

AL[1,2,3,4]. *Assyriche Lesestüke*, von Friedrich Delitzsch, 1st, 2d, 3d, and 4th editions.

BA. *Beiträge zur Assyriologie und semitischen Sprachwissenschaft*, herausgegeben von Friedrich Delitzsch und Paul Haupt.

CIS. *Corpus Inscriptionum Semiticarum.*

CTBM. *Cuneiform Texts from Babylonian Tablets, etc., in the British Museum*, London, 1896–1901.

HWB. *Assyrisches Handwörterbuch*, von Friedrich Delitzsch, Leipsig, 1896.

JAOS. *Journal of the American Oriental Society.*

JBL. *Journal of Biblical Literature.*

KAT[2]. *Keilinschriften und das alte Testament*, von E. Schrader, 2d edition.

KB. *Keilinschriftliche Bibliothek*, herausgegeben von E. Schrader.

OBI. *The Babylonian Expedition of the University of Pennsylvania. Series A: Cuneiform Texts. Vol. I, Old Babylonian Inscriptions*, edited by H. V. Hilprecht, Philadelphia, 1893 to 1896.

PAOS. *Proceedings of the American Oriental Society.*

Petermann's Mittheilungen; i.e. *Mittheilungen aus Justes Perthes geographischer Anstalt wichtige neue Erforschungen auf dem gesammelt Gebiete der Geographie*, von A. Petermann.

R. *The Cuneiform Inscriptions of Western Asia*, edited by Henry Rawlinson. I R., II R., etc., Vols. I, II, etc., of the same.

SBOT. *The Sacred Books of the Old and New Testaments*, edited by Paul Haupt.

ZA. *Zeitschrifte für Assyriologie.*

ZATW. *Zeitschrift der alttestamentliche Wissenschaft*, edited by Stade.

ZDMG. *Zeitschrift der deutschen Morgenländischen Gesellschaft.*

HAMITO-SEMITIC WORLD

A SKETCH OF SEMITIC ORIGINS, SOCIAL AND RELIGIOUS

CHAPTER I

THE CRADLE OF THE SEMITES

IN approaching a study of the social and religious origins of the Semitic peoples, it is necessary, first of all, to ask: Where did the Semitic race take its rise? Where was it differentiated from other races, and in what environment of climate and soil were its early institutions born? Man, like all other creatures, is profoundly influenced by his surroundings. The sturdy character of the Anglo-Saxon, though for a time it may survive in the tropics, is not created there; nor has the careless laziness of the negro been bred in the arctic north. To understand the earliest religious conceptions of the Semitic peoples, we must study the social organization in which they had their birth; and to form a correct theory of their social organization, it is necessary to study its physical environment.

Our inquiry is, however, beset at the very threshold with grave difficulties. The evidence with which we have to deal is very slight, and is differently interpreted by different scholars. The best authorities widely differ. In recent years, four different theories as to the location of the Semitic cradle land have been put forward, in which Babylonia, Arabia, and North Africa are respectively made the primitive home of these peoples.

1. The advocates of the Babylonian theory have been von Kremer, Guidi, and Hommel.

Von Kremer set forth his views in two articles published in 1875, in *Das Ausland*.¹ He reached his results from a comparison of the vocabularies of the different Semitic tongues. He concluded that before the formation of the different Semitic dialects, they had a name for the camel which appears in all of them; whereas they had no common names for the date-palm and its fruit or for the ostrich. The camel the Semites knew while they were yet one people, dwelling together; the date-palm and ostrich they did not know. Now the region where there is neither date-palm nor ostrich, and yet where the camel has been known from the remotest antiquity, is the great central tableland of Asia, near the sources of the Oxus and the Jaxartes, the Jaiḥūn and Saiḥūn. Von Kremer thinks the Semitic emigration from this region preceded the Aryan or Indo-European, perhaps under pressure from the latter race; and he holds that the Semites first settled in Mesopotamia and Babylonia, which he looks upon as the oldest Semitic centre of civilization.

Similarly, the Italian Orientalist, Ignazio Guidi, wrote in 1879 a memoir upon the primitive seat of the Semitic peoples, which appeared among the publications of the Reale Academia dei Lincei.² His line of argument and his conclusions are similar to those of von Kremer. His method of induction appears to have been somewhat broader than von Kremer's, whose work seems to have been unknown to him. He took into consideration the words in the various Semitic languages which denote the configuration of the earth's surface, the varieties of soil, the changes of the seasons and climate, the names of minerals and animals. He concluded that Babylonia was the first centre of

---

¹ This article was published in *Das Ausland*, Vol. IV, Nos. 1 and 2, and was entitled "Semitische Culturentlehnungen aus dem Pflanzen und Thierreiche."

² The title of Guidi's paper was "Della sede primitiva dei popoli Semitici." It is inaccessible to me; my account of it is drawn from Wright's *Comparative Grammar of the Semitic Languages*, p. 5.

Semitic life, and that the primitive Semites in Babylonia were immigrants from the lands south and southwest of the Caspian Sea. This conclusion Driver, in the second edition of his *Use of the Tenses in Hebrew*,[1] was inclined to accept.

Not radically different from this is the view of Hommel, also published in 1879. Like Guidi, he held that lower Mesopotamia, i.e. Babylonia, and not upper Mesopotamia on the one hand nor Arabia on the other, was the home of the primitive Semitic people.[2] This view was accepted by Vlock in the article "Semites," in Herzog's *Real-Encyclopedie*.[3] Hommel has since shifted the primitive home to upper Mesopotamia, and now holds that it was the home of these peoples before the separation of the Semites from the Hamites, or, at least, from the Egyptian branch of that stock. Egypt was, he thinks, colonized from Babylonia, so that the civilization of the former country was derived from that of the latter.[4]

This linguistic method of investigation is, however, precarious. As Nöldeke has pointed out, the fact that one word now denotes an object in all the Semitic languages, may be due to borrowing from one tongue by another in remote centuries, the causes of which we cannot now trace, while the fact that a word is not common to all the languages of the group may not necessarily signify that the primitive Semites were ignorant of the object which it connotes, but may be due to the displace-

---

[1] Cf. p. 250 n.

[2] See his *Die Namen der Säugthiere bei den südsemitischen Völkern*, Leipzig, 1879, p. 406 ff.; and *Die semitischen Völkern und Sprachen*, I, 1881, p. 63.

[3] For a translation of Vlock's article see *Hebraica*, II, p. 147 f.

[4] See his article "Ueber den Grad der Verwandtschaft des Altägyptischen mit dem Semitischen," *Beiträge zur Assyriologie*, II, p. 342 ff. (1891-2); also "Die Identität der ältesten babylonischen und ägyptischen Gottergenealogie und der babylonischen Ursprung der ägyptischen Kultur," *Transactions of the International Congress of Orientalists*, London, 1892, pp. 218-244; and his article, "Babylonia," Hastings's *Dictionary of the Bible*, 1898.

ment of the term by another under circumstances which now escape us.¹

2. Opposed to the view that Mesopotamia is the cradle of the Semites, is the view that Arabia was the primitive home. This theory was defended by Sprenger in 1861² and has since been reaffirmed by him. He regards it as an historical law that agriculturists do not become nomads, and declares that he would as soon think that the dolphin formerly dwelt on the height of the Alps, or the goat in the sea, as to think that mountaineers would become nomadic. Then, after describing the Nafûd and the general features of central Arabia, he concludes: "It is of no importance whether the inhabitants are autochthones or are from other neighboring tribes, the Nejd is the fastness of the above-mentioned lands (Syria and Mesopotamia), which has impressed its character upon the Semites."³ In like manner, in his later work, he says: "All Semites are, according to my conviction, successive layers of Arabs. They deposited themselves layer on layer; and who knows, for example, how many layers had preceded the Canaanites whom we encounter at the very beginning of history?"⁴

Sayce also, in 1872,⁵ declared: "The Semitic traditions all point to Arabia as the original home of the race. It is the only part of the world which has remained exclu-

---

¹ See Nöldeke's *Semitischen Sprachen*, Leipzig, 1887, p. 3 ff. (2d ed. 1899), and his article, "Semitic Languages," in the *Encyclopædia Britannica*, 9th ed.

² See his *Das Leben und Lehre des Mohammad*, Berlin, 1861, I, p. 241 ff.; also his *Alte Geographie Arabiens*, 1875, p. 293.

³ "Gleichveil ob die Einwohner Autochthonen sind oder aus andern Gegenden stammen, das Nejd ist die Veste jener Länder, welche den Semiten ihren Charakter aufgedruct haben." *Leben und Lehre des Mohammad*, Vol. I, pp. 242, 243.

⁴ "Alle Semiten sind nach meiner Ueberzeugung abgelagerte Araber. Sie lagerten sich Schichte auf Schichte, und wer weiss, die wie vielte Schichte zum Beispiel die Kanaaniter, welche wir zu Anfang der Geschichte wahrnehmen, waren." *Alte Geog. Arabiens*, p. 293.

⁵ *Assyrian Grammar*, p. 13.

sively Semite." The racial characteristics — intensity of faith, ferocity, exclusiveness, imagination — can best be explained, he thinks, by a desert origin.

Schrader, in 1873,[1] expressed views of the same nature. As a result of a long examination of the religious, linguistic, and historico-geographical relations of the Semitic nations to one another, he concludes that Arabia is the cradle of these peoples.

De Goeje also, in his academical address for 1882,[2] declared himself in favor of the view that central Arabia is the home of the Semitic race, as a whole. Like Sprenger, he lays it down as a rule that mountaineers never become inhabitants of the steppe and nomadic shepherds, and so rejects the notion that the Semites can have descended from the mountains of Arrapachitis to become dwellers in the plains and swamps of Babylonia. He shows, in contrast, how nomads are constantly passing over into agriculturalists with settled habitations; how villages and towns are gradually formed, with cultivated lands around them; and how the space needful for the pasture land of the nomad is gradually curtailed until, for want of land, he is compelled to go elsewhere. So it was, he holds, with central Arabia; and, as a result, its nomadic population was continually overstepping bounds in every direction and planting itself in Oman, Yemen, Syria, and Babylonia. Successive layers of emigrants would push their predecessors farther forward until the whole of Mesopotamia, and even portions of Africa, shared the same fate.

Wright, whose account of De Goeje's work I have largely reproduced, after giving a résumé of this argument, observes[3] that this process has often been repeated in historical times, in which Arabic emigration has flooded

---

[1] See his article, "Die Abstammung der Chaldäer und die Ursitz der Semiten," *ZDMG.*, XXVII, pp. 397–424, especially p. 420 ff.
[2] *Het Vaderland der Semitische Volken.*
[3] *Comparative Grammar of the Semitic Languages*, p. 8.

Syria and Mesopotamia. He therefore accepts the view that Arabia is the cradle land of the Semitic race.

3. Still another theory, which is, in some respects, as will appear later, a modification of the foregoing, is that the earliest home of the Semites is to be found in Africa. Thus Palgrave holds [1] that the strong racial resemblances between the Arabs, Abyssinians, Berbers, etc., — especially the form of the jaw and the small calf of the leg, — together with their social affinity and linguistic similarity, lead to the view that the pure Semites of the peninsula originally came from an African rather than an Asiatic direction.

Similarly, Gerland reaches, on the basis of physical resemblances, such as the formation of the skull, and on linguistic grounds, the conclusion that all the Asiatic Semites can be traced in their beginnings to the North African regions. Gerland's view is in some respects peculiar. He holds to the racial unity of the African races, and regards the Semites as one of them. The Hamites and the Semites are to him one people, and even the Bantus are, he thinks, related to them.[2]

So G. Bertin advocated, in 1882, the view that the Semites and Hamites originated together in Africa, that the Semites crossed into Arabia, via Suez, and developed their special racial characteristics in Arabia Petra.[3]

Nöldeke, too, in 1887,[4] accepted the same view; but he put it forth not as a fixed theory, but as a modest hypothesis. Brinton, in 1890,[5] championed this hypothesis. He

---

[1] Article "Arabia," *Encyc. Brit.*, 9th ed.

[2] See the exhaustive article "Ethnography," *Iconographic Encyc.*, Vol. I, which is a translation of the author's German work on the same subject. He holds that sporadic traces of prognathism and woolly hair among the Semites is an argument in favor of his view (cf. pp. 369, 370).

[3] *Journal of the Anthropological Institute*, Vol. XI, p. 431 ff.

[4] *Die semitischen Sprache*, p. 9. Also his article "Semitic Languages," *Encyc. Brit.*, 9th ed.

[5] See his *Cradle of the Semites*, Philadelphia, 1890; also his *Races and Peoples*, New York, 1890, p. 132.

attempted to localize, somewhat more specifically, the place in North Africa whence the progenitors of the Semites migrated. He argued that popular tradition, comparative philology, ethnology, and archæology, all point to "those picturesque valleys of the Atlas which look forth to the Great Ocean and the setting sun." His argument from popular tradition is based on a passage in the early chapters of Genesis, and is, as will be pointed out below, irrelevant; but his philological and ethnological arguments are valid, as will be shown in the proper place.

Morris Jastrow also, in a paper published under the same cover with Brinton's,[1] accepts the African origin of the Semites, although he rejects Brinton's special locality in the African northwest as unsupported by the evidence.

Likewise, Keane,[2] who regards Mauritania as the original home and centre of dispersion, not of the Hamites and Semites only, but of the whole Caucasian race, naturally holds that the Semites are of African origin. In his latest work,[3] he regards south Arabia as the earliest home of the Semites after their migration from African soil, and therefore their point of departure for their several national homes. Ripley, after reviewing the various opinions, concludes that "the physical traits of the Arabs fully corroborate Brinton's and Jastrow's hypothesis of African descent."[4]

This theory, that the primitive Semitic home was in Africa, is, as the late Robinson Smith pointed out,[5] not inconsistent with the theory that Arabia was their earliest Asiatic home, and the point from which they dispersed. If they orginated in Africa, the arguments for the view that the Arabian peninsula was their cradle land after

[1] *Cradle of the Semites.*
[2] *Ethnology,* Cambridge, 1896, p. 392.
[3] *Man, Past and Present,* 1899, p. 490.
[4] *The Races of Europe,* New York, 1899, p. 376.
[5] Wright's *Comparative Semitic Grammar,* p. 9 n.

their migration from the neighboring continent are, in a good degree, reënforced.

Lastly, Nathaniel Schmidt suggests, in a paper read at the Congress of Religions in Paris in 1900, that the Semites may have entered Arabia originally from Puaint, — Abyssinia and Somali, — and that they lived in Arabia long enough to have received their special characteristics from its environment.

4. Another view — that Arabia was the original home of the Hamites and Semites, and that the former migrated thence to Africa — finds supporters among some Egyptologists. Thus, Wiedemann holds that the autochthones of Egpyt were a race kindred to the Lybians, and that the Egyptians of the historical period came into the country from Arabia,[1] — an opinion which de Morgan shares.[2]

Similarly, Erman has recently expressed his conviction [3] that Arabia is the home of the whole Hamito-Semitic race, that the Egyptian, the Berber languages, and the languages of Somaliland and East Africa are Semitic in origin, though of course corrupted by admixture with African elements. On this view, Arabia was the cradle land of the Hamites as well as the Semites, the Hamitic migrations to the westward antedating the Semitic migrations to the eastward and northward. Erman holds that this westward migration took place in two streams, one to Egypt and North Africa, the other to East Africa; while the poor region of Nubia possessed nothing to attract Semitic settlers.

---

[1] Cf. de Morgan's *Recherches sur les origines de l'Egypte*, Vol. II (1897), pp. 219, 223, and 228.

[2] Cf. *op. cit.*, Vol. I, p. 196 ; Vol. II, pp. 52, 53. But cf. W. Max Müller's review in *Oriental Literaturzeitung*, I, 78 ff. This theory has also been successfully combatted by Sergi (*The Mediterranean Race*, pp. 90–100) who has shown that the Naqada tombs do not reveal a race different from the later Egyptian, but simply in an earlier stage of development.

[3] Cf. Erman's article "Die Flexion des ägyptischen Verbums," in *Sitzungsberichte der kg. Ak. d. Wiss. zu Berlin*, 1900, pp. 317–353, especially pp. 350–353.

Is it possible, in view of such slight and contradictory evidence, and such conflicting opinions, to find on this matter any secure standing ground? In endeavoring to answer this question, we may take our point of departure from the kinship and differences between the Hamitic and Semitic languages. These groups of languages, strikingly different in many respects, present, notwithstanding, some striking resemblances. Two Egyptologists, Erman and W. Max Müller, hold that the roots of the Hamitic, like those of the Semitic tongues, were originally triliteral.[1] The pronoun, ordinarily the most *sui generis* of the parts of speech in a group of languages, presents, in these groups, a similarity so striking as to point to an original identity. The verbs in each of these groups are, in broad outline, constructed on the same method. They have, for example, in each group but two inflexional forms for tenses, — a perfect or aorist, which denotes that an action is completed, and an imperfect or durative, which denotes that it is incomplete. Each group treats the weak verbs and derivatives in analogous ways. Each group forms intensive stems by doubling a letter or reduplicating a root and reflexive stems in which, in each group, the letter *t* is usually an important feature; causative and reciprocal stems are also common to both groups. Moreover, the general method of verbal inflexion — the combination of a fragment of a personal pronoun with the stem — is also common to both groups. The two groups have also the same endings for gender (masc. *w*, fem. *t*). Four or five of the numerals are identical, and fifty, or possibly seventy-five, of the actual words of the Old Egyptian are identical with Semitic words.[2] Both

---

[1] Cf. Erman, *op. cit.*, p. 350. W. Max Müller made the same statement at a meeting of the Oriental Club of Philadelphia in November, 1899.

[2] Thus, in Semitic, "two" is expressed by the root *šn* (Arabic *in*); in Old Egyptian, Coptic, and Tamešeq, by *sn;* "six," in Semitic, by the root *šdš* (contracted except in Ethiopic, as *e.g.* in the Heb. *šš*), in Hamitic, by *sds* (which appears in Tamešeq), contracted in Egyptian to

groups of languages form verbal nouns with a prefix *m*; each regards a certain accented syllable in each word, or group of words, as important, and each has therefore a construct state. Each group has several consonants in common (*Aleph*, *Waw*, *Yodh*, '*Ayin*), and each writes without expressing the vowels in written character.[1]

These linguistic facts prove that the Semitic and Hamitic races formed one group of peoples for a considerable period of time after the art of speech had been developed, during which time the pronoun was fixed and the main outlines of verbal and noun inflexion were formed; but that they separated at a period so remote that the individual names for objects in the two groups of languages are, with few exceptions, absolutely different.

Friedrich Müller says concerning this: "The separa-

---

ss; "seven," in North Semitic by *šbʿ*, South Semitic, *sbʿ*, Egyptian, *sfḫ;* "eight," Semitic, *šmn*, *smn*, *tmn*, *ĭmn*, Coptic, *smn;* "nine," North Semitic, *tšʿ*, South Semitic, *tsʿ*, Tamešeq, *tzz*. For other identical words common to Egyptian and Semitic, see Erman, *ZDMG.*, Vol. XLVI, pp. 107–126.

[1] For full proof of these statements, the reader is referred to Friedrich Müller's *Grundriss der Sprachwissenschaft*, Bd. III, Wien, 1884, pp. 226–417, Erman's article "Das Verhaltness des aegyptischen zu den semitischen Sprachen," in *ZDMG.*, Vol. XLVI (1892), pp. 93–126, and his *Aegyptische Grammatik*, Berlin, 1894, "Die Flexion des ägyptischen Verbums," in *Sitzungsberichte d. Kg. Als. d. Wiss. zu Berlin*, 1900, pp. 317–353; Steindorf's *Koptische Grammatik*, Berlin, 1894, Brugsch's *Grammaire Hieroglyphique*, Leipzig, 1872, Giovanni Collizza's *Lingua 'Afar*, Vienna, 1887, Belkassen ben Sedira's *Langue Kabyle*, Alger, 1887, Wright's *Lectures on the Comparative Grammar of the Semitic Languages*, Cambridge, 1890, and Zimmern's *Vergleichende Grammatik der semitischen Sprachen*, Berlin, 1898, *passim*, and esp. p. 181. Müller finds three groups of Hamitic languages: the Egyptian, embracing Old Egyptian and Coptic; the Lybian, embracing the Tamešeq; and the Ethiopic, embracing the Bedza, Galla, Somali, Saho, Belin, and Chamir tongues. Sometimes he includes, as on p. 225, the Dankali or 'Afar language, which ought always to be included. To the Lybian group the Kabyle and other Berber tongues should be added. Müller's list of Semitic languages is not as large as it should be, but this does not affect his argument.

The argument for the kinship of these tongues is well stated in Crum's article, "Egypt," in Hastings's *Dictionary of the Bible*.

tion of the individual languages from the common original occurred in such a way that the primitive language was divided into two dialects, of which one might be called Hamitic and the other Semitic. While the primitive Hamitic language was, at an early time, divided into individual tongues, probably because of the great number of the individuals who spoke it, and the wide dispersion of the races which used it, the primitive Semitic speech preserved for a long time a compact unity, probably because of the small number of individuals speaking it, and the narrow limits in which they lived. While, also, the primitive Semitic language could develop itself uniformly without foreign influx within the whole of the race which spoke it, the Hamitic primitive language must at an early time have broken up into a series of individual tongues, in consequence of the separation of the peoples who spoke it and the influx of strong foreign influences. Therefore, it happens that to-day the unity of the Semitic languages runs not only through the similarity of the articulation and the grammatical foundation, but also to the identity of roots and word-forms; while, on the other hand, the Hamitic languages betray the fact that they belong together merely by the similarity of their foundation and the form of their roots, less often by the identity of the material of the roots, and still less often by the identity of the roots themselves.[1] This opinion is borne out by an

[1] See Müller, *op. cit.*, p. 225: "Die Loslösung der einzelnen Sprachen von gemeinsamen Grundstocke ging derart von sich, dass sich zunächst die Grundsprache in zwei Dialekte spaltete, von denen der eine als hamitische, der andere als semitische Stammsprache bezeichnet werden kann. Während die hamitische Stammsprache weiderum frühzeitig, wahrscheinlich in Folge der grossen Anzahl der sie redenden Individuen und der weiten Verbreitung der sie redenden Geschlechter, in mehrer Dialekte, respective Einzelsprachen sich spaltete, bildete die semitischen Grundsprache, wahrscheinlich in Folge der geringen Zahl der sie redenden Individuen und der beschränkten Verbreitung derselben, lange Zeit eine geschlossene Einheit. Während also die semitische Grundsprache sich gleichmässig ohne fremde Einflüsse innerhalb des ganzen sie redenden Stammes entwickeln konnte, musste die hamitische Grundsprache in

examination of the facts upon which it is based, and is accepted by scholars of eminence.[1]

If we accept it, we are led thereby to one of two alternatives. Either the united Hamito-Semitic race lived at some prehistoric time in western Asia, whence a large number of them migrated to Africa, or they were all resident in northern Africa, whence the ancestors of the Semites migrated to Asia. It will be noted that the linguistic evidence, as stated by Friedrich Müller, favors the latter conclusion. The threads of identity which bind the Semitic languages together are, as Müller says, such as to make it clear that the primitive Semitic speech was spoken by a comparatively small number of people who were for a long time sheltered from outside influences; while the Hamitic languages, which are much less closely bound together, must have been spoken by a larger and more widely scattered body of people. Now, it is more probable that a small number of people separated from the main body and settled in Arabia, than that the race as a whole originated in the latter country and the majority migrated to Africa. While the latter supposition is not impossible, it is far less likely to represent the true order of events.

Gerland and others have adduced the ethnological argument in favor of the North African origin of the Semites. It will be well, therefore, to ask what anthropology has to tell us of the larger question of the origin of man,—or at least of the white race,—of its primitive home, and its

---

Folge der Trennung der Stämme und der mächtig einwirkenden fremden Einflüsse frühzeitig in eine Reihe von Einzelsprachen zerfallen. Daher kommt es, dass die einheit der semitischen Sprachen nicht nur in der Gleichheit der Articulation und der grammatischen Anlage, sondern auch in die Identität der Stämme und Wortformen zutage tritt, während dem gegenüber die hamitischen Sprachen ihrer Zusammengehörigkeit blos durch die Gleichheit der Anlage und Identität der Stoff-wurtzeln, noch seltener in der Identität der Stamme selbst verrathen."

[1] Cf. Peschal, *Races of Men*, New York, 1888, p. 493, and Ratzel, *History of Mankind*, London, 1898, Vol. III, p. 182.

differentiation from other races, in order to see whether any confirmation of the solution of our problem to which philology points can be found.

As to the part of the globe in which human life first appeared, no unanimous verdict has been reached. Several scientists assign the beginnings of humanity, with considerable probability, to a continent which they believe once occupied the site of the Indian Ocean, and which stretched away from Borneo and the Philippines to Madagascar. This view is supported by Hæckel,[1] Peschel,[2] Ridpath,[3] and Keane.[4] Quatrefages, on the other hand, holds[5] that man was developed from a lower order of life in the region "bounded on the south and southwest by the Himalayas, on the west by the Bolor Mountains, on the northwest by the Ala-Tau, on the north by the Altai range and its offshoots, on the east by the Kingkhan, on the south and southeast by the Felina and Kuen-Loun."

Gerland and Brinton hold still a different theory. They maintain that the Mediterranean basin, including southern Europe and northern Africa, is the part of the earth where man first appeared.[6] Finally, Giddings[7] after a thorough discussion of the evidence, concludes that "the habitat of the homine species was probably a tropical or subtropical zone, which reached half-way around the earth from Java northwesterly to England." The discovery, in 1894, of *Pithecanthropus erectus*, a kind of missing link, in Java,

---

[1] *History of Creation*, New York, 1884, Vol. II, p. 326.
[2] *The Races of Men*, New York, 1888, p. 32.
[3] *Great Races of Mankind*, Cincinnati, 1893, Vol. I, pp. 173-182.
[4] *Ethnology*, Cambridge, 1896, p. 229 ; cf. also Suess, *Anlitz der Erde*, Leipzig, 1883, Vol. I, p. 535.
[5] *The Human Species*, New York, 1890, pp. 175-177.
[6] *Inconographic Encyclopædia*, Vol. I, p. 29, gives Gerland's view. Brinton's is found in his *Races and Peoples, New York*, 1890, pp. 82-94. Gerland is not so specific as Brinton. He places the cradle of the race in Europe, but a Europe differing greatly from the present continent.
[7] *Principles of Sociology*, The Macmillan Co., 1896, p. 219.

would lend some plausibility to the first or the last of these views.[1]

Fortunately our subject does not compel us to decide between these contending scientists. It is becoming clear that the beginning of the human species is so remote that man was distributed at an early date over practically the whole earth, and that the processes of race formation have been so gradual and so long that it is as unnecessary as it is impossible to connect the cradle of the Semites with the birthplace of the race.

Croll,[2] by showing that the glacial epochs have been caused by variations in the eccentricity of the earth's orbit, which, from astronomical data, can be computed in terms of years, has given us some idea how long ago those men lived whose remains go back to the glacial and to earlier periods. This method of investigation has been widely accepted by scientists, many of whom have applied the results in ways of their own. While, therefore, their estimates of the antiquity of man do not agree, they are all sufficiently large to remove the beginnings of the species far from the beginnings of any of the races which now exist. Thus, Quatrefages[3] supposes that man goes back to Miocene times, a geologic epoch which Croll[4] believes ended about 720,000 years ago. Fiske,[5] on the basis of the discovery of the fossil remains of man by Ribeiro and Whitney in the Pliocene rocks of Portugal and California,

---

[1] Cf. Giddings, *op. cit.*, p. 217.

[2] See his *Climate and Time in their Geological Relations*, London, 1890, 4th ed. This work is a collection of papers, many of which had appeared earlier in the *Philosophical Magazine* and other journals during the ten or twelve years prior to the first edition of the book.

[3] *The Human Species*, p. 152.

[4] *Climate and Time*, p. 359.

[5] *Excursions of an Evolutionist*, Boston, 1890, pp. 36, 75-77, and 148. Recent investigation tends to undermine the correctness of Whitney's inferences; cf. William H. Holmes in *American Anthropologist*, new series, Vol. I, p. 107 ff. Payne, however, holds (*History of the New World Called America*, Vol. II, p. 64 ff.) that by the glacial epoch man was present in both the old and the new worlds.

THE CRADLE OF THE SEMITES

is led, by Croll's calculations, to believe that man was as widely scattered over the earth as the distance between California and Portugal as long as 400,000 years ago. Keane[1] estimates the age of man as from 240,000 to 1,000,000 years, — a latitude rather startling, — Ridpath[2] at 200,000 years, Lubbock[3] at hundreds of thousands of years; while Gerland[4] thinks that the facts of ethnology point to at least 240,000 years.

Some have objected that man could not have lived so long upon the earth without undergoing great physical modifications. Since Miocene times natural selection has transformed all the animals, and why should it not have transformed man, too? Yet the oldest fossil remains are almost identical in form with the existing races of men. This difficulty disappears when we remember that, as Wallace has pointed out,[5] when once man's mind was developed, natural selection would cease to act upon his body, and would expend itself in expanding his mind. The approach of a glacial epoch instead of rendering him extinct, or developing a hairy covering for his body, would sharpen his wits to enable him to provide food and clothing for himself. During the time of his existence, therefore, every other form of physical life may have been entirely transformed by those laws of natural selection which have ripened his mental power.

It is clear, from the foregoing summary of opinion, that we may, with perfect propriety for the purpose of the present inquiry, dismiss this larger subject of the origin of man and confine ourselves to the investigation of a smaller part of the question.

If we turn our attention to the origin of the white races, the problem appears about as difficult for one not a profes-

[1] *Ethnology*, pp. 56–70.
[2] *Great Races of Mankind*, Vol. I, p. 150.
[3] *Prehistoric Times*, 5th ed., London, 1890, pp. 383–425.
[4] *Iconographic Encyclopædia*, Vol. I, p. 28.
[5] *Natural Selection and Tropical Nature*, The Macmillan Co., 1891, p. 180.

sional anthropologist to handle, so little agreement has been reached by those who have given the subject special attention. Thus, Hæckel,[1] Peschel,[2] Brinton,[3] Keane,[4] and Sergi[5] regard the Mediterranean basin as the cradle of the white races, while Ripley[6] gives convincing evidence that there is no white race, but that at least three distinct white races are traceable in Europe: the Teutonic, or Homo Europæus, most distinctly preserved in Scandinavia; the Alpine (for which he rejects the name Celtic), most clearly preserved among the lower classes of Austria and Bavaria, and clearly of the same type as the prehistoric lake-dwellers of Switzerland;[7] and the Mediterranean race, most clearly defined in Corsica, Sardinia, and the Iberian peninsula, and clearly identical with the Berber race.[8] Ripley recognizes, as the others do, that the race of the south of Europe is identical with that of North Africa, and that it is a white race. These are, after all, the only points which affect our problem. Sergi holds that the substratum of all the population of Europe is composed of this Mediterranean, or Eurafric race.[9]

Gerland introduces a difficulty into the problem, however, by denying that the Semites belong to the white race, and would connect them with the black. Thus he says: " The Arabic-Africans are one ethnological race, or division of mankind. . . . Kai-Koin, Bantu, and Negro tribes exhibit the same physical characteristics as the Semites; and their languages show the path by which the Semitic reached its goal."[10] This opinion does not seem

[1] *History of Creation*, Vol. II, p. 321.
[2] *Races of Men*, pp. 480-518.
[3] *Races and Peoples*, pp. 97-139.
[4] *Ethnology*, ch. xiv.
[5] *Mediterranean Race*, New York, 1901.
[6] *The Races of Europe*, ch. vi, especially pp. 121-130.
[7] Cf. *The Lake Dwellings of Europe*, by Robert C. Monro, London, Paris, Melbourne, 1890.
[8] See *op. cit.*, pp. 247 and 276.
[9] *The Mediterranean Race*, New York, Scribners, 1901.
[10] *Iconographic Encyclopædia*, Vol. I, pp. 369, 370.

to rest on a sufficiently secure basis. The occasional prognathism and woolly hair observed among the modern Arabs, on which he relies,[1] is much more likely due to mixture brought about in recent times by the Arabic slave raids into Africa, which have been going on for centuries. Travellers in Arabia testify that, in consequence of this, amalgamation of races is still going on there.[2]

The Bantu languages, as described by Müller,[3] exhibit, so far as I can see, no real kinship to the Semitic tongues. The pronouns are not similar to the Semitic, as is the case with the Hamitic pronouns; the tenses of the verbs are more like those of the Aryan than those of the Semitic tongues, so that the similarity seems to be reduced to the fact that the Bantu languages have causative, reflexive, reciprocal, and causative-reflexive stems. These are, however, formed, for the most part, by afformatives instead of preformatives, as in Semitic, and cannot be held to prove kinship. It seems safe, therefore, to follow the prevailing opinion and class the Semites with the white races. Sergi, moreover, has pointed out that many of the Hamites in North Africa are to-day blonds, and that they are probably native there. The pigmentation of the skin is, he believes, due to the altitude of the country in which a people lives.[4] If this be true, the question of complexion need not seriously trouble us.

If now, with Ripley, we conclude that the Alpine race is identical with the race of the prehistoric lake-dwellers, we shall also look for the perpetuation of very ancient racial types in the Mediterranean race. The Mediterranean basin has at different times undergone such changes of level that its north and south shores have been united at Gibraltar, or by way of Italy, Sicily, and Tunis, or in

---

[1] See above, p. 6 note 2.
[2] Cf. Palgrave's *Central and Eastern Arabia*, Vol. I, p. 452, Vol. II, pp. 242, 272, and 302; also Doughty's *Travels in Arabia Deserta*, Cambridge, 1889, Vol. I, p. 553, Vol. II, pp. 80, 171, and 337.
[3] Cf. *Grundriss der Sprachwissenschaft*, Vol. I, Pt. II, pp. 238 ff.
[4] *The Mediterranean Race*, pp. 59–75.

both places.¹ This fact accounts for the unity of the fauna and flora on the two sides of the sea. At the same time the Sahara desert was, at least in part, submerged, so that the northern part of Africa was separated from the southern and, through long lapse of time, the life of the two parts of the continent became distinct. This condition was probably terminated by the beginning of the last glacial epoch. It is probable that the Mediterranean race was, in this far-off time and under these conditions, developed.

Boyd Dawkins,² who is followed by Fiske,³ tells the story of the succession of the races of men in Europe in a most attractive way. If we could follow him we might enter upon some very pleasing speculations. His results are not admitted by the great number of anthropologists, however, and seem to be based on insufficient data. We must therefore be content to follow a more sober path.

If we take the more sober statement of Ripley and Sergi, that the race still distinctly marked in Corsica, Sardinia, and the Spanish peninsula is identical with the Berber race of North Africa, we have the clew for which we have been seeking. The late Count von der Gabelenz,⁴ following the lead of certain ethnologists who thought they detected racial affinities between the Basques and Berbers, endeavored to go further, and to show that the tongue of this little people of the Pyrenees is kindred to that of the Berbers of North Africa. If this could be established,⁵

---

[1] Cf. Suess's *Anlitz der Erde*, Leipzig und Prag, 1883, Vol. I, p. 771; Neumahr's *Erdgeschichte*, Leipzig und Wien, 1890, Vol. II, p. 698; and Wallace's *Geographical Distribution of Animals*, The Macmillan Co., 1876, Vol. I, pp. 113-115, and 201 ff.

[2] Cf. his *Man in Britain and his Place in the Tertiary Period*, London, 1880, pp. 161-172, and ch. vii.

[3] Cf. his *Excursions of an Evolutionist*, pp. 39, 44-46.

[4] See *Die Verwandtschaft der Baskischen mit den Berber-sprachen Nord-Afrikas*, Brunswick, 1894. He published a previous essay on the subject in the *Sitzungsberichte der Ak. d. Wiss. zu Berlin*, 1893, pp. 593-613.

[5] See Brinton's *Races and Peoples*, p. 112, and Keane's *Ethnology*, p. 378.

the threads which connect the Berbers with the races of the Iberian peninsula would be greatly strengthened; but his effort cannot be pronounced a success. He admits that the languages differ in structure of speech, in gender, and in most of the formatives; but urges that they have certain analogous laws of phonetic change, and that there is a resemblance in a few culture words, such as the names of animals and of articles of dress. These names, however, afford no basis of argument whatever, as they may all have been borrowed during the Arabic-Berber occupation. Stumme[1] has pointed out that they seem quite as much Arabic as Berber — a fact which seems to make the hypothesis just advanced the more probable. The labor of von der Gabelenz seems to have been suggested by a mistake, for Ripley now comes forward and proves that there is no pure Basque type.[2] Without the aid of philological arguments, however, we may rely upon the fact, in which all anthropologists agree, that the race on the two sides of the Mediterranean is identical.

We noted above that the geologic changes which separated North Africa from Europe occurred by the beginning of the last glacial epoch. Croll[3] calculates that that epoch began about 240,000 and ended about 80,000 years ago. The free interchange by land necessary to make this identity of race must, therefore, have occurred before this remote period, and must have been going on before that for a time sufficiently long to fix a racial type so constant that it still persists on both sides of the Mediterranean. During the millenniums which have elapsed since this epoch this race has persisted in these regions, has absorbed all foreign elements which have been injected into it, and has maintained its identity in the face of everything.

[1] Cf. *Literarisches Centralblatt* for 1895, p. 581. For other criticisms of von der Gabelenz's work, see *Berlin philologisches Wochenschrift*, Vol. XXV, p. 784, *The Academy*, Vol. XLIV, p. 93, and *Science*, Vol. XXII, p. 77.
[2] *Op. cit.*, ch. viii.
[3] *Climate and Time*, chs. xix and xx, especially pp. 328 and 342.

So far as I know, the general unity of the Hamito-Semitic stock is not seriously questioned.[1] We may grant that, as they moved out from their original home, they may have imposed their languages upon foreign tribes, and thus have become, in course of time, somewhat modified at the extremities;[2] nevertheless, the general racial type is well marked, showing that, on the whole, they are rightly classed together. Among the Hamitic peoples we may expect to find traces of racial mixture in Somaliland, among the Dankils, and the people of that region; but for the rest of the Hamitic stock a purer racial type appears to exist, and the kinship of the Hamitic tongues, which links the Berber languages to the ancient Egyptian and to those of East Africa, and through these to the Semites, proves that there exists either a real kinship, or that through conquest one race has imposed its language upon the rest. The latter alternative is ruled out, it seems to me, notwithstanding the views of Erman[3] and others, by the consideration that the records of a part of the Hamitic race go back to the very dawn of history, and that in these records from Egypt we have no trace of such an extensive conquest as would be required to account for this unity of language. Such a conquest would have to be early to allow time for the tongues to develop their striking differences. At such an early time we have no record of a conquest of large parts of North Africa, and the conditions for it did not exist. Further, as Sergi has pointed out,[4] the fact that the Berbers developed an independent system

---

[1] Sergi seems to imply that they are distinct, for example in his discussion of the Hittites and Phœnicians (*Mediterranean Race*, pp. 150-153), but he does not enter fully into the subject.

[2] See Ripley's *Races of Europe*, p. 376.

[3] See *Sitzungsberichte d. kgl. Ak. d. Wiss. zu Berlin*, 1900, pp. 350-353. Cf. also de Morgan and Wiedemann, in de Morgan's *Recherches sur les Origines de l'Egypte*, Vol. I, p. 196. Deniker accepts de Morgan's views, but is in doubt whether the Hamitic peoples originated in Asia or Europe. Cf. his *Races of Man*, London, 1900, pp. 426, 428.

[4] *Mediterranean Race*, p. 56 ff.

of writing, wholly uninfluenced by hieroglyphic Egpytian, proves that no such conquest can ever have taken place. We must therefore conclude that the real explanation is in the fact of kinship.

If, then, the Berbers are a real part of the Hamitic race, and at the same time are a part of that Mediterranean race which has been resident in this region since the last glacial epoch, we have at last some secure ground on which to tread. It becomes clear that the southern shore of the Mediterranean was the original home of the Hamito-Semitic race;[1] that at some time since the glacial period, but after the germ of languages still spoken had begun to develop, the Semites were separated from their Hamitic brethren, and in their migrations ultimately reached Arabia, and that the more numerous Hamites gradually spread themselves over the northern part of Africa. Ethnology thus confirms the conclusion to which the linguistic phenomena of the two families of languages — the Semitic and Hamitic — had led us; viz. that the Semites migrated from Africa, and not the Hamites from Asia. How long ago these movements began we cannot tell. If the glacial epoch ended 80,000 years ago, who knows how much of the period which has elapsed since then may not have been occupied by the various movements which have transformed the Hamito-Semitic family into the nations known to history?

In this connection we may note that the arguments of Hommel in favor of the Babylonian origin of the Egyptian civilization,[2] even if they were much stronger than they are, would have no bearing on the point in question; for if it could be proven that the oldest monuments of Egyp-

---

[1] So Paulitschke holds that the Hamites were autochthenes of the northern coast of the African continent, *Beiträge zur Ethnographie und Anthropologie der Somâl Galla und Horarî*, 2d ed., Leipzig, 1888, p. 7.

[2] See his article, "Ueber den Grad der Verwandtschaft des Altägyptischen mit dem Semitischen," in *Beiträge zur Assyriologie*, Vol. II, pp. 342-358, and his article, "Babylonische Ursprung der ägyptischen Kultur," in *Trans. Inter. Cong. Orient.*, London, 1892, pp. 218-257.

tian culture were inspired by influences from Mesopotamia, it would only demonstrate that there was a western movement of migration from the Tigris-Euphrates valley thousands of years later than the time of which we are speaking. That there have been many migrations of Semites in various directions, no one acquainted with early history will deny. Should Hommel's contention be granted, then (and I am by no means convinced that it should be), it has no more bearing on the movement in the opposite direction, in the remote period under discussion, than the Mohammedan conquest of Egypt has.

The arguments of von Kremer, Guidi, and Hommel, referred to above, in favor of regarding Babylonia as the earliest centre of Semitic culture — the cradle of the Semitic race into which it was put soon after its birth in the high regions east of the Caspian Sea — cannot be regarded as credible in opposition to the Afro-Arabic origin.

Their argument is met by the following objections: (1) It is based on linguistic data, which Bertin[1] and Nöldeke[2] have shown to be precarious. It is, as Bertin points out, precisely the objects which are most common for which most synonyms exist in a language, some of which would survive in one of its derived tongues and others in another. (2) It places the primitive Semitic home in a region where, at the dawn of history, the Semites were in conflict with other races, from one of which many scholars hold that the resident Semites borrowed much of their civilization. These races so profoundly modified the Semitic spoken in the region that it has suffered more deterioration than any other Semitic tongue. Surely it will take more than linguistic evidence to convince us that the primitive home, in which the Semites developed those special characteristics which so strikingly differentiate them from other races, was in such

---

[1] See *Journal of the Anthropological Institute*, Vol. XI, p. 426.
[2] *Die semitischen Sprachen*, p. 3 ff.

a region. (3) This theory would compel us to believe that the Semites migrated from the fertile plains of Babylonia to the wastes of Arabia; and it offers no sufficient motive for such migration, although it necessarily puts the entrance into Arabia at a comparatively late date, and has to face the fact that in historic times the movement has been all the other way. (4) It in no way satisfactorily accounts for the connection between the Semitic and Hamitic stock, and leaves utterly unexplained the fact that the Hamitic languages are less closely related to one another than the Semitic, though all the tongues of the two groups are kindred. (5) The anthropological argument, as we have seen, is against it.

Of the four classes of arguments by which Brinton [1] supports his theory of the North African origin of the Semites, two — the traditional and the archæological — may be dismissed at once. The Biblical traditions embodied in Genesis ii and iii, even if the word *qedem* could be translated "eastward," as he supposes,[2] cannot possibly refer to events so far in the past as the original movement of the Semitic from the Hamitic races. This event must have been separated from the Biblical writer by at least several thousand years — a period through which the memory of no uncivilized people carries a reliable tradition. The memory of the Biblical tradition may go back to Babylonia, and may, as we shall see in a subsequent chapter, refer to practices born in Arabia and perpetuated in Babylonia and elsewhere; but it certainly refers to far later events in the history of the Semites than their primal migration. His archæological argument from the method of using the bow known as the "arrow-release"[3] is, for similar reasons, of little if any significance. It is a practice found in many parts of the world.

The linguistic and ethnological arguments on which

---

[1] *The Cradle of the Semites*, Philadelphia, 1890.
[2] *Op. cit.*, pp. 5, 6.
[3] *Op. cit.*, p. 11. Cf. Jastrow's criticism of it, *ibid.*, p. 23.

others had laid stress before him are, as we have seen, valid, and in the absence of weighty reasons for any other view must be considered convincing. We therefore hold that North Africa was the home of the Hamito-Semitic stock.[1] We cannot, so far as I can see, with our present knowledge, settle upon any special locality there and claim that this rather than another was the place where this race first appeared.[2] Its habitat must have included the Mediterranean coast lands, from whence it could pass into southern Europe.

As has been already pointed out, the theory that Africa was the primitive home of the Hamito-Semitic race in no way conflicts with the theory of Sprenger, Sayce, De Goeje, and Wright, that Arabia was the specific home of the Semites, — the country where their peculiar characteristics were developed and the centre from whence the Semitic nations radiated to other lands. All the arguments they have urged seem to me valid, so that, as the late Robertson Smith perceived, though the Semites came from Africa, Arabia is the centre from which they spread.[3]

It will be remembered that Friedrich Müller, in the passage quoted from him above,[4] suggested that the greater unity which the Semitic languages present, when compared with the Hamitic, is probably due to the fact that the primitive Semitic tongue was spoken by a smaller number of people, who lived in a more confined area than was the case with the primitive Hamitic. This suggestion grows naturally out of the nature of the two groups of languages, and commends itself as true. It harmonizes

---

[1] So also Ratzel. See his *History of Mankind*, Vol. III, p. 181; "The Hamites are the aborigines of Africa."

[2] Brinton holds that this race originated in the vicinity of the Atlas Mountains, while Sergi formerly held, and still inclines to believe, that East Africa, in the neighborhood of Somaliland, is their primitive home. Cf. *Mediterranean Race*, pp. 42, 43, 70.

[3] Cf. Wright's *Comparative Grammar of the Semitic Languages*, p. 9 n. Cf. above, p. 7, n. 5.

[4] p. 10 ff.

also with the view that the Semites migrated from Africa (since the emigrants would naturally be few in comparison with those who would remain), and that within the comparatively narrow confines of central Arabia they long lived in close contact with one another and separated from the rest of the world.

One comes occasionally across a writer who holds that the pure Arabs entered Arabia from Abyssinia.[1] If this means that they entered Arabia as Hamites, and were afterward differentiated from the Hamitic peoples, it may possibly be true; but if it means that Abyssinia is the cradle of the Semitic peoples and Arabia only its centre of distribution, the view, not to mention a social argument which will appear in a future chapter, is, for the following reasons, untenable: (1) The physical characteristics of Abyssinia[2] and Somaliland are not such as to have isolated the Semites for a long period from foreign influences in such a way as to produce the linguistic results which appear among them; and (2) Hamitic tribes (the Afars or Dankils, the Gallas, and Somalis) now lie to the south and southeast of the Semitic inhabitants of Abyssinia, so that the Semitic population, driven in like a wedge, separate these Hamites from the Hamites of Egypt.[3] It is clear, therefore, that the Abyssinian Semites are late intruders in this region. The Geez

---

[1] Cf. the article "Arabia" in *Encyc. Brit.*, 9th ed., and Schmidt's paper read before the Congress of Religions in Paris.

[2] Cf. *The Sacred City of the Ethiopians, being a Record of Travel and Research in Abyssinia in 1893*, by J. Theodore Bent, London, 1893, in which are many descriptions of the country. Cf. also Ratzel's *History of Mankind*, Vol. III, p. 222 ff.; and Jules Borelli, *Ethiopie Méridionale*, Paris, 1890, *passim;* also *Modern Abyssinia*, by Augustus B. Wylde, London, 1901, ch. xx.

[3] Brinton's *Races and Peoples*, p. 131; Gerland, *Iconographic Encyclopædia*, Vol. I, p. 352; and Ridpath's *Great Races of Mankind*, Vol. III, pp. 459–472. The objection of Erman (*Sitzsungsberichte der Kgl. Ak. d. Wiss. zu Berlin*, 1900, p. 352), following Lepsius, that the Nubians are non-Hamitic and also intervene between the Hamitic nations may be obviated by one of two considerations: either the Nubians may have

civilization, especially in its ancient form,[1] has so many characteristics in common with that of south Arabia, — characteristics, too, which appear more at home, as we shall show below, in Arabia, — that there can be no doubt but that it is the result of a westward Semitic movement from that country across the straits of Bab-el-Mandeb, and not the unmoved remnant of the primitive Semitic stock.

If now it be asked what can have induced the Semites to enter so sterile a country as Arabia, we can only answer by conjectures. It must be noted that their migration probably occurred so long ago that the Nile valley had not begun to be cultivated, so that they were not tempted on account of the fertility of the country to stop there. This we infer from the fact that the language of the earliest monuments of Egypt is so different from the Semitic. The Hamitic Egyptians must have come into the Nile valley and developed their civilization long after the Semites had passed on to Arabia.[2] It is hardly probable that at that remote period Arabia was a less desolate country than now. Wallace believed that the large treeless tracts of desert in Eastern Africa and Western Asia were once covered with aboriginal forests, which were destroyed by the abundance of camels and goats, — animals which are exceedingly destructive of a woody vegetation, — and that the loss became permanent on account of the absence of irrigation.[3] If Arabia was ever covered with

---

entered this region after the Hamites of East Africa had gone thither, or their country may have been too poor to attract the Hamites, so that they passed them by. As Erman confesses, this is the real explanation.

[1] See below, ch. iv.

[2] Of course it is not impossible, as Erman (*Sitzungsberichte der Ak. d. Wiss. zu Berlin*, 1900, p. 351 ff.) and Wiedemann (in de Morgan's *Recherches sur les Origines de l'Egypte*, Vol. II, pp. 219-228) believe, that a later wave of Semitic migration from Arabia may have formed one element in the formation of the old Egyptian civilization. It was probably not an important element. Cf. Sergi, *Mediterranean Race*, pp. 90-100.

[3] *Geographical Distribution of Animals*, Vol. I, p. 200.

forests, it must have been many thousands of years ago; and it is unlikely that the Semitic migration can be placed far enough back so that such an inducement can be thought to have led its hordes hither. As our investigation proceeds, however, the reasons which led to this migration will become clear.[1]

How long ago the Semites entered Arabia we can now only guess. It must have been, as we have already noted, after the main skeleton of Hamito-Semitic verbal formation was formed and several of their numerals developed. On the other hand, it must have been some considerable time since the change in the contour of the continents had separated those members of the Mediterranean race resident in Europe from those resident in Africa. We infer this because, while the Berbers are connected with the other Hamitic races in language, there is no linguistic connection between them and any member of the Mediterranean race resident in Europe, either in ancient or modern times, except those Arabs and Berbers who migrated into Spain in the early days of Islam. Eighty thousand years ago (or should we say 240,000?[2]) no fixed language (*i.e.* a language sufficiently fixed to survive) had been developed by these Mediterranean peoples. All this might be true, and yet the two great families of Hamito-Semitic speech might have been outlined as much as they were when the Semites branched off, if that event be placed at 20,000, 30,000, or even 50,000 years ago. Any one of these periods would be sufficiently long, so that Arabia may have been a more fertile country then than now, and so that its present conditions may afterward have supervened, and still have occurred long enough ago to allow them thousands of years in which to indelibly impress on the Semite his social organization and religion. We shall, however, see in the next chapter some reason for holding that the conditions of Arabia were what they are now when the Semites entered the country.

[1] See below, ch. iii. [2] See above, p. 19.

However long ago this migration may have occurred, — and any statement in years is a mere guess, — the peculiar conditions of life which the Arabian deserts and oases have presented for millenniums are the matrix in which Semitic character, as it is known to us, was born. It is a land of barren and volcanic mountains,[1] of broad stretches of dry, waste, unproductive soil,[2] and wide areas of shifting sand, interrupted by an occasional oasis, — a land where, for the most part, water is difficult to obtain, where famine is always imminent, where hunger, thirst, heat, and exposure are the constant experience of the inhabitants. The Bedawi are always underfed, they suffer constantly from hunger and thirst, and their bodies thus weakened fall an easy prey to disease;[3] they range the silent desert, almost devoid of life, where the sun is all powerful by day and the stars exceedingly brilliant by night. This environment begets in them intensity of faith of a certain kind, ferocity, exclusiveness, and imagination. These are all Semitic characteristics wherever we find the Semites; and there can be little doubt but that this is the land in which these traits were ingrained in the race. Here, too, the Arabic language, preserved in its purity by the barriers which nature interposed against foreign influences, though it is by no means identical with the primitive Semitic language, has preserved more characteristics of that primitive speech than any other Semitic tongue.[4]

We conclude, then, that we must hold to the Arabic origin of the Semites. Taking Arabia as the Semitic cradle land, the course of distribution of the Semitic nations over the lands occupied by them during the his-

[1] Cf. Doughty's *Travels in Arabia Deserta*, Vol. I, chs. xiii–xvi.
[2] Cf. Doughty, *op. cit.*, Vol. I, p. 56.
[3] See the books on Arabian travel generally; *e.g.* Doughty, *op. cit.*, Vol. I, p. 244.
[4] Cf. Schrader in *ZDMG.*, Vol. XXVII, p. 417; Wright, *Comparative Grammar of the Semitic Languages*, p. 8; and Vlock in *Hebraica*, Vol. II, p. 149.

torical period would be that described by Schrader[1] and Wright[2] on the basis of the relative divergence of the languages from the primitive type. The northern Semites — the Babylonians, Aramæans, and Canaanites — first parted from their brethren in the south and settled in Babylonia and the neighboring regions, where they lived together for a long period. The Aramæans were the first to separate from the main body of emigrants; at a considerably later period the Canaanites, and, last of all, the Assyrians. At the same time an emigration went on in a southern direction. Parting from the main body in central Arabia, these emigrants settled on or near the southern coast of the peninsula, whence a band of them subsequently crossed into Africa and pitched in Abyssinia. These movements must each be considered as processes going on for a considerable period,[3] and, in some cases, as in Mesopotamia and Palestine, subject to a considerable mixture not only of foreigners, but from Arabia directly.

[1] *ZDMG.*, Vol. XXVII, p. 421 ff.
[2] *Op. cit.*, p. 9.
[3] Cf. Robertson Smith's *Kinship and Marriage in Early Arabia*, Cambridge, 1885, p. 244.

CHAPTER II

PRIMITIVE SEMITIC SOCIAL LIFE

IN primitive life the form of the clan depends upon economic conditions. My friend and colleague, Professor L. M. Keasbey, who is engaged upon a work on the economic origins of society, would sketch some of the differences as follows: In protected spots where the beginnings of agriculture or arboriculture are possible, communities are formed of women and the weaker men. The stronger men are drawn away by more hazardous enterprises. Polyandry of the Nair type may prevail, and descent will be reckoned in the female line. This gives us the "communal clan."

Where men organize for hazardous enterprises, such as conquest, conducting a caravan, or hunting the buffalo, the "republican clan" is formed. The success of the enterprise requires the most skilful leader, who must, accordingly, be chosen for his personal qualities. A few hardy women are taken into these clans, and polyandry of the Thibetan type, or communal marriage, may result. Descent is here counted through the father.

Where pastoral life is possible, the care of the flocks leads to the formation of the "patriarchal clan." In this polygamy may prevail, and descent is reckoned through the father.

The late W. Robertson Smith, in beginning his discussion of the relations of gods and men in the oldest Semitic communities, takes the clan as the earliest social unit.[1] For historical times this view is amply justified by the

[1] *The Religion of the Semites*, 2d ed., London, 1894, p. 35.

evidence, and there is much reason to believe, as we shall see, that it extended far back into prehistoric times. In Babylon it is true that at the very dawn of history cities had superseded, at least in form, the communal clan organization; but this was due to the fact that the rich soil and abundant water of the Tigris-Euphrates valley made agriculture easy, and paved the way for a civilization which gradually outgrew the tribal stage. Whether the Semites originated this civilization or borrowed it, has no bearing on the fact that they were influenced by it. In the earliest times, however, the town life did not materially modify the communal clan life. Cities, whether in Babylonia[1] or in Palestine,[2] were at first simply fortified dwellings of clansmen.

Through many sources clan organization may be traced in the other parts of the Semitic domain. Thus, in the genealogical lists of the Old Testament, we can trace, as scholars now generally recognize, the clans of which the Israelitish tribes were composed, since the writers, in accordance with the patriarchal ideas of their own times, have personified the nation as a man, tribes as his sons, and clans as his grandsons or descendants. Sometimes these clans can, with probability, be traced in extra-Biblical sources, as Heber and Malkiel, clans of the tribe of Asher, in the El-Amarna tablets;[3] but whether they can be so traced or not, there is no doubt but that the names represent clans. Clans not mentioned in the Bible, which once dwelt in Syria and Palestine, are also mentioned in the El-Amarna correspondence, such as the "Sons

---

[1] Cf. Winckler's *Altorientalische Forschungen*, 1st ser., p. 232 ff.

[2] See the remarks of Robertson Smith in the *Journal of Philology*, Vol. IX, p. 92.

[3] They appear in several letters as *Ḫabiri* and *Malki-ilu*. For the Hebrew names cf. Gen. 46^{17}, Nu. 26^{45}, 1 Chron. 7^{31}. For the cuneiform references, cf. Schrader's *KB.*, Vol. V, pp. 302–313. On the identification, cf. Jastrow, in *JBL.*, Vol. XI, pp. 119–122. Reisner (*JBL.*, Vol. XVI, pp. 143–145), following Halévy, makes them Cassites, but this does not seem to me so probable.

of Ebed-Ashera,"[1] "Sons of Labapa,"[2] "Sons of Arzawa,"[3] etc. These letters give us a picture of a seething mass of clans, each struggling for the supremacy of Palestine.

Such lists as that of Gen. 36 attest the same organization for ancient Edom. The clan organization of the whole of Arabia is attested in many ways. One evidence of it is the list of names in Gen. $25^{12\text{ ff.}}$, while proof, if possible of a still more convincing character, is found in the Aramaic inscriptions brought from Hegra and vicinity.[4] Claudius Ptolemy, in his "Geography," in describing Arabia, gives a long list of nations which must, as Robertson Smith pointed out, have been clans in an easy state of flux, for by the time of Mohammed their names had all disappeared.[5] The existence of clans for this region is also attested by the Sabæan inscriptions, which have in recent years been recovered.[6]

Wherever in the dawn of history we can catch glimpses of the Semites before the life of the cities had obliterated more primitive traits, the clan is the unit of organization.

In Arabia, where, to the present time, the physical conditions make a high degree of civilization impossible for a large portion of the inhabitants, the same social organization prevails. While the tribe has become the larger unit of organization in the community, the conditions of existence are such that clans, often exceedingly small, live, move, and act together under the guidance of their own sheik, who holds a position of somewhat ill-defined subordination to the sheik of the tribe.[7] This organization is so ingrained into the constitution of Arabic life,

---

[1] *KB.*, Vol. V, pp. 154, 155, *e.g.* Perhaps afterward the tribe of Asher. See Chapter VI.

[2] *Ibid.*, pp. 306, 307, and 310–311.

[3] *Ibid.*, pp. 310–311.

[4] See *CIS.*, Pt. II, Vol. I, Nos. 197, 198, 209, 215, and 221.

[5] See his *Kinship*, etc., p. 239.

[6] Cf. *CIS.*, Pt. IV, Vol. I, Nos. 2^{17}, $29^{2,3}$ (emended text), 40^6, 41^4, etc.

[7] Cf. Doughty's *Arabia Deserta*, Vol. I, pp. 136, 251, and chs. ix–xii and xiv–xvi, *passim*.

that it has survived the influences of Islam, of migration, and of exposure to civilization, and still appears wherever Arabs are found to-day. Clan organization exists, or has existed in all parts of the world, and is recognized by sociologists as the simplest and earliest form of social integration.[1] We may assume, therefore, that it existed among the primitive Semites in their united home. Indeed, if Keasbey is right in his estimate of the forces which have made man social,[2] Arabia never could have supported a population of any size without it. A semi-agricultural cultivation of the palm in the oases was, as will be shown below, the chief food supply of the Arabs almost, if not quite, from the time of their settlement in the peninsula. No company of men could gain possession of an oasis and hold it for cultivation without organization for defence. Such an oasis would not support them the year around; they must either hunt or keep flocks and herds. In Arabia, as will be pointed out below, there was little hunting. If flocks and herds were kept, they must be led forth to pasture. While some were cultivating the oasis, others must take the more dangerous part of leading the flocks and herds out to graze. This latter task would naturally fall on the younger and more hardy men. Keasbey has shown that it was under such conditions that clans, or artificial brotherhoods, were formed.[3] We have present, therefore, in Arabia from the start those economic conditions in which the clan is forced into existence, and may rest assured that we are treading on firm ground when we assert that the clan organization was a part of primitive Semitic life.

Giddings[4] regards the clan as having for its nucleus an actual group of brothers and sisters, who form a totemic

---

[1] See, *e.g.* Giddings's *Principles of Sociology*, p. 258 ff.
[2] See his article, "The Institution of Society" in the *International Monthly*, Vol. I, pp. 355–398.
[3] *Ibid.*, pp. 385–398.
[4] *Principles of Sociology*, pp. 270–272.

D

kindred and constitute a household; Keasbey,[1] as a brotherhood, artificial in organization, though not necessarily of different stocks, who have selected the totem as a kind of Shibboleth. Whatever the beginning of such a brotherhood, its development is admirably sketched by Giddings.[2] It forms at first an economic group, who aid one another in obtaining food and redressing wrongs. The kinship of such families is usually, among savages, reckoned through the mother and not through the father. At a time too remote for us to detect the origin of the practice, says Giddings, natural brotherhoods are, by expulsion and adoption, arising doubtless from economic causes, converted into artificial fraternities; according to Keasbey they were such from the first. These brotherhoods acquire, in the animistic stage of culture, a peculiar sanctity through the belief that men are akin to supernatural beings. The belief that the individual is akin to his totem reacts on his conception of human relationship; and in time, though the members of a family may have individual totems, the household regards itself as a unit, and comes to have its collective totem in addition to these. Adoption, then, becomes a more sacred ceremony; exogamy, if practised before for other reasons, now becomes a religious obligation, since it is sanctified by the totem; thus, all the practices of the fraternal group assume a more obligatory character. From time to time, the members of such a household would encounter others who had accidentally hit upon the same totem. These, they reason, must be their brothers and sisters, since they are kindred to the same totem as themselves. Thus, the brotherhood, with all its privileges, rules of marriage, and obligations for mutual protection, is enlarged. In a generation or two there exists in such a group all varying degrees of kinship, and the totemic clan is complete.

These descriptions of the genesis of the clan in general may be taken as a tolerably accurate description of the

[1] *Op. cit.*, p. 393 ff.   [2] *Op. cit.*, pp. 270–272.

Semitic clan. The proof of this on the social and economic side will appear as we proceed. We may note now, however, some of the proofs of Semitic totemism. These have been more fully presented by the late Robertson Smith than by any other writer.[1] He regards the proof of totemism complete when we find: (1) "Stocks named after plants and animals; (2) the prevalence of the conception that the members of the stock are of the blood of the eponym animal, or are sprung from a plant of the species chosen as totem; (3) the ascription to the totem of a sacred character, which may result in its being regarded as the god of a stock, but at any rate makes it to be regarded with veneration, so that, for example, a totem animal is not used for ordinary food."[2] Taking these as guides, Smith found many Arabic tribes bearing the names of animals as stock names,[3] and many traces in the Old Testament of the same thing.[4] These names form a striking and impressive list, and form, with the names derived from gods, a large proportion of Arabic personal and stock names.[5] He also found that many Arabs believed themselves to be descended from such animals as the fox, wolf, and hyena, and that some of them bewailed a dead gazelle as a relative.[6] The third link in the proof is nearly wanting because of the veil which Mohammedan sources draw as far as they can over the old heathenism. The nearest approach to it which he found in Arabia was the existence of two or three gods in animal form. Thus, Yaguth, the lion-god, was worshipped in the time of the prophet by

---

[1] In an article in the *Journal of Philology,* Vol. IX, entitled "Animal Worship and Animal Tribes among the Arabs and in the Old Testament," and in his *Kinship and Marriage in Early Arabia,* ch. vii. He has been followed by Jacobs in his *Studies in Biblical Archæology,* London, 1894.

[2] *Kinship,* p. 188.

[3] *Journal of Philology,* Vol. IX, pp. 79-88, and *Kinship,* pp. 192-201.

[4] *Journal of Philology,* Vol. IX, pp. 89-100.

[5] Cf. Smith's *Kinship,* p. 202.

[6] *Ibid.,* pp. 203-205.

several different tribes. Ya'uq, according to commentators, was an idol in the form of a horse, while Nasr was said to have the figure of a vulture.[1] This is as near as we can come to direct proof. As Smith pointed out, there is some indirect proof in the fact that the jinn, who are said in the Qur'an (6^{100}) to have been partners with God, and therefore probably old deities degraded, are generally conceived in monstrous and hairy forms.[2]

Among the Hebrews the survivals of totemism do not form so complete a chain of proof for its existence, but there are a number of sporadic traces of it in the Old Testament which confirm the argument drawn from the Arabic material. There are a number of animal names, like Leah, Rachel, and Caleb, which were borne by reputed ancestors of clans; and in Ezekiel (8^{10}) and Isaiah (66^{17}) we have traces of an old animal worship revived in times of distress, which seems to be a survival of totemistic deities.[3]

The Old Testament affords some evidence that similar conceptions were entertained by neighboring Semitic tribes. Thus Oreb and Zeeb (the Raven and the Wolf) are, in Judges (7^{25}), the names of Midianitish chieftains. So Epher (the fawn or calf of the wild cow) is a Midianite, Judæan, and Manassite clan.[4] Many others might be cited if space permitted the reproduction of the investigations on this subject.[5] Although the proof from the Old Testament is not so complete as from Arabia, yet two out of the three necessary classes of evidence are found.

---

[1] Cf. *Kinship*, pp. 208, 209, and Wellhausen's *Reste arabische Heidentums*, 2d ed., Berlin, 1897, pp. 19–23.

[2] *Kinship*, p. 211.

[3] Cf. Smith's *Religion of the Semites*, 2d ed., p. 357, Cheyne's "Isaiah," in Haupt's *SBOT.*, p. 200, n. 5, and Toy's "Ezekiel," in *SBOT.*, p. 110, n. 7.

[4] Cf. Gen. 25^4, 1 Chron. 4^{17}, 5^{24}, and Robertson Smith in the *Journal of Philology*, Vol. IX, p. 91. See also Gesenius, *Handwörterbuch*, 13th ed., Leipzig, 1899, which follows Smith.

[5] Cf., in addition to Smith and Wellhausen, the list in Jacobs's *Studies in Biblical Archæology*.

In other Semitic countries occasional sporadic traces are found which point in the same direction. Thus, among the Guti or Suti, a tribe on the east of Babylonia, the goddess Ishtar was represented in the form of a lion or riding on a lion.[1] In the Gilgamish epic, which, as we now have it, centres in the city of Erech in southern Babylonia, Ishtar marries now a bird, now a lion, now a horse, and tries to marry a man,[2] — facts which point to a totemistic circle of ideas. At Eryx, in Sicily, Ashtart was thought to have the form of a dove,[3] and at Tyre, the head of a bull.[4] It is to such a conception that the book of Tobit (1[5]) alludes when it tells how people sacrificed to "She-Baal, the cow."[5] In the same class of evidence we should probably put the calves at Bethel and Dan which were said to be images of Yahwe (1 Kgs. 12[28]).

These reasons, slight as they may seem, come from widely different parts of the Semitic territory, and are, for that reason, significant. Sporadic traces of totemism so widely scattered can only be explained by supposing that the primitive clans in their old Arabian home were totemistic. Indeed, it is possible that this stage had been reached before the Hamites separated from them, for the well-known animal worship of the Egyptian nomes, in which each nome worshipped a different animal, is positive proof of the existence of totemism among that people.[6]

---

[1] Cf. *Hebraica*, Vol. X, pp. 26, 27. This and other evidence of a similar character was collected in my "Semitic Ishtar Cult," published in Vols. IX and X of *Hebraica*.

[2] Cf. *Hebraica*, Vol. X, p. 5, and Jastrow's *Religion of Babylonia and Assyria*, Boston, 1898, p. 482.

[3] Cf. Ælian, *De Natura Anamalium*, IV, also *Hebraica*, Vol. X, p. 49.

[4] Cf. the extracts from Philo of Biblos, published by Orelli as *Sanchoniathonis Fragmenta*, p. 30, really taken from the *Præp. Evang.* of Eusebius, Bk. I, 10, 31, Josephus's *Antiquities*, 8, 5, 3, *Against Apion*, 1, 18, also *Hebraica*, Vol. X, p. 31.

[5] Τῇ Βάαλ τῇ δαμάλει.

[6] The attempt of Robert Brown, Jun., *Semitic Influence in Hellenic Mythology*, Williams & Norgate, London, 1898, p. 56 ff., to prove that

The early culture of Egypt embalmed this system for our study as the amber of the Baltic sometimes embalms a fly; and the fact that the totemic system of thought appears both among the Semites and the Hamites makes it possible that before the separation of the two branches of the Hamito-Semitic race the totemic clan had already been developed. This possibility will again confront us at a later point; but however it may be determined, we are justified in holding that the totemic clan was the primitive Semitic social organization.

The economic purpose for which the clan organization was formed by the primitive Semitic folk was the defence of their date-growing oases and their domestic animals in their pasture lands, or for the attack of similar possessions of their neighbors. In a country where the conditions of life are as hard as they are in Arabia, the population has again and again, far back into prehistoric times, become too numerous to be supported by the sterile soil. Some who were pushed away from the oases or better pasture lands were compelled to plunder others for a living, until at last the pressure from within forced a wave of emigration through some convenient channel into another territory. These conditions down to the present time force many Arabs to become robbers, and make bands armed for plunder the terror and often the destruction of

totemism never existed in Egypt, (1) because no real Egyptologist believes it, and (2) because Strabo (XVII, 40) says that *all* worshipped the ox, cat, hawk, and ibis, is a signal failure. Were it true that no Egyptologist believes totemism to have existed in Egypt, it would only prove that Egyptologists allow themselves a narrow range of studies, so that the facts of anthropology escape them. It is doubtful whether this charge can justly be brought against them. Cf. *e.g.* Maspero's *Études de Mythologie d'Archéologie Égyptienne*, Paris, 1893, Vol. II, p. 277. Maspero's statement that their myths are of the same sort as those of the savages of the old and new world, is very like a confession of a belief in totemism. Strabo was a late writer, and, by his time, political unity had created syncretism so that the gods of some localities had obtained universal recognition; accordingly his statement proves nothing.

the nomad's life,[1] and must have operated among the primitive Semites much as they do to-day. Thus, then as now, clans must exist for mutual protection. Some of these would settle on an oasis, and their older and weaker men would aid the women in cultivating the date-palm, while the more hardy of the men led the small flocks and herds out into the neighboring pasture lands.[2] Those who were so unfortunate as to obtain no oasis would wander up and down with their flocks and herds seeking pasturage and plunder as opportunity offered.

In theory, such economic conditions should produce all three classes of clans: the communal, for the cultivation of the oases; the republican, for defence and for caravan trade; and the pastoral, for the part of the population which could obtain no oasis. All these types were, as we shall see, in time produced, but the dependence of all classes on the oases would, in Arabia, long hold the formation of the republican and patriarchal type of clan in check, and enable the communistic clan to exert such an influence as to leave its stamp upon the organization of society. Indeed, it is probable that for unnumbered centuries the clans which were deprived of the privileges of oases found life so hard that the conquest of other countries became for them a necessity, even before the republican or patriarchal type had become fully fixed. These facts will come out more fully as we proceed.

When we go a step farther back and seek to determine the constitution of the primitive Semitic family, we are met by greater difficulties. Those who have labored in this field hitherto have worked with the sociological theory of McLennan,[3] who held that in the primitive con-

[1] Cf. Doughty's *Arabia Deserta*, Vol. I, pp. 345, 489, 505, etc.; also Sale's *The Koran*, p. 24.

[2] Cf. Payne's *History of the New World called America*, Vol. II, p. 7 ff., and Keasbey, in the *International Monthly*, Vol. I, p. 390 ff., for analogous examples.

[3] Cf. G. A. Wilken's *Het Matriarchaat bij de Oude Arabieren*, Amsterdam, 1884; W. R. Smith's *Kinship and Marriage in Early Arabia*,

dition of man the relation of the sexes to one another was one of unrestrained promiscuous intercourse; that this was succeeded by a state of polyandry, and this, in turn, by the practice of polygamy, out of which monogamic marriage has grown.[1] This view presupposed that in the development of society the relation between the sexes had everywhere advanced according to one general law. In the polyandrous state of society it was found that kinship was reckoned through the mother, and it was inferred that woman, and not man, was the head of the clan. Thus, it was supposed that a matriarchate everywhere preceded a patriarchate, and that in the evolution of society the relative position of the sexes has been reversed.

More recent investigators of social problems are, however, unanimous in the opinion that polyandry is not a social condition through which all mankind has passed, but a phenomenon of social evolution which, under very special conditions, has appeared among a few races only.[2] The evidence on the matter seems overwhelmingly in favor of the latter view. It cannot, however, be reproduced here, but must, to be appreciated, be studied in the works of special students of the subject.[3] It appears, therefore, that the real matriarchate is comparatively rare. Among a few peoples, like the Nairs of the Malabar coast, it seems really to exist,[4] and in such families as those of the

---

Cambridge, 1885; and an article of the writer's, "The Kinship of Gods and Men among the Early Semites," in the *JBL.*, Vol. XV, p. 168 ff.

[1] See, *e.g.*, McLennan's *Studies in Ancient History*, Macmillan & Co., 1886, ch. viii.

[2] See Spencer's *Principles of Sociology*, Vol. I, p. 660 (Am. ed., New York, 1897); Starcke's *Primitive Family*, New York, 1889, p. 139 ff.; Letourneau's *The Evolution of Marriage and the Family*, New York, p. 320 ff.; Westermarck's *The History of Human Marriage*, Macmillan & Co., 1891, pp. 459 and 505–508; Lubbock's *The Origin of Civilization and the Primitive Condition of Man*, 5th ed., New York, 1892, p. 143 ff.; and Giddings's *Principles of Sociology*, pp. 155 and 276.

[3] *Ibid.*

[4] Cf. Reclus's *Primitive Folk*, New York, 1891, p. 165.

Andaman islanders[1] it would be the natural outcome of the unorganized condition of society. It frequently happens where polyandry is practised that the brother of the mother is the head of the family, and rears his sister's children, so that there is an avunculate rather than a matriarchate.

The late W. Robertson Smith, the great investigator of this phase of Semitic life, in whose tracks others of us have followed at a distance, and "non passibus æquis," based his investigations on the theory of McLennan; and though many of his results are permanent, and the mass of material he collected invaluable, yet, in the light of the present state of the science of sociology, the whole subject merits a new examination.

Westermarck[2] and Giddings[3] appear to be right in holding that the family of primitive man was an intermediate development between that of the highest animals and the lowest living men. In the lowest existing human societies the usual form of marriage is a temporary monogamy.[4] It is improbable that back of this there was a time when the marriage relations, taking mankind as a whole, were less clearly defined, since temporary marriages of this character appear among the higher apes.[5] It is possible — and a possibility of which writers on sociology take too little notice — that increased intelligence on the part of man may in some races have introduced into sexual relations degenerate practices. Higher mental power is, in the first instance, usually devoted to increased gratification of appetite, until the growth of moral sentiment brings the power of intelligence under the sway of worthy aims. It may easily have been, therefore, that human intelligence first, in some instances, exercised

---

[1] See Giddings's *Principles of Sociology*, p. 266.
[2] *History of Human Marriage*, pp. 14, 15, and 50.
[3] *Principles of Sociology*, p. 264.
[4] *Ibid.*
[5] *History of Human Marriage*, pp. 14, 15, and 50.

itself in gaining more frequent gratification for sexual desire. It is not likely that this would overthrow the kind of family organization which had obtained among our prehuman ancestors, since the economic necessities of life would be sufficient, in most parts of the world, to insure the union of father and mother until the mother and child could obtain food for themselves. It would, however, tend to produce lawlessness in sexual relations, which would bring into existence a sort of promiscuity by the side of the primitive temporary monogomy. This promiscuous intercourse would, on the part of the men, be participated in by those of all ages; while among the women it would be more often the young who would indulge, for these would more often attract by their beauty, — which in such communities quickly fades, — and both desire and inexperience of the consequences would lead them in this direction. This freedom has, I think, been perpetuated among those peoples who attach a religious significance to an act of free love on the part of their women before marriage.

That something like this occurred in the development of the Semites, two facts make probable: (1) the tendency of the early Semitic peoples to sexual excesses, a trait which points to an early bent in this direction; and (2) the fact that in the Ishtar cult in several different Semitic countries a religious importance was attached to an act of free love on the part of woman before she entered wedlock. Thus, Herodotus, Strabo, and the apocryphal letter of Jeremiah tell us that every Babylonian woman must once in her life offer herself in the temple of the goddess to whatever man might come.[1] Ephraim,[2] the Syrian, affirms the same practice among the Arabians in their worship of the mother goddess; and Augustine, in describing the

---

[1] See Herodotus, Bk. I, ch. 199; Strabo, Bk. XVI, ch. 1^{20}, and the *Epistle of Jeremiah*, vv. 42, 43. Cf. *Hebraica*, Vol. X, pp. 20, 21, and *JBL.*, Vol. X, p. 79 ff.

[2] *Opera*, Vol. II, pp. 458, 459. Cf. *Hebraica*, Vol. X, pp. 58, 59.

feast of the mother of the gods among the Carthaginians, makes it probable that the custom also existed there.[1] Herodotus, in the passage cited, says that the custom is also found in parts of Cyprus. We know that a kindred goddess was worshipped there,[2] and it was no doubt in connection with her worship. Lucian vouches for the existence of the custom at Byblos, the old Phœnician Gebal, but tells us enough to show that it had there undergone certain modifications; a woman who did not wish to sacrifice her chastity might sacrifice her hair.[3]

This custom, thus widely extended, is pretty good proof that the practice in question goes back to primitive Semitic times. This view is confirmed by a passage in the Gilgamish epic. In the second tablet of this poem there is a description of how Eabani, a wild man of the mountains or a primitive man, was enticed from the beast with which he had previously satisfied his passion,[4] by an emissary of the goddess Ishtar.[5] The fact that primitive man is here regarded as having promiscuous intercourse with the animals is in itself a testimony to its existence among human beings. Jastrow holds that there is a reflection of this, or a similar story, in Gen. 2, where he believes the original form of the narrative represented man as having intercourse with the beasts until woman was brought to him; and that then he abandoned the animals and became "one flesh" with her.[6] This view has much to commend

---

[1] See his *De Civitate Dei*, Bk. II, ch. iv. Cf. *Hebraica*, Vol. X, pp. 50, 51.
[2] Cf. *Hebraica*, Vol. X, pp. 42–47, and *Journal of Hellenic Studies* for 1888, pp. 175–206.
[3] Lucian's *De Syria Dea*, § 6 ff.
[4] That this is the meaning of the passage Jastrow has pointed out, *AJSL.*, Vol. XV, p. 202.
[5] See Haupt's *Nimrodepos*, Leipzig, 1884, pp. 10, 11; Jeremias's *Izdubar-Nimrod*, Leipzig, 1891, pp. 15–18; *Hebraica*, Vol. X, pp. 2, 3; Jastrow's *Religion of Babylonia and Assyria*, pp. 477, 478; and Jensen, in Schrader's *KB.*, Vol. VI, Berlin, 1900, pp. 125–127. According to Jensen's reconstruction of the poem, the passage is in the first tablet.
[6] See Jastrow's article, "Adam and Eve in Babylonian Literature," *AJSL.*, Vol. XV, pp. 207, 208.

it. The presence in the Gilgamish epic of a female priestess whose life is consecrated to this impure service reveals the existence of an institution which could hardly fail to grow out of the conditions which we have supposed to exist. From the earliest times there must have been, as there are now, women who, for one reason or another, gave their lives to the satisfaction of desire. Under primitive conditions this would be done much more freely than now, since there could not be much, if any, public opinion against it. Such religion as these early men had would, in the lapse of time, preserve, through the conservatism of mankind with regard to religious practices, these conditions under the guise of sacred service far beyond the state of society in which they had their birth; and thus present the anomaly which we find in so much of ancient Semitic life, of an impure priestess ministering in a community whose marriage ideal was relatively pure.

The Eabani episode is one of the oldest strata[1] of a poem, the later parts of which are some four thousand years old, and may well be held to reflect tolerably primitive ideas. We cannot be far wrong, therefore, if we hold, on the evidence presented, that in one of the earliest stages of Semitic development — a stage reached perhaps before their separation from the Hamites — such a strong tendency to unregulated intercourse existed, and that its results are seen in the religious practices which survived here and there far down into historic times. In Oman, where Mohammedan influences are felt less than in the most of Arabia, maiden virtue is, according to Palgrave, still of little account.[2] Sprenger cites a curious passage from Yaqut,[3] with regard to the town of Mirbât,

---

[1] Cf. Jastrow's *Religion of Babylonia and Assyria*, pp. 474–478, 513.
[2] Cf. Palgrave's *Central and Eastern Arabia*, Vol. II, p. 267.
[3] Cf. Sprenger's *Alte Geographie Arabiens*, p. 97. For the original see Jacut's *Geographisches Wörterbuch*, ed. Wüstenfeld, Leipzig, 1869, Vol. IV, p. 482. Nöldeke also admits (*ZDMG.*, Vol. XLV, p. 155), that among the Semites a kind of prostitution was practised without shame.

in the course of which it is said: "Their women go each night to the outer part of the city and devote themselves to strange men, and sport with them the greater part of the night. The husband, brother, son, and nephew goes by without taking notice, and entertains himself with another." This must have been a survival, under somewhat changed conditions, of the primitive tendency of the Semites to unregulated indulgence.

That there existed a temporary monogamy, such as sociologists postulate for the earliest human families, side by side with this unregulated intercourse, can also be shown to be true. Whether living in an oasis or wandering from place to place in the deserts of Arabia, women would be, from the earliest times, needed to perform the drudgery of the household and the camp, that the men might be free for those duties everywhere considered more manly by savages and barbarians — the duties of fighting for defence or plunder. These women must have been, in the earliest period, the mothers and sisters of the men, and not their wives, for ancient Semitic marriage was everywhere exceedingly temporary and divorce extremely common, — facts which show that the primitive Semitic marriage tie was an evanescent bond. These facts are abundantly attested by the Old Testament, the Babylonian contracts, the Qur'an, by numerous instances in Arabic life, and by the condition of Abyssinian society at the present time.

Among the Israelites of the Old Testament the sentiment seems to have been somewhat against divorce; and yet the law of Deuteronomy [1] makes it so exceedingly easy that it evidently points back to a time when divorce was much more common.

Among the Babylonians the frequency of divorce is not so easy to trace, since we have not, as in Deuteronomy, general statements of law, but must draw our inferences from the study of special cases. Nevertheless, in the few

---

[1] Deut. 24^{1-3}. Cf. Isa. 50^1.

marriage contracts and records of Babylonian divorce which have been studied, a sufficient number of instances appear to make it clear that divorce was not uncommon. Peiser has pointed out that two tablets in the British Museum reveal, upon comparison, that a woman who had been married to one man was within eight months married to another, while the first was still living.[1] The fact, too, that provisions for divorce were usually introduced into the marriage contracts of those women who married without a dowry, is clear proof that divorce was so common in Babylonia that women were compelled to protect themselves against it in the marriage contract.[2] Where the woman carried to the husband a dower, this was not necessary, since in Babylonian law the dowry was always hers, so that in case the husband divorced her he would lose it. In such cases the self-interest of the husband was thought to be a sufficient protection to the wife.[3]

The evidence from the Arabs is more abundant and, from sources both ancient and modern, is of the same character. The Qur'an contains two passages which attest the frequency of divorce. Sura 65$^{1-6}$ takes it for granted that divorces will be frequent, and provides that the woman shall not be sent forth burdened with the prospects of motherhood; while Sura 33^{48} supposes that men may frequently divorce their wives for whims after marrying them, but before marriage relations have really been established. The custom of divorce for any cause, at the wish of the husband, was, in the time of the prophet, too thoroughly fixed in Arabic custom, and too congenial

---

[1] See his *Babylonische Rechtsleben*, Berlin, 1890–8, Vol. II, pp. 13–15. The first of these texts is published in Strassmaier's *Babylonische Texte*, Heft VII, No. 111; the second is, so far as I know, unpublished.

[2] Cf. Strassmaier, *ibid.*, No. 183, and *Inschriften Nabuchodonosor*, No. 101; also, Peiser, *op. cit.*, Vol. IV, pp. 12, 13; and Merx in *Beiträge zur Assyriologie*, Vol. IV, pp. 4–8; and my article on "Contracts," §§ viii, ix, in *Assyrian and Babylonian Literature*, Aldine ed., New York, 1901.

[3] See my remarks in the article on "Contracts," § ix, in *Assyrian and Babylonian Literature*.

to the natures of the prophet and his followers, to be
changed; hence it was crystallized in Mohammed's law
and passed on to other generations.[1] This liberty has
been fully exercised by many of the faithful. Thus Ali,
the son-in-law of the prophet, married, including all that
he married and divorced, more than two hundred women.
Sometimes he included as many as four wives in one contract, and divorced four at one time, taking four others in
their stead.[2] A certain Mughayrah b. Sha'abah is reported
to have married eighty women in the course of his life,[3]
while Mohammed b. Aṭ-Ṭayib, the dyer of Baghdad, who
died in the year A.H. 423, at the age of eighty-five, is
said to have married in all more than nine hundred
women. If he began his marital career at the age of
fifteen, he must have had on the average nearly thirteen
new wives a year through his whole life.[4] This liberty
is exercised in Arabian countries still. Palgrave relates
that the Sultan of Qaṭar in eastern Arabia married a new
wife every month or fortnight, on whom the brief honors
of matrimony were bestowed for a like period, and who
was then retired on a pension.[5] Doughty also tells [6] how
Zeyd, his host, a petty sheik of the Bedawi, not only
permitted one of his wives to be courted by another Arab,
but offered to divorce her that Doughty might marry her.
Indeed, in parts of Arabia divorces are, in certain cases,
not necessary, since the marriages are contracted for a
limited period of definite length. Ammianus Marcellinus
(XIV. 4) gives this as their usual type of marriage. After
a certain day, he says, the wife may withdraw if she

[1] For an excellent account of divorce among the Arabs, see Wellhausen
in the *Nachrichten der Kgl. Gesell. d. Wiss. zu Gött.*, 1893, p. 452 ff.

[2] Cf. Lane's translation of the *Thousand and One Nights*, Vol. I, p.
318 ff., cited by Wilken, *Het Matriarchaat bij de Oude Arabieren*, p. 18.

[3] *Ibid.*

[4] *Ibid.*

[5] *Central and Eastern Arabia*, Vol. II, pp. 232, 233.

[6] *Arabia Deserta*, Vol. I, pp. 320, 321. Zeyd had once before found
a husband for a divorced wife of his, see *ibid.*, p. 237.

pleases. Somewhat of the same character is a temporary form of marriage which still exists in Sunan, a town fifteen days from Mocha in south Arabia. It is described as follows: "In all the streets there are brokers for wives, so that a stranger, who has not the conveniency of a house in the city to lodge in, may marry and be made a free burgher for a small sum. When the man sees his spouse and likes her, they agree on the price and term of weeks, months, or years, and then appear before the Kadi (qâdhi), or judge of the place, and enter their names and terms in his book, which costs a shilling or thereabout. And joining hands before him the marriage is valid, for better or for worse, till the expiration of the term agreed upon. And if they have a mind to part or renew the contract, they are at liberty to choose for themselves what they judge most proper; but if either wants to separate during the term limited, there must be a commutation of money paid by the separating party to the other according as they can agree; and so they become free to make a new marriage elsewhere."[1]

In Mecca, whither throngs of pilgrims regularly resort, some of whom tarry for longer or shorter spaces of time, marriages of similarly short duration are still entered into; and women go thither from Egypt with the avowed purpose of entering into such alliances.[2]

In Abyssinia civil marriages, into which ordinary people enter, are still dissoluble at will, and divorce is very frequent. It is nothing unusual for husbands and wives to exchange partners, all remaining as before on the best of terms. Sometimes marriages are contracted for a fixed

[1] Quoted by Wilken in *Het Matriarchaat bij de Oude Arabieren*, p. 15, from Hamilton's *New Account of the East Indies*, Vol. I, pp. 52, 53.
[2] See C. Snouck Hurgronje's *Mekka*, Haag, 1888-9, Vol. II, p. 5 ff., and 109-112, and S. M. Zwemer's *Arabia, the Cradle of Islam*, New York (Revell), 1900, p. 41. Zwemer is, however, dependent on Hurgronje. In Somaliland, where the native customs have been shaped by Arabic immigration, till it is not easy to tell always how much is native and how much is not, divorce is very common. Cf. *Südarabische Expedition*, Bd. I, *Die Somali-Sprache* von Leo Reinisch, Wien, 1900, p. 109.

period, at the end of which husband and wife separate. No stigma attaches to those who find a change of partners desirable. Inconstancy is common and chastity not highly valued.[1]

When now we find in all Semitic countries a tendency to make the term of marriage brief, — a tendency which it requires a high degree of civilization to subdue in them, — the inference is surely valid, that among the primitive Semites marriage relations were in like degree temporary. It is contrary to all analogy to suppose that the affections of the primitive Semite were more constant than those of his semicivilized descendant, or that there were in ancient times stronger inducements than in more recent centuries for the perpetuation of the marriage tie.

This fact is one of great importance, since its effect upon the constitution of the primitive Semitic family must have been serious. When marriages were of brief duration, and the same man had several wives in succession, the most of them cannot have been his sisters, even if such marriages had been permitted. There are, as we shall see by and by, some possible instances of such marriages among the Semites; but for the most part the feeling against mating with members of the same family, which is so widely disseminated among the races of the world,[2] appears also among the Semitic peoples. Even if this feeling had been absent, the transitory character of marriage and the frequency with which men took new wives would make it certain that most of them would be of other families, if not of other clans.

These wives would, when discarded, return to their kindred, if indeed they had ever left it, and would there,

---

[1] Cf. Bent's *Sacred City of the Ethiopians*, 1893, pp. 31 and 35 ff., and *A Visit to Abyssinia*, by W. Winstanley, London, 1881, Vol. II, pp. 73, 74, also *Modern Abyssinia*, by Augustus B. Wylde, London, 1901, pp. 161 and 254.

[2] See Starcke, *Primitive Family*, pp. 210, 211; Westermarck, *History of Human Marriage*, pp. 544, 545; and Giddings, *Principles of Sociology*, p. 267.

if they did not marry again, find support. Since the period of a woman's life during which she was desired in marriage was much shorter than the corresponding period in the life of a man, many of these discarded wives must, in any event, have been ultimately left with their own kindred;[1] where, if they carried their children with them, they would be esteemed, on account of the children, as the real perpetuators of the clan. It is therefore altogether probable, as was remarked above, that the women who, in the primitive Semitic clan, performed the drudgery, whether in oasis or in desert life, were usually the sisters and mothers, and not the wives, of the men.

Before, however, we accept this conclusion, with all its consequences, it is necessary to examine two other points which are closely connected: (1) the residence of the wife during her marriage; and (2) the method of reckoning kinship. In marriages of a temporary nature four different cases are possible: (1) the wife may live with her husband's kindred while married and return to her own when divorced, he retaining the children; (2) she may live while married with her husband's kindred, but on returning to her own take the children with her; (3) she may live in her own clan, whither the husband goes to live with her, she retaining the children when he withdraws; and (4) she may reside in her own clan and the husband in his, simply receiving visits from him from time to time, in which case the children remain with her. In the first of these cases the children would belong to the clan of the father, while in the last three they would belong to the clan of the mother.

The first of these conditions is that which has prevailed in the Arabian world from the time of the prophet to the present. The Qur'an (Sura 65^6) specifically provides that the children shall be reared for the father, and at his expense. Many interesting instances of this might be cited in the history of Mohammedan families; for exam-

---

[1] Cf. Giddings, *op. cit.*, p. 264 ff.

ple, Zeyd es-Sheychan, the sheik who was Doughty's host, and to whom reference has already been made, divorced the mother of his son Selim, but reared the son in his own family.[1] If this system of paternal kinship were primitive, we might suppose that the Semitic family had always existed in much the form of the Arabic family of to-day. If, however, it can be shown that descent was once reckoned through the mother, and that the present patronymic family has superseded a metronymic organization, we shall then be at liberty to inquire which of the last three positions we supposed above to be possible actually represents the status of the primitive Semitic wife.

The late Robertson Smith and others have established the fact, as well as the state of the evidence will permit it to be established, that back of the custom of tracing descent through males there was a time when the Semites traced it through females.[2] It is true that the first point which Smith makes, that if kinship were reckoned by blood it would have to be reckoned through the mother, because in primitive times paternity was uncertain, — owing to the state of promiscuity,[3] — is one which, in the light of recent sociological investigation [4] must be abandoned, for it is altogether likely that in most cases the father was known. Of his arguments, which still remain valid, a summary may be made as follows: (1) The well-known Biblical phrase for relationship is "bone of my bone and flesh of my flesh." "Flesh" is explained in Lev. 25^{49} by the word for clan. The Arabs attach great importance to a bond created by eating together; we must suppose, therefore, that the bond between those born of the same womb and nurtured at the same breast would be

---

[1] Doughty's *Arabia Deserta*, Vol. I, pp. 101, 217, 237, etc.
[2] See his *Kinship*, pp. 145-165.
[3] *Ibid.*, pp. 146-148.
[4] See Starcke's *Primitive Family*, p. 25, his article in the *International Journal of Ethics*, Vol. III, p. 455, and Westermarck's *History of Human Marriage*, pp. 108, 109.

more nearly of the same "flesh" and the same "clan" than any others. (2) The word *raḥim*, womb, is the most general word for kinship, and points to a primitive kinship through the mother. (3) The custom called *'acîca*, by which a child is consecrated to the god of his father's tribe, cannot have been primitive. It must have sprung up in a state of transition to insure the counting of the offspring to the father's side of the house. (4) Cases occur in the historical period in which a boy when grown attaches himself to his mother's tribe. The poet Zohair is a case in point, and Arabic antiquarians appear to have known that such cases were not uncommon.[1] (5) The fear that sons would choose their mother's clans led men who were wealthy to marry within their own kin. (6) The relation between a man and his maternal uncle is still considered closer than between a man and his paternal uncle. (7) Joseph's sons born of his Egyptian wife were not regarded as members of Israel's clan until formally adopted by him (Gen. 48$^{5.6}$). (8) Abraham married his paternal sister, who was not the daughter of his own mother. Tamar might have legally been the wife of her half-brother Amnon, the relationship being on the father's side (2 Sam. 13^{13}). Such unions were known in Judah as late as the time of Ezekiel (see ch. 22^{11}). Tabnith, king of Sidon, married his father's daughter,[2] and such marriages were known in Mecca. Since the marriage of those really regarded as brothers and sisters was abhorrent to the Semites, kinship must in these cases have been counted through the mother. (9) In the Arabic genealogical tables metronymic groups are still found. (10) In Aramaic inscriptions found at Hegra metronymic clans appear.[3]

Although these arguments of Smith are interwoven

---

[1] Cf. Smith's *Kinship*, pp. 155, 246–253.

[2] Cf. *CIS.*, Pt. I, Vol. I, No. 3, ll. 13–15.

[3] Cf. *CIS.*, Pt. II, Vol. I, Nos. 198 and 209. See also Smith's *Kinship*, pp. 313–316.

PRIMITIVE SEMITIC SOCIAL LIFE 53

with some theories of polyandry, the consideration of which must be postponed a little, and with some arguments which do not appear to be valid, these which we have summarized present facts which, regardless of any theories of marriage, prove that at one time kinship was reckoned through the mother.

This conclusion is corroborated by evidence gathered by other scholars. Nöldeke noted that in the religious texts of the Mandæans a man is described as the son of his mother, which indicates that among them kinship was reckoned through the mother.[1] Peiser has pointed out[2] that among the Babylonians a man could if he chose renounce his family and join the kindred of his wife, which is a relic of the same custom. Wellhausen has observed[3] that in the genealogies of the Pentateuch the J document reckons descent through the mother, while in the P document it is traced through the father.

These arguments may be confirmed by several important considerations. If descent had not been reckoned through the mother, the position which, as will be pointed out below, woman held among the early Semites would have been impossible, as would also a type of marriage for which there is considerable proof, and which will be considered in its place.

If, now, the fact be accepted that kinship was counted through the female line, their habit in this respect is found to conform to that of most other primitive peoples,[4] and a vantage ground is obtained from which the social phenomena which remain to be considered become intelligible to us. If children did not belong to the clan of the father, the first of the possible forms of marriage men-

---

[1] *Monatsschrift*, 1884, p. 304.
[2] *Mittheilungen der vorderasiatische Gesellschaft*, 1896, p. 155.
[3] *Nachrichten d. Kgl. Gesell. d. Wiss. zu Gött.*, 1893, p. 478, n. 2.
[4] See Spencer's *Principles of Sociology*, Vol. I, pp. 698, 703; Lubbock's *Origin of Civilization*, etc., 5th ed., pp. 151-157; Starcke's *Primitive Family*, pp. 18, 25, 37, 39, 74; Westermarck's *History of Human Marriage*, pp. 96, 97, 539; and Giddings's *Principles of Sociology*, p. 265.

tioned above is clearly eliminated. The mother, as a rule, when she left her husband's residence (if she had lived there at all) must have taken the children with her; and if she resided in her own clan, it is clear that she retained the children. Of course it is possible that from the earliest times a man might, when the clans were well disposed to one another, induce a woman to leave her own kindred and go to live with his. Of this we have almost no evidence, and in the nature of the case can obtain little. The point proved by Smith,[1] however, that in early pre-Mohammedan times the natural protectors of a woman were not her husband and his kindred, but her own relatives, makes it improbable that in the earliest Semitic communities the woman left her own people at all. Probably, therefore, the second of our possible arrangements of Semitic marriage should also be eliminated.

Of the third possibility — the residence of the husband in the wife's tribe — we have more direct evidence. The classical instance of this, which all writers cite, is the case of Jacob and his wives, Leah and Rachel.[2] Jacob lived with them in Laban's clan, and when he left was blamed for taking away the children. Laban declared, "the daughters are my daughters and the children are my children" (Gen. 31^{43}), *i.e.* they belong to my clan. A second argument, and one which proves that the case of Jacob and Laban is not an isolated instance, is found in the fact that the phrase for marriage which is used throughout the Old Testament, which is found in Syriac, and is still used in south Arabia,[3] is "he went in unto her." Smith has shown[4] that this phrase originated when it was the custom for a man to go to reside in his wife's tent in her tribe. In Yemen it is still the custom for the "going in" to take place in the bride's house; and the bridegroom, if home-born, must stay some nights in the bride's home, and if a foreigner, must settle with

---

[1] *Kinship*, pp. 101–103.
[2] Gen., chs. 29–31.
[3] Smith's *Kinship*, pp. 167, 168.
[4] *Ibid.*, pp. 167–172.

the tribe.[1] Smith also pointed out that the custom in north Arabia which compels a man to build a new tent for his wife, is an outgrowth of the older practice of entering the wife's tent. In the same region it sometimes happens still that the wife refuses to leave her tribe, and the husband is compelled to leave his and go and join hers. Lady Blunt relates such an instance which came under her own observation.[2] That this also occurred in ancient Babylonia, the case cited above of the man who joined his wife's family is sufficient to prove. Such evidence as this, coming from so many portions of the Semitic territory, makes it clear that this kind of marriage was a primitive Semitic practice.

In such marriages many circumstances might arise to call the husband away and interrupt the marriage relations. The clans might become hostile, so that it would be unsafe for him to remain, or his fancy might weary of the bride's attractions, or of her people, and then he would wander elsewhere to contract a similar alliance. Such marriages are called *beena* marriage, the name given them in Ceylon, where they were first studied. They are found in many parts of the world.[3] The children in such cases remain of course with the mother, are reared by her kindred, and become a part of her clan. The net result, therefore, of our discussion up to this point is the establishment of the fact that the primitive Semites practised *beena* marriage, that the children belonged to the tribe of

---

[1] Smith, *ibid.*, p. 168. Among the Hamitic Somalis of East Africa, among whom the Arabs have penetrated and by whom many Arabic customs have been adopted (cf. *Beiträge zur Ethnographie und Anthropologie der Somâl, Galla und Harari*, von Philipp Paulitschke, 2d ed., Leipzig, 1888, p. 2 ff.), it is still customary, when a young man marries, for the bride, aided by the kinswomen of the groom, to build before the marriage feast a new hut, in which after marriage they establish their new home. Cf. *Südarabische Expedition*, Bd. I, *Die Somali-Sprache*, von Leo Reinisch, Wien, 1900, p. 107.

[2] *A Pilgrimage to Nejd*, by Lady Anne Blunt, London, 1881, Vol. I, p. 92.

[3] Cf. Giddings's *Principles of Sociology*, p. 268.

the mother, and that the women of the household were the mothers and sisters, and not the wives and daughters, of the men. The third of the possible arrangements of Semitic marriage mentioned above turns out, therefore, to be a true one.

Evidence is also at hand to prove that the fourth of the possible arrangements was also realized in practice. In three of the Muʻallakāt poems there are specific statements that the women whom the poets visited only occasionally were members of other clans, and that often they visited them at personal risk,[1] on account of the strained relations of the clans. The marriage of Samson (Judges 14) was also an alliance of this character. His wife resided in her own clan, and he visited her there. In such cases as these the marriages were often terminated by the migration of the tribes in different directions.[2] This is the general type of marriage which Ammianus Marcellinus describes when speaking of the Arabs, though he is probably speaking of a somewhat later development of it. He says the bride presents her husband with a spear and a tent, and if she chooses withdraws after a certain day.[3]

This last phase of the marriage relation of the Semites is probably but a modification of the *beena* marriage, or the *beena* marriage a modification of it, brought about at times by the hostile relation of the clans, as in the case of Samson; at times, by considerations of personal attachment to his own clan, which made a man unwilling, even temporarily, to leave it; and at times, by economic necessities, as will be pointed out below.

The general view which we have been led to take of the marriage tie among the Semites is confirmed by the position held among them by women in ancient times. So

---

[1] See *Muʻallakāt of Labîd*, ll. 16-19; that of *ʼAntarah*, ll. 5-11; and that of *Harith*, ll. 1-9.

[2] *Muʻallakāt of Labîd*, ll. 16-19.

[3] See Bk. XIV, ch. 4. He also remarks on the temporary character of Arabic marriages.

far from being the creature of man and almost his chattel, as the system of selling daughters to become wives of the *baal* marriages has made her, she occupied a position of comparative dignity, equality, and independence. Smith has shown that in Arabia, in pre-Islamic times, women were frequently chosen as judges; that they were sometimes queens (of whom the queen of Sheba of Biblical fame is best known); that they were regarded as the most sacred trust of the tribe; and that, in spite of Mohammed's humanitarian laws in behalf of women, their position steadily declined under Islam in consequence of the system of *baal* marriage, which practically made the husband her lord.[1] This view is confirmed by Wellsted[2] and Palgrave,[3] who found that in Oman and Hasa, where Islam is not so rigorously observed as in northern Arabia, women were much more free and respected than in other parts of the peninsula. In several places they did not wear the veils even in the towns; and in some, where it was worn, the practice was voluntary.[4] This freedom is, without doubt, a survival from pre-Islamic times.

In ancient Israel we also catch glimpses of a similar freedom and dignity for women. In what appears to be the oldest bit of literature in the Old Testament,[5] Deborah figures as the inspirer and director of the people in the movement for freedom. She assumes here a position as free and prominent as any that woman occupied in Arabia.

In Babylonia, too, the contract tablets reveal the fact that at the close of the New Babylonian Empire, and in the early Persian period, after many centuries of *baal* marriage, women still held a position of great importance

---

[1] Cf. Smith's *Kinship*, pp. 100–106, 171, and 275.
[2] Cf. Wellsted's *Travels in Arabia*, Vol. I, pp. 351–354.
[3] *Central and Eastern Arabia*, Vol. II, p. 177.
[4] Wellsted, *op. cit.*, Vol. I, pp. 101, 118, and 146; also Palgrave as in n. 4.
[5] The poem in Judges 5.

and freedom. Married women appear with their husbands as joint partners in buying, selling, borrowing, and loaning; married women appear alone in business contracts relating to money, real estate, and slaves; they make contracts concerning merchandise with men not their husbands, and appear in lawsuits.[1] This dignity, which the Babylonian of the seventh and sixth centuries B.C. accorded to woman, must be regarded as a survival of the comparatively independent position which she held among their early Semitic ancestors. Thus Arabia, Palestine, and Babylonia each contribute to the proof of this position.

These arguments, taken in connection with the evidence concerning the nature of primitive Semitic marriage, are sufficient to make it clear that in the course of Semitic progress the position of woman, in the family and in the clan, has been greatly modified, and that she has lost in the process much of her primitive importance. This point will be still further confirmed when we come to consider, in subsequent chapters,[2] the religious argument. It will then appear that in different parts of the Semitic territory, notably in Arabia and Babylonia, goddesses survived till a comparatively late time, who held a position of independence of male deities, without parallel in later Semitic social organization; and whose birth would therefore compel us, even if there were no other evidence on the matter, to postulate a condition of society among the primitive Semites in which woman should hold a position similar to that described in the preceding pages. In many ways free of restraint; often the head of her family, if not of her clan; usually leaving her maidenhood behind by one or more acts of free love; contracting marriages at will as fancy dictated, but each of which was of short duration; cherished as the mother of her children and the perpetuator of her family; performing the drudgery of nomadic

---

[1] See the monograph of Victor Merx, "Die Stellung der Frauen in Babylonien," etc., in *Beiträge zur Assyriologie*, Vol. IV, pp. 1-72.

[2] Chs. III and VI.

life, but mingling in, even when she did not direct, the counsels of her uncles, brothers, and sons, — the primitive Semitic woman was a picturesque figure, if not a model for more modern days.

It is now time to inquire whether the primitive Semites practised polyandry. Robertson Smith, following in the footsteps of McLennan, interpreted many of the phenomena we have passed in review as evidence of polyandrous practices. This, as is evident from the treatment accorded the subject above, is not necessary. Such facts as we have thus far examined may all be explained on the basis of a temporary monogamy of the *beena* type, intermixed with considerable sexual irregularity. Some of these facts are not inconsistent, however, with the institution of polyandry; and there are others still to be considered which make its presence at some periods and in some localities certain.

Polyandry, in one form or another, has existed in many parts of the world. It is found in India, both ancient and modern, where it finds reflection in the ancient Mahabharata epic and other records; and it still appears among some existing tribes.[1] The most famous instance from this land is that of the Nairs of the Malabar coast, whose life has been most fully studied, and who represent one type of the polyandric institution most completely.[2] It is also found in Thibet, though the kind of polyandry practised there is of another type.[3] Still another type was,

[1] On polyandry in India, see Hopkins's monograph, "The Ruling Caste in Ancient India," *JAOS.*, Vol. XIII, pp. 170, 354 ff.; his *Religions of India*, Boston, 1895, pp. 467, 535 n.; and his *Great Epic of India*, N.Y., 1901, pp. 376, 399; Jolly's *Recht und Sitte* (in Bühler's *Grundriss der Indo-Arischen Philologie und Altertumskunde*, Bd. II, Heft 8), pp. 47–49; Hilderbrand's *Recht und Sitte auf den verschiedenen wirtschaftlichen Kulturstufen*, Jena, 1896, pp. 15, 16; Reclus's *Primitive Folk*, pp. 143–177, and Starcke's *Primitive Family*, pp. 79–87.

[2] For description see Reclus, as in n. 1. All writers on marriage and sociology, from McLennan down, have much to say of them.

[3] Cf. Spencer's *Principles of Sociology*, Vol. I, p. 659, and Starcke's *Primitive Family*, p. 134.

according to Cæsar, found among the ancient Britons,[1] and is still found among the Todas.[2] Polyandry is also found in the Polynesian Islands,[3] until recently in Ceylon and New Zealand, in the Aleutian Islands, among the Konyaks north of the Okhotsk, and among the Cossacks. Humboldt observed it among the Indian tribes of the Orinoco; it was common in the Canary Isles; in Africa it has been found among the Hottentots, the Demaras, and among the mountain tribes of the Bantu race. It formerly prevailed among the Picts and Irish.[4]

The explanations offered for polyandry are various. McLennan believed that all races had passed through it as a necessary stage on the way from promiscuity to monogamy. Those who reject this view have assigned it to different causes: some to poverty,[5] others to natural excess of males where tribes interbreed,[6] and others regard it as a mere incident of family communism.[7] Poverty cannot be the sole cause, since it is sometimes found among the rich.[8] It can hardly be explained by a natural excess of males, since such excess is very improbable.[9] As a matter of fact, no one cause is sufficient to explain it in all localities.[10] Each instance of it must be studied by itself in its peculiar environment and in the light of its antecedents.

Before we return to Semitic polyandry it will be helpful to glance at some of the different types of it which have developed in different countries. These types are three

[1] Cf. *De Bello Gallico*, V, 14, and Starcke, *op. cit.*, p. 139.
[2] Cf. Spencer, *op. cit.*, Vol. I, p. 654.
[3] Cf. Waitz, *Anthropologie*, Vol. VI, pp. 128, 129.
[4] McLennan's *Studies in Ancient History*, p. 97 ff., and Giddings's *Principles of Sociology*, p. 155 ff.
[5] So Hilderbrand, *Recht und Sitte*, etc., pp. 15, 16, and, in part, Giddings, *op. cit.*, pp. 155, 156, and 276.
[6] So Westermarck, *History of Human Marriage*, pp. 476–483.
[7] So Starcke, *Primitive Family*, pp. 139, 140.
[8] Cf. Westermarck, *op. cit.*, pp. 476, 477, and 482.
[9] Cf. Starcke, in the *International Journal of Ethics*, Vol. III, p. 464.
[10] Cf. Spencer, *op. cit.*, Vol. I, p. 663.

in number: Nair polyandry, in which a woman may have as many as a dozen husbands, whom she receives in succession or as fancy dictates, but who in turn are free to have as many mistresses as they can secure;[1] Thibetan polyandry, in which a group of brothers share one wife; and British polyandry, in which a group of sisters become in common the wives of a group of brothers. These three types represent three different forms of the institution. Of these the Nair type is the most primitive. The Thibetan and British types may be considered as modifications of the same form, since they are in principle the same.

Returning now to the Semites, we may note that the type of temporary marriage, of which traces are found in the Muʻallakāt poems and in Ammianus Marcellinus,[2] is not necessarily monogamous or monandrous. In such temporary unions, in which the husband and wife belonged to different tribes, it would very probably be that each would have acknowledged lovers in other tribes, with whom they would have intimate relations whenever the tribes approached one another so as to make it possible. When we consider the sexual bent of the early Semites and the lightness with which the marriage tie was regarded, we can hardly hesitate to believe that this was so. Such an arrangement might be classed as temporary monandry, or as polyandry of the Nair type, according to the point of view from which it is regarded. Like Nair polyandry, it was at the same time polygamy. It differed, however, from Nair polyandry in being exogamous; the Nairs regarded intercourse with one of another caste as adultery.[3] In all probability, there was more polyandry than polygamy in these marriages, for the practice of putting

---

[1] Cf. Reclus, *Primitive Folk*, p. 163.

[2] See above, p. 56. These temporary marriages, where the wife received visits from her lovers with the consent of her kinsmen, were called *motʻa* marriages, *i.e.* marriages of pleasure or convenience. It is given this name in some of the Arabic commentaries to Sura 4^{28}. See Wilken's *Matriarchaat*, p. 9, n. 3.

[3] Reclus, *ap. cit.*, p. 164.

to death infant girls, which prevailed down to the time of Mohammed (see Sura 16[61]), was in all probability a primitive Semitic practice. Where the conditions of life were as hard as they always were in the Arabian peninsula, more warriors than women would usually be needed by the tribe; and this mode of preventing not only too many women, but too rapid an increase of the tribe, in view of the limited means of sustenance, would be very natural. Such a custom is not inconsistent with the high honor in which the women who were permitted to live were held, especially to a semi-savage mind not sensitive to incongruities. Inevitably an excess of males would thus be produced, which, among a sexually lax people, would be sure to lead to polyandry. We cannot be sure that such marriages, especially in later times, were always exogamous. Those already cited from the Mu'allakāt poems certainly were, but there are others to be found in the same collection which were endogamous. Imr-ul-Kais alludes in his Mu'allakāt to the fact that he followed the women of his tribe and spent a day in their company,[1] and the Unaizah, whose fruit he boasts he had repeatedly tasted, was the daughter of his uncle. In like manner Laila, the woman celebrated in the poem of Amr b. Kulthum, was Amr's kinswoman.[2] In polyandrous marriages of the general Nair type, there might exist both endogamous and exogamous alliances; and so far as this form of marriage existed among the Semites, it would appear from extant evidence to have combined the two kinds of marriage, that from within and that from without the tribe. In so far as Semitic feeling on this point can be historically traced, it was in favor of endogamy; Semitic parents were always grieved if their children married outside their tribe.[3]

[1] See the Arabic commentator's explanation of v. 11 of Imr-ul-Kais's *Mu'allakāt* in Arnold's edition of the *Mu'allakāt*. For a translation of the poems, see *The Seven Poems suspended in the Temple at Mecca*, by F. E. Johnson, London, 1894.
[2] See *Mu'allakāt*, V, 11, 13, 14.
[3] See Genesis 24[3, 4], 26[34, 35], 28[1, 2], Judges 14[3], etc.

This is, however, probably a late feeling, which sprung up when totemism was decaying, when primitive conditions of marriage and kinship were breaking up, and when, in disregard of earlier customs and ideas, the desire to keep the children for one's tribe was gaining the ascendency. In a totemic clan where real sisters are not taken as wives, totemic sisters cannot be.[1] As the Semitic clans were totemic and did not, as a rule, marry sisters,[2] we must infer that in the earlier stages of development they were exogamous; and that Nair polyandry, in so far as it existed among them, existed as an exogamous institution. The mixed variety with which we meet in the Mu'allakāt poems is explained by the break-up of the old religious ideas which was in progress, and the social transition which the introduction of male kinship was introducing.[3]

Perhaps the kind of marriage which is practised by the Hassenyeh Arabs of the White Nile is a relic of the Nair type of polyandry, though it might equally well be regarded as a slight limitation of the promiscuity of the primitive Semitic girls, which we discussed above. Among these Arabs, the marriages of the most respectable are not for more than four days in the week, and may be for less time. During these days the wife must observe the rules for matrimonial chastity; but on other days she is free to receive any man whom she may fancy, and the husbands seem pleased with any attention paid to their wives during their free and easy days, taking it as evidence that their wives are attractive.[4]

It is safe to conclude, from the evidence presented, that in early Semitic life a combined polyandry and polygamy,

---

[1] See Giddings's *Principles of Sociology*, p. 271.

[2] See Lev. 20[17, 18], Qur'an 4[27], Yaqut, Vol. IV, p. 620, and Robertson Smith's discussion, *Kinship*, p. 162 ff.

[3] Wellhausen holds also that Arabic endogamy was preceded by exogamy; see *Nachrichten d. kgl. Gesell. d. Wiss. zu Gött.*, 1893, pp. 473 ff.

[4] See Wilken's *Matriarchaat*, p. 24, and Spencer's *Principles of Sociology*, Vol. I, p. 617.

approaching the Nair type, but originally exogamous, existed. It has, however, passed away, leaving few results behind it which might not have been produced by a system of temporary marriage, combined with a large degree of that sexual laxity which exists among all peoples, in greater or less degree, but which among the early Semites was regarded as a religious duty.

Of the Thibetan type of polyandry we have more abundant evidence. The most striking is the passage in Strabo's description of Arabia Felix, often quoted by writers in recent years:[1] "All the kindred have property in common, the eldest being lord; all have one wife, and it is first come first served, the man who enters to her leaving at the door the stick which it is customary for every one to carry; but the night she spends with the eldest. Hence, all are brothers of all; they also have conjugal intercourse with mothers;[2] an adulterer is punished with death; an adulterer is a man of another stock." This passage is strong testimony of the existence in Yemen of fraternal polyandry of the Thibetan type. It has recently been confirmed by the testimony of inscriptions brought from the same region. Glaser stated, in 1897, that he had epigraphic evidence of polyandry, or communal marriage, among the Sabæans,[3] and Winckler, in the next year, pointed out that in a Minæan inscription published by Halévy, the genealogy demonstrated a fraternal polyandry.[4] The evidence for this type of marriage for Yemen is therefore indisputable.

The late Robertson Smith collected considerable evidence to show that this type of polyandry was also known

[1] Strabo, Bk. XVI, ch. 4, p. 783.

[2] This is probably not to be taken literally, but to be explained by Qur'an 4^{26}, where it appears that men had married wives of their fathers. Cf. Robertson Smith in *Journal of Philology*, Vol. IX, p. 86, n. 2.

[3] See his note "Polyandrie oder Gesellschaftschen bei den alten Sabäern" in the Beilagen of *Allgemeine Zeitung*, München, December 6, 1897.

[4] "Die Polyandrie bei den Minäern," in Winckler's *Altorientalische Forschungen*, 2te Reihe, Vol. I, pp. 81–83.

in North Arabia and in other parts of the Semitic territory. His arguments are: (1) Bokhari relates that two men made a covenant of brotherhood, which resulted in their sharing their goods and wives, — a fact which would seem to show a survival of a custom of fraternal polyandry.[1] (2) In Arabia *kanna* means the wife of a son or brother, but is used also to denote one's own wife. In Hebrew *kăllāh* means both betrothed and daughter-in-law; while in Syriac *kaltha* means both bride and daughter-in-law. These facts can be explained most easily as remnants of fraternal polyandry.[2] (3) The Arabic law that a man has the first right to the hand of his cousin, as well as the fact which the 4th Sura of the Qur'an and its attendant traditions attest, that in case a man died and left only female children, the father's male relatives inherited his property and married his daughters, are regarded as the results of a previously existing polyandrous condition of society like that described by Strabo.[3] (4) The Qur'an (4^{23}) forbids men to inherit women against their will, and forbids (4^{26}) them to take their step-mothers in marriage "except what has passed." This is regarded as evidence that down to the time of Mohammed these attendant circumstances of polyandry had continued, and that the prophet did not dare to annul existing unions, though he forbade such marriages in the future.[4]

The last two points quoted from Smith may not at first sight seem to be valid arguments, but a little consideration of the circumstances which would inevitably attend polyandry of this sort, and the transition from it to polygamy, will vindicate their character. In fraternal polyandry the oldest brother is the head of the family, and the wife is, or in time becomes, the property of the

---

[1] *Kinship*, p. 135.

[2] *Ibid.*, p. 136. I have modified the statements slightly in quoting because, in the form in which Smith made them, they are not lexically defensible.

[3] *Ibid.*, pp. 138, 139.

[4] *Ibid.*, pp. 86, 87.

F

group of brothers. In case the oldest brother dies, the next in age succeeds to his prerogatives and to his larger claim on the wife. Thus, the idea is established that inheritance carries with it not only rights of property, but marital rights as well. Endogamous customs of marriage extend this idea. A man comes to think of his paternal cousin as by right his wife, so that the conception of inheriting women is strengthened and extends. Under this system of polyandry the conception of male kinship grows up and is firmly established, so that when polygamy succeeds polyandry the social soil is prepared for such customs as those urged by Smith as evidences of polyandry.

In this connection Smith also, following in the footsteps of McLennan, urged that the Levirate custom of marrying the wife of a dead brother to raise up seed to him, of which we have such a beautiful idyl in Ruth 3, 4, of which he also found traces in Arabia,[1] and which still exists in Abyssinia,[2] was an outgrowth of fraternal polyandry. It seemed to him and McLennan that no one would have thought of counting the son of one brother as the son of another, if previously the sons had not been the property of all in common. Spencer, Starcke, and Westermarck have all contested this position. Spencer suggests that it is one of the results of inheriting women as one would inherit other property;[3] to which Starcke justly replies that this view leaves unexplained the real point of the custom, the counting of the children as the offspring of the dead brother. Starcke[4] and Westermarck[5] point out that the Levirate, or institutions of a similar character, have existed in many parts of the world where there was no suspicion of polyandry, and that therefore another explanation must be sought. That which they offer is

[1] *Kinship*, p. 87.
[2] Letourneau's *Evolution of Marriage*, p. 265.
[3] *Principles of Sociology*, Vol. I, p. 661.
[4] *The Primitive Family*, pp. 157, 158, and the *International Journal of Ethics*, Vol. III, p. 465.
[5] *The History of Human Marriage*, pp. 510–514.

that in primitive communities the idea of fatherhood is juridical, and not based on actual fatherhood, and that this fact, combined with the desire to keep intact the dead man's estate, produced the institution in question. The view of Letourneau,[1] that the Levirate, though not necessarily produced by polyandry, is practised under a polyandric régime, seems to come nearer to the truth. Possibly other customs and causes may have sometimes produced an institution of a similar character; but when we find absolutely certain evidence of the existence of fraternal polyandry, such as we have for south Arabia, it is but fair to interpret an institution which grows, as we have seen, so naturally out of polyandry, as evidence of its existence in another branch of the Semitic race.

The explanations which Starcke and Westermarck give of the Levirate seem inadequate in two respects: (1) They leave unexplained why any one should desire to keep the dead brother's estate intact, when it would be for the self-interest of all the other brothers to have it divided; and (2) they assume that in all parts of the world similar institutions must be produced by identical causes. Let it be granted that polyandry does not offer a complete explanation of why seed should be desired for an individual brother, McLennan's contention that it did so is still so far valid, that it may be said that polyandry supplies some probable cause, while the juridical theory affords none. It is not for an outsider to fight the battles of the sociologists, but to me it seems more scientific to study each institution in the light of its antecedents and environment, than to heap instances together from every quarter of the globe, and assume that because their external character is similar one cause must have produced them all. Studied in the light of the characteristics of the Semitic race, we may still hold that for them the presence of the Levirate system argues a previous polyandric con-

[1] *The Evolution of Marriage*, p. 265.

dition. This is the opinion of Wellhausen,[1] Buhl,[2] and Benzinger,[3] all of whom recognize that back of Arabic and Hebrew life, as we know it, there lay a condition of polyandry.

It is in this type of polyandry, where the wife is the recipient of the favors of all the brothers, that the individual father may not be known. It is always known that a child is connected with a certain paternal stock, but which one of the brothers begat him is a matter of doubt. This led Robertson Smith to point out[4] that the Semitic word *abu* must have originally meant "nourisher," not procreator, and that in fraternal polyandry it must have been applied to the elder brother. It thus acquired the value of "husband" before it had the value of "father," and is actually employed in the former sense by Jeremiah (ch. 3⁴). This observation led me to point out[5] that in a Babylonian contract, which dates from more than two thousand years B.C., the word *abu* is also used in the sense of "husband." This affords us at least one trace of this system in Babylonia. It seems safe, therefore, to conclude that this type of polyandry began before the dispersion of the Semitic nations, or was developed by similar circumstances, or was carried by later emigrants from Arabia to the other nations. It seems probable that it was developed before the later separations from the parent stock occurred, and if not before the earliest, it was carried to those countries by later migrations.

[1] Cf. *Nachrichten d. kgl. Gesell. d. Wiss. zu Gött.*, 1893, pp. 460 ff., 474 ff., and 479 ff.
[2] *Die sociale Verhältnisse der Israeliten*, von Franz Buhl, Berlin, 1899, p. 28 ff.
[3] *Hebraische Archæologie*, Leipzig, 1894, p. 134.
[4] *Kinship*, pp. 117, 134. Cf. also my article, "The Kinship of Gods and Men among the Early Semites," in *JBL.*, Vol. XV, especially p. 181 ff.
[5] See my "Note on Meissner's *Altbabylonische Privatrecht*, No. 7," in *JAOS.*, Vol. XX, p. 326. The point of the article is that in line 24 of this tablet a woman's father is called her *abu*, while in line 28 her husband is

PRIMITIVE SEMITIC SOCIAL LIFE

Of British polyandry, or communal marriage (the marriage of a group of women to a group of men), there is not, so far as I know, much evidence. Euting[1] describes a caravan which he saw on its way from Haurân to Kâf, which contained 170 men and more than 20 young women. This suggests the possibility that in the exigencies of caravan life communal unions may have been formed. Dozy[2] cites a case which occurred under Omar I, where an old Arab gave to a young one a share in his wife, in return for which the young man was to do gardening for him; and when reproved for it, both men professed to be ignorant that they were acting contrary to law. This was, of course, not communal marriage, but it indicates a point of view which would make it possible, for convenience, to produce such unions. If this type of marriage ever existed among the Semites, it has left behind no sure traces of itself.

Having established the existence of Thibetan polyandry, as well as that of the Nair type, we must inquire into their relation to one another. Smith held[3] that Thibetan polyandry was a transition stage from the maternal to the paternal family. As has been pointed out,[4] the Nair type of polyandry is consistent with the conditions of very early Semitic life, when marriage was exogamous. The type of polyandry described by Strabo could only be introduced, as endogamous Nair polyandry could be,[5] when these conditions were breaking up, when totemism was losing its hold, and endogamy had taken the place of exogamy. Smith also claims[6] that the capture of women, of which there is abundant evidence,[7] had an important influence in

also called her *abu*, showing that the word was used in the same elastic manner as it is in Jeremiah.

[1] *Tagbuch einer Reise in Inner-Arabien*, Leiden, 1896, p. 38.
[2] *Histoire des Musselmans d'Espagne*, par R. Dozy, Leiden, 1861, Vol. I, p. 36.
[3] *Kinship*, p. 144 ff.
[4] Above, p. 63 ff.
[5] See above, p. 57.
[6] *Kinship*, pp. 74, 75.
[7] See also Wellhausen, *Nachrichten d. kgl. Gesell. d. Wiss. zu Gött.*, 1893, p. 473.

developing it.   The sons of such women were, as Arabian poets declare, brought up with their father's tribe.   The mother could not dismiss her husband at will, as in the older *mot'a* marriage, but became subject to his power. This power over her was sweet; and the advantage of having their children to themselves, and not being compelled to abandon them to the tribe of the mother, appealed to them.   But women were not always to be captured; often, too, the conditions of life were too hard to allow of the support of more than one in a whole family of brothers, so the feeling against letting the children of sons go out of the tribe would of course nurture the older feeling that the children of the daughters were members of it; and thus gradually marriage with a kinswoman took, for the most part, the place of extra-tribal, or clan marriages.

While the forces which transformed Nair polyandry into that of the Thibetan type may have been, in part, those which Smith supposed, there were other economic reasons which, in Arabia, must have had a tendency to act in this direction from the beginning. It is clear from Keasbey's analysis of the clan organization, with which this chapter opened, that the matriarchal clans, which we have in the subsequent discussion proven to exist, must have had their habitat in the oases of Arabia.   There the women and the weaker men would remain, thither other men would from time to time repair, there Nair polyandry would be practised, and there woman would be held in the high esteem in which we have shown her to have been regarded in Arabia. Such was the Arabic communal clan; and to it most of the evidence collected above applies.

From the beginning, however, there must have been a tendency to the republican clan.   Expeditions into the desert with the flocks in search of pasturage, or caravans from place to place for the purposes of trade, would consist, as did the one which Euting saw, of a considerable number of men and a much smaller number of women. This would, from the beginning, have a tendency toward the formation of clans in which polyandry of the Thibetan or British type would prevail. The women of the wealthy Arabians of the oases who to-day accompany their husbands on their expeditions into the desert are as a rule those of lower social position. A princess in a harem may have it understood that she is to remain always in the oasis.[1] Probably it was so in ancient times. Such a band of men would take with them some daring young women, who had not much position at home, or who were captives from another tribe. In such clans, where the men were the most important element, and where Thibetan or British polyandry would be almost certain, there would be a tendency from the beginning to count the children to the father's stock. The men of such clans, like some modern sailors, would be certain, too, to have mistresses in every oasis which they visited; so that, while they formed an important element in the social life of that Nair type which we have traced above as the prevailing type among the primitive Semites, they might also, in their own migratory clans, have been laying the foundation of Thibetan polyandry and paternal kinship.

The evidence passed in review goes to show that in the most primitive times this tendency did not make itself much felt. The reason why it did not is obvious. Arabia is such a poor country, outside the oases, that the life of the people is practically bound up in these fertile spots. For a long time these adventurous bands were too dependent upon the oases, and too much overshadowed by their more numerous population, to make any marked impress on the social order. As trade increased, however, and the population, through numbers, was in places crowded out permanently into the desert, such clans would become more permanent; and thus clans practising Thibetan

[1] Cf. Blunt, *Pilgrimage to Nejd*, Vol. I, p. 232. Only one of the three wives of the emir of Ḥail at the time of Lady Blunt's visit was bound to accompany her lord on his expeditions into the desert. The other two, who never left the oasis, looked down on this one as an inferior.

polyandry and counting kinship through the father might be produced from economic causes.[1] Wars would of course be produced as a part of this process, so that marriage by capture may have been one element of the transformation; but the economic element was probably earlier, and equally prominent.

By these factors fraternal polyandry was produced. Wellhausen[2] ascribes to this feeling for one's tribe alone the change from exogamy to endogamy. Fraternal polyandry adapts itself to a very poor country;[3] and where the murder of female children is added to the conditions just described, it would seem to be the inevitable result of the situation.

The restraint which this type of polyandry imposed on men must always have been exceedingly irksome to those who possessed the Semitic nature; and with them the natural result would be that, whenever plenty permitted the support of more women, and other circumstances threw more of them into their power, polyandry would give place to polygamy. This is what occurred whenever Semites went into countries more fertile than Arabia. We find, as we have seen, here and there traces of a previous polyandry; but wherever circumstances permitted it has given place to polygamy, whether among Arabs, Babylonians, or Hebrews.

Hilderbrand, who has made a careful study of the family type found among peoples who live by hunting, fishing, or as shepherds and agriculturists, lays it down as a general law that, "Among people who are in the lowest stages of domestic development, we never and nowhere meet with promiscuity or community in women."[4] This statement,

---

[1] Such clans seem to exist in Arabia to-day and to have an organization of their own. *Samn*, or melted butter, the produce of their flocks, is their chief article of exchange. Cf. Doughty, *Arabia Deserta*, Vol. II, pp. 71, 206–207, 209, 267, 268, 281, 289, 457.

[2] *Op. cit.*, p. 437 ff.

[3] Cf. Spencer's *Principles of Sociology*, Vol. I, p. 659.

[4] "Bei Völkern, welche sich noch auf der untersten wirtschaftlichen Stufe befinden, begegnen wir niemals und nirgens einem Zustande der

I am told by good authorities in sociology, may be taken as authoritative. He also tells us that, "The purchase of wives is first found among peoples who have already reached the condition of shepherd or agricultural life, and individual property in land. Also, marriage by capture is first frequently found in this stage of development."[1] In like manner, with reference to polyandry, he deduces from the cases he has observed this law, "Among peoples who have already reached the shepherd or agricultural stage of development and have individual property in land, we not seldom find the phenomena that a number of brothers or kinsmen possess one wife in common, or even individuals live in complete celibacy."[2] Similarly, Giddings remarks, "The polyandrian family is found in very many parts of the world, usually in tribes that have passed beyond savagery into barbarism."[3]

If, now, we apply the laws deduced by these students of sociology to the ancient Semites, a part of the observations already made are confirmed, and, in some respects, our knowledge of the earlier prehistoric period of Semitic residence in Arabia is advanced. Hilderbrand's laws confirm our view that the Thibetan type of polyandry is a comparatively late development; but they also lead us to suspect that when the Semites separated from their Hamitic brethren of North Africa, they had already passed beyond the lowest stages of social culture, since all our data point to a sexual looseness for the primitive Semite

Frauengemeinschaft oder Promiscuität." See *Recht und Sitte*, etc., p. 11.

[1] "Der Sitte des Frauenkaufs begegnen wir ernst bei Völkern, welche schon auf der Stufe des Hirtenlebens oder aber des Ackerbaues und Grundeigentums stehen. Und auch der Frauenraub kommt erst auf diesen Stufen häufiger vor." *Op. cit.*, p. 9.

[2] "Erst bei Völkern, welche schon auf der Stufe des Hirtenlebens oder aber des Ackerbaues und Grundeigentums stehen, stossen wir nicht selten auf die Erscheinung, dass häufig mehrere Brüder oder Verwandte eine Frau gemeinsam besitzen, oder sogar Einzelne in einem Zustande vollkommener Ehelosigkeit leben." *Op. cit.*, p. 13.

[3] *Principles of Sociology*, p. 155.

which borders upon promiscuity. This observation is confirmed by two considerations: (1) There are certain features in the Egyptian, as well as in the Semitic, religion, which point to a previous condition of polyandry;[1] and it is possible that the institution was developed before the separation of the Semites from the Hamites. (2) The conditions of life in Arabia and, to a certain extent, in North Africa outside of Egypt, where, as in Arabia, there are many deserts with occasional oases, are such that no people could live long by hunting and fishing. The first of these considerations will be more fully discussed in the next chapter, but to the second some space may be devoted here.

Fishing could never have been an important feature of life in Arabia except upon the sea coasts, for the absence of large rivers, and indeed, except in the oases, of water of any sort, would render it impossible. Hunting has, down to the present time, played some part in Arabian life. Hares, wild goats, gazelles, wild cows, and ostriches may still be found in small numbers; and the Solluby tribe, who have no real home, but pay tribute to all the tribes, still live largely by hunting.[2] If the theory of Wallace,[3] that this region once contained larger forests and more abundant water, be true, it can only have been many, many centuries ago. Probably the camel and goat, to which he ascribes the destruction of the forests, were in Arabia before the Semites were. It is tolerably certain that, since the Semites entered it, the conditions of the peninsula have been practically what they are to-day. Here and there oases are found where a little water produces grass, trees, and vegetation, but in many of these nothing of importance is produced without irrigation.[4]

---

[1] Cf. Maspero's *Dawn of Civilization*, New York, 1897, p. 50 ff.

[2] See Doughty's *Arabia Deserta*, Vol. I, pp. 281 ff., 362 ff., 487 ff., Vol. II, pp. 9 ff., 70, and 216-218.

[3] See above, p. 26.

[4] On Arabian oases, cf. Wellsted's *Travels in Arabia*, Vol. I, pp. 92 ff. and 272 ff.; Palgrave's *Central and Eastern Arabia*, Vol. I, pp. 20, 48 ff.,

Here and there, however, palms grow without artificial watering.¹ Much of the country is covered with volcanic mountains, from which protrude bare crags of igneous rocks, and which produce almost no vegetation. The intervening plains are covered with dry gravel, which is exceedingly unproductive, while between the central and eastern portions of the peninsula there extend immense deserts of shifting sand.² The lack of water and the intense heat must have always made it difficult for savage man to venture far from a spring. It is clear that in such a country no large population could live by hunting; the game itself would find the conditions of life too severe to exist in large quantities. The Semite must have been compelled to domesticate the goat and camel at an early date, in order to obtain the milk which is so important a part of Arabian diet. The date palm, which extended, so Fischer and Hehn declare,³ in prehistoric times, from the Canaries to Penjab, and which now produces the staple article of diet of so much of the Arabian population, must have early revealed its virtues to the Semitic mind, and thus called forth Semitic ingenuity for its cultivation.⁴

258 ff., Vol. II, p. 360; Blunt's *Pilgrimage to Nejd*, Vol. I, p. 113; and Euting's *Tagbuch einer Reise in Inner-Arabien*, pp. 68, 121, 123 ff.

¹ See Doughty's *Arabia Deserta*, Vol. II, p. 10, and Theobald Fischer in Petermann's *Mittheilungen*, Ergänzungsband XIV, No. 64, p. 10.

² Cf. Wellsted, *op. cit.*, Vol. I, p. 241; Palgrave, *op. cit.*, Vol. II, pp. 132 ff., 136 ff., 153, 356–358; Blunt, *op. cit.*, Vol. I, pp. 67, 156–185; Doughty, *op. cit.*, Vol. I, pp. 419–422, 424, 425; and Euting, *op. cit.*, p. 142 ff.

³ See Theobald Fischer in Petermann's *Mittheilungen*, Ergänzungsband XIV, No. 64, p. 1, and Hehn's *Culturpflanzen und Hausthiere*, 6th ed., p. 273.

⁴ There should be no real doubt that the date-palm was known to the primitive Semites in ancient Arabia. It extended in prehistoric times from the Canaries to Penjab (see Hehn's *Culturpflanzen und Hausthiere*, 6th ed., p. 273), or "from the Atlantic to the Himalayas" (so Theobald Fischer, in Petermann's *Mittheilungen*, Ergänzungsband, XIV, No. 64, p. 1), and "belonged to the desert and oasis peoples of the Semites" (Hehn, *op cit.*, p. 263). This fact was doubted by von Kremer and Guidi, as noted above in ch. i, on linguistic grounds, but without sufficient reason.

Thus in Arabia, as has so often been the case in other
countries where the conditions of life are hard, necessity
compelled man at an early period to form a somewhat
advanced social organization. The conditions in which
such relations between the sexes as we have described

It is true the Semitic tongues have no common word for palm; it is *gishimmaru* in Babylonian and Assyrian, *diqlā* in Aramaic, *tamar* in Hebrew, *nakhlu*^{n} in Arabic, and *tamrt* in Ethiopic; but as we pointed out above (p. 22), Bertin has correctly observed (*Journal of the Anthropological Institute*, Vol. XI, pp. 423-433), that it is the animals and plants which are most common which always have the most names, and that some of these may have survived in one dialect and others in others. It will be noticed that the Hebrew and Ethiopic words for palm tree are identical. Such a resemblance in two such widely separated dialects of the North and South Semites shows, as Hommel long ago pointed out (*Die Namen der Säugthiere*, p. 412), that this word was the name of it in the primitive Semitic tongue. This is confirmed by the fact that in Arabic *tamr* means "date," and then "fruit" in general, while *tamara* means to "feed with dates." The use of *tamr* as date must have been a specialization of the term for palm, when *nakhlu*^{n}, the word for "tree," was narrowed to mean "palm tree." That *nakhlu*^{n}, the more general term, could be narrowed to the palm shows that that was the tree par excellence. The Babylo-Assyrian term is apparently borrowed from a non-Semitic people. Whence the Aramaic *daqlā* came, it is not easy to say. Yaqut (in his *Geographical Dictionary*, Vol. II, p. 580) speaks of a place, *Daqala*, in south Arabia. "where date palms are found," which would show that this term was also used in Sabæa. Perhaps it is this fact which led Robertson Smith to say (*Religion of the Semites*, 2d ed., p. 109), that the date-palm was introduced into Arabia from Yemen and Syria, — a statement impossible of proof. Surely the word *daqlā* is not proof. One could more plausibly prove from *tamr* that it was introduced from Palestine and Ethiopia, which would surely be false. Hommel, when he wrote *Die Namen der Säugthiere*, held that the date palm was a native of Babylonia, but now says that it was introduced thither from Arabia (Hastings's *Dictionary of the Bible*, Vol. I, p. 214). It is much more likely, as Hehn says, that the palm was native throughout all North Africa and Southwestern Asia. The culture of it would probably arise first in an oasis country like Arabia, and may have been introduced thence to Babylonia, as Hommel believes, and also to Egypt, as Hehn thinks (*op. cit.*, p. 274). Theobald Fischer, the scholar who has most thoroughly investigated the date palm, holds that Arabia was the original home of its culture, and it was thence introduced into Babylonia and Egypt (*op. cit.*, p. 11). The position taken in the text is therefore thoroughly justified.

could exist, even if, with Hilderbrand and Giddings, we recognize that they can exist only in a pastoral and semi-agricultural life, must have been present in the peninsula not long, at most, after the Semitic occupation of the country.

The importance of the date palm, for the sustenance and development of Semitic life, can hardly be overestimated. The palm leaves are to-day plaited into string mats and baskets, and the bark into ropes. The dates themselves form a staple article of Arabian diet, some of the people having almost no other source of sustenance;[1] they are exported as far as Damascus and Baghdad,[2] and in return the Arabs are able to obtain a few articles from the outside world. The stones are ground and used for the food of cows, sheep, and camels;[3] syrup and vinegar are made from old dates, and, by some who disregard the Qur'an, a kind of brandy;[4] and altogether the statement of Palgrave is not too strong: "They are the bread of the land, the staff of life, and the staple of commerce."[5] They still serve, in some parts of Arabia, as the standard of value, as cattle do among shepherd peoples.[6] They cast a dense shade, which, in contrast to the hot Arabian atmosphere, must be exceedingly grateful.[7] Europeans regard the dates as a not altogether pleasing staple of diet;[8] but in a land which produces so sparingly it is regarded as a divine gift. An Arabic proverb declares that a good housewife knows how to set before her husband a new

---

[1] Cf. Doughty, *Arabia Deserta*, Vol. I, p. 148, Vol. II, p. 178.

[2] *Central and Eastern Arabia*, Vol. I, p. 60.

[3] In addition to the references in the two preceding notes, cf. Wellsted's *Travels in Arabia*, Vol. I, pp. 94, 164 ff., 241, 288 ff., Vol. II, pp. 112, 122, 419; Euting's *Tagbuch einer Reise in Inner-Arabien*, pp. 52, 53; Palgrave, *op. cit.*, Vol. I, p. 263; and Zwemer, *Arabia*, p. 123. For the statement about vinegar and brandy, see Zwemer.

[4] *Ibid.*

[5] *Central and Eastern Arabia*, Vol. I, p. 60.

[6] Doughty, *op. cit.*, Vol. I, p. 332.

[7] Wellsted, *op. cit.*, Vol. I, p. 94.

[8] Palgrave, *op. cit.*, Vol. I, p. 60; and Doughty, *op. cit.*, Vol. I, p. 148.

preparation of date food each day in the month.[1] Much thought has to be devoted to the culture of the date palm in many places in order to make it grow. In many parts of the peninsula it must be irrigated, and in some parts water for the purpose must be conducted considerable distances.[2] The female flowers of the date palm must be artificially impregnated from the male flowers, unless a male tree happens to grow where the winds will naturally carry the pollen to the female flowers. This is now sometimes done by planting a male tree in the midst of the female ones; but even as late as the early part of the present century, Wellsted observed in the Sinaitic peninsula an old method, once perhaps more widely used in Arabia, of fastening a bunch of the male flowers on a branch exposed to the wind, and so placed that it would disseminate the pollen over the flowers to be fertilized.[3] In Mesopotamia the method which the ancient sculptures attest, and which is still employed,[4] was to climb the tree and sprinkle the pollen over the flowers. This insured the fertilization of each flower. That this tree and its culture played a very important part in the development of ancient Semitic life we may therefore well believe. Mohammed is said to have addressed his followers thus: "Honor your paternal aunt, the date palm. It was named our paternal aunt because it was created of what was left from the clay of Adam; and it resembles mankind because it stands upright in figure and height, and it distinguishes between its male and female, and has the peculiarity (among plants) of impregnating the latter."[5] This high estimation of the

[1] *Erdekunde*, von Carl Ritter, Berlin, 1779–1857, Vol. XIII, p. 804. Cf. Zwemer's *Arabia*, p. 123.

[2] Cf. Wellsted, *op. cit.*, Vol. I, pp. 92–94; Euting, *op. cit.*, pp. 52, 53; and Glaser in *Mittheilungen der vorderasiatische Gesellschaft*, 1897, pp. 373–376 and 425.

[3] Wellsted, *op. cit.*, Vol. II, p. 12.

[4] Zwemer's *Arabia, the Cradle of Islam*, p. 123.

[5] Reported by Qazwini (1203–83, cf. Brockelmann's *Geschichte der arabischen Literatur*, Bd. I, Weimar, 1898, p. 481). The text is published

palm is confirmed by an Aramaic inscription from Taima, which, though much mutilated, shows that a part of the fruit of a date orchard was consecrated to a god,[1] and by the further fact that Nakhla, one of the seats of the worship of the goddess Al-Uzza,[2] derived its name from the date palm. The connection of the date palm with the goddess will be established in the next chapter, and it will there appear that the part played by this tree in the evolution of Semitic civilization was of the greatest importance. Fischer declares that the rôle which the Arabic people have played in the world's history is closely bound up with this, its sacred tree.[3] If we substitute Semitic people for Arabic, the statement remains equally true. We can understand, from the economic value of this tree and from the demand which its artificial propagation made upon the Semite, as an increasing population made such artificial culture necessary, something of the importance it would assume in his eyes; but to fully appreciate it, we must learn the divine significance which he attached to it, the reflex of his own social life which he saw in it, and how he attributed to it all his knowledge, especially the knowledge of sex and procreation. The social and the religious life of the people are always interwoven. These conceptions, which are so important for the social life, as well as the religious feasts, which form so large a part of the social intercourse of any people, will be considered in the next chapter.

The discussion in the present chapter has, I think, made the following points clear: The Semites, perhaps

in S. de Sacy's *Chrestomathie arabe*, Vol. III, p. 175, French translation, Vol. III, p. 395.

[1] Cf. *CIS.*, Pt. II, Vol. I, No. 113.

[2] Cf. Wellhausen's *Reste arabische Heidentums*, 2d ed., p. 36; and *Hebraica*, Vol. X, p. 64.

[3] " Wir können daher sagen, das auch die weltgeschichtliche Rolle, welche das arabische Volk gespielt hat, in engstem Zugammenhange mit diesem seinem heiligen Baum steht." Petermann's *Mittheilungen*, Ergänzungsband XIV, Heft. 64, p. 10.

as early as the time of their separation from the Hamites, had reached the animistic stage of culture, and formed totemistic clans. Their family relations were exceedingly vague. Marriage was for a short term, women resided in the homes of their own kindred, and descent was reckoned through them; the killing of female infants created a paucity of women, which produced a condition of polyandry resembling the Nair type. At the same time there was much sexual irregularity, which was regarded as innocent. Out of this there grew, through the formation of small trading clans and the influence of the capture of women, a system of Thibetan polyandry and, later, a system of male kinship. Perhaps at the time of their separation from the Hamites, and at all events comparatively early, they had entered the pastoral and semi-agricultural stage of culture, in which the cultivation of the date palm played an important part.

CHAPTER III

SEMITIC RELIGIOUS ORIGINS

MANY features of the religion of the primitive Semitic people were successfully elucidated by the late Robertson Smith in his epoch-making work, *The Religion of the Semites*. In most respects it is, as yet, impossible to advance beyond the position there taken. The primitive Semitic community was, as he has so well shown, thought by them to be made up of gods, men, and animals, all of whom were akin to one another. All nature was peopled with spirits, but the god of a people was the chief spirit of the locality where that people dwelt. The gods were confined each to its own tribe or clan, and in their activities they were limited to certain localities. They were originally chthonic, and were identified with objects on the earth before they were associated with heavenly bodies. In this chthonic period they were especially associated with springs, wells, and trees, and were regarded as the proprietors of naturally watered land. The bond between them and their worshippers was thought to be one of physical kinship, and was believed to be renewed by sacrifice. The latter was originally conceived as a meal at which both the gods and their worshippers partook of the flesh of a victim which was akin to them both. Each clan had its own god which it especially worshipped, though it did not deny the reality of the gods of other clans. Each god was limited in his activities largely to his own soil; and when one lived in the territory of a clan not his own he must, in addition to his own god, worship the god of the soil on which he resided.

These positions Smith has satisfactorily established, and it is not necessary to reopen their discussion here. In one respect, however, it is possible to carry the investigation farther than Smith did, and to determine the gender of the chief deities of the primitive Semites, the connection of their gods with the social organization outlined in the preceding chapter, and some of the transformations wrought in the conception of their nature by changed economic conditions, migrations, and syncretism.

It is a law which may be regarded as practically universal, that the religious conceptions of a people are expressed in forms which are modelled, in large degree, on those political and social institutions which the economical conditions of their situation have produced. Thus, a god could not be conceived as a father where marriage was so unstable that fatherhood was no recognized feature of the social structure, nor as a king among a people into whose experience the institution of kingship had never entered. An illustration of this principle may be found in the fact that republican institutions are, by their influence, gradually banishing the kingly idea of God from theological discussions, and are leading to an emphasis of the fatherhood, and even brotherhood of God.[1] We should therefore, on general principles, be led to suppose that the prominence of the mother and the institutions of maternal kinship among the primitive Semitic clans, as well as their tendency to unregulated intercourse and the important functions of the date palm, all left a deep impress on their religious ideas and practices. Indeed, we may be sure that this is the case, especially as a large mass of evidence has survived which is only intelligible when interpreted in the light of these general laws.

A considerable mass of this evidence was presented in

[1] Cf. *Can I believe in God the Father?* by W. N. Clarke, Scribners, 1899, ch. iii; and "Fides et Spes Medici," by Dr. R. H. Thomas in *Present Day Papers*, London, Vol. III (1900), p. 377.

the writer's study, "The Semitic Ishtar Cult,"[1] the main conclusions of which are confirmed by further investigation. Additional material has also now been collected, so that it is possible, in several respects, to carry the subject farther, and to prove more clearly than in 1894 that the primitive Semitic religion was organized on the analogies of its economic and social life. In the article mentioned the Ishtar cult was shown to be coextensive with the Semitic peoples, traces of it appearing in Assyria, Babylonia, north and south Arabia, Ethiopia, Nabathæa, Moab, Palestine, Phœnicia, Cyprus, Malta, Sicily, and Carthage. With three exceptions, the deity in all these countries which received the largest share of the popular homage was a mother goddess, and a patroness of unmarried love. In Babylonia, Arabia, and Cyprus virgins must sacrifice to her their chastity by an act of free love; at Byblos this might be commuted to a sacrifice of the hair; and at Carthage and elsewhere her feasts were attended by impure ceremonies, in which sexual excesses formed a prominent feature. The Israelites found this cult among the Canaanites, and adopted, as most scholars hold, many features of its ritual. At all events, by the time of the prophets the feasts of Yahwe were foul with deeds most subversive of spiritual ideas.

Connected with this worship in historical times were bands of priestesses (and often of priests) consecrated to a service which, judged by modern standards, would be prostitution. Ukhat, the creature who in the Eabani episode[2] enticed that primitive man from his animals, was a prototype and model of this order. With primitive simplicity she unblushingly enticed him to the satisfaction of desire, and is, in the Gilgamish epic, celebrated for her act.[3]

[1] Published in *Hebraica*, Vol. IX, pp. 131-165, and Vol. X, pp. 1-74. Cf. also notes on the same topic in *Hebraica*, Vol. X, pp. 202-205.

[2] See above, p. 43.

[3] Cf. Haupt's *Nimrodepos*, p. 11, ll. 16-21. For translations of the passage, cf. Jastrow, *Religion of Babylonia and Assyria*, p. 477; Jensen in

There can be no doubt that the mother goddess whose worship is thus widely diffused is a survival from primitive Semitic times, when the mother held the chief place in the clan, and all women shared a measure of free love. As social conditions changed, the women who adhered to the old practices would all have lost caste and become despised harlots but for the fact that the social character of the service of the goddess protected some of them. As civilization advanced, it is probable that religious conservatism became a cloak for much that was vile and debasing. In the beginning, however, the practices which were thus perpetuated must have been comparatively innocent, since they but reflected the best thought of primitive man with reference to manifestations of the divine.

The goddess Ishtar reflects, as was noted in the preceding chapter, by her various unions the brevity of the marriage tie among the primitive Semites. She married a lion, a horse, and a bird, each for a brief space. She desired to unite herself to Gilgamish, the hero of Uruk (Erech), but he declined her advances. Thus, the myth concerning her and the ritual by which she was served reflect two different phases of primitive Semitic life, — the temporary marriage and the consecration of the functions of woman to the service of childbearing by one or more acts of free love.

These features of her worship, taken in connection with its universal diffusion among the Semites, renders us certain of its existence in the primitive Semitic home.

It is important for us to note, also, that Ishtar was not only the divinity who presided over human love, but over all animal desire as well. Once when, according to an ancient poem, she abandoned the earth for the lower world, animals as well as men lost desire altogether.[1]

KB., Vol. VI, p. 127; and Muss-Arnolt in *Assyrian and Babylonian Literature*, Aldine ed., p. 330.

[1] Cf. *Hebraica*, Vol. IX, p. 147; and Jeremias's *Leben nach dem Tode*, p. 17.

SEMITIC RELIGIOUS ORIGINS 85

Connected with the worship of Ishtar was the worship of the god called in Babylonia Dumu-zi or Tammuz. The fourth month was named for him, and one of the chief features of his worship was a ceremony of wailing for his death, which was followed by wild rejoicing that he had come to life. Prominent among the forms under which this joy manifested itself was indulgence in unwedded love.[1] Tammuz is variously represented in Semitic mythology as son of Ishtar, as the first of her series of rejected husbands, and as the beloved and lost husband of her youth, whom she went to the under world to rescue.[2] These myths represent conceptions which were formed by three different stages of social progress. That which sees in Tammuz Ishtar's son is a reflection of the primitive Semitic family, the head of which is the mother, and the chief male her son. The second, which makes him a rejected husband, comes from a time a little later, when marriage was still temporary and women quite free, but when the original kindly relations between Ishtar and Tammuz had been forgotten. According to this view, the Tammuz wailing was a consequence of Ishtar's hatred and vengeance, and not of her grief at his loss, as in the former case. The third form of the myth reflects the later conception of marriage as a more permanent and less sensual relation. In the light of primitive Semitic social conditions, there can be no doubt but that the first of these conceptions is the original one.

Many scholars agree that Tammuz was in some way connected with vegetation, and that the legend of his death was a reflection of the annual dying of the leaves.[3] To

[1] Cf. Lucian's *De Syria Dea*, § 6; Ez. 8^{14}; and *Hebraica*, Vol. X, pp. 31, 35, 73.
[2] Cf. II R. 36, 54; II R. 59, col. ii, l. 9; IV R. 31, esp. col. ii, l. 46 ff.; Haupt's *Nimrodepos*, p. 44, l. 46 ff.; and *Hebraica*, Vol. X, pp. 73, 74.
[3] Cf. Jensen, *Kosmologie der Babylonier*, pp. 197, 227; Frazer, *Golden Bough*, Vol. I, pp. 278–296; Jeremias, *Leben nach dem Tode*, pp. 32, 41; Nowack, *Archæologie*, Vol. II, p. 310; Bertholet, *Das Buch Hezekiel*,

this opinion I adhered when the "Ishtar Cult"[1] was written, and further study confirms it. Robertson Smith was probably right in the opinion that the wailing at first began as a mourning for the death of a theanthropic victim,[2] but there can be little doubt but that it was very shortly associated with the death of vegetation. Lenormant[3] and Halévy[4] are, I now think, wrong in claiming a Semitic origin for the name, and it is not probable that this origin was connected with vegetation except indirectly.[5] Adonis, the name under which Lucian mentions him, is but an epithet which, in Phœnicia, had displaced the original name, as other epithets displaced it elsewhere. The original name is hopelessly lost.

The opinion expressed in the "Ishtar Cult" that Ishtar was originally a water goddess, the divinity of some never failing spring or springs, and that some sacred tree to which the spring gave life represented her son,[5] can now be confirmed by additional arguments.

The reasons which led to the adoption of that opinion were: (1) that Athtar, in a number of Sabæan inscriptions, is called "lord of the water supply";[6] (2) an old

p. 49; Jastrow, *Religion of Babylonia and Assyria*, p. 682 ff.; and Toy, *Ezekiel* in *SBOT.*, p. 111 ff.

[1] *Hebraica*, Vol. X, pp. 73, 74. The hymn to Tammuz, IV R. 27, No. 1, specifically connects 'him with vegetation. Cf. Ball's translation, *PSBA.*, Vol. XVI, p. 196. The name is, however, Sumerian, and means "child of life" or "living child." It probably refers to Tammuz as the child of the goddess of fertility.

[2] *Religion of the Semites*, 2d ed., p. 411.

[3] *Sur le nom Tammuz*.

[4] *Recherches bibliques*, p. 95, and *Mélanges de critique et d'histoire*, p. 177.

[5] *Hebraica*, Vol. X, p. 73. I am now convinced, however, that the name Tammuz is not primitive, but Sumerian Babylonian. It was at times even applied to a goddess (see below, Chapter V). While the name Tammuz was local (cf. my article, "The Genesis of the God Eshmun," in *JAOS.*, Vol. XXI,[2] p. 188 ff.), the god was, I believe, primitive, though a less permanent and fundamental factor in the religion than the goddess.

[6] See *CIS.*, Pt. IV, Vol. I, No. 47, and Fell, in *ZDMG.*, Vol. LIV, p. 245.

Babylonian hymn calls Ishtar "the producer of verdure";[1] (3) the god Baal, with whom Ashtart in Phœnicia was closely associated, was the god of well-watered land; (4) the evident connection of Tammuz with vegetation; and (5) the series of tree-like representations of the goddess found by Ohnefalsch-Richter in Cyprus.

To these arguments we may now add the following considerations: the fact that in two inscriptions from Gebal-Dîn, Athtar is the god of field fertility, which is in Arabia especially connected with the water supply,[2] forms another link connecting this cult with water and vegetation. Ilmaqqâhu, who, as is shown below,[3] was really Athtar under another name, was also the god of field fertility.[4] Traces of tree-worship also appear, which, if the Ishtar Cult represents the religion of the primitive Semites, must be regarded as survivals from that time. Trees were thought to be animate and to have perceptions and passions, and were not infrequently taken as totems.[5] In the latter case, all the attributes were ascribed to them which under like circumstances were ascribed to sacred animals. This proves the existence of that attitude of mind on the part of the Semites which could easily see a god in a tree. It still survives in Arabia, where certain trees are thought to be inhabited by the jinn even to the present time.[6] Such trees were probably in the pre-Islamic days regarded as the residences of gods, who, upon the introduction of Islam, shared the fate of other deities and were deposed to the rank of evil spirits. In like manner the Jews and early Christians regarded the gods of the heathen as demons.[7] Sometimes, however, it is not jinn

[1] Cf. Zimmern's *Babylonische Busspsalmen*, p. 33, and *Hebraica*, Vol. X, p. 15.
[2] See *CIS.*, Pt. IV, Vol. I, Nos. 104, 105. [3] Chapter IV.
[4] Cf. *CIS.*, Pt. IV, Vol. I, Nos. 72–102, and Fell, in *ZDMG.*, Vol. LIV, p. 244 ff.
[5] Smith's *Religion of the Semites*, 2d ed., p. 132.
[6] Doughty's *Arabia Deserta*, Vol. I, p. 365.
[7] Cf. Deut. 32^{17} and 1 Cor. 10^{20}.

but angels who are thought to come down to tabernacle in the trees; and it is still the custom in parts of Arabia for the sick to go to trees which are thus visited and offer sacrifice and prayer for the recovery of their health. The offering is usually a sheep or a goat, the blood is sprinkled, the flesh cooked at the place, a part of it is divided among the friends of the sick man and a part left hanging on the branches of the tree. The worshipper then lies down and sleeps, confident that the angels will come in vision and speak precepts for his health so that he will rise whole.[1] Such possessed trees are behung with old beads, votive shreds of calico, lappets of colored stuffs and other such things.[1] This is a relic of old Arabian heathenism, in which offerings were made in the same manner. The traditions tell that Mohammed referred to such a tree as "a tree to hang things on."[2]

Such traces of worship are not now found in connection with the palm tree in Arabia, but more often with the acacia, though at times with other trees and even with shrubs. Some evidences of the worship of the palm tree in ancient times are still extant. Tabari refers to the sacred date-palm of Negran, where the tree was in all respects treated as a god.[3] The residence of Al-Uzza at Nakhla, who was in reality an Athtar,[4] is said by Ibn Abbas to have been a group of *Samura* trees, in one of which the goddess especially dwelt. The *Samura* tree is explained by a scholion to Ibn Hisham (p. 145) to be a palm tree.[5] The reliabil-

---

[1] Doughty's *Arabia Deserta*, Vol. I, p. 449 ff.

[2] Smith's *Religion of the Semites*, 2d ed., p. 185.

[3] Cf. *Annales quos scripsit at-Tabari*, van M. J. de Goeje, Leyden, 1879–1897, Vol. I, p. 922, and *Geschichte der Perser und Araber zur Zeit der Sassniden aus der arabisch Chronik des Tabari*, von Th. Nöldeke, Leyden, 1879, p. 181. Smith (*op. cit.*, p. 185) holds that the statement is incredible because it rests on the authority of a liar; but liars sometimes tell the truth.

[4] Cf. *Hebraica*, Vol. X, pp. 58–66.

[5] Wellhausen's *Reste arabische Heidentums*, 2d ed., p. 38. Wellhausen suspects this statement, because the vale of Nakhla (Palms) was so near. That, however, does not prove the statement wrong.

ity of these statements has been unjustly suspected by Wellhausen and Robertson Smith. The story of the birth of Jesus, as told in the Qur'an, vouches for the ancient sacredness of the palm. According to the statement of Mohammed, which probably comes from Arabian Christians, Mary retired to a palm tree (Sura, 19^{23}) as the time of her delivery drew near, and was miraculously nourished by dates produced out of season (19^{25}). Such a statement reveals the conception that the palm tree was closely related to the divine. All these references coincide with a number of facts from other parts of the Semitic world which indicate that the date palm was sacred, and thus receive a confirmation which establishes a strong presumption of their truth.

In Abyssinia as in Egypt the sycamore was a sacred tree, and in some instances still maintains this character.[1]

The terebinth was a sacred tree in Palestine. It plays a prominent part in the traditions concerning Abraham (Gen. 13^{18}, 14^{13}, 18^1), Gideon received a message from an angel under one (Jud. 6^{11}), and in the days of Hosea incense was burned under terebinths (Hos. 4^{13}). There are traces also that the date-palm was a sacred tree in Israel. Deborah is said to have sat under a palm tree, and is called a prophetess (Jud. 4^5), the inference being that the palm was sacred, and that it helped her inspiration to be near it. Some scholars endeavor to identify this with the terebinth of Gen. 35^8, but without sufficient ground.[2] There is reason, as will appear below, to believe that the tree of knowledge in Gen. 3 was a date palm. Evidence of this also comes to us from the Jewish book of Enoch. In the oldest portion of the Ethiopic Enoch we are told (ch. 24) how Enoch visited paradise, and found that the tree of life was a date-palm.[3] The full significance of this statement

---

[1] Cf. Bent's *Sacred City of the Ethiopians*, p. 210.

[2] So Moore, *Judges* in *Inter. Crit. Comm.*, p. 113, and Budde, *Richter*, in Marti's *Kurzer Hand Commentar*, p. 35. On the other hand, cf. H. P. Smith's *Samuel* in *Inter. Crit. Comm.*, p. 67.

[3] Cf. Charles's *The Book of Enoch*, 1893. Charles rightly dates this portion of the book before 170 B.C.

will appear at a later point; it is enough to note at present that it affords evidence that the date-palm as a sacred tree played a very important rôle in the thought of ancient Israel. Other evidence of this is not wanting. The story of Judah and Tamar (Gen. 38) indicates, since Tamar means palm, that a clan was incorporated into the tribe of Judah which made the palm a totem, and therefore regarded it as a sacred tree. Further, on the confines of Judah and Benjamin, there was a place, Baal-Tamar, which took its name from a god who must have been called "lord of the palm" (Jud. 20^{33}). Earlier it seems to have been called Baalat-Tamar, or "lady of the palm." In all probability the name was derived from an early connection of a deity with a sacred tree.

At Elim, one of the stations at which the Israelites are said to have stopped on the way out of Egypt, the palm had a sacred significance, since it is connected with the sacred number seventy and with twelve sacred wells (Ex. 15^{27}). Jericho, too, was called the "city of palm trees" (Deut. 34^3, Jud. 1^{16}, 3^{13}), and it is probable that there in early times the palm had a sacred significance. The fact that the palm tree and cherub formed part of the adornment of the interior of the temple of Ezekiel (Ez. 41^{18}) and of the temple of Solomon affords further proof of the same thing. We cannot doubt, therefore, that the palm was a sacred tree among the Hebrews or their immediate ancestors.

The numerous representations of trees on Babylonian and Assyrian cylinders and monuments attest, as several scholars have recognized, a primitive tree worship for the ancient Babylonians or their ancestors. The tree most represented, however, is the date-palm, and this is shown to be in most instances the female date-palm by the hanging clusters of dates.[1] Many of the representations on

---

[1] Cf. Schrader in *Monatsbericht d. kgl. preus. Ak. d. Wiss. zu Berlin*, 1882, p. 426 ff. Other trees were also sacred; cf. Bonavia's article, "Sacred Trees of the Assyrian Monuments" in the *Babylonian and Oriental Record*, Vol. III.

the monuments picture a winged being, sometimes with a human face and sometimes with an eagle's face, holding in one hand a basket or bucket, and in the other a cone which he is applying to the tree. That the difference in sex of the date-palms was known to the ancient Assyrians is attested by a fragment of a list of trees which was found in the library of Assurbanipal, but which was probably copied from a Babylonian list of much greater antiquity, and in which *gishimmaru zakiru*, or "the male date-palm," is distinguished from *gishimmaru zinnishtu*, or "the female date-palm."[1] E. B. Tylor first suggested that the winged figures which apply the mysterious cones to the trees are representations of the winds — personified as divine agencies — in carrying the pollen of the male flowers to the stigmata of the female flowers, so as to fertilize them.[2] He found in these figures the explanation of the cherubim of Ezekiel and of Genesis, as well as of other parts of the Old Testament. This seemed especially appropriate, since Ps. 18^{10}, in a description of the coming of Yahwe on a thunder cloud, equates the cherub with the wind. This view has since been accepted by others,[3] and affords a most satisfactory explanation of these interesting representations. Some of these portray a fish god, *i.e.* Ea in the act of performing this fecundation. Ea was a water god — a god of fertility, originally connected, as will be shown by and by, with the primitive Semitic mother goddess.[4] In the legend of Oannes, as preserved in Berossos, and which is in reality a myth of Ea, a fish-like monster came, we are told, from the sea, and taught the Babylonians the

[1] Cf. II R., p. 46, No. 2, ll. 29, 30.
[2] See *PSBA.*, Vol. XII, pp. 383–393.
[3] Cf. Jastrow's *Religion of Babylonia and Assyria*, p. 662, and Haupt in Toy's *Ezekiel* in *SBOT.*, pp. 181–184.
[4] See Chapter V. The fertilization of the date-palm in Mesopotamia has to be performed in part by hand unto the present time. (See Zwemer's *Arabia, the Cradle of Islam*, p. 123.) This fact explains the anthropomorphic form of the cherub. The wind is conceived as a supernatural man applying the fertilization by hand.

beginnings of civilization. Among other arts he made them distinguish seeds, and taught them how to collect fruit. In his hands, therefore, the cone and bucket would properly have a place.

The fact that the sacred character of trees is established for so many parts of the Semitic area is good evidence that tree worship existed in the primitive Semitic home, and the traces of the sacred character of the date-palm which have been adduced above lead us to think, when taken in connection with what we learned in the previous chapter of that tree, that it was the sacred tree *par excellence*.

In the same way the idea that perennial springs and wells were connected with divinities is found in many parts of the Semitic territory, and is no doubt primitive. At Beersheba, Dan, Sidon,[1] on Mount Lebanon,[2] and at Mecca sacred wells and springs were found, not to mention many others. That they do not appear in Babylonia is due to the presence of the great rivers and the nature of the irrigation of the country; but the fact that Ea was a water god attests there the same circle of ideas. We cannot therefore be far wrong in coupling the two — the palm tree and the spring — and in seeing a mythological representation of them in the primitive mother goddess, Ishtar, and her son Tammuz. Indeed, the well at or near Sidon was sacred to Eshmun, a god who, as I have pointed out elsewhere,[3] was probably developed out of Tammuz by the use of an epithet.

That this is a correct view is confirmed from another quarter. The Assyriologists of a score of years ago[4] regarded the pictures of the sacred tree on Babylonian and

---

[1] *CIS.*, Pt. I, Vol. I, No. 3, l. 17.

[2] Cf. *Hebraica*, Vol. X, pp. 33 and 61–66, and Smith's *Religion of the Semites*, 2d ed., pp. 166 ff. and 177 f.

[3] See the article "Ashmun" (Eshmun) in the *Jewish Encyclopedia*, and "The Genesis of the God Eshmun" in *PAOS.*, Vol. XXI[2], p. 188 ff., and below, Chapter VI.

[4] So George Smith in his *Chaldæan Genesis;* see the German translation, p. 84; also Lenormant in his *Origines de l'histoire*, Vol. I, p. 90.

Assyrian monuments as the prototype of the tree of life in Gen. 2 and 3, and though this view is rejected by some[1] who see in these pictures the date-palm, it is, I believe, a hint in the right direction. The Yahwistic writer of Gen. 2 and 3 gives us a twofold representation of the circumstances of the union of Adam and Eve and its effect. In ch. 2 we are told how man, after consorting with the beasts, left them for the woman and became "one flesh" with her. That this was the original form of the story the parallelism of the Eabani and Ukhat episode in the Gilgamish epic enables us to determine.[2] It also enables us to see that the Rabbis were right in explaining "cleave to his wife and become one flesh" as referring to connubial intercourse.[3]

In ch. 3 the same thing is differently represented. A serpent tells the woman to pluck the fruit from a forbidden tree, she does it, the man and woman both eat of it, their eyes are opened, and they know good and evil. The first effect of this knowledge was the perception of the difference of sex — the perception that they were naked. The Rabbis thought that the serpent here represented the sexual passion,[4] but it is doubtful whether this is correct. As among many other peoples, the serpent was sacred[5] among practically all the Semites. He belonged no doubt to that primitive totemistic circle of society of which we have seen the primitive Semitic community to consist. He is here represented as living in the primitive garden or oasis, where serpents no doubt abounded, and as urging man to partake of an act which seemed to him a divinely provided joy. In ch. 2 and its Babylonian parallel, woman enticed man from in-

[1] So Bonavia, *Babylonian and Oriental Record*, Vol. III, p. 36 ff.

[2] Cf. Jastrow's "Adam and Eve in Babylonian Literature" in *AJSL.*, Vol. XV, pp. 192–214.

[3] Cf. Jastrow, *AJSL.*, Vol. XV, p. 207, n. 44.

[4] *AJSL.*, Vol. XV, p. 209.

[5] Cf. Pietschmann's *Geschichte der Phönizier*, p. 227, and Kittel's *Könige* in Nowack's *Hand-Kommentar*, p. 278 ff.

tercourse with the beasts, so here a beast is represented as urging man to union with woman. The two representations arose no doubt because of the union of two originally independent explanations. The effect of tasting this divine fruit was that man was thereby brought to the knowledge of good and evil, *i.e.* to the exercise of a virile manhood; he was led to adopt clothing, to till the soil, and to a knowledge of the various features of civilization. This view of the meaning of good and evil is confirmed by the fact that in Deut. 1[39] "having no knowledge of good and evil" is equivalent to not having reached the age of puberty.

But why in this case should the tree appear at all? Why should its fruit even symbolically represent such an act? The answer is, I believe, to be found in the fact that the beginnings of Semitic civilization were connected with the date-palm, that a knowledge of the difference of sex in these trees was known at a very early time, and that the marvellous effect on the palms of the fertilization wrought by the wind, appeared to the primitive Semitic mind as a divine exhibition of sexual fertilization and divine approval of it. Thus, the two would become associated in the Semitic mind, and in time the act would naturally be pictured as the fruit of the tree. That this view represents the truth is shown by the fact that in the Biblical narrative cherubim are placed in the gate of the garden to prevent the return of man to his Eden of sexual unconsciousness. The cherubim were, as we have seen, representations of the wind, which bore the fructifying pollen of the male flowers to the female, and the introduction of the cherubim at this point represents the primitive feeling, that the constant enaction of this divine process of fertilization in the tree, which stood in the garden of his god and which sustained life, forced man onward by its divine example to similar acts with all their consequences. The ever-present cherubim of the palm kept alive, he thought, the sexual passion in himself which made abstinence and a return to conditions which he regarded as primitive (*i.e.* a life in which woman played no part) impossible.¹

Thus the Assyrio-Babylonian sacred tree becomes not the prototype in the first instance of the tree of life, but of the tree of knowledge of good and evil. A comparison of Gen. $3^{3.9}$ with Gen. 2^9 and 3^{22} reveals the fact that in the original form of the story only one tree is mentioned. The tree of life in the two latter verses is a later addition.² That such additions should be made to the substructure we have supposed is shown to have been very natural by the following facts. The idea of a future life played no important part in primitive Semitic thought. The life of the spirit after death was thought by the Babylonians and Hebrews to be a colorless and undesirable one, and to the Arabs of the desert, the idea of an under world, seems to have been wholly lacking.³ The problem which confronted them was the cause of present suffering, and not the problem of an immortal life. As the thirst for an immortal life was felt, but before it had been accepted as a fact, the story of the cause of human suffering would naturally be modified to make it explain why man could not live forever, and this is the form which we have in Genesis. As time went on and a provisional immortality of five hun-

---

¹ Thus an Arabic poet describes and addresses the palm: —

"He lifts his leaves in the sunbeam glance
As the Almehs lift their arms in dance;
A slumbersome motion, a passionate sigh,
That works in the cells of the blood like wine.
O tree of love, by that love of thine
Teach me how I shall soften mine."

— Translated by Zwemer, *Arabia, the Cradle of Islam*, p. 121 ff.

² See *Die Biblische Urgeschichte*, von Karl Budde, Giessen, 1883, p. 53 ff., and Toy, *JBL.*, Vol. X, p. 12 ff.

³ See *Der Ahnenkultus und die Urreligion Israels*, von Carl Grüneisen, Halle, 1900, p. 55. This seems true notwithstanding Stade (*Geschichte*, Vol. I, p. 395, n. 2), and Schwally (*Leben nach dem Tode*, p. 46, etc.). For Babylonian view see Jeremias, *Leben nach dem Tode*, and for the Hebrew, Charles, *Eschatology*, p. 33 ff.

dred years was accepted (Eth. Enoch, 10^{10}), the tree of knowledge disappeared from Eden and the tree of life took its place (Eth. Enoch, 24, 25). Thus did Hebrew thought transfer the story from an explanation of toil to the promise of future reward.[1] This transfer was easy; for, in another sense, the tree was to the primitive Semite always a tree of life as well as a tree of knowledge. The parallels which the Eabani story affords to the narrative of Genesis vouch for the Babylonian derivation of the latter. This is also shown in the fact that the garden is situated in the East (Gen. 2^8), and that the Tigris and Euphrates rivers are mentioned in connection with it[2] (Gen. 2$^{14.15}$).

There are in the Eabani episode, as has been already pointed out, features which were derived from the primitive conditions of Semitic social life. Although these features have been somewhat veiled in the Biblical narrative, they are nevertheless present, and that narrative also contains another primitive feature which is still more prominent. The narrative in Gen. 3 represents God, man, and the serpent as forming one social circle. The

[1] On the view presented in the text the historical origin of the Hebrew ideas of Eden and the heavenly paradise or New Jerusalem are as follows: The primitive conceptions of a sacred enclosure, where the god dwelt and the sacred tree was, grew out of an Arabian oasis, or possibly a North African, at a still earlier time (see below). This was transferred to Babylonia, where it became a garden. This conception was taken over by the Hebrews and is represented in Gen. 2 and 3. As time passed on and Jerusalem was destroyed and rebuilt, the Jewish ideal passed from a garden to a city. A garden may have been the home in the beginning, but a city became their ideal for the future. As Apocalypses were written and their authors sought for imagery under which to shadow forth their hopes of the heavenly future, they sometimes took the picture of Eden as did the author of Eth. Enoch, 24, 25 ; sometimes the city of Jerusalem, as did the author of Psal. Sol. 17 ; and sometimes the two were combined as in the Apocalypse of John, where it is a city with twelve gates (ch. 21), and yet it has a river with a tree of life, *i.e.* a garden (ch. 22$^{1.2}$). Thus the imagery born in prehistoric times in the Arabian oasis with its palm tree appears, transformed and elevated it is true, but still appears on the last page of the New Testament.

[2] See Delitzsch's *Wo Lag das Paradies,* Leipzig, 1881, and Haupt, in *Ueber Land und Meer,* 1894-95, No. 15.

serpent is wiser than man; he talks to the woman, and his power of speech causes her no astonishment. These elements of the tale must have taken shape in a primitive totemistic society in which animals were really believed to possess such powers; *i.e.* it reflects the conditions of primitive Semitic, and not of Hebrew thought.

The fact that in Genesis Yahwe is represented as forbidding the acquisition of the knowledge of good and evil on the part of man, has, I think, nothing to do with the primitive form of the story; it is but the local coloring given to the tale by the Yahwistic writer. This writer, in the stories of Cain and his descendants which follow, attributes the beginnings of civilization in every instance to those who disobeyed Yahwe. When he does so in the narrative of Eden, he is but following out his prevailing tendency. An opportunity was afforded him to thus interpret the tale by one of the features of the Babylonian story, preserved on a fragmentary tablet, which may form a part of the Gilgamish epic. This represents Eabani as cursing Ukhat, who had promised to make him like a god and who had instead brought him to death.[1] This story probably reflects the evil effects of the unrestrained sexual practices of the Semites, as does also that passage in the sixth tablet of the epic where Ishtar's love is represented as so terrible that she has smitten and crippled all her husbands. Such loose sexual habits as those traced above would necessarily produce venereal disease and death, and such dire effects might well be interpreted as evidences of the anger of the god. In the Eabani episode this view is, so far as we can tell, not taken. Eabani's anger is directed against the woman alone; he does not seem to be conscious that he has angered a god. This latter inference, however, lay close at hand, and could hardly fail to be made by a writer whose attitude toward civilization was like

[1] Cf Haupt, *Nimrodepos*, pp. 16, 17, and *BA.*, Vol. I, pp. 318, 319; also Jastrow, *Religion of Babylonia and Assyria*, p. 478, and *AJSL.*, Vol. XV, p. 209.

that of the Yahwist. Side by side with the Babylonian view just described, and older than it, was another, which attributed civilization to the knowledge of sex and which regarded both as a blessing. Divine approval was manifested through the example of the sacred tree, which was the home of the divinity. It is thus only that we can account for the reference of civilization to sexual relations, for the sacred character attached to those relations among the Semites, and for the connection of both with the sacred tree.[1]

Thus our view of the original form of Ishtar is confirmed since in the palm tree, which grows by every Arabian spring, and which has grown there since man inhabitated Arabia,[2] we find that the Semite saw the embodiment of all those features of vegetable and animal fertility which characterize this primitive Semitic cult, and which found such expression at a later time in its religious practices and in its mythology. Since we are led by such reasons to these conclusions, it seems most natural to find in the rite of circumcision, which has survived among the Arabs, Abyssinians, Syrians, Phœnicians, and Hebrews, a confirmation of them, and in them an explanation of Semitic circumcision. Circumcision has been found among many peoples of the world, and is usually explained like tattooing, cutting off a finger joint, and other mutilations, as embracing the twofold idea of offering a sacrifice to the god and furnishing a tribal mark by which the god may easily know his followers, and they may be known to each other. That it had this latter force among the Semites is attested by its history among the Hebrews. The Yahwistic writer represents Yahwe

---

[1] The Biblical writer is in this representation also paralleled by another Babylonian tale, the Adapa myth (cf. *KB.*, Vol. VI, pp. 92–101). This myth represents the god Ea as preventing by a deception the eating of the bread and water of life (*i.e.* the gaining of immortality), by a mortal. Cf. Gunkel, *Schöffing und Chaos*, p. 148 ff., and Jastrow, *Religion of Babylonia and Assyria*, p. 549 ff.

[2] See Theobald Fischer in Petermann's *Mittheilungen*, Ergänzunungsband XIV, No. 64, p. 11, and above, Chapter II, p. 75, n. 4.

(Ex. $4^{24, 25}$) as trying to kill Moses or his son as though he were of a foreign stock until Gershom was circumcised, when Yahwe desisted; while the priestly writer regarded circumcision as the sign of Yahwe's covenant with his people (Gen. 17^{10-12}, Ex. 12^{48}). Such passages attest the religious importance of the rite among the Israelites, and the struggle which Paul and the early Christians who thought like him were compelled to undertake to gain emancipation is sufficient, to mention no other evidence, to show the importance attached to it by the Jews as the visible sign to their god and to one another of their fidelity.[1] Herodotus mentions the Syrians and Phœnicians among those who practise circumcision,[2] but of the details of its practice among them we know nothing. Of its practice among the ancient Arabs we have fuller information. It is mentioned by Josephus and Sozomen as a practice of the northern Arabs, and by Philostorgius as a practice of the Sabæans.[3] Sharastani mentions it as one of the practices which Islam confirmed as a religious duty.[4] The way in which it is observed in Arabia at the present time attests the truth of this statement. Among the Bedawi it is the occasion of a feast at which the rite is performed on children of three full years. There is dancing on the part of the maidens, while the young men stand about and select from the dancing throng their wives. A sheep is sacrificed, its flesh cooked and eaten near sundown at a feast, while the entrails are left hanging on a trophy bush, or sacred tree. After the feast the dancing begins again and continues into the evening.[5] Among

---

[1] For a concise sketch of the history of the rite in Israel see the article "circumcision" by McAllister in Hastings's *Dictionary of the Bible*, or by Benzinger in the *Encyclopedia Biblica*. For the Abyssinian custom, cf. Wylde's *Modern Abyssinian*, p. 161.

[2] Bk. II, ch. 104.

[3] Josephus, *Ant.* I, 12^2; Sozomen, *H. E.*, VI, 38; Philostorgius, *H. E.*, III, 4. Cf. also Nowack's *Archäologie*, Vol. I, p. 167.

[4] See Haarbrücker's translation of Sharastani, Vol. II, p. 354.

[5] Doughty's *Arabia Deserta*, Vol. I, pp. 340, 341.

other Arabs it is the custom to make the child ride on the back of the sacrificial sheep.[1] At Mecca there still exists a similar custom of performing circumcision in connection with a sacrificial feast.[2] Here the operation is performed from the third to the seventh year, and is performed on female children as well as upon male.

The circumstances under which it is performed in Arabia point to the origin of circumcision as a sacrifice to the goddess of fertility, by which the child was placed under her protection and its reproductive powers consecrated to her service. The slaughter of the sheep was originally not simply for domestic purposes, since all slaughter of domestic animals was sacrificial.[3] The consecration of the child by such an offering, in addition to the regular sacrificial victim, is parallel to the sacrifice of chastity by which women consecrated their wombs to the goddess of childbearing at Babylonia and Byblos.[4] In the dance and the selection of future wives by the young Arabs in the Bedawi ritual we see a survival in a purified form of an old love feast, such as must have accompanied in one form or another all the feasts of the Semitic mother goddess, and to which Augustine and Ephraem bear witness.[5] Originally circumcision seems to have been a preparation for connubium.[6] Its transfer to infancy may, as W. R.

---

[1] Doughty, *op. cit.*, Vol. I, p. 391.

[2] See Snouck Hurgronje's *Mekka*, Vol. II, pp. 141–143. Among the Hamitic Somalis of East Africa, who are deeply penetrated with Arabic influence, boys are circumcised at seven years of age, and girls are infibulated at ten. The hair is cut short at the same time, so that a long-haired person and an uncircumcised are identical. Cf. Reinisch, *Somali-Sprache*, pp. 110, 111, etc.; Bd. I of his *Südarabische Expedition*. Wien, 1900.

[3] See Smith's *Religion of the Semites*, 2d ed., pp. 234, 241, and 307.

[4] Herodotus, I, 199, and Lucian's *De Syria Dea*, § 6. Cf. *Hebraica*, Vol. X, pp. 21 and 31.

[5] Cf. Ephraem, *Opera*, Vol. II, pp. 458, 459; Augustine, *De Civitate Dei*, II, 4; also *Hebraica*, Vol. X, pp. 51 and 59.

[6] Cf. Gen. 34, and also Ex. 4^{25}, where circumcision is connected with the idea of "bridegroom."

Smith suggests,[1] have been a later development. Circumcision thus receives for the Semitic peoples a fitting explanation, and an explanation not out of harmony with that usually given it by modern scholars for other peoples.

Circumcision was also practised by the Egyptians at a very early date,[2] and Herodotus was so impressed by their practice of it that he claims that others learned it from them.[3] According to Strabo they, like the modern Meccans, circumcised both men and women.[4] The Gallas, another Hamitic tribe, also practise it.[5] The connection of this Hamitic practice with the Semitic will be considered with some other similar matters at a future point in the discussion.

In a system of religious thought, in which the sexual functions of the animal world found a counterpart and an apotheosis in the processes of the sacred tree, and in which free love was at certain times a religious duty, what more natural than that the organs of reproduction should be placed under the care of the tutelary divinity by such a sacrifice? Indeed, the Arabs to-day, who are much with flocks and herds, declare that only in man is an impediment like the foreskin found, and wonder how it is possible for reproduction to occur among uncircumcised Christians.[6] Possibly their remote Semitic ancestors reasoned in the same way, and so conceived the necessity of making this sacrifice to the goddess of productivity, that they as well as other creatures might receive the blessing of fertility.

Trumbull has collected a convincing array of instances of the sacred character of the threshold among the Babylonians, Phœnicians, Hebrews, and Arabs,[7] which prove

---

[1] Cf. *Rel. of Sem.*, 2 ed., p. 328; Wellhausen, *Heidentum*, 2 ed., p. 175.
[2] Ebers, *Aegypten und die Bücher Moses*, Vol. I, p. 283.
[3] Bk. II, 104.
[4] Strabo, Bk. XVII, 2^5.
[5] Macalister in Hastings's *Dictionary of the Bible*, Vol. I, p. 444.
[6] Doughty's *Arabia Deserta*, Vol. I, pp. 341 and 410.
[7] *The Threshold Covenant*, Philadelphia, 1896, pp. 108–164.

that the threshold among the Semites, as among people in many parts of the world, had the sanctity of an altar. The explanation which Trumbull offers for the sacredness of the threshold throughout the world is that primitive men everywhere make, by some common psychological process, a connection between the relation between the threshold and doorpost on the one hand, and the relation of the sexes on the other.[1] The result of our investigation into Semitic religious origins confirms this conclusion in so far as it applies to the Semites. A people who, like them, attributed to the sexual relation the beginnings of intelligent life, the knowledge of clothing, agriculture, and the arts of civilization, and who, in their conceptions of divinity, in their religious rites, and in their social organization, gave such prominence to sexual relations and functions, would most naturally invest the threshold, the approach to the tent or house where the fruits of these divinely ordained functions were sheltered, with something of the sanctity of the function itself. This would be especially easy for early man as soon as any structure beyond a mere tent formed his dwelling. The old Semitic door sockets and posts would by their very form readily suggest the organs of fertility. No doubt the *nosb* or *masseba*, which bore a general resemblance to a phallus, afterward became the symbol of Semitic deity for a similar reason.

With the view of the nature of Ishtar here set forth, the meaning of her name, I believe, coincides. It is true that so many varying etymologies of the name have been offered that it is precarious to build much on an argument derived from this source, and yet the confirmation afforded to the views expressed above by what I believe to be the true etymology renders it worthy of a little discussion.

Driver[2] still refers the name, as Schrader[3] and Sayce[4]

---

[1] *Op. cit.*, pp. 193–203.
[2] "Ashtoreth" in Hastings's *Dictionary of the Bible*.
[3] *KAT.*[2], p. 179.   [4] *Hibbert Lectures* for 1887, p. 252 ff.

did a decade or two ago, to a non-Semitic origin. Delitzsch, who held this view in 1883 and 1886, had abandoned it as long ago as 1889.[1] That so admirable a scholar as Driver can still hold this view is no doubt due to the fact that the historical and religious bearings of the problem have not sufficiently claimed his attention. It can hardly be regarded as probable that a divinity so primitive as Ishtar and whose cult was so widely diffused as to be worshipped in every Semitic territory, should be known in them all by a name borrowed from a foreign source by one of the Semitic nations after the Semitic dispersion had begun. Such an improbable view ought not to be maintained if a Semitic etymology which is even plausible can be suggested. That this borrowing did not occur is indicated by the presence of the letter 'ayin at the beginning of the name in all the Semitic languages except the Babylonian-Assyrian. From this latter tongue the 'ayin had disappeared, and it is hardly conceivable that the 'ayin would be present in all the other languages if the name had come to them from a Babylonian source.

Most scholars regard the name as of Semitic origin and have offered for it various etymologies.[2] The etymology proposed in my "Ishtar Cult" derived the name from the

[1] Cf. his *Hebrew Language viewed in the Light of Assyrian Research*, p. 11, and *Prolegomena eines neues Hebraisch-Aramaisches Wörterbuch*, p. 138, with his *Assyrian Grammar*, p. 181.

[2] See, *e.g.*, Haupt, *ZDMG.*, Vol. XXXIV, p. 758, and Moore's "Ashtoreth" in the *Encyc. Bib.* in addition to references below. The following proposed etymologies are worthy of mention: 1. Haupt holds that it is a feminine form of the stem of the name of the Assyrian god Ashur (Asshur), Ishtar being written for Itshar (quoted by Tiele, *Actes d. 6me Cong. Inter. d. Orient.*, Pt. II, p. 497, n., and reiterated by Haupt, *Amer. Jour. of Philology*, Vol. VIII, p. 278, n., also his *Assyrian E Vowel*, 1887, p. 16, n.). If the name of the god Ashur be derived, as is supposed below (Chapter V), from the 'ashera or post which marked the limits of the primitive sanctuary, this view would be plausible, were it not for the confusion which it assumes from 'aleph to 'ayin. That confusion, however natural in Assyrian and Babylonian, can hardly have occurred in primitive Semitic. 2. Jensen (*Zeit. f. Keilschr. For.*, Vol. I, p. 306), and Zimmern (*Babylonische Busspsalmen*, p. 39), hold that the *t* is inserted after

root ʻ*athara*, "to fall,"¹ and took the name to be a reflexive with both a transitive and an intransitive meaning; the former of which meant to "cast forth" or "cause to fall," applying to the mother; the latter, "that which is cast forth," or offspring, being applied in Deut. 7¹³, 28⁴·¹⁸ to lambs. To this derivation Driver objects² — and the objection is a forcible one — that the root ʻ*athara* means not simply "to fall," but "to stumble," "to trip," which, he urges, makes the etymology unsatisfactory. This objection applies, as I now think, not to the etymology itself, but to the particular meaning which I attached to it. Lagarde had pointed the way to the true solution in a short article published as long ago as 1881,³ but when the "Ishtar Cult" was written his article escaped my attention. He connected the name, as I did, with the root ʻ*athara*, but called attention also to some important variations in the meaning of the root which Lane had exhibited in his lexicon,⁴ and which the connection of the goddess with the palm tree now enables us to appreciate. While in Arabic literature the stem ordinarily has the meaning "fall" or "stumble," ʻ*âthûr* means "a channel that is dug for the purpose of irrigating a palm tree such as is termed *baʻal*"; ʻ*athr*, "such as is watered by rain alone"; and ʻ*athîr*, "dust," "earth," or "mud."

The idea that Baʻal was the lord of self-irrigated land has been shown by Robertson Smith to belong to Syria.⁵

the second radical and that the name is to be derived from the root *hashar* = ʻ*ashar*, "to unite." This etymology is far less objectionable and much might be said in its favor. Another one will, however, be found to fit the conditions more perfectly. 3. Georg Hoffmann derives it (*Ueber einige phon. Inschriften*, Göttingen, 1889, p. 22, n.), by a like method of formation from the root ʻ*ashar*, Aramaic ʻ*athar*, "to be voluptuous," a derivation too abstract in its meaning to be primitive.

¹ *Hebraica*, Vol. X, pp. 69–71.
² Hastings's *Dictionary of the Bible*, Vol. I, p. 169, n.
³ "Astarte" in *Nachrichten v. d. Königl. Gesellschaft der Wissenschaften zu Gött.*, 1881, pp. 396–400.
⁴ *Arabic Lexicon*, p. 1953.
⁵ *Religion of the Semites*, 2d ed., pp. 97 ff. and 109 ff. Smith held

He also held that the term *ba'al* land was afterward borrowed by the Arabs. The term *ba'al* for an irrigated palm tree would in any case be late, and must have supplanted an earlier term. That earlier term was, I think, connected with the root ʻ*athara*. This is borne out by the statement which Robertson Smith cites from Bokhari (Bulac vocalized edition) which makes ʻ*athari* synonymous with "what is watered by the sky and by fountains."[1] Smith thought that this term was derived from the name of the god Athtar, but from our preceding discussion it seems more probable that the derivation was the other way, or that both came simultaneously from a common root. It is probable, therefore, that in primitive Semitic ʻ*athara* was connected with naturally watered land, and that ʻ*athtar* meant, in its transitive sense, "she who waters," or "she who makes fruitful," while in the intransitive sense it might apply to that which was "watered," "fertilized," or "produced," and so could come in course of time to mean "offspring," and as in Deut. 7¹³, etc., "lambs."[2] This view suits the agricultural and social conditions which the foregoing pages have shown to have been prevalent in Arabia. The Bedawi, coming in from the arid desert to a green and fruit-

that agriculture, even to the cultivation of the date-palm, was borrowed by the Sabæans from Syria. Since the latter has been proven above to be incorrect, it may well be that the term *ba'al* originated in Sabæa or Arabia. It could not even then, however, be as old as ʼ*âthûr*. See below, Chapter IV.

[1] Smith, *Ibid.* p. 99, n 2.

[2] On this view of the etymology the meaning of the Arabic ʻ*athara*, Heb. ʻ*ashar*, and Aram. ʻ*athar* are all explained. ʼ*Athûr* means according to Lane "a pit dug for a lion or other animal that he may fall into it in order that he may be taken." As noted in the text another form of the word signifies "irrigating ditch for a palm tree." The idea of falling may have become connected with the root from the catching of wild animals in deep irrigating ditches. In time this meaning supplanted the original one. The idea of stumbling would naturally connect itself with the root from the idea of falling into such ditches. From the idea of irrigation would come the idea of fertility, whence the Hebrew, Aram., and Syr. meanings "to be rich," "voluptuous," etc., would easily follow.

ful oasis, would naturally say, "the self-irrigating or fruit-producing goddess has her abode here." That oasis thus became to him a garden of his god, its water and trees visible representatives of his deities. The society in which he lived was one of great sexual freedom in which the mother was the head of the family; he therefore naturally thought of his gods as a mother and son. The trees in the oasis were palm trees; the sex relations of the trees and of human beings were all combined in his mind in the way already described, so that the "self-waterer" was for him the "fruit-producer," "the creator of life," "the mother goddess," the goddess of love. Such was the religion of the Semites in their primitive home while they were yet one people.

Robertson Smith's picture of their sanctuaries, their gods, their totemistic clan organization, their sacrifices, and their animistic conception of spirits, abides; we only see more clearly that the chief deity of the clan was at this primitive time a goddess, and that in so far as a male deity played any considerable part he was her son and reflex.[1]

No doubt it will be distasteful to many to believe that

[1] I have pointed out elsewhere (article "Asherah" in *Jewish Encyclopedia*), that in all probability the limits of the primitive Semitic sanctuary were marked, even before the Semitic dispersion, by wooden posts called "*asherahs*" or "*athrahs*," and that in course of time the name of the post was in certain localities, as in South Arabia and the Lebanon region of Syria, applied to the goddess herself. The evidence for this statement is that *asherah* means "sanctuary" in the Phœnician inscription from Ma'sub, and its philological equivalent *ashirtu*, *ashrâti* or *eshritu*, *eshrâti* is commonly used in Assyrian for sanctuary, while a goddess *Atherat* has been found in a Minæan inscription (Hommel in *Expository Times*, Jan., 1900, p. 190), and a goddess *Ashirta* in the region of Lebanon (Sayce, *ZA.*, Vol. VI, p. 161, Epping and Strassmaier, *ZA.*, Vol. VI, p. 241; Winckler in Schrader's *KB.*, Vol. V, p. 124, and *passim;* Reisner in *Mittheilungen* of the Berlin Museum, p. 92, and Jensen, *ZA.*, Vol. XI, p. 302 ff.). Cf. also below, Chapter VI. Hommel (*op. cit.*) fancies that he sees in the original form of the ideogram for Ishtar a post on which hangs the skin of an animal (cf. Thureau Dangin's *L'Ecriture cunéiforme*, No. 294, and Smith's *Religion of the Semites*, 2d ed., p. 435 ff.

the beginnings of Semitic religion as they were conceived
by the Semites themselves go back to sexual relations. It
must be remembered that such things were thought of
and treated much more innocently in primitive times than
would be indicated by a similar treatment now. In reality,
too, the Semite actually hit upon a feature of human life
which is, as scientific investigation is showing us, intimately connected with religious feeling at the present
day [1] and has had more real influence in developing
moral, altruistic, and humanitarian feeling in the past than
any other. The prolongation of the period of helplessness
in infancy and the consequent development of maternal
love out of which feelings of obligation and conscience
have grown is now seen to lie at the root of the moral and
religious progress of the race.[2] The primitive Semite's
conception of his goddess and her service, to which he
attributed the beginnings of intelligence and civilization,
was in a rude, blind way an emphasis of the same truth.
Considering the animal passions of human nature, it is
little wonder that the processes of procreation often attracted more attention than the offspring itself; but the
delight which all Semites took, and still take, in their
children, is witness to the fact that such religion was
never wholly degenerate. Semitic sacrifice, commensal as
Robertson Smith has shown it to be,[3] embodies in a gross
way the principle of the religious life which is expressed
in the highest spiritual form in John 17^{23}: "I in them
and thou in me that they may be perfected into one;" so
the Semitic conception of deity as we have traced it embodies the truth — grossly indeed, but nevertheless embodies it — that "God is love."

This religion, containing a kernel of perpetual truth,

[1] See Leuba in *Journal of Psychology*, 1896; Starbuck's *Psychology of Religion*, New York, 1900, Part I, on conversion; and Coe's *Spiritual Life*, New York, 1900.
[2] See Drummond's *Ascent of Man*, New York, 1895, chs. vii and viii, and Fiske's *Through Nature to God*, Boston, 1899, pp. 96–130.
[3] *Religion of the Semites*, Lectures VII to XI.

although it was formulated thus crudely, formed the substratum of the religion of the Semites in historical times. It was modified here and there by economic changes and the consequent change in social conditions which followed. At other times foreign influences combined with these to effect a transformation. In Israel its baser elements were eliminated by the prophets, who erected on its foundation a structure of spiritual religion.[1] Traces of these primitive conceptions appear throughout the Semitic world as witnesses to the perpetual influence of these fundamental conceptions of religion and life; and owing to its influence through the Phœnicians upon the Greeks and through Greek society upon the early Christians, and also its influence on the Hebrews and through them upon the church, its effects in many ways abide to the present hour.[2]

In all Semitic life, religious and social, the ḥag or religious festival has always played an important part. Among the ancient Hebrews there were three such festivals which all readers of the Bible will readily recall, — the Passover, near the vernal equinox, the feast of Weeks at the end of the harvest, seven weeks after the Passover, and the feast of Ingathering or Tabernacles at the time of the grape harvest in the seventh month. Of these, recent Biblical scholars regard the first only as primitive, and hold that the others were agricultural festivals adopted by the Israelites after the settlement in Canaan.[3] There is much evidence, however, to show that two of these three festivals have their roots in primitive Semitic practices, and that what the settlement in Canaan did for them was not to originate them, but to give them a new interpretation.

---

[1] See below, Chapter VII.

[2] See below, Chapter VIII.

[3] Wellhausen, *Prolegomena zur Geschichte Israels*, 5th ed., 1899, p. 91; *Reste arabische Heidentums*, 2d ed., p. 98; W. Robertson Smith, *Prophets of Israel*, 2d ed., pp. 38, 56, and 384, also *Old Testament in the Jewish Church*, 2d ed., pp. 240, 269; Harding in Hastings's *Dictionary of the Bible*, Vol. I, p. 860; and Budde, *Religion of Israel to the Exile*, p. 73.

All scholars agree that the paschal portion of the Passover festival, as distinguished from the unleavened bread features of it, existed in the nomadic life of pre-Canaanitish days. This sacrifice of a sheep occurred in the month Nisan, *i.e.* in the spring, or at the beginning of the Oriental summer. Similarly in Cyprus, as we learn from Johannes Lydus,[1] a sacrifice of a sheep was made to Ashtart. This occurred also in the spring, on the 2d of April. In Babylonia there was also a New Year's festival, which was held in Nisan, which, at different times and in different places, was associated with different gods. When we can first trace it in the days of Gudea, it is the festival of Bau,[2] one of the mother goddesses, into which the primitive Semitic mother goddess had developed in the peculiar Babylonian conditions.[3] Later, in consequence of the forces which wrought the transformations described below,[4] it appears as a feast of Marduk of Babylon.[5] In the earlier time when we can trace it as a festival of the goddess, the offerings were lambs, sheep, cattle, etc. Wellhausen, Robertson Smith, and Winckler have shown that in Arabia the festival in the month Ragab originally corresponded both in time and in character to these spring festivals among the other Semites.[6] Two characteristics are common to all these festivals, — they occurred in the springtime, and they involved the sacrifice of lambs. In Arabia the domestic animals bring forth once a year, and the yeaning time is in the spring.[7] In Ex. 34, the Yah-

---

[1] Cf. his *De Mensibus*, Bk. IV, 45, and *Hebraica*, Vol. X, p. 45.

[2] See *KB.*, Vol. III¹, pp. 59, 61, 69, and 71; also Jastrow's *Religion of Babylonia and Assyria*, pp. 59 and 677 ff.

[3] See below, Chapter V.

[4] Chapter V.

[5] *KB.*, Vol. III², p. 15, and Jastrow, *ibid.*, p. 677.

[6] Wellhausen, *Reste arabische Heidentums*, 2d ed., p. 97 ff.; Robertson Smith, *Religion of the Semites*, 2d ed., p. 227 ff.; and Winckler, *Altorientalische Forschungen*, 2te Reihe, Vol. II, pp. 324–350, especially p. 344. On the character of the offerings at the Regab feast, cf. Smith, *ibid.*, n.

[7] Doughty's *Arabia Deserta*, Vol. I, p. 429.

wistic Decalogue, the earliest of existing Hebrew law-books, this spring festival is connected with the gift of firstlings to Yahwe (vv. 18-20). There can be little doubt, in view of these facts, that originally the nomadic Semites kept a spring festival to the mother goddess of fertility. The lambs, kids, and young camels were her gifts, and to her it was right that a joyous feast should be held in honor of her gracious blessings.

The circumcision festivals which were witnessed by Doughty occurred at the same time of the year.[1] Those feasts are still accompanied, as we noted above, by the sacrifice of a sheep, the dancing of girls, and the selection of wives. We cannot, therefore, be far wrong in regarding them as a survival of this old spring festival. As already pointed out, Ephraem and Augustine described the festival of the Semitic mother goddess, as it was known to them, as lewd.[2] Originally, therefore, the spring festival was accompanied by the sacrifice of maiden virtue, — a sacrifice out of which grew the custom described by Herodotus,[3] as well as the sacrifice of the foreskin of youths. Probably acts of free love on the part of all were also a part of the primitive ritual.[4]

The spring festival in this far-off primeval time was then an occasion when the mother goddess was honored by sacrifices to her of some of all her many gifts of animal fertility in the ways which were thought to be pleasing to her. The time was appropriate, since she was revealing in the spring her power through the offspring of the flocks and herds, through the flowering date-palms where her acts of fertilization were taking place, and through the nature which she had given men.

So the infant was consecrated to her service by circum-

[1] Doughty's, *Arabia Deserta*, Vol. I, pp. 340-342.
[2] Ephraem, *Opera*, Vol. II, p. 458 ff., and Augustine, *De Civitate Dei*, Bk. II, 4. Cf. *Hebraica*, Vol. X, pp. 51 and 59.
[3] Bk. I, 199. Cf. *Hebraica*, Vol. X, p. 20.
[4] Such, as I take it, was the original meaning of the dance described by Doughty, *ibid.*, p. 341.

cision, the maiden by the sacrifice of her chastity, and all by acts of free love. At the same time the bonds of tribal kinship were more closely knit by the commensal meal, which was no doubt accompanied by boisterous manifestations of joy, and by songs, which would be extremely coarse when judged by the more refined standards of later ages.

Wellhausen has made it tolerably clear that in the pre-Islamic days the Arabs divided the year roughly into halves,[1] and that the second half which originally began in the autumn was inaugurated by the Safar festival as the other half was by the Ragab festival. This feast he coördinates with the Hebrew feast of Tabernacles, which came in the month Tishri and which represented to the Palestinian Hebrews the conclusion of the grape gathering. No trace of this feast is found in Babylonia, though Jastrow conjectures[2] with some probability that at some time a sacred New Year's feast occurred in the autumn in some part of Babylonia, since the Jews, who derived their method of reckoning time from thence, begin their New Year with Tishri. The character of this feast among the primitive Semites it is not hard to guess. The harvest of the date-palm comes at just this time,[3] when the Arabs give themselves to gladness and hospitality,[4] and the nomads visit the oases to lay in a supply of dates for the winter.[5] We cannot doubt but that in ancient times such an occasion was made a festival to the goddess of the palm tree or that it was characterized by orgies such

---

[1] *Reste arabische Heidentums*, 2d ed., p. 96 ff. Cf. Winckler, *Altorientalische Forschungen*, 2te Reihe, Vol. II, p. 344, who makes the same division as Wellhausen, but makes it begin with Muḥarran, the month before Safar.

[2] *Religion of Babylonia and Assyria*, p. 681. Cf. Muss-Arnolt in *JBL.*, Vol. XI, p. 160 ff.

[3] See Doughty's *Arabia Deserta*, Vol. I, pp. 557 and 561; also Zwemer's *Arabia*, p. 125.

[4] Wellsted's *Travels in Arabia*, Vol. II, p. 122.

[5] Doughty, *ibid.*, as n. 3.

as would befit the rejoicings of a people possessing such a social organization and pervaded by such religious ideas. In the earliest times the oases were *ḥimas*,[1] or tracts sacred to the gods; the gathering of the dates took place therefore in a sacred tract as well as from a sacred tree and would accordingly be naturally regarded as a religious act. This autumn festival still survives in Abyssinia. It has been Christianized and is called *Mascal*, or the Cross. It is celebrated in September, and a part of its ritual includes the lighting of fires on high places before dawn, when oxen are slaughtered as in a heathen festival. It is celebrated, too, with dancing, drumming and playing the sistra during the whole night.[2] Considerable elements of heathenish rites have entered into all the phases of the ritual of the Abyssinian church, but it is not difficult to detect the source whence this feast has come.

Of a third festival we cannot be so confident. If it existed in primitive times, it must have been connected with the god Tammuz. Traces of a festival of the god Tammuz, preceded by wailing for him, are found in Babylonia, Palestine, and Phœnicia. It appears from the poem known as "Ishtar's Descent," that there was in Babylonia a "day of Tammuz."[3] It is usually held, since the fourth of the Babylonian months bore the name of this god, that it was then that his festival was celebrated, and Jastrow on this basis holds that it was a solar festival, celebrated in the fourth month at the approach of the summer solstice.[4] He, like many others, connects this feast, which was preceded by wailing for the death of the god and celebrated by rejoicings at his resurrection,[5] as significant

---

[1] Smith's *Religion of the Semites*, 2d ed., pp. 112, 142-144, and 156-157; Wellhausen, *Heidentums*, 2d ed., p. 105 ff.

[2] See Bent's *Sacred City of the Ethiopians*, pp. 53, 83, 84.

[3] Cf. IV R., p. 31, rev. l. 56; *Hebraica*, Vol. IX, p. 151; and **Jeremias's** *Leben nach dem Tode*, p. 23.

[4] *Religion of Babylonia and Assyria*, p. 682.

[5] Cf. Lucian, *De Syria Dea*, § 6; *Hebraica*, Vol. X, p. 31; and Pietschmann's *Geschichte der Phoenizier*, p. 219.

of the annual death of vegetation, which on Jastrow's interpretation would be due to the burning heat of the summer sun. It appears, however, that in Phœnicia and Palestine the festival was celebrated not in the fourth but in the sixth month. Ezekiel (ch. 8¹) dates it according to the Massoretic text at that time, though the LXX place it in the fifth month. Many modern scholars follow the LXX, but, as it seems to me, without sufficient reason.[1] The cuneiform non-Semitic expression for the sixth month was "the month of the message of Ishtar," as though it was then that she descended to the lower world.[2] The name of the sixth month, Elul, has been explained from the wailing for Tammuz,[2] and altogether it seems probable that the wailing originally occurred in the sixth month, and was followed by the festival of date harvest at the beginning of the seventh, of which we have already spoken. If this be the case, the sacrifice of chastity of which Lucian speaks in connection with these rites at Biblos was a survival from the rites of joy with which the date harvest was celebrated in primitive Semitic times. That the feast of Tammuz should in some form go back to primitive Semitic conditions is indicated by the myth which makes Tammuz the son of Ishtar and which, as we have noted, could only have been formed in a society organized on the lines of the so-called matriarchal clan. Winckler's conclusions as to the old Arabic calendar include the opinion that there was in Arabia a similar summer festival in July-August.[3] The special characteristics of this festival are not clearly known. It seems likely, however, that it was a survival from the old wailing for the death of vegetation which preceded the glad festival of the date harvest. Primarily, then, this feast was a sort of lent preceding the glad time of the

[1] Cf. Toy's *Ezekiel*, in Haupt's *SBOT*.
[2] Cf. Muss-Arnolt in *JBL.*, Vol. XI, pp. 88, 89; and Brünnow's *Classified List of Cuneiform Idiographs*, No. 10759.
[3] *Altorientalische Forschungen*, 2te Reihe, Vol. II, pp. 336–344.

I

autumn festival, when the tree of Tammuz and Ishtar yielded its fruit.

Following Robertson Smith,[1] I expressed in the "Ishtar Cult" the opinion that the wailing for Tammuz was originally the wailing for a sacrificial victim.[2] I still incline to think that this view is right, although, as then, I think that at a very early period it may have received a new explanation which connected it with the death of vegetation. In the deserts of Arabia when the burning summer sun dries up the pastures and in consequence the milk of the domestic animals largely fails, while the summer heat renders life almost unendurable,[3] it may well have seemed to the nomads that Tammuz was dead. Thus the wailing, which originally accompanied the death of the victim at the festival, was, I think, extended to cover a portion of time preceding harvest. This produced a period of gloom to be turned to life when harvest came with its evidences of the god's returning life.

Robertson Smith has with great plausibility connected the fasting and humiliation of the Jewish Day of Atonement with this Tammuz wailing.[4] Such connection is from every point of view exceedingly probable. The Day of Atonement came at the beginning of autumn, a fact which confirms our view that it originally occurred in connection with the autumn feast.[5]

If this view be correct, it is not difficult to understand how the Tammuz wailing and ritual may have been transferred in Babylonia to the fourth month. The first harvest of wheat and barley is in that country reaped at the time of the summer solstice, and at such a time a festival

---

[1] *Religion of the Semites*, 1st ed., p. 392, n.
[2] *Hebraica*, Vol. X, p. 74.
[3] Doughty's *Arabia Deserta*, Vol. I, chs. xvii and xviii, esp. p. 472 ff.
[4] *Religion of the Semites*, Lect. XI, esp. p. 411.
[5] Fraser, *Golden Bough*, ch. iii, connects the death of Tammuz with the corn (wheat) harvest, — the slaying of the divine grain. This cannot have been primitive, on account of the economic conditions of Arabia, though possibly it was a later agricultural explanation.

among an agricultural people is a most natural occurrence. If in order to meet this need the Tammuz festival were put forward a few weeks, the influence of Babylonia on Palestine in the El-Amarna period would lead (if local influences had not already done so) to the establishment of a festival at the end of harvest there. This afterwards the Hebrews adopted as the feast of weeks. Meantime the direct influence of Arabia seems to have been sufficient in Phœnicia and Palestine to keep the original Tammuz festival at its own period in the autumn separate from the festival at the end of barley harvest. Something like this may have been the course of development in Babylonia. The fact that the fourth month bore the name of Tammuz is a somewhat slight basis for such conjecture, since the month may have been given the name for other reasons.

We conclude, however, that but two Semitic festivals were primitive, the festival of the yeaning time in the spring and the festival of the date harvest in the autumn. Out of these the other festivals of the Semitic world have been developed, except as some of them have been borrowed from the peoples of the lands in which they settled.

If now we turn to the Hamites, from whom originally the Semites separated themselves, we find some indications that their primitive institutions were similar to those of the primitive Semites, if not identical with them. Circumcision was, as we have already noticed,[1] practised by the Egyptians and the Hamitic Gallas, and Nowack[2] and Benzinger[3] still hold with Herodotus that the Semitic rite was borrowed from Egypt. Down to the time of the Cæsars women and girls were licensed to a life of immorality by consecration to the service of Amon at Thebes. These women were held in such high esteem that this public course of life did not prevent them from making good marriages when age compelled them to withdraw from this service.[4] Maspéro interprets this rightly as a relic of

[1] See above, p. 101.
[2] *Archæologie*, Vol. I, p. 167.
[3] *Archæologie*, p. 154.
[4] Strabo, Bk. XVII, 46.

polyandry.¹ In its later stages this polyandry was endogamous, like the later polyandry of the Semites, since it permitted the marriage of brother and sister, and sometimes of father and daughter. One of the legacies left to Egypt by this type of polyandry is the use of the words "brother" and "sister" in the sense of "lover" and "mistress."² This stage of the civilization is further indicated by the fact that in the temples of the chief gods there were women devoted to purposes similar to those for which they were attached to the temple of Amon, while in the temples of the female divinities they held the chief places.³

Another reflection in the Egyptian religion of this state of society is found in the conception of the goddess Isis. The oldest myths concerning her represent her as an independent deity, dwelling in the midst of the ponds without husband or lover, who gave birth spontaneously to a son, whom she suckled among the reeds,⁴ — a tale which can only be properly interpreted as the reflection of a society in which exogamous polyandry, of a type resembling the earliest Semitic polyandry, was practised. In later times she was said to be married to Osiris, a fact which one school of mythologists interpret as the marriage of Isis, the Dawn, to Osiris, the Sun,⁵ but which Maspéro, with more probability, takes to mean the marriage of Isis, the Earth, to Osiris, the Nile.⁶ There can be no doubt but that this latter myth is the later of the two, and is the reflection of a later social organization.

We have then in the oldest Hamitic civilization traces of circumcision, of polyandry, of a mother goddess who represented well-watered land, as among the Semites.

---

[1] Maspéro's *Dawn of Civilization*, p. 50.
[2] Maspéro, *op. cit.*, p. 51.
[3] Maspéro, *op. cit.*, p. 126.
[4] Maspéro, *op. cit.*, p. 131.
[5] So Robert Brown, Jr., *Semitic Influence in Hellenic Mythology*, p. 53. Brown is a disciple of Max Müller in the interpretation of mythology.
[6] Maspéro, *op. cit.*, p. 132.

The date-palm was also known, and there is at least one trace of it as a god.[1]

Among the Hamites who lived to the west of Egypt similar customs appear. Thus Herodotus tells us[2] that the Nasamones, a tribe of Berber Hamites,[3] made yearly expeditions to a date-palm oasis to gather the fruit, and their polyandry and sexual customs in general resembled closely much which we find among the Semites.

With reference to these institutions which the ancient Semites and Hamites had in common, there are three possible opinions: (1) they may have developed them in the early days before the two peoples separated, when as yet the races were one; (2) they may have developed them independently through the influence of similar environments; or (3) one race may have borrowed from the other at a comparatively late period.

The last of these possibilities must be rejected at once. We have shown above how all these institutions of primitive Semitic life, including even circumcision, grew naturally out of the desert and oasis life such as they were subjected to in Arabia. It is purely arbitrary, therefore, to assume without positive proof that any one of these institutions was a late intruder into Semitic practice. The theory of Herodotus with reference to circumcision must therefore be abandoned. On the other hand, few will be found to maintain that it or any of the other institutions under discussion were borrowed by the Egyptians from the Semites. A people which reached such a high state of culture at such an early epoch is not likely to have borrowed a religious and social practice from so rude a people as the Semitic Arabs at a time when the two must have been separated by sea and desert.

Of the other two possibilities, the first is, under the circumstances, by far the most probable. While, of course,

[1] Maspéro, *ibid.*, pp. 27 and 121, n. 1.
[2] Book IV, 172.
[3] Sergi, *Mediterranean Race*, p. 47.

two peoples of kindred race may in similar environments have developed similar institutions independently of one another, it must be remembered that the environment of the Egyptians, from the time of their settlement in Egypt, was not similar to that of the Semites, or of a character to produce institutions similar to theirs. Egypt is not a land of oases, but a river-land similar to Mesopotamia. It was an agricultural country, rich and productive. As we shall show below, the civilization produced in such a land was not polyandrous, and differed consequently, as to all the features which grow out of polyandry, from that which the desert-oasis life produced. North Africa, outside of Egypt, was for the most part a barren country, with occasional oases, in its general features not unlike Arabia.[1] It is altogether probable that, as these regions filled up, conditions were produced by the crowded populations similar to those which we have proven for Arabia,[2] and that in consequence a similar culture of the date-palm,[3] a similar organization of the clan, a similar worship for the feminine productive principle, and in general, similar institutions were in some portions produced, though the fertile valleys in some portions of North Africa probably

---

[1] For a description of North Africa and its oases, see *The International Geography*, ed. by Hugh Robert Mill, London, 1899; for Morocco, p. 905; for Algeria, p. 907; for Tunesia, pp. 913, 914; for Tripoli, p. 916 ff.

[2] Above, p. 73 ff.

[3] My friend, Professor W. Max Müller, tells me that the whole Paradise story of Genesis, which, as we have seen, reflects primitive Semitic ideas, has a parallel in the hieroglyphic Egyptian. This indicates that what we have proven for the primitive Semitic conceptions of religion which grew out of oasis life, could in like manner be proven for the Hamites. In other words, the institutions which we have proven in Arabia were born earlier in North Africa. Sayce (*PSBA.*, Vol. XXII, p. 278) describes a vase taken from a predynastic tomb, on which a palm tree is pictured. It is, therefore, unnecessary to account for such phenomena in the Egyptian religion on the ground of Semitic influence from Arabia. It is in the highest degree doubtful whether such foreign influence, exercised apart from conquest or settlement, produced such results anywhere in the ancient world. Semitic words in later Egyptian inscriptions are no argument against this view.

prevented the production of these institutions on so wide and so uniform a scale as in Arabia.

Now such crowding of the country must have occurred before the Semitic migration, and must have been its cause. Some such force must have impelled the first immigrants to enter the unattractive Arabian peninsula. We have, then, in the primitive Hamito-Semitic home the elements present for the birth of these institutions before the separation of the two grand divisions of the race. We hold it probable, therefore, that the totemistic clan, the culture of the date-palm with its worship, the mother goddess as the typical divinity, and circumcision, had to some extent their beginnings at the time when the Hamites and Semites were living in that common home of their infancy, in which their kindred tongues were born, notwithstanding that the differences in those tongues bear witness to the fact that they separated in prehistoric time, thousands of years ago.

If this be so, we find, by applying Hilderbrand's law referred to above,[1] that, at the time of the separation of the Semites from the Hamites, the pastoral and semi-agricultural stage of life had been reached, with some rude cultivation of the date-palm. This conclusion removes the time of Hamito-Semitic savagery some thousands of years farther back into remote antiquity than it has usually been placed, but it is not on that account to be rejected. It must, it seems to me, be regarded as highly probable.[2]

The conclusions reached in this discussion inevitably lead to another, of no little importance to the correct understanding of the Semitic religions. If we regard it as a

[1] pp. 72, 73.
[2] The writer makes no pretence to a knowledge of Egyptology. The facts quoted above are quoted on the authority of reputable Egyptologists. An interpretation has been given them in the text, such as is compatible with the results made probable by the interpretation of the Semitic material in the light of economic and social laws. It is to be hoped that some Egyptologist will take the matter up and do the same for the material of his science.

law, that religious institutions are in some important respects patterned on those social and political institutions which economic environment makes possible, we should naturally expect the Semites, as they modified their environment or moved to new ones and developed a system of male kinship, to make masculine instead of feminine deities the chief objects of their worship.

The feminine deities thus displaced were the earliest principal deities which the Semites had, for even in their savage state, their monogamy was too temporary to permit of a system of male kinship. We regard it, therefore, as a general principle which may be safely applied, that those phases of Semitic religion which reflect a polyandrous state of society are more primitive than any of those which reflect a patriarchal. The latter are either of later birth, are borrowed from foreign peoples, or are formed from a mother goddess, by changing her gender but retaining many of her attributes. As society, in consequence of changed environment, was transformed from the matriarchal to the patriarchal form, such transformations of deities actually occurred, as will be shown in the next two chapters. Here and there the old mother goddess survived in something of her pristine independence, preserved by the forces of religious conservatism. Where transformations into a masculine deity occurred she was often in part retained as the consort and companion of the male deity.

Thus by classifying the deities on this principle and following out the lines of economical and social development, much light will be thrown upon the problems of Semitic religion, and gods which have been considered to be borrowed by one Semitic nation from another will frequently appear to be independent developments from a common mother goddess of the primitive time.[1]

---

[1] It does not fall within the scope of this investigation to account for the origin of the idea of a god or of supernatural spirits among the primitive Semites. It is probable, however, that among them religion did not originate in ancestor worship. Cf. Frey's *Tod Seelenglaube und Seelen-*

kult in alten Israel, and Grüneisen's *Der Ahnencultus und die Urreligion Israels.* For arguments on the other side, cf. Stade *Geschichte,* Vol. I, pp. 387–427; Schwally, *Leben nach dem Tode,* ch. I; Charles, *Eschatology,* p. 20 ff., and G. A. Smith, *Preaching of the Old Testament,* p. 184, n. 2.

CHRONOLOGICAL TABLE

South Semitic Chronology

Minæan kingdom, cir. 1250–600 B.C.
Sabæan kingdom, cir. 750–115 B.C.
Kingdom of Saba and Raidan, 115 B.C. to cir. 350 A.D. (south Arabia and Abyssinia).
Kingdom of Aksum, cir. 350 A.D. onward (Abyssinia).
Mohammed born, 571 A.D.
Mohammed began preaching, 610 A.D.
Mohammed left Mecca, 622 A.D.
Mohammed's death, 632 A.D.
Medina Caliphate, 632–661 A.D.

West Semitic Chronology

El-Amarna Tablets, cir. 1400 B.C. (Tyre, Sidon, Gebal, Jerusalem, Lacish, and Ashtoreth then flourished).
Kingdom of Tyre, cir. 1300–332 B.C. (Hiram, king, cir. 1000; Eth-Baal, cir. 880; Baali, cir. 660).
Israel invaded Canaan, cir. 1200 B.C.
Yakhwemelek, king of Gebal, cir. 400 B.C.
Eshmunazer, Tabnith, and Eshmunazer II, kings of Sidon, cir. 380–332 B.C.
Greek rule of Phœnicia, 332 B.C. onward.
Phœnician kings of Citium and Idalion in Cyprus, 479–312 B.C.
Græco-Egyptian kings rule in Cyprus, 312 B.C. onward.
Carthage founded, cir. 825 B.C.
Carthage subject to Rome, 201 B.C.

CHAPTER IV

TRANSFORMATIONS AMONG THE SOUTHERN AND WESTERN SEMITES

WE have traced above [1] the general lines of social development in Arabia and have noted how the vague polyandry of the Nair type and descent through the mother were, through economic causes, and possibly the influence of war and marriage by capture, transformed into ba'al marriage and descent through the father; polyandry of the Thibetan type forming in certain localities an intermediate stage of social development. Robertson Smith is no doubt right in holding that this transformation did not take place before the Semitic dispersion.[2] Much evidence will be presented in Chapter VI in support of this view. The transformation had, however, taken place by the time of Mohammed, who provided that wives whom their husbands could not trust might be rebuked, secluded in lonely apartments, and even flogged by the husband.[3] Of course, in parts of Arabia the older liberties of women may have been retained much longer than they were at Mecca and Medina, but the trend of social development, as the passage quoted above [4] from Strabo indicates, had been for some time in the direction of the patriarchal family. It must have been well advanced in Mecca and Medina before the prophet could make such a law as that referred to.

This transformation of the family and the exaltation of the father left its impress upon the Arabic conception of

[1] Chapter II.   [2] *Kinship*, p. 179.   [3] *Qur'an*, 4^{39}.
[4] p. 64. See Strabo, Bk. XVI, p. 783.

divinity. In South Arabia, the old mother goddess, even while she retained her feminine name, became a masculine deity and a father god.[1] He is frequently designated as lord (*ba'al*) Athtar, and is at least once called "father."[2]

In Yemen, in the southwestern corner of Arabia, this impress can be most clearly traced. The country is of volcanic formation, consisting of extensive uplands, broken by mountain ranges and interspersed with valleys of surpassing richness, where from time immemorial the land has been laid out in terraces, the water of the rainy season stored in cisterns for irrigation, and many natural rivulets course down the hills.[3] These valleys produce wheat, barley, maize, millet, and coffee, as well as palm trees, orange, lemon, quince, mango, plum, apricot, peach, apple, pomegranate, and fig trees. The vine also grows there luxuriantly.[4] This is the Arabia Felix of the ancients. Here a Semitic kingdom had been established, probably as early as 1250 years before the Christian era, and perhaps earlier. The claims of Glaser and Hommel that a Minæan kingdom preceded the Sabæan on this soil seem to me to be well made out. The Minæan sarcophagus of the Ptolemaic period, discovered some years since in Egypt,[5] is no objection to this; it only shows that the city of Ma'in kept its identity some time after it was dominated by the Sabæan power. Tradition has it that a queen of Sabæa visited Solomon,[6] and Sargon, king of Assyria, counted It'amara (Jetha'-amara), king of Sabæa, among his tribute-

---

[1] Cf. *Hebraica*, Vol. X, pp. 52–59 and 202–205.

[2] Mordtmann's *Himjarische Inschriften und Alterhümer-Mittheilungen kgl. Museen zu Berlin*, Heft VII, No. 862.

[3] Cf. Reclus, *The Earth and its Inhabitants*, New York, 1885, Vol. IV, p. 438 ff., and Zwemer, *Arabia, the Cradle of Islam*, chs. v and vi.

[4] Zwemer, *op. cit.*, p. 57.

[5] Cf. Golenischeff, in the St. Petersburg *Sapiski*, 1893, p. 219 ff.; D. H. Müller, in Wiener's *Zeitschrift f. d. Kunde des Morganländes*, 1894, p. 1 ff.; Hommel, *PSBA.*, Vol. XVI, 145 ff.; Derenbourg, in *Jour. asiatique*, 1894; and Weber, *Mitteilungen vorderasiat. Gesellschaft*, 1901, Heft I, p. 42.

[6] 1 Kgs. 10¹ ff.

payers in the year 715 B.C.,¹ but it seems probable that these references are to a North Arabian precursor of the Sabæan kingdom.² In the rich valleys of southwestern Arabia, agricultural communities must have been formed at a very early time. Semitic social life would therefore be transformed here far sooner than in other parts of Arabia. Reclus declares³ that in this mountainous region the very soil and climate render a nomadic life almost impossible. There are vast uplands between the mountains and valleys where the Bedawi have settled into a pastoral life.⁴ To this region the Semites from central Arabia came, here their social structure underwent in course of time, and in consequence of their new conditions, a transformation. Descent was reckoned through the father, and in time the old mother goddess was transformed into a god. He became, of course, a father, and is frequently called lord (*ba'al*) Athtar.

Not only is this true, but we are able in one inscription to catch a glimpse of the deity in the very process of transformation. This interesting document was published some years since by the Derenbourgs,⁵ and is of sufficient importance to be reproduced here. It reads: —

1. Yaṣbakh of Riyam, son of Mauqis and Baus, and his wife Karibat of M. . . .
2. of the tribe Ṣirwakh, a royal vassal, — they have consecrated to their lady 'Umm-Athtar for
3. four sons four images of pure gold, because 'Umm-Athtar blessed
4. them with the boys and three daughters and they lived — all these chil-
5. dren — and they two themselves have acquired gain through these children. May 'Umm-
6. Athtar continue to bless his servants, Yaṣbakh and Karibat with well-formed children, and to favor them

[1] Cf. *KB.*, Vol. II, pp. 54, 55; and Glaser, *Die Abessinier in Arabia und Afrika*, p. 29.
[2] Cf. Weber, in *Mitteil. der vorderasiat. Gesell.*, 1901, I, 32.
[3] *Op. cit.*, p. 438.
[4] Zwemer, *op. cit.*, p. 68.
[5] *Journal asiatique*, 8 Ser., Vol. II, pp. 256–266.

7. themselves, and to favor their children. May 'Umm-Athtar be gracious
8. and grant complete safety to the sons of Yaṣbakh, Kharif Magda'al, Ra-
9. balat and 'Am'atiq, the descendants of Mauqis, and to their harvests and good fruits in
10. the land Nakhla Kharif, and in the pastures of their camels. To 'Umm-Athtar.

The value of this inscription to our subject can scarcely be overrated. 'Umm-Athtar is not a new female divinity as the Derenbourgs thought,[1] but is as Mordtmann has rightly seen, simply "mother Athtar."[2] 'Umm-Athtar is also in l. 2 called "lady."[3]

It is therefore clear that she is, in the thought of these worshippers, still a goddess. No doubt, therefore, it was an Athtar thus conceived who was invoked in such proper names as Yasma'um, meaning "may mother hear."[4] Although the parents, who caused the inscription under discussion to be written, addressed Athtar as "lady" and as "mother," they nevertheless describe themselves as "his servants,"[5] showing that they were conscious that at times, or possibly that in neighboring places, the deity was regarded as a god, and that the transition was beginning to make itself felt in their own thought. At the same time the character of the old mother goddess, or deity of sexual love and fertility, was still strictly maintained; they give thanks for the birth of their seven children, and while they pray for more they pray also for their harvests and pasture lands, over which the same goddess has power. It is also an interesting fact that the name of the place where this "mother Athtar," who is called "he," was worshipped was Nakhla Kharif, which

---

[1] *Op. cit.*, p. 259.
[2] *Himjarische Inschriften*, p. 25.
[3] Sabæan, מראת.
[4] Sabæan, יסמעאם. Cf. *Journal asiatique*, 6 Ser., Vol. XIX, p. 213, No. 417¹.
[5] Sabæan, עבדיהו.

means "the palm tree of ripe fruit," — a fact which connects this deity with the date-palm, as we have done in the preceding chapter.

The evidence that Athtar in Sabæa was transformed into a god is abundant. He is called *ba'al* or "lord" in a considerable number of inscriptions which come from several different localities,[1] and is at least once, as already noted, called "father." Robertson Smith was of the opinion that the term *ba'al* originated in Syria and was borrowed by the Yemenites from thence.[2] If this be true, the application of the term *ba'al* to Athtar would be decidedly late. Smith's argument is, however, based on the supposition that all agricultural processes were borrowed from Syria, even to the cultivation of the date-palm, — an opinion which our investigation has proven[3] to be, in part at least, untenable. The primitive Semitic social and religious institutions presuppose the culture of the date-palm and a semi-agricultural life. The course of development which Semitic social life underwent, however, assures us that the *ba'al* form of marriage made its appearance at a comparatively late time, and that therefore the *ba'al* conception of deity is likewise late whether it was borrowed by the Yemenites from Syria or not. We are safe, then, in assuming that the *ba'al* Athtar is later than the *'umm* Athtar and was developed out of her.

This masculine Athtar was in places called "lord of the water supply,"[4] and like the feminine Athtar described above, was a god of fertility, whose blessing was necessary to abundant harvests.[5] That Athtar became localized in different places in each of which slightly different conceptions of him were entertained, so that there were

---

[1] See *CIS.*, Pt. IV, Vol. I, Nos. 40¹, 41⁸, 46⁵; Mordtmann, *op. cit.*, No. 886², and *ZDMG.*, Vol. XXXVII, pp. 4 and 326.
[2] *Religion of the Semites*, 2d ed., p. 107 ff.
[3] See p. 75, n. 4.
[4] Cf. *CIS.*, Pt. IV, Vol. I, No. 41, and Fell, *ZDMG.*, Vol. LIV, p. 245.
[5] *CIS.*, Pt. IV, Vol. I, Nos. 104 and 105.

different gods of this name just as there were different Ishtars in Assyria and different Virgin Marys in modern Europe, I have shown elsewhere.[1]

It frequently happens in such cases that some favorite epithet of the deity is used so constantly to designate him that it finally displaces his original name: thus Tammuz (or whatever the primitive name was) became Adōn, as did Yahwe in Israel. Fell has shown[2] how frequently the Sabæans attached epithets to their gods, but his investigation of the subject is not sufficiently thoroughgoing. He stops at what are still epithets only, and does not attempt to distinguish those divine names which originated as epithets. It is possible to show how several divine names in Arabia originated in this way. At 'Amrân the epithet Ilmaqqâhu, "the divine protector," very nearly displaced the older name of Athtar.[3] In thirty inscriptions, Ilmaqqâhu has displaced the name Athtar except in two instances,[4] and in the former of these[5] the meaning of the inscription equates Ilmaqqâhu with Athtar. Ilmaqqâhu is, moreover, throughout this group of inscriptions, a protector of children and a giver of fertility, — functions not only performed by Athtar elsewhere, as we have seen, but also performed by Athtar in this very town, as one of the inscriptions from which the epithet Ilmaqqâhu is omitted proves.[6] This epithet was known elsewhere, *e.g.* at San'â,[7] but at 'Amrân it nearly displaced every other name of Athtar. At times, as in some of the inscriptions published by Mordtmann,[8] the personification of the epithet goes so far that Athtar and Ilmaqqâhu are put side by side as separate gods. Thus the evolution of a new deity from an old, by the use of an epithet, was completed.

From this phenomenon it is safe to infer that if other South Arabian, or indeed Semitic, gods appear, whose

---

[1] *Hebraica*, Vol. X, pp. 57, 203, 204.
[2] *ZDMG.*, Vol. LIV, p. 238 ff.
[3] See *CIS.*, Pt. IV, Vol. I, Nos. 72–102.
[4] Nos. 74 and 102.
[5] No. 74.
[6] No. 102.
[7] Cf. *CIS.*, Pt. IV, Vol. I, No. 18.
[8] *ZDMG.*, Vol. LII, pp. 394–400.

names are epithets, and whose characteristics and functions are clearly those of Athtar, that they are offshoots from him and have arisen in a similar manner. Another instance of this may be seen in the god Tâlab Riyâm, "The Strong One of Riyâm," [1] (analogous to the "Mighty One of Jacob"[2] as a name for Yahwe). The South Arabic epithet has, however, gone so far that the combination of the name of the locality with the adjective is complete, and the two have so fully displaced the name of Athtar that in one instance [3] Athtar is enumerated in the same sentence as a separate deity. That the two were originally one appears from the fact that they both have the same functions of fertility.[4]

Thus Yemen developed many masculine deities, — how many, we do not yet know, and probably shall not when all the inscriptions which South Arabia can yield are found and read, for many of them no doubt passed away without leaving any monument behind to commemorate them.

The old mother goddess was not, however, lost in consequence of this transformation. She was retained as the consort of the male deity; or to speak more accurately, she was divided into two deities, a masculine and a feminine. This masculine deity was identified in the age from which our inscriptions come with the morning star, and was often known as "Athtar Sharqan,"[5] while the feminine deity was identified with the sun, and called "Shams." That Shams should be a goddess in South Arabia while Shamash was elsewhere a god, was due, perhaps, as we shall see, to the absence of foreign influences; but whatever its explanation, it is a fact. The expression "to the goddess Shams, the Lady" (baʻalat) occurs in one inscription,[6]

---

[1] Mordtmann, *Himjarische Inschriften*, etc., Nos. 825, 826, 830, 860, 866, 875, and 879.
[2] Isa. 49^{26} and 60^{16}. [3] No. 866. [4] Cf. No. 825$^{27-29}$.
[5] Cf. *Hebraica*, Vol. X, p. 204. Fell, however, thinks that Sebæan analogies would lead us to regard Sharqan as a place. See *ZDMG.*, Vol. LIV, pp. 241, 242.
[6] Mordtmann and Muller's *Sabäische Denkmälern*, No. 13.

K

while the term *ba'alat* is applied to her in others.[1] She is therefore clearly feminine. She was further thought to be the spouse of the masculine god of fertility, and they together were thought to be the parents of their worshippers. Thus one inscription, published by Mordtmann, read in its original form, as he has pointed out, "with Tâlab Riyâm and with Shams, their parents, are the sons of דהרם."[2] Here Shams is undoubtedly the spouse of a deity which, as we have seen, sprung from Athtar. This passage makes it clear that when "Athtar Sharqan and Shams" are coupled together in another inscription, as objects of devotion,[3] they were worshipped as the union of male and female in the divine circle, analogous to the union of husband and wife in the patriarchal home, which had become the basis of Arabian society.

The material upon which these observations are founded comes from the Sabæan and later periods. The same was probably also true of the religion of the earlier Minæan kingdom. At least that is the conclusion forced upon me by an examination of the material accessible to me. The Minæan kingdom was composed of a number of tribes, each of which had its local deity. In what is probably one of the earliest Minæan inscriptions,[4] coming from Waqhail, the second king of Ma'in whose name is recovered,[5] three deities are mentioned, — Athtar of Qabḍ, Wadd, and Nakrakh. That this Athtar was not originally a member of the Pantheon of the city of Ma'in seems certain, from the

---

[1] *E.g.* in Mordtmann's *Himjarische Inschriften*, No. 880.

[2] *Op. cit.*, No. 869.

[3] *CIS.*, Pt. IV, Vol. I, No. 74. There are two or three interesting passages in which Shams is associated with a masculine form of Athtar (in two cases it is Ilmaqqâhu) and is called "his Shams." See *CIS.*, Nos. 106; 143 and 149. Winckler has endeavored to show (*ZDMG.*, Vol. LIV, pp. 408–420) that Shams also meant "goddess" at times, as Ishtar did among the Assyrians. Even if this be so, it, like Ishtar, also designated a definite goddess.

[4] Halévy, No. 255 (*Journal asiatique*, 1872).

[5] Cf. Weber, in *Mitteilungen der vorderasiat. Gesell.*, 1901, Heft I, p. 59, and Mordtmann, *ZDMG.*, Vol. XLVII, pp. 395–417.

fact that she (or he) is connected with another place, and also from the fact that a king who reigned three or four steps down the list mentions only Wadd and Muraḍawahi as the deities of Ma'in.[1] In the inscriptions of other kings a number of Athtars of other places are included; it is natural to conclude, therefore, that at Ma'in the native deities were Wadd and a feminine deity called by various epithets. That the primitive Semitic order of society and of thought had largely passed away is shown by the presence of the *ba'al* idea in these inscriptions.[2]

The name Wadd is an epithet formed from a root meaning "love," and there can be no doubt that Wadd is but another name for a masculinized Athtar, or for an Arabian Tammuz. Another Minæan inscription makes him the consort of the old mother goddess under the name of Athirat,[3] a name derived from the posts which marked the old Semitic sanctuary. There can be little doubt, therefore, that the transformation which we trace elsewhere in later inscriptions, had taken place at Ma'in by the beginning of the period of the Minæan kingdom.

If now we pass to North Arabia and assume that the same laws of religious development were at work there, it will appear that a number of deities were evolved by the same social forces out of the transformed mother goddess, and that Allah himself, the one true God of Mohammedanism, was originally one of these gods. That Mohammed introduced a large spiritual element into the Islamic conception of Allah cannot be denied. The strong assertion of the unity of God, his eternity and aloneness, made, for example, in Sura 112, distinctly and immeasurably exalted the Arabian conception of divinity. Mohammed's earnest effort to make the association of any other divinity with Allah impossible[4] dealt a death blow to the old heathenism.

[1] Halévy, No. 229.
[2] Cf. the proper name "Ba'alat," in Halévy, No. 234.
[3] Cf. Hommel, *Expository Times*, Vol. XI, p. 190, and *Aufsätze und Abhandlungen*, Vol. II, p. 206 ff.; also below, Chapter VI.
[4] See, *e.g.*, Suras 4 and 53, *passim*.

No one who reads the Qur'an can doubt that for much of the purity and loftiness of this monotheism Mohammed was indebted to Judaism and Christianity.[1] It is also clear that the pure monotheism of the early years of his ministry was not attractive to his fellow countrymen, and that in the later years of his career several concessions were made to the older Arabian religious ideas. Thus after his migration to Medina the qibla, or direction of the face in prayer, was changed from Jerusalem to Mecca.[2] In consequence, the Qaʻaba became for the Mohammedan the sanctuary of Allah, so that Mohammed could subsequently call it "the holy house," "the holy sanctuary."[3] He also provided that if, while on a pilgrimage to Mecca, one killed game, — an act which violated an old taboo,[4] — a sacrifice of atonement for it must be offered to Allah in the Qaʻaba.[5] The one God, Allah, was thus identified with the god of the Qaʻaba, and it became his sanctuary, which it has remained to the present time. One of the evidences of borrowing is that, though Mohammedanism knows no necessity of atonement, yet a part of the ritual to which every pilgrim to Mecca must conform is the offering of a sacrifice.[6] This is a camel, bullock, goat, or sheep, according to the wealth of the pilgrim. Such a custom is clearly a survival from heathen ritual.

This identification of Allah with the god of the Qaʻaba could, however, not have been made had not a god been previously worshipped at the Qaʻaba who could be thus fused with Mohammed's Allah without doing serious violence to religious feeling. It has been frequently pointed out that

---

[1] Cf. Geiger's *Was hat Mohammed aus dem Judenthum aufgenommen?* 1833, and *The Bible and Islam*, by Henry Preserved Smith, New York, 1897.

[2] Sura 2^{140}.

[3] Sura 5$^{2.3}$.

[4] Robertson Smith's *Religion of the Semites*, 2d ed., p. 112 ff., and 144 ff.

[5] Sura 5$^{96-98}$.

[6] Cf. Zwemer's *Arabia, the Cradle of Islam*, 1900, p. 39.

the goddess Al-Uzza was especially connected with the sanctuary at Mecca.[1] It is clear, however, from one of Mohammed's Meccan Suras which dates from the earlier years of his ministry ($53^{19\,\mathrm{ff.}}$), that the popular mythology made Al-Uzza, Al-Lat, and Manât daughters of a male deity which, even at this early period, Mohammed identified with Allah. This is not surprising, for what is more natural than that Mohammed should believe that the god of his childhood's tribal faith was after all one with the God of his larger thought and prophetic ministry? That a goddess should be at Mecca the daughter of a god is the reverse of the conception which prevailed among the primitive Semites, and which was preserved among the Nabathæans, where Al-Lat was regarded as the mother of Dhu-'l-Shara.[2] These facts and the course of development in the conception of deity which we have traced in south Arabia lead us to suggest the following as the probable history of the conception of deity at Mecca. The shrine with its sacred spring, the Zemzem, was originally the shrine of the mother goddess, Athtar. By processes identical with those which operated in Yemen she was divided into a masculine and a feminine deity, or by influences similar to those which appear in the Gilgamish epic in Babylonia, Tammuz had become her husband. This is not a mere conjecture, since the memory of this masculine and feminine pair under the names Isâf and Nâila has actually been preserved in Mohammedan tradition.[3] To this feminine deity different epithets were applied. Whether these epithets grew out of the thought of the Meccans themselves, or were in part the result of syncretism with other Arabic tribes, we cannot now determine. These epithets became so fixed that in time they were regarded as the

[1] Cf. Robertson Smith's *Kinship*, p. 294, Wellhausen's *Heidentum* 2d ed., p. 36 ff., and *Hebraica*, Vol. X, p. 64 ff.
[2] See Smith, *Kinship*, p. 292; and *Religion of the Semites*, p. 56 ff.; and *Hebraica*, Vol. X, p. 64; and below, Chapter VI.
[3] Cf. Wellhausen, *Heidentum*, 2d ed., p. 77.

names of different goddesses. In course of time the male phase of the Athtar at Mecca so overshadowed the female, just as the patriarchate had in human society overshadowed the matriarchate, that the feminine deity, the mother, was to such a degree subordinated that the male could be called *Al-lahu*, or "the god." This god was also known as Hubal, and there was an idol of him in the Qaʻaba. Wellhausen has anticipated me in identifying him with Allah.[1] For a long time one of the epithets applied to the old mother goddess was thought to be the name of Hubal's spouse, while others were thought to be the names of their daughters. By the time of the prophet, however, if we may judge by the one allusion made to it, Allah and his daughters were thought by the Meccans to constitute their pantheon.

At this juncture Mohammed appeared and endeavored to exalt and purify the conception of Allah possessed by his countrymen. Finding himself after years of preaching unable to banish the old heathenism, he compromised, — banishing the goddesses who still were the patrons of social impurity, and persuading the people to regard them as mere names, — he led them to identify the god of the Qaʻaba with the one God of the universe. Thus the God of Islam was engrafted onto a natural stock, which had its root in the primitive Semitic mother goddess.

No doubt the few gods of Arabic heathenism which are known to us through Mohammedan sources originated, at least most of them, in the same way. Their names are epithets, as Dhu-'l-Khalaṣa, Al-Fals, Al-Galsad, Al-Uqaiṣir, etc.[2] They were each connected with some idol which

---

[1] *Op. cit.*, pp. 75, 76. Among the customs which Mohammedanism inherited from this old cult is that which requires the pilgrim to make a circuit seven times around the Qa'aba. He must lay aside his own clothes and put on two pieces of cloth, one around the loins and the other over the back, but in the more shameless days of heathenism it was done without any clothing whatever. Cf. Zwemer's *Arabia, the Cradle of Islam*, p. 38.

[2] Cf. Wellhausen's *Heidentum*, 2d ed., pp. 45–64.

was often a natural crag or stone. The details of their history are unknown to us, but if we could ascertain them we should no doubt find that these gods were developed out of the primitive Semitic mother goddess by the same laws of progress and differentiation, the action of which we have already traced.

Passing now to Abyssinia, we find the worship of the same deity, known here as Astar, the form which the name of the primitive mother goddess assumed in Ethiopic. The worship of Astar is vouched for in an inscription from Aksum, fragmentary copies of which were brought to Europe as long ago as 1833, and of which other fragments have been secured at various times since. Bent in 1892 secured an almost perfect copy. The inscription was written a little later than 400 A.D.[1] There is also much in Abyssinia besides the name to connect this deity with the Athtar of south Arabia. At the site of the city of Yeha, Bent found some fragmentary inscriptions which made allusion to a place called Ava or Awa, apparently situated on the present site of Yeha. Bent concludes that Awa was the original name of Yeha. One of these fragmentary inscriptions reads "his house (temple), Awa."[2] This inscription is written in the Sabæan script, evidently by an immigrant from south Arabia. D. H. Müller has also pointed out that in two inscriptions from ʿAmrân (and there are really more than two) Ilmaqqâhu is called "Lord of Awa^m."[3] Awa^m was probably a temple, since it was situated in the city, Alw.[4] This confirms Bent's conjecture[5] that Yeha was formerly called Awa, and was

---

[1] Cf. D. H. Müller's *Epigraphische Denkmälern aus Abessinien*, Wien, 1894, pp. 37, 38.

[2] Cf. Theodore Bent's *Sacred City of the Ethiopians*, pp. 145, 235, and Müller, *op. cit.*, in n. 7, p. 61.

[3] Müller, *op. cit.*, p. 61, Bent, *op. cit.*, p. 237. Cf. *CIS.*, Pt. IV, Vol. I, Nos. 74, 80, 99, 126, 147, and 155. Cf. Glaser's *Die Abessinier in Arabia und Afrika*, pp. 103–105, and Halévy in *Revue semitique*, Vol. IV, pp. 78–79.

[4] *CIS.*, Pt. IV, Vol. I, No. 74^4.

[5] Bent, *op. cit.*, p. 145.

founded by immigrants from south Arabia who brought the cultus of that country with them. Ilmaqqâhu, who is described as " Lord of Awa^m " we have already found to be a local development of Athtar, so that a chain of epigraphic evidence connects the worship in ancient Yeha with the old Arabian mother goddess.

The deities of this cult in Arabia were often thought to reside in a crag or stone,[1] one of which may still be seen near Taif, in which Al-Lat was once thought to make her home.[2] These stones corresponded to the *maṣṣebas* of the northern Semites. The temple at Yeha still exhibits traces of monoliths which answered a similar purpose, and like those at Aksum, to be mentioned presently, help us to identify the widely extended traces of this ancient cult.[3]

The two countries on the opposite shores of the Red Sea were at this time closely united, as the epigraphic evidence shows,[4] and Glaser contends that Habashat, the old Semitic name of which Abyssinia is a corruption, was not confined to the African side of the sea, but designated a part of the Arabian peninsula as well.[5] It is, however, beyond dispute, in consequence of the monumental evidence, that migration to Africa took place after the masculine Athtar had been developed, and that close political relations were maintained between the two regions for a considerable period of time.

Bent has shown that when hard pressed by their foes at Yeha, the Semitic Abyssinians removed their capital to Aksum and transferred their shrine thither. This shrine

---

[1] Cf. Wellhausen, *Heidentum*, 2d ed., pp. 45–64, and Smith, *Religion of the Semites*, 2d ed., pp. 201, 204, and 340.

[2] Cf. Doughty's *Arabia Deserta*, Vol. II, pp. 515 and 517.

[3] See Bent, *op. cit.*, p. 139, and Wylde, *Modern Abyssinia*, pp. 150 ff., 154 ff.

[4] Cf. D. H. Müller, *Epigraphische Denkmälern aus Abessinien*, pp. 75–79, and *Hebraica*, Vol. X, p. 202 ff.

[5] See his book, *Die Abessinier in Arabia und Afrika, passim*, and *ZDMG.*, Vol. L, pp. 294, 295.

was marked by a large number of monoliths which served as *nosbs* or *maṣṣebas*, though like those at Yeha they were somewhat more developed than those of the Israelites and Cypriotes, since they had altars at their bases.[1] They are taller than the monoliths found by Bliss at Tell-es-Safi in Palestine,[2] but like them seem to have been *maṣṣebas*. These objects, whether called *nosbs* or *maṣṣebas*, or by whatever name, were in general in the form of rude phalli, and were no doubt chosen as the symbol of Semitic deity because of their resemblance to the organ of the god of life. Bent noted that the altars attached to the monoliths at Aksum, as well as certain decorations which they bore, were on the side of the rising sun.[3] This, he inferred, connected them with sun worship. The presence of the name Astar at Aksum, together with the chain of evidence which connects Athtar with Yeha, enables us to see in the orientation of these monoliths an evidence of the worship of Athtar Sharqan, with whom, as in Arabia, Shams was probably associated. This inference is confirmed by the traces of heathen ritual which have survived in the Abyssinian church. All the church festivals are celebrated with music and dancing like heathen orgies.[4] On entering the church the threshold and door posts are kissed, showing that they are held to be sacred.[5] The great festival of the year is the feast of the Cross, which occurs in September, the month of the old Semitic date harvest festival, and which we have already identified with it.[6] An important part of the celebration of this festival is the building of fires on the high places and the slaughter of oxen before sunrise, — traits not only heathen in their origin, but which connect themselves in form with

[1] Bent, *op. cit.*, pp. 180, 182, and 185.
[2] Cf. Pal. Expl. Fund's *Quarterly Statement* for October, 1899, pp. 317–320.
[3] Bent, *op. cit.*, p. 190.
[4] Bent, *ibid.*, pp. 53, 83, 84, and 165, also *A Visit to Abyssinia*, by W. Winstanley, London, 1881, Vol. II, p. 127.
[5] Winstanley, *op. cit.*, p. 127.
[6] Above, p. 112.

the morning sacrifice of the camel to Al-Uzza by the Arabs of Sinai, which the son of Nilus witnessed.[1] The autumn festival of the old mother goddess is scarcely disguised by its Christian name. The church at Aksum is also probably the old temple; and to this day the old Semitic right of asylum is enjoyed there by the wrong-doer[2] as it was in Israel at the altars of Yahwe.[3]

Abyssinia consists for the most part of a high tableland on which crops are easily grown. The country is therefore an agricultural one, and subsistence is decidedly easier than in Arabia.[4] The central and southern portions are especially fertile.[5] These conditions of life wrought, so far as we can tell, no change in the Semitic family or the Semitic conception of deity. The migration occurred so late that the development traced in Arabia had already taken place, and the cult was transplanted bodily to Africa.

The inscription of Ezana, which contains the name of Astar, couples with it two other deities, Barrâṣ and Medr. These gods are, I believe, not otherwise known, but it is probable that one or both of them arose from Athtar, first having been used as an epithet, and coming afterwards to be regarded as a distinct god on account of its separate name. In an inscription published by Halévy,[6] Illmaqqâhu, whom we have already shown to be an Athtar, is called "Lord of Medr." In this expression, Medr is the name of a place.[7] According to a passage in Iklil, quoted by Sprenger,[8] there stood opposite the mosque of Medr a large castle with a marble slab on which was a picture of

---

[1] Smith, *Religion of the Semites*, 2d ed., pp. 166, 281, etc.
[2] Bent, *op. cit.*, p. 163.
[3] Cf. Ex. 21$^{12-14}$, and 1 Kgs. 1 and 2.
[4] Bent, *op. cit.*, pp. 67, 79, 90, 91, 135, 136, 154, and 202, also Wylde, *op. cit.*, ch. xi.
[5] *Geology and Zoology of Abyssinia*, by W. T. Blandford, The Macmillan Co., 1870, p. 196.
[6] *Journal asiatique*, Ser. 6, Vol. XIX, p. 164, No. 172.
[7] Cf. Mordtmann and Müller's *Sabäische Denkmäler*, p. 59.
[8] *Alte Geographie Arabiens*, p. 221.

the sun and moon. It is conceivable that Athtar was called "Lord of Medr" until the title was abbreviated to Medr, who, when his devotees had removed to Africa, was in time regarded as a god separate from Astar.

The case of Barrâṣ is even more obscure. D. H. Müller has conjectured[1] that he was the god of thunder and lightning because the Arabic *baraṣa* means to gleam or flash (micare). If there be any value in this guess, the name "Thunderer" may well have been an epithet of Athtar. These are, however, only possibilities, and the gods may have originated in ways quite different, — they may, for example, have been native Abyssinian deities, whose place was fixed before the Semitic immigration, whose favor the Semites felt bound to propitiate, as the Babylonians whom Sargon settled in Samaria felt bound to propitiate Yahwe.[2]

Turning now to the countries north of Arabia, we come first to the land of Moab. This country forms part of the fertile strip at the eastern end of the Mediterranean which we call Syria. This region is cut off from those sterile influences which render Arabia a desert by the proximity of the sea and by its two ranges of mountains.[3] A rainfall is thus secured and the country redeemed from the encroachments of the desert. The most easterly of the mountain ranges of Syria forms the eastern bulwark of Moab toward the desert, bringing its high plateaus within the region of rain and fertility.[4] The elevated plains of Moab must have been from time immemorial excellent pasture lands; and the few glimpses which the Old Testament and the Moabite Stone give us of its industry, confirm us in the belief that the Moabites were engaged mostly in pastoral pursuits. Thus the tribute paid by Mesha to Omri and

---

[1] *Epigraphische Denkmäler aus Abessinien*, p. 44.
[2] Cf. 2 Kgs. 17$^{24-34}$.
[3] See G. A. Smith's *Historical Geography of the Holy Land*, pp. 45-48.
[4] Cf. G. A. Smith, as above, and Hull's "Geology of Palestine" in Hastings's *Dictionary of the Bible*.

Ahab was paid in wool,[1] while the sacrifices which Mesha claims to have offered to his god consisted of sheep alone.[2]

The conditions of life in a country like this must have been far easier than in Arabia. How far back in antiquity the Semites began to overrun Moab, no one knows. The language of the Moabite Stone is practically identical with the Hebrew of the Old Testament. A dialect identical with both was spoken in Canaan in the fifteenth century B.C., and has influenced the Babylonian of the El-Amarna letters.[3] In their traditions the Israelites also recognize the Moabites as their kinsmen.[4] These facts, together with the character of the Hebrew-Moabitish language, which belongs to the north Semitic group, — languages which have undergone a long development independently of Arabic, — make it evident that the Moabitish emigration was part of a movement which took place many centuries before the date of the Moabite Stone.

In a country like Moab, where the conditions of life are not as severe as in Arabia, social evolution would proceed, even if undisturbed by outside foreign influences, much more rapidly than in the Arabian peninsula itself. Keasbey's researches into the formation of the clan[5] have shown that in the pastoral stage of civilization the patriarchal clan is formed as the natural result of the environment. The conditions, therefore, in Moab must have produced a patriarchal family centuries earlier than it was produced in Arabia. The few references to Moab in the Old Testament and the text of the Moabite Stone confirm this view. The patriarchate was fully established there before the ninth century B.C. How long before we

---

[1] Cf. 2 Kgs. 3⁴ and Moabite Stone (*e.g.* Smend and Socin's *Inschrift des Königs Mesa von Moab*, Freiburg, 1886), ll. 3–9.

[2] Cf. Moabite Stone, ll. 30, 31. נקד and צאן are the terms used.

[3] Cf. Zimmern in *Zeit. d. deutsch. Palastina-Vereins*, Vol. XIII, H. 3, and *ZA.*, Vol. VI, pp. 245–263; also my "Peculiar Use of *Ilâni*," in *PAOS.*, 1892, p. cxcix.

[4] See Gen. 18 and 19.   [5] See above, p. 30.

do not know. Their chief divinity, Chemosh, is a male deity, — a fact which presupposes a patriarchal society for a time sufficiently long to influence their religious conceptions.[1]

Contrary to the opinion of many scholars, I believe Chemosh to be genetically connected with the old Semitic mother goddess. This opinion rests in part on the analogy of the south Arabian development already traced, but largely on the interpretation of the name, Ashtar-Chemosh of l. 17 of Mesha's inscription. Baethgen,[2] Driver,[3] Moore,[4] and Peake,[5] hold that this deity Ashtar is not identical with Chemosh, but is an Ashtar, or Astarte, who was associated in worship with him. Moore suggests that it is parallel to Malik-Ashtart[6] and to the Ashtart worshipped in the shrine of the god Hamman of the Ma'sub inscription.[7] This view appears to me untenable on the following grounds: 1. The parallels urged are all much later in date than the Mesha inscription. They represent movements of thought influenced by Persian or Greek ideas, or by both. The combination Ashtar-Chemosh may fittingly be compared with the combination Yahwe-Elohim with which it is approximately contemporary,[8] but not with Melek-Ashtart, which is considerably later. Such comparison suggests the identification of god with god on account of political union, but not the union of a god with a goddess. 2. Ashtar in the inscription of Mesha lacks the feminine termination, and is therefore

[1] Cf. Moabite Stone, ll. 1, 3, 5, 6, 9, 11, 12, and Nu. 21^{29}, 1 Kgs. 11$^{7.33}$, Jer. 48$^{7.13.46}$, etc.

[2] *Beiträge zur semitischen Religionsgeschichte*, 1888, p. 14.

[3] Article "Ashtoreth," Hastings's *Dictionary of the Bible*, p. 171a.

[4] "Chemosh" in *Encyc. Bib.*

[5] "Chemosh" in Hastings's *Dictionary of the Bible*.

[6] *CIS.*, Pt. I, Vol. I, No. 8.

[7] Cf. G. Hoffmann, *Über einige phoen. Ins.*, p. 20.

[8] This statement is based, not on the form Yahwe-Elohim as it appears in our present Biblical text, where it is made to appear to be a harmonization with the late P document, but on the practical identification of the two when the J and E documents were united about 650 B.C.

a god and not a goddess. True, in primitive Semitic the name designated a goddess without the help of a feminine ending; it is also true that in Babylonia and Assyria the name continued to do so down to the latest times; but wherever the name has been found among the southern Semites without the feminine termination, it designates either an actual or a nascent god, and wherever it is found among the western Semites designating a goddess it has the feminine ending. It seems safe to conclude, therefore, that the name in Moab which was on the border of Arabia and Canaan and intimately connected with the latter, would, when lacking a feminine termination, designate a god. To break the force of this consideration one of two things should be clearly proven, either that the feminine ending was added to the name by the rest of the western Semites after the time of Mesha, or that Babylonian influence is responsible for its disuse here. Although all the Biblical and Phœnician material containing the name is later than the Moabite Stone, the name occurs twice in the El-Amarna tablets[1] as the name of a city, — no doubt the Biblical place which bore the name "Ashtaroth," named from the goddess, — and here the feminine ending appears. The west Semitic custom had attached the feminine termination to the name by the fourteenth century B.C., and that too on Moab's very border. The only reason for suspecting Babylonian influence in Moab is the possible connection of a proper name or two with Babylonian names, such as Mount Nebo with the name of the Babylonian god Nabu. But even if the name of a mountain and a city survived from the time of Babylonian occupation (which is uncertain), that is insufficient ground for supposing that the name, Ishtar, survived for six hundred years without modification, when all the neighboring

---

[1] Cf. *KB.*, Vol. V, pp. 263 (No. 142^{10}), and 353 (No. 237^{21}), also Gen. 14^5, and Josh. 13^{31}. For the identification of the localities mentioned in these letters, and the demonstration of their east Jordan situation, see Sayce's *Patriarchal Palestine*, pp. 133 ff. and 152 ff.

people, with whom the Moabites were intimately associated, used it with the feminine termination. 3. Mesha equates Ashtar-Chemosh with Chemosh. He says (l. 14 ff.), "And Chemosh said to me 'go and take Nebo against Israel,' and I went by night and fought against it from break of dawn till noon, and I took it and killed all of them, seven thousand men and boys and the women and girls and slave-girls, for I had made them *ḥarim* to Ashtar-Chemosh." Now it seems clear that the king would devote his victims to the god who sent him forth to battle, — the god who held, as the inscription shows throughout, the same relation to the nation as a whole, which Yahwe bore to Israel. Chemosh appears alone at the end of the inscription, ll. 32, 33. Ashtar-Chemosh cannot, therefore, be even in part a different god from Chemosh. If under such circumstances he had desired to associate a goddess with Chemosh, he would hardly have put her before him. It seems more natural to suppose that Ashtar-Chemosh like Yahwe-Elohim is the union of two names into one compound designation, either element of which might be used for the god alone.

The course of religious development in Moab must, therefore, have been not unlike that in south Arabia; the mother goddess under the pressure of social transformation became a father god, and through the use of epithets gradually came to be called by another name. This development, as already observed, was earlier by centuries than that in Arabia.

If this be true we should expect Chemosh to be a god of fertility. There is even in the very scanty material extant, some indication that this was the case. An old poem, twice quoted in the Old Testament,[1] makes the Moabites his sons and daughters. He seems also to have been a *ba'al*, or god of the land. I can see no good reason for denying with Moore,[2] a real identity between Chemosh

---

[1] Nu. 21 27-30 and Jer. 48 45. 46.

[2] "Chemosh," in *Encyc. Bib.* Moore's denial probably is intended to

and Baal Maon,[1] nor for his denial of the substantial identity of Chemosh and Baal Peor (Nu. 25³, Hos. 9¹⁰), long ago perceived by Jerome. Baethgen is nearer the truth when he regards both of them as forms of Baal.[2] We do not need to insist that the people always thought of the absolute identity of the god who was worshipped at one shrine with the god who was worshipped at another, any more than the untutored Catholic in modern Europe always is conscious of the identity of the Virgins adored at different shrines; but the analogy of the Athtars of south Arabia and of the Baals of Syria make it practically certain that all had their root in the same god of fertility, by whatsoever name each may have been called.

We learn from the prophet Hosea (9¹⁰), that the gross practices characteristic of the worship of the Semitic mother goddess in other localities, and which were so abhorrent to the prophets, were a part of the cult of this Moabitish god. No doubt therefore as in south Arabia a form of this goddess still existed in Moab side by side with the male deity which had grown out of her, and that these two, with slightly varying attributes at different shrines, perpetuated in their worship the features which pertained to this cult in other countries. This result remains even if one were to disagree with the argument given above for the sex of Ashtar in Moab; for if Ashtar were a goddess, Chemosh, who is joined with her, would of necessity be her male counterpart, or he could not be so joined. The term *ba'al* would apply to him as aptly as we shall see that it applied in Syria and Phœnicia. How the name Chemosh came to be applied to this god we cannot tell; it is still a puzzle.

If now we turn to Phœnicia and Palestine, we come to a land different in many ways from any of those hitherto studied. Its contour is much more broken, and within

mean no more than that the gods were worshipped at different shrines and therefore often thought of as practically distinct.

[1] Moabite Stone, l. 30.   [2] *Op. cit.*, p. 15.

comparatively narrow limits there is greater variety of scenery and climate than elsewhere in the Semitic world. It is a maritime country, bordering as it does on the Mediterranean coastland. Its two mountain ranges,— the Lebanon, with its hills tapering off into southern Judæa, and the range east of Jordan,— intercept the moisture from the sea and give an abundant rainfall. The deeply depressed valley of the Jordan and Dead Sea affords a climate of tropical warmth, while the snow-capped heights of Lebanon present the opposite extreme.[1] The soil along the maritime plain and in the valleys of Esdrælon and the Jordan is very fertile, while that of the hillsides is well adapted to the vine. Trees have always grown in abundance on the hills, especially in the Lebanon region. The Assyrian kings boast often that they took from here beams with which to adorn their palaces.[2] The low-lying lands have always been well adapted to grain, while in ancient times the palm tree grew in the Jordan valley and along the sea coast. The olive and the vine were the chief fruit bearers, the former being native in this region and the latter probably so.[3] The land has, in historical times, been a land of orchards, the apricot, fig, pomegranate, orange, citron, mulberry, pistachio, and almond being its chief fruits, while the sycamore and carob tree yielded a living for the very poor.[4] Wheat, barley, and many vegetables, such as onions, could be produced in abundance. In such a land agriculture was born in the remote prehistoric past, and its birth was inevitable. As George Adam Smith remarks:[5] "To pass from the desert into Syria is to leave the habits of the nomadic life for those of the agricultural. The process may be gradual, and generally has been so, but the end is inevitable."

[1] G. A. Smith's *Historical Geography of the Holy Land*, ch. ii.
[2] Cf. e.g. *KB.*, Vol. I, pp. 41, 108, and Vol. II, p. 113.
[3] G. A. Smith, *op. cit.*, p. 82.
[4] Cf. Amos 7 [14] (Amos gathered sycamore figs), and Luke 15 [16] (the prodigal son ate carob pods).
[5] *Op. cit.*, p. 85.

L

The beginnings of agricultural life in this region are shrouded in obscurity. In the El-Amarna letters the prince of Kumidi, near Gebal, sent, we are told, a tribute of olive oil to the king of Egypt.[1] The Egyptian monuments of the middle empire tell the same tale. Wine, figs, grain, and olive oil are mentioned as products of Syria and Phœnicia,[2] as well as several minerals, such as lead and copper. Agriculture therefore must have antedated in these lands the fifteenth century before Christ. Agriculture may have been preceded by the pastoral stage of society, and the beginnings of the patriarchate and consequently the general supremacy of male deities may date from this stage of development.[3]

Of the coming of the Semites into this region we know little. Lugalzaggisi, king of Erech 4000 B.C. or earlier, whom Hilprecht believes to have been a Semite,[4] claims to have subdued the country as far west as the Mediterranean Sea.[5] Sargon of Agade, about 3800 B.C., conquered the Westland, or, as scholars generally regard it, the land of the Amurru or Amorites on the north of Canaan.[6] A contract tablet has been discovered which makes reference to it in its date. From this time onward many Babylonian kings claim to have conquered the Westland. That the claim was real the El-Amarna tablets have proven by showing that Babylonian culture had so penetrated the country that the language and script of Babylonia had become the regular vehicle of official communication. In the fifteenth or sixteenth century B.C. the Egyptians over-

---

[1] Cf. *KB.*, Vol. V, p. 261. For location of Kumidi, cf. pp. 141, 187–189, and 201.

[2] Cf. W. Max Müller's *Asien und Europa*, pp. 155 and 183.

[3] Hilderbrand's *Recht und Sitte*, pp. 31–34.

[4] Cf. *OBI.*, Pt. II, p. 54 ff.

[5] Hilprecht, *op. cit.*, p. 53.

[6] Cf. Thureau Dangin in *Comptes rendus de l'academie d'inscriptions*, 1896, p. 358 ff. (identical with his *Tablettes chaldéennes inédites, No. 17*), also Driver in Hogarth's *Authority and Archæology*, p. 40. For the identification of *Martu* (Westland), with *Amurru*, see Schrader in *Sitzungsberichte* of the Berlin Academy, 1894, p. 1301.

ran the region, and at a date which we cannot now determine the Phœnicians had made their way into it. The Hittites also gained a strong foothold in the North earlier than the Egyptian conquest. Great as the mixture of races became, the Amorites appear to have maintained their identity down to the Hebrew period. Their name is still used by Amos and by the Elohist to designate the old inhabitants of Palestine.[1] This people who persisted so long in a region where many races strove for the supremacy had then assumed by 3800 B.C. an importance so great that their land was coveted by the far-off Babylonian. If they had not then developed agriculture, it is difficult to understand why the country should have gained such prominence, unless there were fisheries to make their land conspicuous. There is some probability that the agriculture which we are able to establish by monumental evidence in the El-Amarna period is at least some twenty-five hundred years older than that. The Amorites, like other primitive peoples, must have had many local numina, the most important of which would on the principles already established be masculine deities.

What would happen when a band of Semites entered this land, we may learn from 2 Kgs. 17$^{25\,\mathrm{ff.}}$ We are informed there that the colony of Babylonians whom Sargon settled in Samaria worshipped their own national gods until such disasters overtook them that they felt compelled to learn the worship of the god of the land. The worship of Yahwe which was thus begun by them did not cause them to forsake their old deities, but for a time both were worshipped together, and at last a new composite worship resulted. If one should object that this occurred very late in Semitic history, the objection would only strengthen our argument, for what could happen at so late a date must *a fortiori* have happened in

---

[1] Cf. Wellhausen, *Jahrb. f. deut. Theol.*, Vol. XXI, p. 602; Ed. Meyer in *ZATW.*, Vol. I, pp. 121–127; and Stade, *Geschichte*, Vol. I, p. 110.

more primitive times.[1] Not altogether unlike this in principle was the custom of the Aztecs in Mexico to sacrifice to the gods of conquered countries to propitiate them.[2]

At the period covered by the Old Testament and the Phœnician inscriptions the chief god of each locality was known as a *ba'al*,—a term which denotes the proprietor or inhabitant of some favored place or district. Robertson Smith thought[3] that among the Semites it designated the divine proprietor of naturally irrigated land, and there is much to be said for this view. Every city had its Baal,[4] and there would seem to have been as many of them as there were towns, cities, sanctuaries, or objects which appeared to the worshippers to have a religious significance. Thus there was the Baal of Tyre, the Baal of Sidon, Baal-Hamman, Baal-Barith, Baal-Shamem, Baal-Zebub, etc. In parts of Palestine this god was identified with the sun and called Shemesh. The town of Beth-Shemesh (1 Sam. 6) was named from his worship.

This worship of Baal was in many places connected with the old mother goddess Ashtart; *e.g.* at Sidon an Ashtart of the name of Baal is coupled with Baal as his consort,[5] and in the Old Testament Baal and Ashtoreth are frequently classed together as though they belonged to the same cult.[6] It may be added that in North Africa, which was colonized from Phœnicia, the mother goddess Tanith, whom I have elsewhere shown to be an Ashtart,[7] is constantly mentioned with Baal, and is sometimes called "The Face of Baal."[8] What connection has this worship with the primitive conditions which we have discovered for the Semitic stock?

Moore suggests that these Baals were originally distinct

---

[1] Cf. Budde, *Religion of Israel to the Exile*, 1899, p. 54 ff.
[2] Cf. Réville's *Native Religions of Mexico and Peru* (Hibbert Lectures, 1884), 2d ed., p. 31.
[3] *Rel. of Sem.*, 2d ed., p. 97 ff.
[4] Cf. Jer. 2^{28}, 11^{13}.
[5] Cf. *CIS.*, Pt. I, Vol. I, No. 3^{18}.
[6] See, *e.g.*, Jud. 10^6.
[7] *Hebraica*, Vol. X, pp. 48–53.
[8] Cf. *CIS.*, Pt. I, Vol. I, Nos. 195, 263, and 380.

local numina.¹ In one sense that is no doubt true, just as the Ashtars of the primitive Semites were distinct numina, though each numen in its oasis was formed under conditions so similar to those which prevailed in other oases that all of them possessed a common form.

When the Phœnicians or their ancestors first entered Syria, it is clear that they brought the worship of their Semitic goddess with them; the survival of her worship as an independent deity at Sidon and Gebal² is sufficient to prove this. We have shown that even in Arabia, as society changed to the patriarchal type, this goddess was transformed into a god, and it is clear that in an agricultural country like Syria, already inhabited by a settled and comparatively civilized people, which had for many centuries been swept by wars of conquest,³ the process would be greatly hastened. Each locality would have its local god worshipped by the Amurru, or Amorites, or whoever the previous inhabitants were; the incoming Semites, like the Babylonians settled in Samaria⁴ (2 Kgs. 17$^{25\,f.}$), would feel compelled to worship it; they would at first worship their own goddess also until in time her cult would be blended in greater or less degree with that of the god, as that of Yahwe came in time to be blended in Israel with that of Baal.⁵ That this actually occurred is shown by one of the El-Amarna tablets, which refers to the goddess as "Ba'alat."⁶ Thus syncretism helped the progress of natural development, and made a male deity supreme.

At Tyre the local Baal was called Melqart,⁷ or "King

---

[1] Article "Baal" in *Encyc. Bib.*

[2] See below, Chapter VI.

[3] For a discussion of the effects of war upon the sex of primitive agricultural earth goddesses, see below, Chapter V.

[4] See above, p. 147.

[5] See Budde's *Religion of Israel to the Exile*, Lect. II, and below, Chapter VII.

[6] See *KB.*, Vol. V, p. 139.

[7] Cf. *CIS.*, Pt. I, Vol. 1, No. 122.

of the city." It was doubtless the cult of this god which the Tyrian princess Jezebel introduced into Israel.[1] We learn from Philo of Byblos that Astarte, Zeus Demarous, and Adodos reigned over the countries, and that Astarte took up her abode in Tyre.[2] Zeus Demarous is probably Melqart, while Adodos, or Hadad, does not belong to Tyre, but is the Aramæan equivalent of Melqart. Thus at Tyre a god and a goddess had developed in the cult, although the persistency with which the old mother goddess clung to her independence is shown by the fact that Philo still names her first. From the Old Testament we learn, what we should naturally expect, that in most Canaanitish towns the Baal was the chief deity,[3] and the same appears to have been the case in most of the Phœnician colonies, since Baal is often addressed alone in their votive inscriptions.[4] Perhaps the same was true of North Africa, though there are some peculiar phenomena in the votive inscriptions from that land. In the numerous cippi published in the *Corpus Inscriptionum Semiticarum*, Tanith, though often called "face of Baal," is usually mentioned before him. The goddess is clearly subordinate to the god, but the older Semitic feeling still leads the worshipper to place her name first. The epithet, "face of Baal," probaby survived from a time of transition when both masculine and feminine qualities were ascribed to the goddess, so that she was represented with a female form and a bearded face.[5]

At Sidon still a different development occurred. Sidon had its Baal, to which was attached, as has been remarked,

---

[1] See 1 Kgs. 18.

[2] See Eusebius, *Preparatio Evangelica*, ed. Dindorf, I, 10, 31; Orelli's *Sanchoniathontis Fragmenta*, p. 30; cf. *Hebraica*, Vol. X, p. 31.

[3] Cf. Jer. 11^{13}.

[4] Cf. *CIS.*, Pt. I, Vol. I, Nos. 123, 138, and 147, and the inscriptions published by Philippe Berger, *Actes du XIe cong. d. orent.*, Sec. IV, p. 273 ff.

[5] See below, Chapter VI, and an article, "An Androgynous Babylonian Divinity" in *JOAS.*, Vol. XXI^2 f., 185 ff.

an Ashtart "of the name of Baal"; but side by side with this pair the mother goddess alone held her supremacy also, for separate from the "Ashtart of the name of Baal" was another Ashtart, whose priest king Tabnith was, and whose priestess, his wife.[1] This fact confirms the hint given in the Old Testament phrase: "Ashtoreth, the abomination of the Sidonians."[2] In the midst of changes wrought by syncretism and social transformation the worship of the primitive goddess had survived in comparative purity at Sidon, notwithstanding that in one phase she had been subjected to Baal. We shall see later that this was not an isolated phenomenon.

There are some curious combinations of divinities in the Phœnician inscriptions, such as Melek-Ashtart, Eshmun-Ashtart, and Eshmun-Melqart, but as I have pointed out elsewhere,[3] these are not primitive. They resulted from influences which came into force in the West after contact with Persians and Greeks.

We learn from Old Testament denunciations of Baalized[4] Yahwe worship that Baal was worshipped on hill-tops, under green trees, in spots marked by 'ashēras, masṣebas, and hammanim. Images were not always present, but when there was a shrine the god was often represented by the image of a bull. At his altars offerings of firstfruits and firstlings were made; and beside them fornication was not only licensed, but consecrated. The god had priests who leaped upon the altar and gashed themselves with knives, and also a retinue of prophets. Of the connection of all this with the worship of Yahwe we shall speak in a future chapter. Similar organizations of the Baal cult existed elsewhere. A fragmentary inscription attests a similar

---

[1] Cf. *CIS.*, Pt. I, Vol. I, No. 3; *Revue archeologique*, July, 1887, p. 2; and *Hebraica*, Vol. X, p. 29.

[2] 2 Kgs. 23^{13}.

[3] In an article entitled "West Semitic Deities with Compound Names" in *JBL.*, Vol. XX, pp. 22–27.

[4] Hos. 2$^{5, 12}$.

organization in Cyprus.[1] Among the Edomites the god seems to have been called Edom,[2] and from his high place[3] it seems that his worship was kindred to that of the Baalim. Both he and the god Gad, for whom the tribe of Gad was named,[4] probably at the bottom were Baalim, which originated like the others from the mother goddess.

The conditions in the north of Syria were not strikingly dissimilar to those which prevailed in Phœnicia and Canaan. The chief god of this region was called Hadad, though other gods were not unknown.[5] From the general principles thus far established we should expect the origin of Hadad to be not unlike that of a Baal. For reasons which will appear as we proceed it will be better to postpone the discussion of this great Aramæan god until we have passed in review the gods of Babylonia and Assyria. The problems of these countries are, however, so complex that they merit a chapter to themselves.

[1] *CIS.*, Pt. I, Vol. I, No. 86.
[2] Cf. W. R. Smith, *Rel. of Sem.*, 2d ed., p. 42.
[3] Cf. Robinson's article, "The High Place at Petra," in *Biblical World*, Vol. XVI, p. 66.
[4] Cf. *Oriental Studies of the Oriental Club of Philadelphia*, p. 108.
[5] See the Berlin Museum's *Mittheilungen aus dem orientalische Sammlungen*, Heft XI, p. 83.

CHRONOLOGICAL TABLE

BABYLONIAN CHRONOLOGY B.C.	ASSYRIAN CHRONOLOGY B.C.
E. A. Hoffman tablet and Father Scheil's archaic texts, cir. 6000-5500.	
Blau monuments, cir. 5500-5000.	
En-shag-kush-an-na, king of Kengi, before 4500.	
Urkagina, king of Shirpurla, cir. 4500.	
Ur-Nina, king of Shirpurla, cir. 4300.	
Eannadu I, king of Shirpurla, cir. 4150.	
Entemena, Patesi of Shirpurla, cir. 4125.	
Eannadu II, Patesi of Shirpurla, cir. 4100.	
Lugalzaggisi of Gishban and Erech, cir. 4000.	
Lugaltarsi, king of Kish, cir. 3900.	
Manishtuirba, king of Kish, cir. 3850.	
Alu-usharshid, king of Kish, cir. 3830.	
Sargon, king of Agade, cir. 3800.	
Naran-Sin, king of Agade, cir. 3750.	
Ur-Bau, Patesi of Shirpurla, cir. 3200.	
Gudea, Patesi of Shirpurla, cir. 3000.	
Dynasties of Ur, Erech, Isin, and Larsa, 3000-2400.	
Ur-Gur, king of Ur, cir. 2500.	
Dungi, king of Ur, cir. 2450.	
First dynasty of Babylon, 2399-2094.	
Khammurabi, king of Babylon, 2287-2232.	
Second dynasty of Babylon, 2094-cir. 1730.	Ishmi-Dagan, Patesi of Assyria, cir. 1840.
Third dynasty of Babylon, cir. 1730-1150.	Shamshi-Ramman, Patesi of Assyria, cir. 1820.
Agum-kak-rimi, king of Babylon, cir. 1700.	
Kurigalzu II, king of Babylon, cir. 1300.	Shalmeneser I, king of Assyria, cir. 1330-1300.

CHRONOLOGICAL TABLE — *Continued*

BABYLONIAN CHRONOLOGY B.C.	ASSYRIAN CHRONOLOGY B.C.
Nebuchadnezzar I, king of Babylon, 1140 (founder of Pashi dynasty).	Tiglath-pileser I, king of Assyria, cir. 1120–1100.
Nabu-apal-iddin, king of Babylon, cir. 880.	Assur-nasir-pal, king of Assyria, 885–860.
	Shalmeneser II, king of Assyria, 860–824.
	Tiglath-pileser III, king of Assyria, 745–727.
	Sargon, king of Assyria, 722–705.
	Sennacherib, king of Assyria, 705–681.
	Esarhaddon, king of Assyria, 681–668.
Nabopolasser, king of Babylon, 625–604.	Assurbanipal, king of Assyria, 668–626.
Nebuchadnezzar II, king of Babylon, 604–562.	Assyria conquered by Babylon, 606.
Nabonidos, king of Babylon, 555–538.	
Cyrus conquered Babylon, 538.	
Babylon under the Persians, 538–331.	
Babylon under Greeks, from 331 onward.	
Inscription of Antiochus Soter (latest dated cuneiform inscription) from between 280–260.	

CHAPTER V

TRANSFORMATIONS IN BABYLONIA

It is no easy task to apply the principles which have been traced in the preceding pages to the phenomena of the religion of Babylonia. The civilization of the Mesopotamian valley is so old that its beginnings can only be conjectured; our information is so fragmentary concerning the various periods of which we know something that no complete history of the country can yet be written, while the problem of its racial and linguistic origins is so complicated that it has become the subject of heated controversy. Notwithstanding all these obstacles, the principles of economic and social development can be applied with considerable certainty, and by their application much light is shed upon some of the complicated problems connected with the genesis of Babylonian civilization.

The most ancient civilizations of the old world were developed in the great river basins of the Nile, the Tigris-Euphrates, the Ganges, and the Yang-tske rivers, where the soil was rendered fertile by new material brought down by the water.[1] The civilization of Babylonia was probably the oldest of these. In the judgment of most Assyriologists we have written inscriptions from Babylonia dating from a time as remote as 4500 B.C.,[2] and it is probable that

---

[1] Cf. *The International Geography*, ed. by Hugh Robert Mill, London, 1899, p. 436.

[2] The writer holds with most Assyriologists that the statement of Nabonidos (*KB.*, Vol. III, Pt. 2, p. 105), that 3200 years elapsed between him and Naram-Sin, the son of Sargon, may safely be taken as a working hypothesis. Lehmann's acute suggestion in his *Zwei Hauptprobleme d. altorientalische Chronologie*, p. 175 ff. (Leipsig, 1898), that it is a scribal

the oldest picture writing is at least a thousand years older than that, and a previous history of considerable length is required for the development of this system of writing.

The beginnings of agricultural life in these regions can only be conjectured. In far-off geologic time the Persian Gulf extended far up toward the Mediterranean Sea.[1] The whole valley of Mesopotamia has been gradually formed, and in recent geologic time this has been done largely by the detritus brought down by the rivers. About seventy feet a year[2] is added to the land in this way, or a mile in seventy years. Both the Tigris and Euphrates have annual periods of overflow on account of the melting of the snow in the mountains of Armenia near their sources. The Tigris begins to rise about the first of March, and the Euphrates the middle of March; the water of the former is at its height in May and recedes in June or July, while that of the latter rises till June, and not till September has receded to its ordinary proportions.[3] The soil has thus been formed of rich materials, and the retreating flood leaves it each year pulverized and well manured. There is a considerable rainfall in November and December, and

---

error for 2200 is based largely on our ignorance. Peters (*PSBA.*, Vol. VIII, p. 142) suggested that it was a round number, made up of an estimate of eighty generations of forty years each. George A. Smith (*Modern Criticism and the Preaching of the Old Testament*, p. 91, n.) holds the same view, and by reducing the generation to thirty-three years, would fix Naram-Sin's date at 3190 B.C. The excavations now going on in the East may falsify Lehmann's view any day. It will be time enough to reduce Nabo-nidos's statement when more of the mounds have been forced to relinquish their secrets, and it has been demonstrated that the gaps in our present knowledge cannot be filled. Cf. Rogers, *History of Babylonia and Assyria*, p. 318 ff. If the oldest historical inscription is 4500 B.C., the Blau Monuments must date from at least 5000 B.C., and probably as early as 5500 B.C. The E. A. Hoffman tablet and Father Schiel's would then seem to be as old as 6000 B.C.

[1] See the map in *Geology, Chemical, Physical, and Stratigraphical*, by Joseph Prestwich, Oxford, Clarendon Press, 1886-8.

[2] *International Geography*, p. 447.

[3] Rawlinson's *Ancient Monarchies*, Vol. I, p. 12, and Jastrow's *Religion of Babylonia and Assyria*, p. 29.

then only occasional showers till May. Wheat and barley, which were indigenous to this region, were probably cultivated first on the outskirts of the inundation, where the soil had been naturally prepared for it. The rainy season comes on just in time to give the grain a start after the river floods have passed, and in the spring the harvest occurs before the water attains its height. Here the natural conditions combine to make agriculture easy, and here there was in consequence developed one of the oldest, if not the very oldest, agricultural communities of which there is any record. Payne holds[1] that agriculture is usually developed before a tribe is settled in the most favorable position for husbandry, and that when they have outgrown the resources of the spot where they became agricultural they migrate to a more favorable environment, where an opportunity is afforded to attain a higher civilization and enter upon a grander history. It is perhaps the case that this is true of the originators of Babylonian agriculture, but there have been so many changes in Babylonia that we cannot now speak with any certainty on this point. No spot more suitable for the beginnings of an agricultural life than Babylonia can well be imagined.

Wheat, barley, and sesame were no doubt the grains first cultivated. They are indigenous to the region, and play an important rôle in the many Babylonian contracts and revenue lists which have come down to us, both those from the dynasties of Ur, about 2500 B.C.,[2] and the numerous contracts which come from the eighth to the fifth centuries

[1] *History of America*, Vol. II, p. 61.
[2] For instance of these grains see *CTBM.*, Pt. I, No. Bu. 94-10-15, 4, l. 1; Pt. II, No. Bu. 91-5-9 2178 A, l. 1; Pt. III, No. 18343, Col. I, l. 1; No. 16368, obv. l. 1; Pt. IV, No. Bu. 88-5-12, 504, l. 1; Pt. VI, Nos. Bu. 91-5-9, 476, l. 1, and 91-5-9, 2421, l. 1; Pt. VII, Nos. 13166, l. 1; 13318, l. 1; 18376, l. 1; 18395, l. 1; 18397 *passim*; 18403, l. 1; 18409, l. 1; 18410, l. 1; 18414, l. 1; 18415, l. 1; 18419, l. 1; Pt. IX, Nos. 21386 *passim*; 17748, l. 1; 20007, l. 1; Pt. X, 14308, rev. Col. VIII, l. 1; 21381, rev. l. 1; 18964 *passim*, etc., the tablets published and translated in Radau's *Early Babylonian History*, pp. 418-433, also, Reisner's *Tempelurkunden aus Telloh*, Berlin, 1901, pp. 16, 137.

B.C.[1] These were always the most abundant grains; they figure largely in the payment of taxes (which were often paid in kind) and are among the most frequent subjects of contract between individuals. Still earlier, in the time of Sargon and Naram-Sin (3800–3700 B.C.), Agade was noted for its perfect grain, and the grain of Agade was in demand at the market of Shirpurla.[2]

Along with these grains there are lists of cattle, sheep, asses, horns, hides, etc., which were given in payment of taxes to the temples of Shirpurla and Ur.[3] Pasturage was therefore combined, as we should expect, with agriculture in the economic life of ancient Babylonia. The fertile valleys which led out from the great valley of the rivers were admirably adapted to pasturage. Individual property in land must have existed here several thousand years ago. Estates were bought, sold, and rented, as the contract tablets show, as early as 2300 B.C.,[4] and we have a plot of an estate of complicated character and peculiar shape, which dates from the fourth millennium before our era.[5] An unpublished archaic tablet in New York, which probably

[1] As an example of the evidence from the latter contracts, see the numerous citations made to the Nabu-na'id contracts in Tallquist's *Sprache der Contracte Nabu-na'ids*, pp. 130 and 138.

[2] Cf. Thureau Dangin's *Tablettes chaldéennes inédites*, Paris, 1897, Nos. 13, l. 1; 29, l. 1; 41, l. 1; 43 *passim*, and p. 9 ff.

[3] Cf. Thureau Dangin's *Tablettes chaldéennes inédites*, Nos. 12: 35, 55, rev. 1 and 70; *CTBM*, Pt. I, No. Bu. 94–10–15, 5, Col. I, ll. 1 and 26, rev. Col. II, l. 1; 94–10–16, 26, rev. Col. II, l. 6; Pt. V, Nos. 12913 *passim;* 18993 *passim;* 19024 *passim;* Pt. VII, Nos. 12938, rev. l. 13; 12944 *passim;* 18383 *passim;* 18434, l. 11; 17766 *passim;* 12939, Col. II, l. 18; 12929 *passim;* 18382 *passim;* Pt. IX, No. 19055 *passim;* Pt. X, Nos. 19064, rev. *passim;* 19772 *passim*, etc., Radau, *Early Babylonian History*, pp. 354–409, where several tablets of the same character are published and translated, and Reisner's *Tempelurkunden aus Telloh*, pp. 24, 25, 26, 28, 30, 31, 33, etc.

[4] See the references in Meissner's *Altababylonische Privatrecht*, pp. 9–11.

[5] Cf. Oppert's article, "Un cadastre chaldéen du quatrième milénium avant l'ére chrétienne" in the *Comptes rendus de l'Académie des Inscriptions et Belle-Lettres*, 4me ser, Vol. XXIV (1896), pp. 331 ff.; and Thureau Dangin's in *Revue d'Assyriologie*, Vol. IV, p. 13 ff.

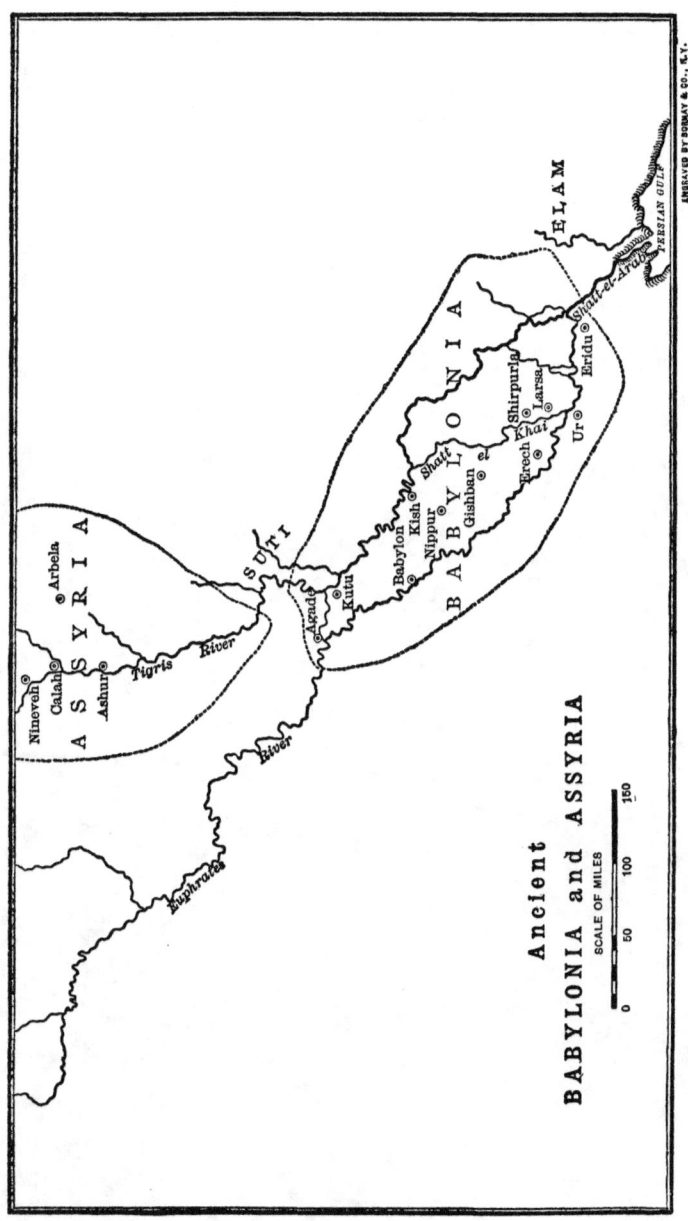

dates about 6000 B.C., presents a plot of ground to a temple and so proves that individual ownership of land even then existed.

As we have learned in the preceding pages, the structure of society in such a community would be in a sense patriarchal. Kinship would naturally be reckoned through the father, and this would as naturally find reflection in the religion by making masculine deities prominent, if not by placing masculine deities at the head of the pantheon.

As we have noted above,[1] the date-palm was a sacred tree in Babylonia, but whether native there or whether its culture was imported from Arabia has been a moot point among scholars.[2] At present the palm is so abundant in lower Mesopotamia that it is said that a proper coat of arms for the country would be a date-palm.[3] Dates were, during the period from which most of our contract tablets come, — the period from the eighth to the fifth centuries before our era, — a staple article of diet and of commerce.[4] We have not as yet so much evidence of their commercial use at an earlier period, but they are mentioned several times in the revenue lists of Gamil-Sin, Bur-Sin, and other kings of the second dynasty of Ur.[5] An interesting tablet from Telloh, dating from the time of Naram-Sin (about 3750 B.C.), informs us that twenty-six and one-half shekels of "dates of Agade" were received at the city of Shirpurla.[6] It follows that dates were cultivated at Agade in the first half of the fourth millennium B.C. which had a sufficient reputation to be

---

[1] P. 90 ff.
[2] See the opinions cited above, Chapter II, p. 75, n. 4.
[3] Cf. Zwemer's *Arabia, the Cradle of Islam*, p. 121.
[4] For examples of the abundant references in the contracts of this period, cf. Tallquist's *Sprache der Contracte Nabu-na'ids*, p. 111.
[5] Cf. *CTBM.*, Pt. III, No. 18958, rev. ll. 18, 22; Pt. VII, No. 17765 *passim;* Pt. IX, Nos. 17748, Col. II, ll. 10, 13; 19054 *passim*. Palm tree wood is also mentioned, Pt. VII, No. 18390, l. 1.
[6] Cf. Thureau Dangin's *Tablettes chaldéennes inédites*, No. 48, Col. II, l. 4, and also p. 9.

distinguished from the dates of other places. That dates
were highly regarded at Shirpurla is further proven by
the fact that Entemena Patesi of that city, who lived
about 4100 B.C., built a house for the storage of dates, —
a fact of sufficient importance to be mentioned among his
titles to fame.[1] That the palm was known long before
that in Babylonia is made probable by the presence of
a sign in Babylonian writing, which is perhaps derived
from the palm tree, and which occurs as early as the
inscription of Lugalzaggisi, about 4000 B.C., in a very
primitive form.[2] It has the values šag=damâqu="to
favor," and gišimmar="palm tree." Delitzsch holds[3]
that the sign is composed of three elements, one meaning
"favor," one "people," and one "open" or "bestow";
and that because of its great usefulness the palm was
designated "(the tree which) is full of favor to men."
Ball on the other hand considers[4] that the sign is derived
from the application of the cone-like instrument borne
and applied to the tree, by the winged figures in the
Babylonian and Assyrian sculptures, and that it is therefore a picture of the fertilization of the date-palm. In
this case the idea of "favor" (šag) would become connected with the sign on account of the peculiarly useful
function which the palm performed in ancient Babylonian
life. The older texts give the sign in a form which favors
Delitzsch's explanation rather than Ball's. This harmonizes also better with other considerations concerning the
culture of the palm in Babylonia which we will now

[1] Cf. *CTBM.*, Pt. X, No. 86900, l. 14. The line reads E-TUR-RA KA-LUM-MA MU-NA-RU, "A house for the accumulation (literally 'abyss,' Brünnow's *List*, No. 10220) of dates he built." Cf. also *Rev. d'Assyr.*, Vol. II, 148, 149; De Sarzec's *Découvertes*, pl. 5, bis No. 1, *a*; and Radau, *op. cit.*, p. 113, for a similar expression.

[2] Cf. *OBI.*, No. 87, Col. III, ll. 30, 32, and Thureau Dangin's *Recherches sur l'origine l'ecriture cunéiforme*, No. 137. For the later form and meanings, cf. Brünnow's *List*, p. 305.

[3] *Entstehung der ältesten Schriftsystems, oder der Ursprung der Keilschriftzeichen*, Leipzig, 1897, pp. 144, 145.

[4] Cf. *PSBA.*, Vol. XVI, p. 193.

adduce. We accept the fact of the presence of the palm and the use of the date at the period of Sargon and Naram-Sin, but the fact should be noted that the use of the date and the culture of the palm does not seem to have been general at that time. Of course the fact that the dates of Agade are especially mentioned does not prove that the date was not cultivated elsewhere; it does, however, prove that it was especially cultivated at Agade, whose kings are among the earliest kings to write in Semitic. The fact that a king of Shirpurla built a house for the accumulation of dates, somewhat as another built one for the storage of cedar,[1] — a wood of foreign origin which had to be brought from afar, — gives some ground for the supposition that the fertilization of the date-palm so as to make it produce more abundantly was a comparatively new introduction into Babylonia, and perhaps not generally adopted.[2] It is probable, as Hehn and Fischer contend, that in prehistoric time the date-palm extended from the Canaries to the Penjab,[3] and its presence in Babylonia in about 6000 B.C., is attested by its occurrence as a pictograph in an unpublished text in the E. A. Hoffman collection in New York, translated below, p. 213, n. 5, but it by no means follows that the artificial fertilization of it would become everywhere known at an equally early date.[4] Indeed,

---

[1] Cf. an inscription of Eannadu (Eannatum), published by Thureau Dangin in *Comptes rendus de l'Academie des Inscriptions*, 1899, p. 348, Pl. II, Col. ii; also the translation in Radau's *Early Babylonian History*, p. 72 ff.

[2] As we shall see below, it does not follow that artificial fertilization of the date-palm was introduced at Agade in the time of Sargon into Babylonia for the first time, but only that a strong wave of Semitic influence and Semitic culture helped the date culture of Agade at that time to reach a point of preëminence over that of other places.

[3] See Hehn's *Culturpflanzen und Hausthiere*, 6th ed., p. 273; and Fischer in Petermann's *Mittheilungen*, Ergängungsband XIV, No. 64, p. 11.

[4] The fertilization of the palm in Mesopotamia is still performed by hand. The tree is climbed and the pollen sprinkled over the flowers. See Zwemer's *Arabia, the Cradle of Islam*, p. 123.

we should expect that, in an agricultural country like Babylonia, where grain was indigenous and easily cultivated, that the development of agriculture would remove the spur of necessity which in Arabia compelled men to resort to artificial fertilization of the date-palm to support life. This view is confirmed by a contract of the fifth century B.C., which shows that the process of getting a date orchard started in Babylonia was so expensive that a man was willing to forego the rent of the land for sixty years for the sake of having it done.[1] These general considerations lead us to believe that the process of fertilizing the date-palm was introduced by the Semites from Arabia, and that Arabian or Semitic civilization was characterized by the influences of the date-palm culture, as the earliest civilization of Babylonia was characterized by the more ordinary agricultural pursuits. This conclusion involves the consideration of some knotty problems to which we must soon proceed, and it will be found, when these are considered, that several other considerations will confirm the point of view here taken.

In such an agricultural country villages grow up in protected centres where fortification is possible and where it is accordingly possible to protect the growing crops from the forays of more barbarous tribes. This was the case in Mexico and Peru,[2] in Egpyt, and was also no doubt the origin of the Babylonian cities.[3] These cities were in the first instance the residence of fellow-tribesmen and were built around the temple of their divinity of fertility. All this in the development of Babylonia lies in the prehistoric period. In that period, however, Nippur, Eridu, Ur, Shirpurla, Kutha, Erech, Agade, and other cities had sprung into existence. Before the dawn

---

[1] Cf. Hilprecht and Clay's *Business Documents of Murashû Sons of Nippur*, No. 48. Cf. *ibid.*, p. 36 ff., and *Assyrian and Babylonian Literature*, N. Y., Appleton, 1901, p. 260 ff.

[2] Cf. Payne's *History of America*, Vol. II, p. 47.

[3] See Winckler's *Altorientalische Forschungen*, Heft III, p. 232 ff.

of our present historical knowledge, about 4500 B.C., the struggle between these cities for supremacy had not only been begun, but had been waged with such varying fortunes that now one city had been supreme in power over the others for a century or two, and now another. This struggle, with its varied results, — Shirpurla being in possession of empire for a time, then Erech, then Agade, then Erech, Ur, Isin, Ur, and Larsa in succession, — continued until terminated by the final supremacy of Babylon, about 2300 B.C.[1] As will appear from arguments to be adduced later, Nippur must have held the supremacy for a long time during the prehistoric period. The political combinations which resulted produced religious syncretism. The city which was fortunate enough to win the leadership for a few centuries would gain a high position for its god in the minds of the inhabitants of the subjugated cities, and the city which was sufficiently fortunate to gain the supremacy first and to hold it for a long period would win for its god the distinction of being the head of the pantheon. That Nippur first held such empire the position of its god Enlil (Bel) indisputably proves, and a few fragments of archaic inscriptions attest.[2] The gods and goddesses of the other cities were grouped around him as sons and daughters or in some other subordinate position.[3] Enlil, who held this position for two thousand years, from the dawn of history to the rise of Babylon, was finally displaced by Marduk, the god of the latter city. How long in prehistoric time this process had been going on we can only estimate. Our task is ren-

---

[1] On this period of Babylonian history cf. Meyer, *Geschichte des Alterthums*, Vol. I, 1884; Tiele, *Babylonische-assyrisch Geschichte*, 1886–8; Mürdter-Delitzsch, *Geschichte Babyloniens und Assyriens*, 2d. ed., 1891; Winckler, *Geschichte Babyloniens und Assyriens;* McCurdy, *History, Prophecy, and the Monuments*, 1894; Rogers, *Outlines of the History of Early Babylonia*, 1895; Radau, *Early Babylonian History*, 1900; and Rogers, *History of Babylonia and Assyria*, Bk. II.

[2] Cf. *OBI.*, Nos. 90–92, 94, 96, and 111; also Pl. XVI.

[3] Cf. Jastrow's *Religion of Babylonia and Assyria*, chs. iii–vi.

dered difficult by the fact that the beginnings which we are seeking are not only, as in other cases, shrouded in prehistoric darkness, but that the traces of them which can for the most part be detected in other parts of the Semitic world were here very largely swept away before the dawn of history by political and religious syncretism.

The difficulty of the problem is increased by the linguistic and paleographic phenomena. As is well known, the cuneiform inscriptions contain what most scholars regard as two distinct languages, the Sumerian and the Semitic Babylonian. It is generally held that the Sumerians invented the cuneiform system of writing. Halévy first, in 1874,[1] and with much persistence in several publications since,[2] has maintained that the so-called Sumerian was only an allographic way of writing Semitic, and that the Semites invented the cuneiform system of writing. Guyard,[3] McCurdy,[4] Price,[5] Jeremias,[6] and Thureau Dangin[7] have come over to his theory, and though Delitzsch had in 1889,[8] in 1896,[9] and 1897,[10] he had returned to his former Sumerian point of view. The Sumerian theory is based on the fact that there exist bilingual syllabaries

---

[1] See *Journal asiatique*, 7th ser., Vol. III, p. 461 ff.

[2] For a list of them cf. Weissbach's *Sumerische Frage*, Leipzig, 1898, p. 25 ff. Halévy's most complete grammatical statement of his point of view is in *Actes du sixième Congrès International des Orientalistes*, Pts. I and II, pp. 535-568. His latest statement is contained in a series of articles in the *Revue sémitique* for 1900.

[3] Cf. *Revue critique*, nouv. ser., Vol. IX (1880), p. 425 ff; and *Revue de l'histoire des religions*, Vol. V, pp. 252-278.

[4] Cf. *Presbyterian and Reformed Review*, Vol. II, 1891, p. 58 ff.; and *History, Prophecy, and the Monuments*, Vol. I, pp. 87-95.

[5] Cf. "Accadians," in Hastings's *Dictionary of the Bible*.

[6] Cf. Chantepie de la Saussaye's *Lehrbuch der Religionsgeschichte*, Vol. I, p. 165 ff.

[7] Cf. *Revue d'assyriologie*, Vol. IV, p. 73 ff.; *Tablettes chaldéennes inédites*, pp. 1-18.

[8] Cf. his *Assyrian Grammar*, pp. 61-71.

[9] Cf. his *Assyrisches Handwörterbuch, passim*.

[10] Cf. his *Entstehung des ältesten Schriftsystems, passim*.

and word lists,[1] bilingual hymns and prayers,[2] bilingual inscriptions of kings,[3] besides many unilingual inscriptions in both languages.[4] The language of the portion of these documents, called Sumerian, is held by most Assyriologists as conclusive evidence of the existence of a non-Semitic people, who gave birth to the language and invented the script. Halévy contends that this was only a priestly method of writing so that the uninitiated should not be able to read it, that the syllabic values are all of Semitic derivation,[5] and that the Babylonian syllabary is perfectly adapted to express the sounds of a Semitic language. Delitzsch held, in 1889,[6] that 106 signs were demonstrably of Semitic derivation. To this number McCurdy has added about forty more.[7] The scholars of this school also urge, that the fact that the Semitic inscriptions occur side by side with the Sumerian back to 3800 B.C., together with the fact that no Sumerians are mentioned in the historical inscriptions, as the Elamites, Kossæans, etc., are, is evidence that no such people existed.

The arguments of these scholars are persuasive, but not quite convincing. We may grant the force of the fact, that such texts as the prayer of Šamaššumukin[8] is influenced by Semitic idiom, and that a number of Semitic

[1] See for example those published in II R., and in *CTBM.*, Pts. XI and XII.

[2] See those published in IV R., and in Haupt's *ASKT.*, and by Reisner in the *Mittheilungen* of the Berlin Museum, Heft X. Cf. also Zimmern's *Babylonische Busspsalmen.*

[3] As, for example, that of Khammurabi. Cf. *KB.*, Vol. III¹, p. 110 ff.

[4] The many royal annals of the Assyrian kings (*KB.*, Vols. I and II) may be cited as Semitic examples, while those of the kings of Shirpurla, published in De Sarzec's *Découvertes en Chaldée*, are examples of the Sumerian.

[5] See Part 3 of his "Nouvelles considerations sur le syllabaire cuneiforme," *Journal asiatique*, 7th ser., Vol. VII, p. 201 ff.

[6] Cf. his *Assyrian Grammar*, § 25.

[7] Cf. *Presbyterian and Reformed Review*, 1891, p. 58 ff.

[8] V R., 62, No. 2, and Lehmann's *Šamaššumukin*, Tafeln I and II. Cf. Pt. II, p. 6 ff.

idioms are found in Sumerian texts even back to the oldest inscriptions,[1] but there are a number of phenomena which are not satisfactorily explained by the arguments of the Halévy school. No satisfactory Semitic origin has as yet been proposed for a considerable number of the oldest and most common signs.[2] The way in which Semitic words have to be torn apart, in order to be expressed in the cuneiform script, is hardly consistent with the supposition that it was the invention of a Semitic people. The peculiar verb prefixes and suffixes, the postpositions instead of prepositions, and the various phenomena of the Sumerian grammar, can by no process of argumentation be made to appear the phenomena of a Semitic language, or the probable invention of a Semitic people. There are not wanting, morever, in the bilingual texts instances in which the Semitic idiom is so peculiarly modified that no explanation of it seems adequate, except that it has resulted from the influence of the idiom of the foreign language, of which it is a translation.[3] When we reflect, too, that most of the oldest inscriptions are written in what Helévy calls the allographic, or hieratic form, we are not only confronted with the difficulty, to which Radau has called attention [4] (viz., that the existence of this double form of writing, as early as 3800 B.C., presupposes an incredibly long anterior cultural development), but are compelled to

---

[1] Cf. Hilprecht, *OBI.*, Pt. II, p. 55; and Radau, *Early Babylonian History*, pp. 145–147.

[2] The value *an*, for example, can hardly have originated, as Delitzsch (*Grammar*, p. 65) would have it, from a Semitic source. Nor can the following be assigned to a Semitic origin: *ud* (*utu*), *uš*, *sal*, *šu*, *pi*, *du*, *ḫa*, *ur*, *kur*, *gir*, *bu*, and many others. In general, the signs which were originally pictographs have values which cannot be explained on a Semitic basis. Cf. my *Studies in the Origin and Development of the Cuneiform Syllabary*, in preparation.

[3] Such, for example, is the phrase, *i-sap-pu-ru-šu-nu* = "they cry out" (IV R., 1, Col. I., l. 15), where *šu-nu* is, contrary to Assyrian idiom, the subject of *i-sap-pu-ru*. It is a literal translation of the Sumerian *GU-BAL-BAL-A-MEŠ*, which stands in the preceding line.

[4] *Early Babylonian History*, p. 148.

suppose, that such kings as Eannadu and Lugalzaggisi, who wrote inscriptions to perpetuate their fame, chose to have them written in a form which only a few could understand. One can hardly believe, as he would thus be compelled to do, that the French *bon mot*, that language was invented to conceal thought, was thus anticipated by these kings at the very dawn of history.

Radau's view [1] is the one which my own studies had led me to adopt, viz., that the Sumerians were the pre-Semitic inhabitants of Babylonia, that they invented the cuneiform system of writing, but that the Semites had entered Babylonia and conquered them before the dawn of history. The situation with which we are confronted in early Babylonia is not altogether unlike that which existed in Palestine in the period from which the El-Amarna tablets come. In the latter country the Canaanites had their own language, but had as yet no method of writing it. The Babylonians had long dominated the country, and their system of writing was well known. To express themselves in written form, therefore, the Canaanites had recourse to the Babylonian language and script, though the Babylonians as a power in Palestine had ceased to be for so long a time that no reference is made to them in the El-Amarna, Palestinian letters. In thus using Babylonian the Canaanites mingled their own idioms with those of the foreign tongue.[2] Similarly, at the dawn of history the Semites had broken the Sumerian power so long before that we find no mention of the Sumerians in the inscriptions of Babylonia, though to express themselves in writing the Semites were at first compelled to resort to the Sumerian language and script. In using these, however, they, like the Canaanites, mingled their own idioms.[3] In some important respects there is

[1] *Ibid.*, p. 149.
[2] For examples see my article " A Peculiar Use of *Ilâni* in the Tablets from El-Amarna " in *PAOS.*, 1892, p. cxcvi ff., especially p. ccxix.
[3] See the references given above, p. 166, n. 1.

no parallel between Babylonia and the Palestine of the period cited. For example, in Babylonia the Semites who did the borrowing were the invaders, while in Palestine the invaders were the people who furnished the script; but the analogy holds for the important point to which we have applied it, and helps us to understand the silence of the inscriptions with reference to the Sumerians.[1]

The linguistic may be reënforced by other considerations. While there are few elements of the Babylonian religion which cannot be explained as Semitic, if one may be permitted to draw analogies from agricultural Semites outside of Arabia, yet there are some features which cannot be so explained. For example, the early kings of Babylonia were frequently deified. Even in their lifetime their names were written with the determinative for deity before them. Naram-Sin calls himself "god of Agade," and votive inscriptions are offered to other kings as gods;[2] while Gudea provided that certain sacrifices should be offered, apparently to his statue, which was erected in the temple of Ningirsu.[3] Radau has tried to trace the growth of this custom,[4] and finds it incipient in the inscription of Lugalzaggisi, full grown in those of Sargon of Agade,

---

[1] The arguments for the existence of the Sumerian language are forcibly stated from the older point of view in Haupt's *Die sumerischen Familiengesetze*, 1879; "Ueber einen Dialekt der sumerischen Sprache," in *Nachrichten d. K. Gesell. d. Wiss. zu Göttingen*, 1880, pp. 513–542; and *ASKT.*, pp. 134–220; Schrader's "Zur Frage nach dem Ursprung der babylonischen Kultur" in *ZDMG.*, Vol. XXIX (1875), pp. 1–52; and Tiele's *Geschichte*, Vol. I, p. 68 ff. For more recent statements of the argument see Lehmann's *Šamaššumukin*, Pt. I, pp. 57 ff., 107 ff., and Weissbach's *Sumerische Frage*, p. 150 ff. The view of the problem taken in the text supposes that the Semites began to use the cuneiform system of writing at a time so early that they exercised a large influence on its later development. Thus the fact that the syllabary contains a sign for Aleph and for other derivatives from sources demonstrably Semitic is fully accounted for.

[2] Cf. Radau, *Early Babylonian History*, pp. 164–166, 240, n. 1, 247, 250, 251, and 308 ff.

[3] Cf. *KB.*, Vol. III¹, p. 27.

[4] *Op. cit.*, p. 308 ff.

and most flourishing in those of Naram-Sin, though it persisted long afterward, as, for example, in the inscriptions of the second dynasty of Ur. On the basis of these facts he builds the theory that it was a point of view characteristic of the Semites, and that Sargon, representing a Semitic migration from Arabia, had revived a Semitic custom.[1] To argue thus is to erect a pyramid on its apex. There is no Semitic analogy elsewhere for the deification of kings, either during their lifetime or afterward. All we know of the culture of Arabia affords no basis whatever for the view that such a custom could originate there. The simple life of the desert and the oasis threw men too closely together for even a sheik to become a god to his fellow-clansmen. If there is a religious idea which we can pronounce absolutely un-Semitic it is this. Thureau Dangin seems to recognize this when he suggests that Egyptian influence led to the deification of themselves on the part of Babylonian kings.[2] As the empire of Naram-Sin extended to Palestine, he thinks contact with Egypt may have occurred in a way to account for the introduction of this practice. Such influence is not intrinsically probable, and if it were, one wonders why in later ages, under Kallima-Sin, Burnaburiash, Esarhaddon, Assurbanipal, and Nebuchadnezzar, when contact with Egypt was close and prolonged, no such consequence of Egyptian influence resulted. In fact, such influence is inadequate to explain the phenomenon. It must have been an influence local, intimate, and prolonged, an influence from a non-Semitic source, but which after a few centuries failed to be felt. It is just such an influence as the Sumerian must have been. Radau seems to think that because it first manifests itself fully at Agade that it cannot be Sumerian,[3] but do we know enough of the habitat of these prehistoric people to be sure of this? I

---

[1] *Op. cit.*, p. 310.
[2] Cf. *Receuil de traveaux*, Vol. XIX, p. 187.
[3] *Op. cit.*, p. 309.

think not. Moreover, evidence will be adduced below to show that the Sumerian power was dominant in the North rather than in the South. The presence of a non-Semitic race in ancient Babylonia is further indicated by the faces pictured on the votive tablet of Ur-Enlil at Nippur.[1] Professor Cope recognized in these peculiar faces the Semitic nose, but a jaw which he regarded as Aryan.[2] He thus bears witness to the existence of a hybrid population in this region at the dawn of history. The Blau Monuments, which are still older, bear witness, as Ward has pointed out, to the presence of two races in Babylonia.[3] This is all we desire. We must confess that the Mongolian affinities of the Sumerians have never been clearly proven. It is enough for our present purpose to show that there was a mixture of races in Babylonia at this period, and to agree to call the non-Semitic portion Sumerian until such time as we can obtain a better name.

Another feature of the civilization of Babylonia points to such a mixture of races. The decimal system of numbers was the native Hamito-Semitic system. Either it or the quintal system, based on the fingers of one hand,[4] is universally present among the Hamites and Semites, and in Babylonia finally prevailed over the sexigesimal system which was used in the earlier inscriptions.[5] In Babylonia the day and night were divided into six equal parts[6] — a

---

[1] *OBI.*, Pl. XVI.

[2] Cf. *OBI.*, Pt. II, p. 48, n. 1.

[3] See *American Journal of Archæology*, 1st ser., Pls. IV and V, and p. 40.

[4] McGee's argument (*American Anthropologist*, New Series, Vol. I [1899], pp. 646–674), although it adduces considerable proof in favor of the influence of mythical or superstitious ideas in giving prominence to certain numbers, really offers no explanation for the adoption of a quintal or decimal system of numbers. The time-honored suggestion which is repeated in the text therefore seems valid.

[5] Cf. the article "Number" in *Encyc. Bib.*, by the writer.

[6] See the interesting astronomical report published in III R., 51, which was made at the time of a vernal equinox. It reads: "3d day of the month Nisan; the day and the night were equal. 6 *Kasbu* was the day;

measurement which, as Ihering has pointed out, cannot have originated with a people who knew the decimal system.[1] We cannot go astray, therefore, in attributing the invention of this system of numbers to the Sumerians who invented also the cuneiform system of writing.

As we find in Babylonia convincing proof of the existence before the coming of the Semites of a non-Semitic people who possessed a high degree of civilization, and from whom the Semites borrowed the elements of their system of writing, we have next to inquire whether there is any test which we can apply to Babylonian religious institutions which will enable us in any degree to distinguish its Semitic from its Sumerian elements. We have seen that the characteristic elements of primitive Semitic religion are those produced in the desert and by the oasis culture of the date-palm. There the feminine element of society held a most important place, and in the religion it was deified. In Babylonia, on the other hand, the economic conditions were such that agriculture flourished from time immemorial. A fertile and almost inexhaustible soil yielded its riches to the husbandman. The date-palm grew wild, and no doubt the fruit which it happened to yield was gladly used; but in all probability it was so easy to raise grains that the pressure which compelled the Semite in Arabia to cultivate the date-palm was lacking in Babylonia. Fischer is probably right in claiming that its culture, in the proper sense of that term, was introduced from Arabia.[2] In such a fertile environment every man can obtain enough to support a wife, especially as in early communities the woman performs much of the labor. Monogamy is in such communities the rule for the common people, while polygamy is practised by the rich, of whom such a community soon produces a considerable

---

6 *Kasbu* was the night. May Nabu and Marduk to the king my lord be gracious!"

[1] See Ihering's *Evolution of the Aryan*, p. 121 ff.
[2] Cf. Petermann's *Mittheilungen*, Ergänzungsband, XIV, No. 64, p. 11.

number.[1] If now we can determine what kind of a religion the civilization of such a country would produce, some light will be thrown upon our problem.

In search of an analogy which will supply our needed clew, we may most profitably turn to the civilizations of ancient Mexico and Peru,—two countries quite isolated from the civilizations of the Eastern hemisphere and from each other, but both of which produced civilizations and religions of a high degree of organization.[2]

Mexico consists of an elevated tableland, the surface of which is covered with lava discharged from its volcanic mountains, and of detritus which the storms of countless centuries have washed down from its lofty ranges and peaks. For the most part it has few rivers, but the region around the city of Mexico is well watered and contains many lakes.[3] The water supply and the subtropical climate in this part make agriculture easy. Here the ancient Mexican tribes developed their civilization. In its completed form it was of a mixed character with Aztec elements in the ascendency; but in its earlier phases simple agricultural communities, especially devoted to the worship of their earth goddesses, or, as they often regarded them, maize goddesses, formed the earliest nuclei.[4] These earth goddesses were, as Payne[5] has pointed out, especially connected in their development with agriculture. They were the original deities of the Totoncas, the Otomi, and the Toltecs; and also of the Aztecs in their

---

[1] Cf. Payne's *History of America*, Vol. II, pp. 13, 15.

[2] We cannot seek the analogy which we desire in Egypt because, as we have seen, the religion of Egypt has back of it some elements of the oasis civilization. Nor can we turn to India, China, or Japan with any success because there the primitive agricultural religious product has long been displaced by more philosophical systems, or tortured by them into unrecognizable forms.

[3] *The International Geography*, p. 776.

[4] Cf. Payne's *History of America*, Vol. I, pp. 462, 516, 520, and Vol. II, p. 480.

[5] Cf. Payne, *op. cit.*, Vol. I, p. 518.

primitive northern home before they migrated to the South and became conquerors.[1]

The civilization resulting from this Aztec conquest was in many respects quite advanced. Property was organized for the nobles on a hereditary basis, and for the common people on a communal basis. Taxes were raised in kind, as was the case in good degree in Babylonia.

Slaves, as in the latter country, did the laborious work. Unlike the Babylonians, the Mexicans had no beasts of burden and did not know the use of iron; only gold, silver, copper, and stone.[2] There were good markets and abundance of wealth. In the cities associations of merchants exercised great political influence. As in Babylonia, polygamy was practised by the rich and by kings. The Aztec emperor is said to have had a thousand wives.[3]

In certain respects the resulting Aztec religion resembled the Babylonian. The assimilation of conquered tribes with the conquerors created religious syncretism, and led to the formation of a pantheon. The form of their temple, though much broader, bears considerable resemblance to a Babylonian ziggurat.[4] The Aztecs, too, like the Semites, thought that sacrifice united the worshipper to his god.[5] At the time when Europeans came into contact with the Aztecs, tribe had conquered tribe till much religious syncretism had resulted, a pantheon had been organized, and as in Babylonia the functions of the various gods had been much specialized. The heads

[1] Cf. Payne, *ibid.*, p. 520. For the Otomi, cf. Payne, *op. cit.*, Vol. II, p. 454 ff.

[2] Cf. *The Native Religions of Mexico and Peru*, Hibbert Lectures, 1884, by Albert Réville, 2d ed., London, 1895, pp. 32, 33.

[3] *Mexico, Aztec, Spanish, and Republican*, by Brantz Mayer, Hartford, 1853, Vol. I, p. 36.

[4] Cf. *The History of Mexico and its Wars*, by John Frost, New Orleans, 1882, Vol. II, p. 40; Brantz Mayer, *op. cit.*, Vol. I, p. 37, and Perrot and Chipiez, *Histoire de l'art en Chaldée et Assyrie*, Vol. II, p. 403 ff.

[5] Cf. Réville, *op. cit.*, p. 89, and W. R. Smith's *Religion of the Semites*, Lect., VI–IX.

of the pantheon were identified with the sun and moon, and were called grandfather and grandmother.[1] These were in theory the chief deities, but in practice those were worshipped more which stood nearer the interests of every-day life.[2] There was a wind god, usually pictured under the form of a serpent,[3] a form which had survived from a previous condition of totemism. Tlaloc was the god of rain — the god of fecundity to whom many children were sacrificed.[4] Tlazolteotl was the goddess of love and sensuality. Originally the wife of Tlaloc, the rain god, the sun had stolen her away.[5] Centeotl was the goddess of the maize; she had a son who bore the same name as herself. She was often represented with this son as a child in her arms, and reminded the Spaniards of the Madonna and the child Jesus.[6] In addition to these principal deities they also had little household gods somewhat like the Hebrew teraphim.[7]

It will be noted from this brief description that the resulting Mexican civilization possessed both gods and goddesses as did the Babylonian, and that, as in the latter country, these were arranged in pairs. The goddesses who had survived from the more primitive period were not, however, supreme, but were subordinate to the gods. There is a story to the effect that Tlazolteotl, the goddess of sensuality, prevailed over the pious hermit Yappan when he had resisted all other temptations,[8] as Ukhat prevailed over Eabani;[9] but Tlazolteotl was herself subject to her divine husband, and was not supreme as was Ishtar.

The conception of the relation between gods and goddesses is reflected in the procedure connected with their great annual human sacrifice. The man chosen for this sacrifice was treated for a year previous to its occurrence

---

[1] Réville, *op. cit.*, p. 35.
[2] Réville, *op. cit.*, p. 68.
[3] Cf. Réville, *op. cit.*, pp. 38, 68.
[4] Réville, *op. cit.*, p. 71.
[5] Réville, *op. cit.*, p. 75.
[6] Réville, *ibid.*, p. 73.
[7] Réville, *ibid.*, p. 77.
[8] Réville, *ibid.*, p. 76.
[9] See above, p. 83.

TRANSFORMATIONS IN BABYLONIA

with divine honors. For at least a month before the sacrifice took place four beautiful girls were given him to share his bed, and he passed his time in dalliance with these until the day of the sacrifice came around.[1] It thus appears that the chief deity to whom this sacrifice was offered was conceived as a polygamous god, the possessor of a harem of goddesses.

The story of the seduction of Yappan bears, therefore, only a superficial resemblance to the story of Eabani. There is no trace among the Aztecs of a general worship of deified polyandry or unwedded love as among the Semites. The deep impress which the Ishtar cult left upon Semitic religious life has no parallel among the Aztecs. Their culture was the product of agriculture and conquest and not the culture of the oasis. Men had long been the head of the family, and gods were at the head of their pantheon. The feminine element entered into their religious, as into their social life under the conceptions of a polygamous, and not of a polyandrous social order. The goddesses may have been, and probably were, supreme in the earlier days of the tribal life, but the conditions of the country made the agricultural tribes an early prey to other clans. Wars and conquests followed, producing clans in which the virile elements of manhood were idealized, and in which gods soon became supreme. This happened so soon that the earth goddesses never gained, as in Arabia, where the environment made outside influences impossible and the deserts made the oasis type of life predominant over everything, a character sufficiently permanent to meet the shock of mixture and to survive and absorb it.

In Peru a similar history can be traced. In the basin of Lake Titicaca tribes known as the Colla[2] worshipped

---

[1] Cf. *History of the Conquest of Mexico*, by William Prescott, Boston, 1858, Vol. I, p. 79; Frost's *History of Mexico and its Wars*, Vol. I, p. 42; and Brantz Mayer's *Mexico, Aztec, Spanish, and Republican*, Vol. I, pp. 39, 40.

[2] Cf. Payne's *History of America*, Vol. I, p. 324.

as a mother, some of them the earth, and some the lake,¹ while the Yuncas or Yuncapata of the Pacific coast thus regarded the ocean.² The dominant race who produced Peruvian civilization, the Amyara and Quichua, whose original home seems to have been in the mountainous regions of what we call Bolivia and Argentina, came thither and conquered the country.³ Like some other tribes,⁴ the Incas were, in later times at least, worshippers of the sun. They conquered the coast lands also, and developed a high degree of civilization. Religious syncretism and a pantheon followed. Their social order was definitely organized. Their lands were divided into the lands of the sun, which supported the temple and priesthood, the lands of the Inca, which supported the king, and the lands of the people. The latter were divided among them per capita.⁵ The priesthood was highly organized and numbered about four thousand.⁶ The usual features of agricultural social life present themselves in their organization. The common people were monogamous, and were not allowed to marry one from beyond the bounds of their own community.⁷ The nobles were polygamous, while the Incas or sovereigns were extravagantly polygamous. Honors practically divine were accorded the Incas. One of the most striking features of the social organization were Homes of the Selected, a kind of nunnery, where several hundred virgins were congregated, and their chastity protected by the most stringent regulations. These were destined to be the Inca's wives, or, if the Inca chose, the wives of some of his nobles, or at times for sacrifice to the sun. When he for any reason discarded one after she had been destined for sacrifice, or after she

---

[1] Cf. Payne, *op. cit.*, pp. 503–509.
[2] Cf. Payne, *ibid.*, pp. 376, 502 ff., also Vol. II, p. 555 ff.
[3] Cf. Payne, *op. cit.*, Vol. II, p. 560 ff.
[4] Cf. Payne, *op. cit.*, Vol. I, pp. 560, 561.
[5] Cf. Prescott, *Conquest of Peru*, Vol. I, pp. 47–50.
[6] Prescott, *ibid.*, p. 101.
[7] Prescott, *ibid.*, p. 112.

had been taken to his palace and had lived with him for a time, she returned to her native village.¹ Like the Semites, they sacrificed only edible animals to their gods,² regarded sacrifice as commensal, and concluded their feasts with music and drinking.³ Like the Semites, too, they had passed through a totemistic stage of development before they reached the point of civilization which has been described.⁴

At the time of the Spanish conquest, when Europeans came in contact with the empire of the Incas, that race had subjugated other tribes, and welded them into a complete organization with its resulting pantheon. In this pantheon the sun god stood at the head, with his sister and consort, the moon goddess.⁵ Virachoca, a lake or rain god, was also worshipped with his sister Choca.⁶ These deities were older than the sun deities, as their myths show.⁷ They were survivals from the more primitive social organization. Pochacoma, the animater of the earth (a kind of Dionysos), also held a conspicuous place.⁸ Cuycha, the god of the rainbow, and Chasca, a male Venus, were also worshipped as attendants of the sun.⁹

In the religion of Peru, then, we find a course of development quite similar to that of Mexico. The primitive goddesses were retained, but in the religious syncretism of

---

¹ Prescott, *op. cit.*, Vol. I, pp. 109–112 ; Réville, *op. cit.*, pp. 204–208 ; and Payne, *History of America*, Vol. I, p. 564 ff.

² Réville, *op. cit.*, p. 219.

³ Prescott, *ibid.*, p. 107.

⁴ Cf. Prescott, *ibid.*, p. 93 ; Réville, *op. cit.*, p. 198 ; *Histoire des Yncas, rois du Peru*, par Jean Baudoin, Amsterdam, 1765, pp. 39 ff., 41 ff.; and Payne's *History of America*, Vol. I, p. 445 ff.

⁵ Réville, *op. cit.*, pp. 153, 154 ; Prescott, *op. cit.*, p. 93 ; and Baudoin, *op. cit.*, p. 80 ff.

⁶ Note that the extreme practice of endogamy in Peru, similar to that of the royal family of Egypt, had projected itself into their conception of the gods, so that the celestials also married their sisters.

⁷ Réville, *ibid.*, pp. 185–188.

⁸ Cf. Prescott, *op. cit.*, p. 91, and Réville, *op. cit.*, p. 189 ff.

⁹ Prescott, *ibid.*, p. 92, and Réville, *ibid.*, p. 194.

the Inca's empire were subordinated even more than in Mexico to male deities. This, as in Mexico, was no doubt due in part to early conquests of the peoples who worshipped the earth as a mother goddess, before that worship became so fixed by long practice as to be able to withstand, as the Semitic cultus of primitive times did, a good proportion of this absorbing power.

If we turn to the gods and goddesses of ancient Greece, we find similar beginnings and a similar result. The various waves of races and of conquest which swept over Greece finally left its pantheon a mixture, in which the male element predominated. There are not wanting, however, evidences that at the beginnings of its agricultural life many goddesses of mother earth were worshipped. The most obvious of these is Demeter, whose name probably meant originally "Earth-mother"; but, as Farnell has shown, Artemis was such a goddess among the Greeks of Asia Minor,[1] Hecate in Ægina,[2] and Athena at one time at Athens.[3] In the civilization which resulted from later mixtures these goddesses lost their supremacy, with the exception of Artemis, who in Asiatic cities like Ephesus maintained her position, though under a somewhat transformed character, till a comparatively late time.

There is some evidence that a similar history was enacted in connection with the pantheon of Rome. Maia seems to have been an earth-mother goddess, whose cult was in a way maintained down to the latest times,[4] but Rome became such a warlike power that the virile gods of battle almost eclipsed in the historical period this primitive goddess.

A similar history can in all probability be traced in the Teutonic pantheon.[5]

---

[1] See Farnell's *Cults of the Greek States*, Vol. II, p. 464 ff.
[2] Farnell, *op. cit.*, Vol. II, p. 507.
[3] Farnell, *op. cit.*, Vol. I, p. 289.
[4] Macrobius, *Saturnalia*, I, 12.
[5] Cf. Gummere's *Germanic Origins*, New York, 1892, ch. xiv.

From such examples as these the following conclusions may be fairly drawn. Where the beginnings of agriculture are possible men naturally worship goddesses which they connect with the earth, or a lake, or some spring which is conceived as the giver of fertility.[1] In all probability as long as such communities remained peaceful such goddesses continued to be supreme, but when other tribes or clans, attracted by their prosperity began to conquer them, all soon became changed. These attacking clans were in some cases pastoral, and consequently patriarchal and worshippers of gods rather than goddesses; in other cases they were clans organized on the republican basis for hazardous undertakings and therefore worshippers of virility. If they had been agricultural communities and worshippers of goddesses, warlike habits in many cases changed these into gods. In the struggles which followed the strong powers of the warrior would in time become idealized by all as the chief powers of the leading deity, and the old goddesses when retained would take a subordinate position.

In an oasis country like Arabia the conditions were somewhat different. The direct dependence of all upon the oasis and the mother goddesses of these fertile spots would keep even the republican clans, organized for the caravan trade, largely dependent upon, and worshippers of, the mother goddesses. The natural barriers of the peninsula protected the clans from outside influences and attacks, so that here even in the midst of long struggles between clan and clan for supremacy the goddess could maintain her position. We have a right therefore to expect that when the Semites went forth in hordes from Arabia into other lands their mother goddesses would present much more fixity of character than the mother goddesses of ordinary agricultural communities such as the Sumerians of Babylonia were. The peculiar emphasis

[1] This is no doubt the origin of the "corn spirit" which Frazer traces through so many countries. Cf. *Golden Bough*, Vol. II, *passim*.

which the deification of the palm tree led them to place upon sexual functions also gives a Semitic goddess a character quite peculiarly her own. In the fragmentary information which has come down to us we may not always be able to distinguish these characteristics, but where our information is full the task is not difficult.

In applying these principles to the gods of Babylonia we are met by another difficulty. Were the Sumerian communities always peaceful and their goddesses consequently left in supremacy until the Semites invaded the country and the struggle with them began? The answer is not easy, as it lies altogether in prehistoric time, but the probabilities are all in favor of a negative answer. From the mountains and high lands on either side of the Mesopotamian valley pastoral or unsettled clans must have poured themselves into the lower and more fertile lands of the agricultural portions from the time when the Sumerians made their first settlements. At the very dawn of history Eannadu and the kings of Kish had frequently fought and conquered the Elamites,[1] Eannadu boasting that he had driven them back to their mountain, and we have no means of knowing how many struggles between Babylonians and Elamites may have preceded. In all probability such wars had been going on for generations before the Semitic advent, and had as in Mexico, Peru, Greece, Rome, and elsewhere transformed or subordinated the Sumerian goddesses. If then we can find in Babylonia gods of tribes or cities whose masculine character seems to have been fully established before the dawn of history and whose traits seem to have no organic connection with Ishtar or Athtar, we may conclude that such deities are Sumerian. If, on the other hand, we find cities where goddesses are supreme and where the peculiar sexual features which were developed in Arabia

---

[1] Cf. *Revue d. assyr.*, Vol. IV, pl. 1, col. iii and col. v; also Radau, *Early Babylonian History*, pp. 85 and 91; de Sarzec's *Découvertes*, pl. 31, No. 2, a and b, col. iii, and Radau, *op. cit.*, p. 94; also *CTBM.*, Pt. IX, pl. 1 and 2; Hilprecht, *OBI.*, No. 5, and Radan, *op. cit.*, p. 128.

are present, or goddesses connected with the culture of the date-palm, or gods developed out of goddesses which were so connected, we may hold that the dominant element of such civilization was Semitic.

In applying this test it will be most convenient to begin with an old Babylonian kingdom, which has been brought to light by the researches of recent years, the kingdom of Kish. True, scholars have wavered as to whether it was really a kingdom,[1] but the fact that the name is followed by the determinative for place when spoken of by those outside its limits,[2] seems to settle the matter. This city or region appears to have been situated east of Babylon and north of Shirpurla on the Tigris River in northern Babylonia.[3] It is the first of the Babylonian states whose kings wrote their inscriptions in Semitic Babylonian, and thereby reveal their Semitic origin.[4] One of the early kings of Kish has left a votive inscription hitherto misunderstood, which proves for the kingdom of Kish a development of the Ishtar cult similar to that which we have already proven by monumental evidence for south Arabia.[5] This inscription reads : —

1. "For the king of countries,
2. Nana, (Ishtar) ;
3. For the lady, Nana, (Ishtar),
4. Lugal-tarsi,
5. king of Kish,
6. the structure of a terrace
7. has made."[6]

[1] Cf. Winckler's *Altorientalische Forschungen*, 1st ser., p. 144, and Hilprecht, *OBI.*, p. 270 (pt. 2, p. 56).

[2] Cf. Radau's *Early Babylonian History*, p. 126.

[3] Cf. Radau, *op. cit.*, p. 112.

[4] Cf. Hilprecht, *OBI.*, Nos. 5-10, and Scheil's *Textes, élamites-sémitiques.* Paris, 1900.

[5] See above, Chapter IV.

[6] This inscription is published in *CTBM.*, Pt. III, pl. 1, No. 12155. In Sumerian it reads: (1) *Dingir* LUGAL-RA KUR-KUR ; (2) *dingir*

In this inscription the name of the deity both in line 2, where it is in apposition with "king," and is consequently masculine, and in line 3, where the fact that it is preceded by the word "lady" proves it to be feminine, is expressed by the sign, which is employed as the ideogram for the name of the goddess Ishtar,[1] as the syllabaries and bilingual hymns testify, but which scholars are accustomed to read in Sumerian texts, "Nana" or "Ninnai."

It is clear from the argument in the first three chapters of this work that the name Ishtar was no late invention of the Semitic peoples, but had its origin in primitive Semitic life. In all probability, therefore, it was carried by the Semites with them to Babylonia, as well as to the other countries whither they went. As the people of Kish were Semitic, it was no doubt their name for the goddess,[2] and

NANA; (3) NIN *dingir* NANA-RA; (4) LUGAL-TAR-SI; (5) LUGAL KISH; (6) GIR KISAL; (7) MU-NA-RU. Thureau Dangin translates (*Rev. d'assyriologie*, Vol. IV, p. 74, n. 15, and *Tablettes chaldéennes inédites*, p. 6, n. 15), " En l'honneur du dieu contrées et de Ishtar, de la dame Ishtar," etc. Radau (*op. cit.*, p. 125, n. 3) would render: " In honor of the god of countries and of Ishtar, the mistress of the divine Innanna," etc. I believe both to have missed the significance of the inscription as to the history of the development of religious conceptions. Cf. my paper, " An Androgynous Babylonian Divinity," in *JAOS.*, Vol. XXI[2], p. 185 ff. Radau's reading " Innanna " is based on Thureau Dangin's translation in *Rev. sémitique*, Vol. V, p. 67 ff., of Eannadu's *Galet* A, of col. ii, l. 5. Thureau Dangin translates the sign for Ishtar " Inanna " there because in col. v, l. 26, he had been unable to render it otherwise. Upon reference to the original publication in *Rev. d'assyriologie*, Vol. IV, pl. 1, it is found, as I have pointed out in the paper referred to above, that it may equally well be read in both passages " Ishtar " instead of " Inanna." Even if the inscription was deposited by the king at a temple in Shirpurla, it vouches for the conceptions prevalent in his own city.

[1] Cf. II R., 59, 12, e.f.; IV R., 1, 33 b; and Brünnow's *List*, No. 3051.

[2] The Sumerian name Nana, I take to be simply an epithet. It is usually written NA-NA-A. NA signifies "exalted" (cf. II R., 30, 24, g, h, Brünnow, *List*, No. 1584, and Haupt, *ASKT.*, p. 136, § 5). Words are in Sumerian frequently repeated for emphasis; thus we get *NA-NA*. This repetition is too frequent in verbs to need illustration, but it also occurs in nouns; cf. UD-UD, *OBI.*, No. 87, col. 1, l. 46; and the final A is the repetition of the final syllable in the emphatic state. Thus

we have a right accordingly to read the sign Ishtar in both places where it occurs in the inscription of Lugaltarsi. Clear evidence is thus presented of the development of the old mother goddess into a masculine and feminine deity at Kish, parallel to that of Athtar in Arabia, — a development produced by the transformation in the social structure caused by the changed environment.

If one is inclined to object to the conclusion just reached, he might urge that this inscription very likely comes from Telloh, and that accordingly it may not represent the religious ideas of Kish at all, and that as Enlil is so constantly called "King of countries" Ishtar may have been written in the first line by a scribal error for Enlil. These are two considerations which certainly deserve to be met. To take the second one first, it may be remarked that in the inscriptions from Telloh, Gudea frequently calls Nana-Ishtar "Mistress of countries,"[1] and that there was at Shirpurla a god Lugal-Erim, who seems to have been but another phase of Nana-Ishtar, "Mistress of Erim."[2] Suppose then that Lugaltarsi was addressing these, our conclusion would still be just, though it would apply to Shirpurla instead of Kish.

But probably it applies to Kish, as the inscriptions from Susa, recently published by Father Scheil,[3] seem to confirm it. The most important of these inscriptions is from

NA-NA-A means "the exalted one," and was applied as naturally to the supreme mother goddess in primitive times as *ṣirtu* (*MAG.*) was applied to the same goddess, with a similar meaning in the Gilgamish epic (cf. Haupt *Nimrodepos*, p. 141, l. 163. Jensen *KB.*, Vol. VI, p. 241 renders it *bêlit ilâni*, "lady of the gods," which is an interpretation rather than a translation).

[1] Cf. *e.g.* Statue C, col. ii, l. 2, and col. iv, l. 10; *i.e.* de Sarzec's *Découvertes*, pl. 13, No. 1. Cf. *Records of the Past*, 2d ser., Vol. II, pp. 87, 89.

[2] See de Sarzec, *Découvertes*, pl. 8, col. ii, l. 2, and col. iv, ll. 8, 9. Cf. also *Records of the Past*, 2d ser., Vol. I, pp. 75, 77, and *KB.*, Vol. III¹, pp. 21, 23.

[3] *Mémoires de la délégation en Perse*, Tom. II. *Textes élamites-sémitiques*, Paris, 1900.

Manishtu-irba, king of Kish. It shows that the kings of
Kish had conquered Susa at a very early date. In other
archaic texts from Susa, written by men who were subject
to some foreign power, probably Kish, the ideogram for
Susa is the ideogram for Ishtar, plus ERIN, which means
"cedar forest."[1] This same combination of signs is also
used to represent the name of a deity, which would accordingly be "Ishtar of the cedar forest."[2] That deity is once
called "Lady" and "King" in the same inscription.[3]
Either, therefore, the Semites of Kish had planted the
worship of their goddess at Susa, where she became
metamorphosed into a god, or they had identified her, after
she had been so metamorphosed at Kish, with a god which
they found already at Susa. The result is for our purpose
the same in either case, for it confirms the development
suggested by the inscription of Lugaltarsi.

It will be best to examine next the gods of Shirpurla
(otherwise called Lagash),[4] since we have more abundant
information concerning its pantheon than we have concerning the gods of any other Babylonian city at a date
equally early. From the inscriptions of Gudea, who was
ruler of Shirpurla about 3000 B.C., it is possible to form a
tolerably clear idea of its principal deities for Gudea's
time, and the occasional glimpses which the inscriptions
of his predecessors give us of these deities, assure us that
substantially the same pantheon extended back to 4500
B.C., or earlier.[5] The city or region of Shirpurla (for it

[1] Scheil, *op. cit.*, 58, 59, 63, 69.

[2] *Ibid.*, pp. 58, 59, l. 8.

[3] *Ibid.*, p. 69. It seems probable that this is the same deity which was later called Khumbaba, and who dwelt in the cedar wood in the midst of such magnificence. Cf. the Gilgamish epic, tablet V, Haupt, *Nimrodepos* pp. 24 ff., 28, 54, 58, and *KB.*, Vol. VI, p. 159 ff.

[4] Cf. Pinches, *Guide to the Kouyunjik Gallery*, London, 1884, p. 7.

[5] See the inscriptions of Urukagina and other early kings in *KB.*, Vol. III¹, p. 10 ff., and in Radau, *op. cit.*, p. 48 ff. Also the B inscription of monument Blau, which must be much older. (Cf. Ward in *PAOS.*, 1885, p. lvii, *Jour. of Am. Arch.*, 1st ser., Vol. IV, pl. v, and my translation, *JAOS.*, Vol. XXII, p. 123.)

is not certain that it was simply one city)¹ was, as Amiaud pointed out ² and as other scholars have also observed,³ composed of four cities or districts, each of which possessed its tutelary deity. These four districts were Girsu, in which the god Ningirsu was the chief deity ; Uruazagga, the chief deity of which was the goddess Bau ; Ninâ, over which the goddess Ninâ presided, and a town the name of which most scholars read as Gishgalla, but which I, with Jensen, would read Erim, the principal divinity of which was the goddess Ishtar or Nana. By the time of Gudea these four places had long been united under one sovereignty, and the four deities had been given places in one mythological family. Ningirsu and Bau were husband and wife, Ninâ was the sister of Ningirsu, while Nana was perhaps his mother.⁴ Shirpurla afforded at this time many other deities beside these, but these were formed into an amicable family, while most of the others were grouped about them as subordinates. A few, like En-lil or Bel of Nippur, were superior to these four. This superiority of the gods of other cities had, however, grown out of previously existing political conditions, while the gods subordinate to this group had either been developed by the application of epithets from a few primary deities, or borrowed from other places.

If now we apply to the principal deities of Shirpurla the rule formulated above,⁵ we reach the conclusion that Uruazagga, Ninâ, and Erim were either Sumerian settlements which had escaped war, or Semitic settlements, because their chief divinities were goddesses. As the former alternative is contrary to all probability, we are driven to regard them as Semitic. This conclusion is con-

---

¹ Cf. Ball, *PSBA.*, Vol. XV, p. 51 ff.; Hommel, *PSBA.*, Vol. XV, p. 108 ff. ; and Davis, *PAOS.*, 1895, p. ccxiii ff.

² *Records of the Past*, 2d ser., Vol. I, p. 46 ff.

³ See Davis in *PAOS.*, 1895, p. ccxiii ff., and Price in *AJSL.*, Vol. XVI, p. 48 ff.

⁴ Cf. Davis in *PAOS.*, 1895, p. ccxv.

⁵ p. 179 ff.

firmed by the traces of Semitic idiom which appear in the inscriptions of Shirpurla.[1] If this be true, these three feminine divinities were three forms of the goddess Ishtar, and it will be instructive to examine them a little more closely.

To begin with Nana, it is clear from the preceding argument that her real name was Ishtar, and that she was probably so called in the popular speech of Erim. The statements made concerning her by the kings would well apply to Ishtar. Ur-Bau calls her "the brilliant, the exalted lady,"[2] and Gudea, "the bearer of the word of life."[3] Davis has pointed out that Ninkharsag was originally the same goddess as Ishtar, but worshipped under a separate epithet, and the inscriptions bear out the statement.[4] Under this epithet Entemena, about 4100 B.C., built a temple to her,[5] Eannadu and Entemena claim to have been nourished by her milk, as does Lugalzaggisi,[6] and Gudea a millennium later calls her the "mother of the city's children."[7] That Nana (Ishtar) was held in high esteem in other ways is shown by the fact that Eannadu claims that she gave him the patesiship of Shirpurla and

---

[1] Cf. Radau, *op. cit.*, pp. 145–147. The language chiefly spoken in Shirpurla was probably Semitic, but writing had been adopted here from the Sumerians at a date long before the use of the cuneiform character for the expression of thought in Semitic had begun in neighboring Babylonian cities. It was apparently conformity to ancient custom which maintained the use of Sumerian for the purpose of written expression so long at Shirpurla, when at Kish, Guti, Lulubi, and Agade writing in Semitic had been going on for some hundreds of years.

[2] Cf. de Sarzec's *Découvertes en Chaldée*, pl. 8, col. iv, l. 9; cf. *KB*, Vol. III¹, p. 23.

[3] See Price's *Great Cylinder Inscriptions A & B of Gudea*, Cyl. A, col. xiv, l. 26.

[4] Cf. *PAOS.*, 1895, p. ccxiv.   [5] See Radau, *op. cit.*, p. 101.

[6] Cf. Galet A, *Rev. d'assyr.*, Vol. IV, pl. i, col. ii, l. 5, and my translation in *JOAS.*, Vol. XXI¹, p. 186, n. 6. Cf. *OBI.*, No. 115, and Radau, *op. cit.*, p. 118, and *OBI.*, No. 87, col. i, ll. 28–29, and Radau, *op. cit.*, p. 133.

[7] Cf. de Sarzec, *op. cit.*, pl. 20, col. i, l. 3; Amiaud, *Records of the Past*, 2d ser., Vol. II, p. 75, and Radau, *op. cit.*, p. 198.

the kingship of Kish.¹ From such statements as these we can, with the knowledge gained in the preceding pages, fill out a tolerably correct picture of her character and worship. She was simply the old Semitic mother goddess. Since she was the tutelary deity of the city Erim, its inhabitants were probably chiefly Semites.

There is also evidence that the Ishtar of the town had, like the goddess worshipped by Lugaltarsi, begun to undergo differentiation into a masculine and a feminine deity. She is several times referred to as Lugal-Erim, *i.e.* "king of Erim," showing that a confusion of thought with reference to her sex had already begun.²

A goddess of this group about whom somewhat more is known is Ninâ, the tutelary deity of the city or district of the same name. She is represented in the inscriptions by an ideogram, which is compounded of the ideogram for house into which that for fish is inserted.³ This indicates that she was previously the goddess of a fishing town. The same ideogram was afterwards employed to write the name of the city of Nineveh in Assyria. It was, of course, used to express the name of the city of Ninâ in Shirpurla. The name of the Assyrian city was pronounced *Nina* or *Ninua*. As *nun* is the Semitic Babylonian for fish, we have in the name Ninua a hint at what men in the Assyrian period considered her name to mean. Perhaps in Sumerian she had been called NIN-A, "lady of waters," which was by a folk etymology afterwards made in Semitic to mean "the fish." The reasons for this we shall have occasion to examine by and by.

[1] Cf. Galet A, col. v, l. 23 to col. vi, l. 5. Text *Rev. d'assyr.*, Vol. IV, pl. i, and my translation *JOAS.*, Vol. XXI¹, p. 186, n. 6.

[2] Cf. *Rev. d'assyr.*, Vol. IV, pl. 1, col. ii, l. 13 (cf. Thureau Dangin in *Rev. Sem.*, Vol. V, p. 67, and Radau, *op. cit.*, p. 85), and de Sarzec, *op. cit.*, pl. 8, col. ii, 1, 2 (cf. Amiaud, *op. cit.*, p. 75, and Jensen, *op. cit.*, pp. 20, 21), also *CTBM.*, Pt. X, No. 86900, ll. 28, 29. The development noted in the inscription of Lugaltarsi (above, p. 181 ff.) should be compared.

[3] Cf. Thureau Dangin's *Recherches*, No. 350.

Our knowledge of the worship of Ninâ begins about 4300 B.C., with the inscriptions of Ur-Nina. He declares that he built her temple, renewed her image, and caused her servants to build for her two high places.[1] The word used for "servants" is expressed by the ideogram for "dog," the Semitic term for sacred prostitute (see below, Chapter VI). Eannadu and Entemena call themselves a little later the "Chosen of her heart,"[2] and Entemena built various buildings for her.[3] Ur-Bau calls her the mother of the goddess Nin-mar,[4] and Gudea, the "mistress of tablet writing,"[5] "the child of Eridu,"[6] and "the supreme lady."[7] He says he built her temple and placed in it the image of a lion.[8] An inscription from the time of Dungi calls that king "the lord whom Ninâ loves," and he calls on an unnamed goddess, who was probably Ninâ, in behalf of his life.[9]

From the general course of our argument we should expect a goddess like Ninâ to be a form of Ishtar. This

---

[1] See de Sarzec, *Découvertes*, pl. 2 in No. 2, *KB.*, Vol. III¹, 11–15, and Radau, *op. cit.*, pp. 61–63. Where Radau reads "his wife for Ninâ" we should read, "the lady Ninâ."

[2] Cf. *Rev. d'assyr.*, Vol. IV, pl. i, col. i, l. 9, and col. ii, l. 1; also *Rev. semitique*, Vol. V, p. 67; also de Sarzec, *Découvertes*, pl. 43, and Radau, *op. cit.*, p. 116.

[3] Cf. *Rev. d'assyr.*, Vol. II, pp. 148, 149, col. iv; Radau, *op. cit.*, p. 113. Also de Sarzec, *Découvertes*, pl. 31, No. 2, and Radau, *op. cit.*, p. 94.

[4] De Sarzec, *op. cit.*, pl. 8, col. v, ll. 8–10; cf. *KB.*, Vol. III¹, p. 25.

[5] Cf. *PSBA.*, Vol. XIII, pp. 62, 64, No. 2; Radau, *op. cit.*, p. 193; Gudea, Statue B in de Sarzec's *Découvertes*, pl. 16 ff., and *KB.*, Vol. III¹, p. 47.

[6] Cylinder A (cf. Price's *Great Cylinder Inscriptions*), col. xx, l. 16.

[7] *PSBA.*, Vol. XIII, pp. 62, 64, No. 2.

[8] *Ibid.*

[9] The text is published in *CTBM.*, Pt. V, No. 12218, and is as follows: (l.¹) *Dingir* (NIN) LIG (2) NIN-A-NI (3) NAM-TI (4) *Dingir* DUN-GI (4) NITAG LIG-GA (5) LUGAL URU-*Ki*-MAMUG-KA (6) *dingir* BA-U-NIN-A-AN (7) ZABAR ZID (8) UR *dingir* NIN-GIR-SU (9) EN KI AKA *dingir* NINA-KA-KID (10) NAM-BA-KA-NI (11) MU-NA-DIM, *i.e.* "To the powerful lady, his mistress for the life of Dungi, the mighty hero, king of Ur, the exalted prince of Bau, lady of heaven, the brilliant, the faithful one, servant of Ningirsu, the lord who is beloved of

expectation is confirmed by the fact that she had a company of prostitutes, and was probably the lady of life. It is further confirmed by the fact that Entemena declares in several different inscriptions that he built a storehouse of dates for Ninâ.[1] The date-palm we have seen to be so closely connected with the Semitic goddess that this becomes another evidence that Ninâ was a form of that divinity. Gudea, as we have noted, says that he placed in Ninâ's temple a statue of a lion. Dr. Ward has called attention to a seal in the Metropolitan Museum in New York, which represents a nude goddess riding on a lion drawing a chariot and holding the lightnings in her hands.[2] He dates the cylinder at 3500 to 4000 B.C. It seems to me probable that this is a representation of Ninâ, and that it gives pictorial evidence of her close relationship to Ishtar.

The worship of the third of these goddesses, Bau, is known to us from the same early sources as that of Ninâ, since she is mentioned in the inscriptions of Urkagina,[3] Ur-Nina,[4] and Gudea.[5] She is easily shown to be a form of Ishtar. Ur-Bau calls her the "good lady,"[6] while Gudea calls her his chief mistress,[7] and has left on record two prayers in which he applies the term mistress in

Ninâ, the beauty of her building constructed." Of course the goddess addressed in the first line may be Ishtar or Bau, but since the prince calls himself the beloved of Ninâ, it seems more probable that he addresses her throughout.

[1] See *e. g. CTBM.*, Pt. X, No. 86900, ll. 14, 15, and de Sarzec's *Découvertes*, Pl. 5 bis, Face, col. iv, ll. 2, 3.

[2] Cf. *AJSL.*, Vol. XIV, p. 95; cf. *PSBA.*, Vol. XVIII, pp. 156, 157.

[3] Cf. Amiaud in *Records of the Past*, 2d ser., Vol. I, p. 69, and Radau, *op. cit.*, p. 50.

[4] Cf. *Rev. d'assyriologie*, Vol. IV, p. 106, No. 11, and Radau, *op. cit.*, p. 65.

[5] See *e. g. KB.*, Vol. III¹, pp. 58, 59.

[6] Cf. de Sarzec *Découvertes*, pl. 8, col. iv, l. 3 ff., Amiaud, *op. cit.*, p. 76, and *KB.*, Vol. III, p. 23.

[7] Cyl. A, col. xxiv, l. 6.

several different ways and prays especially for life,[1] as though she were the life giver. In another passage he calls her "mother Bau."[2] Galalama calls her also "mother (?) of Shirpurla."[3] On New Year's day, probably at the beginning of the first month, Gudea tells us also that he celebrated the festival of the goddess Bau, offering her various sacrifices of oxen, sheep, and lambs; dates and shoots of palm forming also a prominent feature of the offering.[4] This spring festival was, as we have shown in a previous chapter, the old spring festival of the yeaning time, and was a festival of the goddess Ishtar. A mother goddess, whose festival celebrated the birth of young, would, among a Semitic people, be a form of Ishtar. The name BA-U was simply an epithet, meaning "producer of food," and was probably given her as the goddess of the date tree and then of agriculture in general. Bau had a brother, Ningishzida,[5] whose name means "lady (or lord (?)) of the tree of life." Jastrow takes him to be identical with Ningirsu,[6] but Price considers this to be impossible.[7] In view of the development at Kish noted above,[8] where Ishtar was divided into a masculine and a feminine deity, it is probable that Ningishzida was originally an epithet given to Bau in consequence of her connection with the palm tree, and gradually, as she was differentiated, continued to be applied to the masculine portion of her. Possibly it may seem more probable to some that Ningishzida was a name of Tammuz, and that he is, in consequence of this, a brother of Bau-Ishtar; the result is in this case

---

[1] Cf. de Sarzec, *op. cit.*, pl. 13, Nos. 1 and 4, Amiaud, *Records of the Past*, 2d ser., Vol. II, pp. 92, 103, and Radau, *op. cit.*, pp. 202, 208.

[2] Cyl. B, col. xvii, l. 2.

[3] Cf. de Sarzec, *op. cit.*, pl. 21, No. 4, and *KB.*, Vol. III¹, p. 71.

[4] Cf. *KB.*, Vol. III, p. 61, and Amiaud, *op. cit.*, p. 101.

[5] Cf. Cyl. B, col. xxiii, l. 5, and Davis, *PAOS.*, 1895, p. ccxv.

[6] *Religion of Babylonia and Assyria*, p. 92.

[7] *AJSL.*, Vol. XVII, p. 50.

[8] p. 181 ff.

the same, though the goal by which it is reached be slightly different.[1]

At the time from which most of our information comes, the four districts of Shirpurla had long been united under one sovereignty. This had produced religious syncretism, and the gods were formed into a pantheon. In this pantheon Bau was regarded as the wife of Ningirsu, the god of Girsu, the fourth of the districts of Shirpurla.[2] She is also said to be the daughter of Anu,[3] but this, as we shall see by and by, has less historical significance than some of the mythological statements concerning other forms of the goddess.

The view we have taken of the nature of Bau is confirmed in another way. One of her titles was Gatumdug.[4] Indeed, under this name she became almost a separate goddess. As Gatumdug she is frequently called "mother of Shirpurla,"[5] but is shown to be originally identical with Bau since she is said to sit enthroned in Uruazagga,[6] Bau's city.

Ningirsu, the god of Girsu, the fourth district of Shirpurla, is mentioned in the inscriptions much oftener than any of the goddesses of the other districts. Most of the references, important as they are for a knowledge of other phases of the religion, do not materially help us in solving the problem of origins.[7] The application of our econom-

---

[1] Other epithets of Bau were *Ma-ma* (cf. *OBI.*, Pt. II, p. 48, n. 6), and *Gu-la*. In later times, this last name prevailed (cf. Jastrow, *Religion of Babylonia and Assyria*, pp. 60, 105, 166, etc.), and became the goddess of healing and of the nether world.

[2] Cf. Davis, *op. cit.*, p. ccxiv.

[3] Cf. *KB.*, Vol. III¹, p. 53, Amiaud, *op. cit.*, Vol. II, p. 91.

[4] Cf. Amiaud, *op. cit.*, Vol. I, p. 60.

[5] See, *e.g.*, de Sarzec, *op. cit.*, pl. 14, col. i, l. 1 ff., Amiaud, *op. cit.*, Vol. II, p. 97.

[6] Cf. de Sarzec, *op. cit.*, pl. 14, col. iii, l. 6 ff., and Amiaud, *op. cit.*, Vol. II, p. 99. Gatumdug is once an epithet of Nana, see below, p. 260, n. 6.

[7] He is called in them, "the king," "the great warrior of Enlil," etc., epithets which are important as showing his position in the pantheon of Shirpurla, but which throw little light on his original nature.

ico-religious test has made it clear that the towns or districts of Erim, Ninâ, and Uruazagga were peopled mainly by Semites, and probably founded by Semites. At all events, at the very dawn of history, the Semitic element in the civilization is predominant. Is the same true of the remaining district of Shirpurla, Girsu? I think that it is, for the following reasons: 1. The name Ningirsu really means "lady of Girsu."[1] It is true that in at least one phrase the Sumerian NIN seems to mean "lord,"[2] but it has almost universally a feminine signification,[3] which was no doubt its primary meaning. The Sumerians had another word for "lord" (viz. EN), and they can hardly be supposed to be so lacking in the sense of sex as to have expressed at first both "lord" and "lady" by the same word. Confusion between the two words would be very natural, however, if a goddess had been metamorphosed into a god as was done in South Arabia and at Kish. The word in the name which once had a feminine meaning would then seem to have a masculine signification, thus producing the confusion. 2. At the time of Gudea, both masculine and feminine qualities may in one passage still be traced in the conception of this god. Certain gifts are presented in one line to "mother Ningirsu," and two lines

[1] The name of the city or district is usually spelled GIR-SU, but in two or three inscriptions in de Sarzec's *Découvertes* (cf. No. 4 bis., and *KB.*, Vol. III¹, p. 10, col. i, l. 5, and Radau, *op. cit.*, p. 58, n. 6), it is spelled SU-GIR, or SUN-GIR (cf. Hommel, *Sum. Les.*, No. 7). Some scholars have therefore taken it to be identical with the later *Sumir*, cf. Radau, *ibid.*, and Rogers, *History of Babylonia and Assyria*, Vol. I, p. 356, who reads it Sungir. If GIR-SU be the spelling, it probably meant "body lance," perhaps equivalent to "girdle lance." This was at least an early folk interpretation of the name, for in a Babylonian inscription from before 5000 B.C., the Blau Monuments, a certain Khakhatabbar says that Ningirsu's monument of protection, a lance (GIR) he brought and placed in his temple. The inscription is inscribed on an object shaped like a lance blade (cf. *American Journal of Archaeology*, 1st ser., Vol. IV, pl. v, and my article "Notes on the Blau Monuments" in *JAOS.*, Vol. XXII¹, p. 123).

[2] *AL.*,[3] No. 301ª, *AL*,[4] No. 309ᵇ.
[3] Cf. Brünnow's *List*, Nos. 10984–10990.

farther on, to "lord Ningirsu."[1] This confusion can only be accounted for by supposing that there was a time when Ningirsu was the goddess of Girsu, and that she had afterwards been transformed into a god. 3. A bilingual fragment of a later time equates EN-GIR-SI (the word NIN, "lady," having been here changed to EN, "lord"), with Tammuz.[2] This indicates that Ningirsu and Tammuz were closely related, just as Ishtar and Tammuz were. If Ningirsu were a transformed Ishtar, the Tammuz which originally accompanied her may well have been fused with the resultant god either during or after the process of transformation. 4. If Ningirsu had been a Sumerian deity, the prehistoric wars would probably have completely effected his transformation from a goddess before the dawn of history. 5. Ningirsu came to mean husbandman,[3] — a meaning which appears to have been derived from the fact that he was a god of fertility and life, such as a transformed Ishtar would be. 6. Entemena, in a mutilated text on an old gate socket, the reading of which is not quite certain, appears to call him "god of life,"[4] as the goddesses of Shirpurla are called "lady of life." 7. The scores of phallic shaped cones inscribed to Ningirsu, found at Shirpurla, such as are pictured in de Sarzec's *Découvertes en Chaldée*, pl. 38, point to a connection of his cult with the sexual cult of Ishtar. For these

[1] Cyl. B, col. x, ll. 5, 7. The passage reads (l. 3) GIŠTIN-A DA GIŠTIN-TIN-A DA (4) UZ AZAG UZ GA GU BIR-MIR (5) AMA *dingir* NIN-GIR-SU-KA (6) NI-GA-BI EŠ E-ŠI-A-MUS NU-GUB-DA (7) EN IMIR SIBA BIR-IMIR EN *dingir* NIN-GIR-SU-RA (8) MI-NI-DA MU-NA-DA DIB SUM, *i.e.* "Wine he brought up, strong drink he brought up, a goat, a perfect goat, milk, the drink from the asses of mother Ningirsu, the cream of their milk in the temple Eshiamush he offered; to the lord of the asses, the shepherd of the asses, the lord Ningirsu he raised, he lifted up, he brought, he presented it."

[2] IV R., 27, No. 6, col. ii, ll. 42-43.

[3] Cf. V. R., 16, 39 ef, and Brünnow's *List*, No. 10995.

[4] *CTBM.*, Pt. V, No. 12061, ll. 10-12. They read *dingir* NIN-GIR-SU LUGAL(?) DINGIR-A-NI............ DINGIR TI(?), *i.e.* "Ningirsu the king, his god, the god of life." The sign TI, "life," is not quite certain, as it is partly erased.

o

reasons it seems highly probable that Ningirsu was a masculinized Ishtar. The fact that he was transformed, while Nana, Ninâ, and Bau were not, is probably due either to the fact that Girsu was the conquering and the more warlike of the settlements of Shirpurla, or to the presence of a larger Sumerian element there. It seems probable that Girsu was the oldest of the four settlements. Ningirsu, its god, appears already before 5000 B.C., under that name on the Blau Monuments.[1] This presupposes the existence of the city at that early time. There is, however, in the inscription nothing to indicate whether Ningirsu was at that time masculine or feminine (unless the fact that the sacrifice consisted of ewes may point to a goddess), as the suffix used in referring to the deity may be used in either gender.[2] Girsu, too, was the original seat of the monarchy, which afterwards conquered the other districts, for Urkagina, about 4500 B.C., styles himself indifferently king of Girsu or king of Shirpurla. Girsu must have been originally quite separate from the other districts. Indeed, each was no doubt originally quite an independent settlement. That that settlement was predominantly Semitic is shown by the Blau Monuments, for the superior race who are pictured upon them have the Semitic nose, while the inferior or slave race which they show, have quite different features.[3]

The conclusions here reached are not at all in conflict with the view that in the period from which our inscriptions come Ningirsu was a sun god; they simply show that before he was identified with the solar orb he was a chthonic mother goddess.

No doubt some Sumerian elements beside their system of writing entered into the Semitic civilization of

---

[1] Cf. my article "Notes on the Blau Monuments" in *JAOS.*, Vol. XXII¹, p. 123.

[2] It is NI; cf. Brünnow's *List*, Nos. 5330, 5331.

[3] Cf. *American Journal of Archaeology*, 1st ser., Vol. IV, pls. iv and v, and Ward, *ibid.*, p. 40.

Shirpurla, but it is impossible at this distance to tell how great they were. Possibly some of the elements which helped to transform Ningirsu into a god were Sumerian. It is not necessary from the religious point of view to postulate any large amount of such influence; the laws of Semitic social evolution are in the Mesopotamian environment sufficient to account for all that occurred in the realm of the religion.

Before passing from Shirpurla to other parts of Babylonia it will be convenient to remind ourselves that we are seeking origins which lie altogether beyond the horizon of written history and which can only be reconstructed by working backward from sporadic survivals. In this reconstruction help may often be obtained from the myths which grew up around the pantheon of Shirpurla and other cities. Even at the early date when the written history of Babylonia begins, the country had been united in various political organizations till some gods like Enlil and Enki (Ea) had become largely dissociated from their original habitations and had entered into various pantheons as lord of the earth and of the deep. Anu is a god whose local habitation[1] we cannot trace, and who seems in the historical period to have been more of an abstraction than Enlil and Enki He had been added to these, and the three had been formed into a triad. In this triad Anu in theory stood at the head, but in practice the other two were more honored. There are, therefore, three classes of myths to be distinguished at the very dawn of Babylonian history; (1) those which recall migrations of tribes or parts of tribes from earlier places of residence, like the myth that Ninâ is the daughter of Enki or Ea;[2] (2) those which resulted from a long political subjugation, like the

---

[1] See Jastrow's *History of Babylonia and Assyria*, p. 89. The statement of Jeremias (Chantepie de la Saussaye's *Religionsgeschichte*, Vol. I, p. 171), that he was the god of Erech, is a misconception. One might with as much reason call him a god of Shirpurla. See below, p. 218 ff.

[2] IV R. 1, col. ii, l. 38; cf. Davis, *PAOS.*, 1895, p. ccxv.

myth that Ningirsu is the son and warrior of Enlil;[1] and (3) those which have grown up out of the later abstract conceptions, or the identification of the gods with celestial objects, like the myth that Bau is the daughter of Anu.[2] Careful examination will often enable us to distinguish these different classes of myths from one another, and to do so will aid us in following our slender thread of evidence through the tangled mazes of Babylonian life.

Returning now to the first of the three myths just mentioned, we are led to the city of Eridu, the most southerly of the old Babylonian towns, and to its god Ea. Ninâ is called the daughter of Ea and the child of Eridu.[3] Eridu was the city of the god Ea, its ideogram being the same as that of the god with the determinative for place affixed.[4] It was, about 4000 or 5000 B.C. or earlier, situated on the shore of the Persian Gulf.[5] The name of Ninâ was, as we have seen, written with the sign for house around the sign for fish; while Ea was often pictured under the form of a fish, or as clad in a fishskin. A legend preserved for us through Berossos and Eusebius tells us how Oannes (who is certainly identified with Ea[6]) bore the form of a fish, and how he came up by day to the land and taught men how to construct houses, till the earth, collect fruits, compile laws, and all other useful knowledge.[7] In the pictorial representations Ea is seen as part man and part fish.[8] The fact that the fish form enters into the repre-

[1] See *e.g.*, Cyl. A, col. vii, l. 5, col. viii, l. 21, and Cyl. B, col. vi, l. 6; cf. Price, *AJSL.*, Vol. XVII, p. 49.

[2] See above, p. 191, and below.

[3] See above, p. 188.

[4] Cf. Brünnow's *List*, Nos. 2625, 2645, and 2649.

[5] Cf. Sayce, *Hibbert Lectures*, p. 104, and Peters, *Nippur*, Vol. II, p. 299.

[6] Cf. Lenormant, *Histoire ancienne de l'orient*, Vol. V, p. 231 ff., Sayce, *Hibbert Lectures*, p. 131, and Peters, *Nippur*, Vol. II, p. 299.

[7] Cf. Cory's *Ancient Fragments*, p. 23 ff., also a cuneiform original of a part of it, published by Scheil in *Recueil de traveaux*, Vol. XX, p. 126 ff.

[8] Cf. Lenormant, *op. cit.*, pp. 232, 238, and Sayce, *op. cit.*, p. 133.

sentations of both Ninâ and Ea confirms the statement of the mythology that the two were kindred. Sometimes the fish god is pictorially represented as applying the fertilizing cone to the sacred palm tree,[1] and this gives another thread of connection between the two, for as noted above, Ninâ was the goddess to whom dates were sacred.[2] At Eridu, the city of Ea, there was also a sacred tree,[3] no doubt a palm, so that it is no accident that the fish god, or god of the water, is represented as fertilizing the palm. An unpublished cylinder in the British Museum represents Ea thus and calls him "the god of life."[4] George Smith called attention to the fact that an unpublished brick in the same museum is inscribed to Ea under the name Nin-Eridu, or "lady of Eridu."[5] Amiaud doubted whether it really applied to that god,[6] but there can, in view of the development which we have traced elsewhere,[7] be no doubt of it.

The meaning of all these facts and myths would seem to be this: Eridu was probably the oldest Semitic settlement in Babylonia. Hither from Arabia the Semites came and planted their earliest colony, probably selecting the site because they found their sacred palm tree already growing there. The proximity of the Persian Gulf led them in course of time to associate their goddess with that body of water as they had in Arabia associated her with the spring or well of the oasis. If a Sumerian fishing goddess preceded her here, identification of the two may have hastened the process. That in time she should be associated with the fish symbol was perfectly natural. In the lapse of years colonies were sent out to other points, partly in consequence of the natural multiplication of the populace, and partly in consequence of new immigration from

[1] See Lenormant, *op. cit.*, p. 232.   [2] p. 189.
[3] Cf. Jensen, *Kosmologie*, p. 99 ff., 249, n.; Hilprecht, *OBI.*, pt. 1, p. 28, and Radau, *Early Babylonian History*, p. 231.
[4] Sayce, *op. cit.*, p. 133.   [5] *TSBA.*, Vol. I, p. 32.
[6] *Records of the Past*, 2d ser., Vol. I, p. 60.
[7] *E.g.*, that in Athtar, Ishtar at Kish, and Ningirsu.

Arabia. Ninâ was one of these, but probably by no means the earliest. The first colonists at Eridu brought with them the artificial culture of the palm tree, a culture probably before unknown to the country, and this addition to such knowledge of agricultural pursuits as the country may have possessed before led in process of time to the myth that Ea was the source whence all knowledge of agriculture and civilized pursuits came. As this myth grew Ea became in consequence the god of wisdom. He was so regarded by Eannadu,[1] Entemena,[2] Lugalzaggisi,[3] and through all the subsequent history. As Semitic society was in this environment organized on another basis, the Ishtar of Eridu was transformed into a god, as happened also at Kish and Girsu. As early as the time of Eannadu the transformation had occurred, since he is called "king"[4] by that monarch as he is centuries later by Ur-Bau[5] and Dungi.[6]

The worship of Ea is so widespread in Babylonia at the first dawn of history that we are compelled to suppose that in prehistoric time Eridu had been the seat of an empire which held sway over all of southern Babylonia. There is no improbability to offset this necessary inference from the phenomena of the religion, but on the other hand as the oldest Semitic settlement it would be very natural for it to become the head of a kingdom.

After the time of Khammurabi (about 2300 B.C.) Ea was regarded as having for a spouse the goddess Damkina, "the lady of the earth." She does not appear in the older

---

[1] Cf. *Rev. d'assyriologie*, Vol. IV, pl. i, col. ii, ll. 6, 7; *Rev. semitique*, Vol. V, p. 67; and Radau, *Early Babylonian History*, p. 84.

[2] *Rev. d'assyriologie*, Vol. IV, pl. ii, col. v, ll. 24, 25; cf. Thureau Dangin's translation, *ibid.*, p. 49, and Radau's *op. cit.*, p. 108.

[3] See Hilprecht, *OBI.*, No. 87, col. i, ll. 17, 18; cf. Radau's translation, *op. cit.*, p. 132.

[4] Cf. Radau, *op. cit.*, p. 80.

[5] Cf. de Sarzec, *Découvertes*, pl. 8, col. iv, l. 11; cf. *KB.*, Vol. III¹, p. 23.

[6] See Winckler's *Altorientalische Forschungen*, 1st ser., p. 547, No. 8; and Radau, *op. cit.*, p. 224.

literature,[1] and is clearly simply a female outgrowth or counterpart of the Ea who two thousand years earlier had become a male deity, and who had as the necessities of the pantheons required, taken on more specialized functions. His own reflection was at last assigned to him in female form for a spouse, that he might not stand alone.

Returning to the pantheon of Shirpurla and following another mythological clew, we are led by the statement of Arad-Sin, king of Larsa,[2] that Ishtar (Nana) of Khallabi, which was, perhaps, a colony of Erim,[3] is the daughter of EN-ZU or Sin, to the city of Ur, of which Sin was the chief deity. In the older texts the ideograms for Ur and Sin are as identical as those for Eridu and Ea. Next to Eridu, Ur was the most southerly of the ancient cities of Babylonia. We do hear in mythological poetry of Surippak, farther to the south, which was buried in the flood, but it plays no part in the history. Ur was a little to the westward of Eridu,[4] and is represented by the modern mound of Mugheir. It was a very old city, probably not appreciably younger than Eridu. Its kings at various times held sway over the rest of Babylonia, and probably had done so before the dawn of history, for we find Sin, the god of Ur, a member in high standing of the pantheons of other cities when first the written records give us glimpses of their life. Naram-Sin, king of Agade about 3750 B.C., is said by his name to be the favorite of this god of Ur, and gives us other evidence that Sin was worshipped beyond the borders of Ur.[5] Lasirab[6] of Guti

---

[1] Cf. Jastrow's *Religion of Babylonia and Assyria*, p. 64.

[2] *PSBA.*, Vol. XIII, pp. 158, 159; Davis, *PAOS.*, 1895, p. ccxvi, evidently quoted from memory when he ascribed this statement to Gudea.

[3] See below.

[4] Cf. Peters, *Nippur*, Vol. II, p. 296 ff., and Rogers's *History of Babylonia and Assyria*, Vol. I, p. 290.

[5] Cf. Thureau Dangin, *Comptes rendus de l'acad. inscr.*, 1899, p. 348, and Radau, *op. cit.*, p. 173 ff.

[6] Cf. Winckler, *ZA.*, Vol. IV, p. 406, and Radau, *op. cit.*, p. 175 ff.

and Anu-banani[1] of Lulubi had both worshipped him at a still earlier time. The worship of this god also appears at Shirpurla, where he was probably regarded as the father of Nana or Ishtar.[2] This fact, like the myth that Ninâ was the daughter of Ea, would seem to give a hint that Erim, the district over which Nana ruled may have been colonized from Ur, as Ninâ was colonized from Eridu, or at least that there was some close connection between them. If this be true, we must suppose that Sin was at the first an Ishtar and was transformed into a male like Ishtars in other places. This view cannot be made out as clearly as the cases which have already been treated, but its probability is increased by the following considerations: 1. Dungi calls the chief deity of Ur Nin-Ur, "lady of Ur," and his "mistress," as Ea was called "lady of Eridu."[3] 2. An old hymn to the moon god[4] attributes to him the authorship of all fertility in a way quite explicable if he had first been the chthonic mother goddess, but which would be meaningless were he simply a personification of the moon. He is in this hymn called "lord of increase," "the begetter of everything," "the begetter of gods and men," the "maintainer of the life of the world," the one "at whose command vegetation is created,"[5] etc. These are all epithets not only befitting Ishtar, but which in another old hymn are most of them actually applied to her.[6] 3. Throughout the hymn and in other texts Sin is constantly called "father,"[7] which would be very natural if he had grown out of a mother goddess. 4. His symbol

---

[1] Cf. *Recueil de traveaux*, Vol. XIV, pp. 100–106, since published in *Textes élamites-semitiques*, and Radau, *op. cit.*, p. 177.

[2] Cf. Amiaud in *Records of the Past*, 2d ser., Vol. I, p. 57, and above p. 185.

[3] Cf. Hilprecht, *OBI.*, No. 16, and Radau, *op. cit.*, p. 224.

[4] IV R., 9.

[5] See Jastrow, *Religion of Babylonia and Assyria*, pp. 303, 304.

[6] Cf. Haupt, *ASKT.*, p. 116 ff., Zimmern, *Babylonische Busspsalmen*, p. 33 ff., and *Hebraica*, Vol. X, p. 15.

[7] See, *e.g.*, the text of Nabu-na'id, I R., 69, and *KB.*, Vol. III[2], p. 81 ff.

was the ox. He is called in the hymn (ll.19, 20) "the strong bull with great horns." The symbol of Ishtar, as shown on an old seal, was the cow,[1] and such a transformation as we have supposed would connect the two. Similarly the symbol of Ashtart at Tyre was a cow, that of Baal and Yahwe in Canaan, and of Athtar in South Arabia, a bull.[2] We cannot, however, press this consideration, since the bull and cow are found as divine symbols in many agricultural communities where there is no possibility that an Ishtar or an analogous god had preceded. There can be no doubt though that a large Semitic element entered into the make-up of the moon god of Ur, but the possibility that that Semitic element took on the bull symbol through Sumerian influence must be recognized. The fact that a similar conception prevailed on purely Semitic soil in southern Arabia renders, however, the supposition of Sumerian influence unnecessary. 5. The ideogram by which Sin is represented in many Sumerian texts, EN-ZU, means "lord of knowledge, or of might, or of wisdom, or of increase,"[3] any or all of which are meanings which would naturally spring from the conceptions entertained of Ishtar.

Perhaps we shall get more light on this matter when Mugheir is excavated and its earliest texts recovered, but we are at present justified in regarding Ur as a city predominantly if not altogether Semitic, and its god as in large degree the result of the absorption of an Ishtar, or more probably simply a transformed Semitic goddess. If this be the real origin of Sin, the development must have been completed very early, for a very archaic text[4] dating probably from before 5500 B.C. seems to call Sin Ab, "father."

[1] See Scheil, *Recueil de traveaux*, Vol. XX, p. 62.
[2] Cf. *Hebraica*, Vol. X, p. 31, *ZDMG.*, Vol. XXX, p. 289 (cf. *Hebraica*, Vol. X, p. 56), and the articles "Bull" and "Calf, Golden," in Hastings's *Dictionary of the Bible*, *Encyc. Bib.*, and *Jewish Encyc.*
[3] Cf. Brünnow's *List*, Nos. 130–137.
[4] Cf. below, p. 213, n. 5. The interpretation of the tablet is as yet tentative.

After the deity of Ur had been identified with the moon, the hymns and prayers addressed to him are largely occupied with praises of his brightness and other qualities which were suggested by the brilliance and the movements of the moon.[1] In the pantheons of the historic period Sin, like other gods, was called the son of Enlil.[2] This resulted probably from a long prehistoric hegemony on the part of Nippur, Enlil's city, of which more will be said below. Either the result of this hegemony, or the fact that Sin was a younger deity, prevented him from ever occupying the same exalted position as Enlil, or even as Ea. He was later a member of the second triad in the pantheons of Babylonia, but not like the others of the first.[3]

Taking once more as a point of departure a mythological statement from the pantheon of Shirpurla, we are led by the myth that Ningirsu was the son and warrior of Enlil to consider next the god of Nippur.[4] In antiquity his shrine at Nippur rivals the shrine of any other Babylonian god.[5] Among the earliest inscriptions yet published, except such as the Blau Monuments, are some by a certain Enshagkushanna, lord of Kengi or Sumir, who before 4500 B.C. devoted to Enlil, "king of countries," the spoil of his victories over Kish.[6] This shows that even at that remote period Enlil had come to be regarded far outside the confines of Nippur as the principal god, and from this time

---

[1] See, *e.g.*, King's *Babylonian Magic and Sorcery*, p. 5.

[2] Cf. Ur-Gur, I R., 1, No. 5, *KB.*, Vol. III¹, p. 79.

[3] The inscriptions of the kings of Ur throw little light on the character of Sin beyond the fact that he was regarded as a king (cf. *KB.*, Vol. III¹, pp. 77, 93). The moon god was also worshipped at Harran, but of the origins of his worship there we as yet know nothing. Probably much the same history could be written of his worship there as that which we have sketched for the moon god of Ur, had we the material.

[4] See above, p. 195 ff.

[5] Cf. Hilprecht, *OBI.*, Vol. I, Pt. 2, pp. 44–46, and Peters, *Nippur*, Vol. II, p. 246.

[6] Cf. Hilprecht, *OBI.*, Nos. 90–92; Radau, *op. cit.*, pp. 44, 45; and Rogers, *History of Babylonia and Assyria*, Vol. I, p. 351 ff.

onward he was honored by all worshippers, of whatever city, more than any other god.[1] Even the rulers of Shirpurla made their own god Ningirsu subject to him. This fact can, I think, be adequately accounted for only on the supposition that Nippur had been in prehistoric time the head of a kingdom which included all of Babylonia.

At a time almost as early, — a time before the Sargonic period, — Enlil had a female spouse, Ninlil. Urzaguddu, a king of Kish,[2] and Anu-banini, of Lulubi,[3] both worshipped this pair, and in later times they are often grouped together.

In all probability there is in the Enlil of Nippur a large Sumerian element. The worship which he received from men of all cities is no doubt to be accounted for in part by the political supremacy of Nippur, as already suggested, but in part too by the fact that he was an old pre-Semitic god of the soil. Semites, when first they went into a new country, thought it necessary as late as the eighth century B.C. to learn the worship of the god of the land[4] in order to reside there safely, and in the earlier times they would have this feeling in still larger degree. The Semites in coming into Babylonia would therefore adopt, in some measure, the worship of its native gods wherever they settled, while they kept also the worship of their own goddess. If this foreign worship were practically unorganized, it would make little impression, and would leave the worship of the mother goddess comparatively pure; but if it had assumed a definite form, it would, in fusing

---

[1] Cf. Jastrow, *Religion of Babylonia and Assyria*, p. 52 ff.

[2] Cf. Hilprecht, *OBI.*, No. 93, and Radau, *op. cit.*, p. 125, n. 1.

[3] Cf. *Recueil de traveaux*, Vol. XIV, pp. 100–106, and Radau, *op. cit.*, p. 177.

[4] See 2 Kgs. 17$^{24-34}$; cf. also Budde, *Religion of Israel to the Exile*, pp. 53–55. An instance of fusion, not altogether dissimilar, from a much later time is found in an Aramaic inscription of the second century B.C. from Kappadocia, published in Lidzbarski's *Ephemeris für semitische Epigraphik*, p. 67, which represents the marriage of the Persian religion (*din Mazdianiš*) to the god Bel.

with the Semitic cult, considerably modify it. At Nippur
— assuming a Semitic element in the civilization — the
cult of the mother goddess appears to have been influenced
by such a foreign element, since as early as 3800 B.C. Enlil
was not only of the masculine gender, but had also a female counterpart, which was simply his own reflection. A
transformation, which appears not to have been complete
at Eridu till some two thousand years later, seems to have
occurred at Nippur before the dawn of history. The process was therefore probably hastened by fusion with a
foreign god.[1]

When our written records begin, the Semites appear to
be everywhere dominant in Babylonia; but, as we have
seen, the phenomena of the religion compel us to postulate
a prehistoric kingdom of Nippur, which dominated much
of the surrounding country. This was probably a Sumerian kingdom, into which in its later years a large Semitic
element was infused. If Enlil was originally a Sumerian
god, and Nippur the head of a Sumerian kingdom, the two
forces, religious and political, were then present which in
combination would give Enlil the place at the head of all
the pantheons which he occupied in the later religious
history.

A large Semitic element also entered into the conceptions of Enlil and Ninlil at Nippur. This is shown by
the following facts: 1. A great variety of phallic symbols
were found at Nippur in all the levels of the mound back
to 4000 B.C., or earlier.[2] These symbols are the natural
symbols of a cult like the Ishtar cult, but do not grow so
naturally out of a purely agricultural civilization. We
cannot go astray, therefore, in regarding them as the product of a Semitic element of thought, which entered into
the worship and life at Nippur.

[1] The presence of a non-Semitic element at Nippur is confirmed by the
faces on the votive tablet of Ur-Enlil, which is of about the same age as
the inscriptions of Enshagkushanna, or perhaps a little older. See Hilprecht, *OBI.*, pl. xvi, and Professor Cope's note, *ibid.*, Pt. 2, p. 48, n. 1.

[2] Peters, *Nippur*, Vol. II, p. 236 ff.

An old bilingual incantation contains the following Sumerian expressions: AMA A-A *dingir* EN-LIL, and AMA A-A *dingir* NIN-LIL, *i.e.* "the mother-father Enlil," and "the mother-father Ninlil."[1] The point of this expression is not simply that Enlil and Ninlil were thought of as a pair of parents,[2] but that the qualities of father and mother both are actually attributed to both Enlil and Ninlil.[3] This points to the presence at Nippur of a mother goddess who for a time almost monopolized the thoughts of the worshippers, and who was gradually fused with a masculine deity, with the result that for a time, as in Lugaltarsi's inscription,[4] both masculine and feminine qualities were attributed to the same deity. Enlil was, therefore, probably originally a Sumerian earth goddess, who by the warlike character of his worshippers was transformed to a god, and later given a consort. The confusion of sex probably did not last as long as in the case of the deities Ea and Sin, which were of almost pure Semitic origin, but this little expression in the incantation, a fossil from past strata of thought, has transmitted to us the evidence of its existence. By the time when written records began Enlil and Ninlil were fairly well defined, though even then a Semite sometimes addressed the whole deity under the name of Ninlil.[5] Another point, though it is, as we have seen, indeterminate, is found in the fact that Enlil and Ninlil are in an old bilingual hymn represented under the symbols of an ox and a cow, like Sin and Ishtar.[6]

[1] IV R., 1, col. ii, ll. 23-28.
[2] Delitzsch, *Assyrisches Wörterbuch*, p. 20.
[3] Cf. my article "An Androgynous Babylonian Divinity," in *JAOS.*, Vol. XXI,[2] p. 186 ff.
[4] See above, p. 181.
[5] Cf. Winckler's *Untersuchungen*, p. 157, No. 9; *KB.*, Vol. III,[1] p. 69, and Radau, *op. cit.*, p. 37, and p. 125, n.
[6] See Reisner's *Sumerisch-babylonische Hymnen nach Thontafeln griechischer Zeit* in the Berlin Museum's *Mittheilungen*, Heft X, p. 19, ll. 71-74; cf. the translation in Dr. Banks's dissertation, *Sumerisch-babylonische Hymnen*, Leipzig, 1897, p. 23.

The fusion of Semitic and non-Semitic elements simply hastened, as has been pointed out, the evolution which the processes of social transformation carried on more slowly elsewhere.

The commanding place which Enlil held in the Babylonian pantheon in the earliest period is illustrated by the way in which Enshagkushanna before 4500 B.C. presented to him, as noted above, the spoil of his war with Kish, although so far as appears the seat of Enshagkushanna's government was in the south; and also, by the way Eannadu of Shirpurla some three centuries later claims that Enlil (not Ningursu) gave him victory over the people of Gishban.[1]

The view we have been led to take of these gods throws light on the place which Enlil and Ea afterwards held as the two most prominent members of the triad, Anu, Bel (Enlil), and Ea. In this triad, Bel was the god of the earth, and Ea of the deep. Anu was in part an abstraction added at a later time to represent the third most obvious part of the universe. Bel (Enlil), the old god of the country, though largely permeated by Semitic conceptions, naturally took the lead, because the Sumerian kingdom antedated the Semitic; while Ea, the oldest Semitic god in Babylonia, whose coming brought the artificial culture of the date-palm and infused new elements into the civilization, whose home was on the shore of the great water, assumed naturally a place of importance next to Bel. When the two were united in the first triad, the leading Sumerian and the leading Semitic deities, whose hosts had no doubt in the earlier days struggled in many a bloody conflict, were brought into harmonious accord.

Because of a possible connection with the pantheon of

[1] *CTBM.*, Pt. VII, No. 23580, col. ii, ll. 1–7. It reads: (1) E-AN-NA-DU MEN (2) SA UMUN GAL (3) *dingir* EN-LIL-LAL (4) E-NA SUM (5) NAM-E-NA-TA KUD (6) GAL GISH-BAN-*ki*-KID (7) E-AN-NA-DU-RA, *i.e.*, "Eannadu am I. The temple of the great lord Enlil, its greatness I established. On account of its greatness he subdued the men of Gishban to Eannadu."

Shirpurla, the next deity to be considered is the god Marduk of Babylon, with his spouse Sarpanit. Ball[1] and Hommel[2] have suggested, in consequence of a passage in an old hymn which identifies Gishgalla with Babylon,[3] that the Gishgalla of the kingdom of Shirpurla was really the same place as the Babylon of later history. As Amiaud pointed[4] out, Gudea speaks of the whole of Shirpurla as a city,[5] a fact which precludes the possibility that one of its quarters was as far away as Babylon. The theory also encounters other objections which are equally fatal to it. It is probable that the ideogram which Hommel and Amiaud read Gishgalla should be read Erim.[6] Gishgalla is probably another sign.[7] Eannadu, about 4100 B.C., tells us of his conquest over a city, the name of which he represents by this latter ideogram, and which is probably, therefore, to be read Gishgalla.[8] As he calls himself king of Shirpurla, it was clearly a town outside of that place. He gives us no indication of where it was situated, but from the fact that the ideogram Gishgalla also denoted in later times the direction "south,"[9] it is

---

[1] *PSBA.*, Vol. XV, p. 53 ff.
[2] *PSBA.*, Vol. XV, p. 108 ff.
[3] IV R., 46.
[4] *Records of the Past*, New Series, Vol. I, p. 43.
[5] De Sarzec's *Découvertes*, pl. 14, col. i, ll. 14, 15.
[6] Cf. Thureau Dangin, *Recherches*, No. 359. While he there reads the sign GISHGAL, he reads ERIM in *Revue semitique*, Vol. V, p. 67. As he himself points out (*Recherches*, No. 361), another sign is really equivalent to GISHGAL, and the two signs cannot be identical. This one, as Jensen suggested (*KB.*, Vol. III¹, p. 3 ff.), is probably to be read ERIM (Brünnow's *List*, No. 949), at least provisionally.
[7] Thureau Dangin's *Recherches*, No. 361, and Brünnow's *List*, No. 938.
[8] Cf. the four texts in *CTBM.*, Pt. IX, pls. 1 and 2, col. ii of each text; cf. also Galet A, *Rev. d'assyr.*, Vol. IV, pl. 1, col. iii, ll. 17–19; Cf. Thureau Dangin in *Rev. sem.*, Vol. V, p. 68, and Radau, *op. cit.*, p. 84. The passage reads: TU-ŠU-BI SUM *kur* ELAM *ki*, TU-ŠU-BI SUM GIŠ-GALLA *ki*, TU-ŠU-BI SUM GIŠ-BAN *ki*, TU-ŠU-BI SUM URU *ki*; *i.e.*, "Into his power was given Elam; into his power was given Gishgalla; into his power was given Gishban; into his power was given Ur."
[9] See Brünnow's *List*, No. 947. It probably acquired this meaning, as the word Negebh did in Hebrew, by being a place southward of some

altogether improbable that Gishgalla was as far north as Babylon. It may be that Babylon was a colony of this Gishgalla. That would afford only an indirect connection with Shirpurla, — Gishgalla being not a part of Shirpurla like Erim, but an independent town conquered by Shirpurla in the historical period.

It is clear, therefore, that Hommel's identification of Babylon with Gishgalla, even if interpreted to mean that Babylon was a colony of the latter, will throw little light on the nature of the god Marduk, since we have no information whatever as to the gods of Gishgalla. If there be any connection between the two, the deity of Babylon might throw light on the religion of Gishgalla, but not that of Gishgalla upon Babylon.

From other considerations, however, it can be shown that Marduk is in all probability a Semitic god, evolved, like the Semitic gods already discussed, out of a preceding Ishtar. The considerations which support this view are as follows: —

1. Marduk is called in the hymns "the life giver,"[1] "possessor of the foundation of life,"[2] and is asked to give life.[3] In other words, he is, like Ishtar, a deity of life.
2. Nebuchadnezzar tells us[4] that the Zagmukhu, which in the time of Gudea was, as we have seen, a festival of Bau, was at Babylon a festival of Marduk. It is not necessary to suppose with Jastrow[5] that it was transferred to Marduk; this festival of the yeaning time in spring is another link connecting Marduk with the Ishtar from which he sprang.[6] 3. Marduk comes first to our knowledge in the inscriptions of Sumula-ilu and Khammurabi,

---

other important place in Babylonia, so that Gishgallaward came to mean southward.

[1] IV R., 29, No. 1, Rev. ll. 5, 6 (cf. Sayce, *Hibbert Lectures*, p. 502).
[2] *Ibid.*, Obv. l. 38 (cf. Sayce, *ibid.*, p. 501).
[3] IV R., 18, No. 2, Rev. l. 12 (cf. Sayce, *op. cit.*, p. 489).
[4] I R., 54, col. ii, 54 ff. (cf. Jensen, *Kosmologie*, p. 84 ff., and *KB.*, Vol. III², p. 15).
[5] *Religion of Babylonia and Assyria*, pp. 121, 631.
[6] See above, p. 109 ff.

kings who belonged, as all recognize, to a Semitic dynasty. Their god would be a Semitic god, so that it is in consequence more than probable that Marduk is developed from the Semitic mother goddess like other Semitic deities.

From the time of Khammurabi Marduk was the chief deity in the eyes of all Babylonians. They worshipped other gods as the inhabitants of other cities had done, but unlike them, they practically placed Marduk, not Enlil, first. Jastrow has already pointed out[1] how, in consequence of this, Marduk absorbed in time many of the attributes of Bel (Enlil) and even of Ea. This movement perhaps had its origin in a myth that Marduk was the son of Ea.[2] Sayce infers from this[3] that Babylon was originally a colony of Eridu. This can hardly have been the case, for, as will be pointed out below,[4] the myth was probably in the first place a myth of Nabu which Marduk absorbed. The name Marduk is with some probability explained as "young" or "early sun,"[5] *i.e.*, "child of the day,"[6] and perhaps arose from the association of the primitive Semitic goddess at Babylon with the sun.

Marduk had a consort, Sarpanitum, who first appears in the reign of Sumula-ilu about 2360 B.C.[7] Her name, according to Delitzsch,[8] comes, like that of Marduk, from her solar character, and means "silver brightness." In the historical inscriptions she appears to have been

---

[1] *Religion of Babylon and Assyria*, p. 117 ff.

[2] Cf. Winckler, *Untersuchungen*, p. 140, and *KB.*, Vol. III¹, p. 131.

[3] *Hibbert Lectures*, p. 104.

[4] See below, p. 212, and on the subjugation of Nabu to Marduk, Jastrow, *op. cit.*, cf. 126 ff.

[5] Sayce, *op. cit.*, p. 98, Jensen, *Kosmologie*, p. 88, and Jastrow, *op. cit.*, p. 119.

[6] Delitzsch, *BA.*, Vol. II, p. 623 n.

[7] King's *Letters and Inscriptions of Ḥammurabi*, No. 101, col. i, l. 41; cf. Vol. III, p. 218 ff.

[8] *Ibid.*, Contra, cf. Halévy, *Recherches critique*, p. 260, and Muss-Arnolt in *JBL.*, Vol. XI, p. 165. In consequence of a folk etymology the name of the goddess was sometimes written Ziru-bani-ti, or "creator of seed." (Cf. II R., 67 ¹².)

little more than a reflection of Marduk, but that she was originally more than that appears from the fact that Nebuchadnezzar appeals to her as the goddess of childbearing.¹ That she always played a large rôle in the popular imagination is shown by the fact that in the middle Babylonian period the image of a nude goddess holding her breasts was very popular in Babylonian art.² These are in all probability representations of Sarpanit, and indicate that in the rise of the god Marduk the feminine side of the old mother goddess lost nothing of her popularity. This is further confirmed by what Herodotus and Strabo tell us of her service by the women of Babylon.³ Sarpanitum was then the feminine counterpart of Marduk, as Damkina was the feminine counterpart of Ea. The pair at Babylon, as at Eridu, were probably produced by the differentiation of the old mother goddess Ishtar. If Babylon were a colony of Gishgalla, this conclusion would involve the view that the latter city was also a Semitic settlement.

Another god the origin of whose worship may with some plausibility be traced through Shirpurla is Nabu, the god of the city Borsippa. Hommel has suggested[4] that the Kinnir, which is equated with Borsippa in the hymn which calls Babylon Gishgalla,[5] is the same town as that mentioned in the inscription of Ur-Bau as Kinunir,[6] which Hommel declares was situated in Gishgalla. The enthusiasm of a discoverer has here led Hommel into a slight error, for Ur-Bau does not say that Kinunir was

[1] Oppert, *Expedition en Mesopotamie*, Vol. II, p. 295; *Hebraica*, Vol. X, pp. 18, 19.
[2] Cf. Ward in *American Journal of Archæology*, 1900, pp. 291, 292.
[3] See Herodotus, Bk. I, 199; Strabo, Bk. XVI, 1, 20; Apocryphal Epistle of Jeremiah, vs. 42, 43; cf. *Hebraica*, Vol. X, pp. 20, 21, and *JBL.*, Vol. X, p. 79 ff.
[4] *PSBA.*, Vol. XV, p. 108.
[5] IV R., 46, cf. ll. 15, 16.
[6] De Sarzec's *Découvertes*, pl. 8, col. vi, ll. 9-11. Cf. Amiaud in *Records of the Past*, New Ser., Vol. I, p. 77, and Jensen, *KB.*, Vol. III¹, pp. 24, 25.

situated in Gishgalla, but in Girsu. It is natural to see in Kinnir or Borsippa a colony from Girsu. The emigrants from Kinunir, which would seem to have been a portion or suburb of Girsu, would of course take with them the worship of their deity. Ur-Bau tells us that the deity of Kinunir was the goddess Dumuzizuab[1] (*i.e.*, "the living child of the abyss," or "the Tammuz of the deep"). He makes it clear that she was a goddess by calling her "lady of Kinunir."[2]

Now if we take Hommel's identification to mean that Borsippa was a colony from this portion of Girsu, then the goddess "Tammuz of the deep" must have been the real deity of Borsippa out of which Nabu was developed by processes with which we are already familiar. That Nabu had some such genesis is made probable by an old hymn which makes him a water god and a god of fertility, such as we have seen Ishtar to be.[3] This view is further confirmed by a list of gods[4] in which Nabu is identified with a deity of the island Dilmun, an island in the Persian Gulf near Bahrein.[5] It would seem, therefore, that the people of Kinunir brought their goddess from one of the islands of the Persian Gulf, to which they had previously migrated from Arabia, and settled in or near Girsu, and that thence a band moved onward to Borsippa. The settlement at Girsu was made before the time of Eannadu, for he was acquainted with their deity.[6]

The proof that Nabu originated in this way is only enough to furnish a basis for conjecture, but in the light of the analogies we have traced elsewhere it seems highly probable.

[1] De Sarzec, *ibid.*
[2] Jensen's idea that Dumuzizuab must be a god (*KB.*, Vol. III[1], p. 25 n.) is, if the line of reasoning in the preceding pages be at all correct, groundless.
[3] IV R., 14, No. 3, ll. 10-14. Cf. Sayce, *Hibbert Lectures*, p. 448.
[4] II R., 60, 30; cf. also 54, 66, and Brünnow's *List*, 5372.
[5] Cf. Sayce, *Hibbert Lectures*, p. 114, n. 1.
[6] See *Revue d'assyriologie*, Vol. IV, pl. 1, col. ii, l. 9; cf. also *Revue semitique*, Vol. V, p. 67, and Radau, *Early Babylonian History*, p. 84.

The name "Living child of the deep"—Dumuzizuab, —would naturally suggest a connection of this goddess, and hence of Nabu, with Ea. This probably took first the form of a myth which made Nabu the son of Ea, which would be "child of the deep" put into slightly different terms—a myth which, as has been suggested, was probably afterward appropriated by Marduk.[1] It was probably this genesis of Nabu and his association with Ea, the god of wisdom, which afterward made Nabu the god of learning and wisdom to the Babylonians and Assyrians.

Nabu does not appear in extant inscriptions till the time of Khammurabi,[2] and Jastrow supposes that that monarch tried to suppress his worship in favor of that of Marduk.[3] The date of his appearance and his functions as god of fertility and wisdom all point to such an origin as has here been supposed.[4] His consort Tashmit is of still later origin, and is clearly only a feminine counterpart of Nabu. Her name means "hearing" or "revelation," and is derived from Nabu's function as god of wisdom. Her origin is therefore quite parallel to that of Damkina from Ea.

The worship of the god Shamash, as we know it from the inscriptions, was the native religion of two cities of ancient Babylonia, Larsa and Agade, or Sippar. Of the details of this worship in either city we know very little. At Larsa, Ur-Gur, king of Ur about 2500 B.C., repaired the temple of Shamash,[5] as did also Khammurabi of Babylon some two hundred years later.[6] The latter calls the Sha-

---

[1] Above, p. 209.
[2] *KB.*, Vol. III¹, p. 123.
[3] See Jastrow's *Religion of Babylonia and Assyria*, p. 125 ff.
[4] Jensen's endeavor to make Nabu a sun god (*Kosmologie*, p. 239) certainly does not explain all the functions ascribed to him. The goddess Erua, whom Sayce (*Hibbert Lectures*, p. 111 ff.) connects with Sarpanit and Tashmit, and whom Jastrow (*op. cit.*, p. 130) supposes to be the older consort of Nabu, is probably the goddess Dumuzizuab under another name.
[5] Cf. I R., No. 7 ; also *KB.*, Vol. III¹, p. 79.
[6] See King's *Letters and Inscriptions of Hammurabi*, No. 62.

mash of Larsa "lord of heaven and earth" and "shepherd"[1] — expressions also used of the other Shamash. It is hard to say whether the worship at Larsa or at Agade is the older. If, as Jastrow supposes,[2] antiquity and fame went hand in hand in Babylonia, he is right in the view that the palm of antiquity should be ascribed to Agade. In this latter city we find the worship of Shamash and Ishtar side by side in the inscriptions of Sargon of Agade, about 3800 B.C.[3] At that early time the worship of Shamash had begun to overshadow somewhat the worship of Ishtar, for we find Sargon making offerings and appeals to him in which the goddess is not included.[4]

A very archaic tablet in the E. A. Hoffmann collection at the General Theological Seminary in New York, which records the gift of a field to a deity, which has not yet been identified, speaks of Shamash as "the lady who pours forth brightness, the mistress." There is nothing in the tablet except a sign which is still unidentified to indicate whence the tablet comes; we cannot tell, therefore, whether it refers to the Shamash of Agade or of Larsa. If, however, I interpret it correctly (a matter of some doubt in the case of writing as old as any yet discovered), it not only records a time when Shamash was a goddess, but shows that even then another deity, which is possibly Ishtar, was worshipped beside her.[5] Analogy makes it probable that Shamash was

[1] Cf. King, *ibid.*, l. 2.   [2] *Religion of Babylonia and Assyria*, p. 70.
[3] Cf. Hilprecht's *OBI.*, No. 1, and Radau, *op. cit.*, p. 167 ff.
[4] Cf. *PSBA.*, Vol. VII, p. 66, and *KB.*, Vol. III¹, pp. 100, 101; also Hilprecht, *OBI.*, No. 2, and Radau, *op. cit.*, p. 170.
[5] The inscription which is unpublished I interpret as follows: —
Col. I, 1. IIIMV GANA DUK-KA DINGIR ?-KI LAG
2. SAL-LAL-TUR
Col. II, 1. IIIMVICL URTU-NI-A SIG LIK-A
2. IIIMVICL ĞAL PI NER-A DA-KU GUR DIMMENA BABBAR NIN-A TAB BAR UMUN(?)
[I, 1.] "3005 Bur of a field, (a bed) of clay(?), to the god of ? presented [2.] Sallaltur. [II, 1.] 36,050 cubits in its Akkadward side, the lower (side), from the beginning; [2.] 36,050 cubits running along the breadth of the ziggurat to the side of the great terrace of Shamash, the lady, who pours forth brightness, the mistress(?)." [Continued on p. 214.]

here a goddess beside whom Ishtar was worshipped. Whether Shamash was a Sumerian goddess and Ishtar a Semitic, we have no means of determining. Shamash may have been an epithet of Ishtar which hardened, as epithets so often did afterward, into a separate deity; or two tribes, a Semitic and a Sumerian, may have composed the community from which our inscription comes, and Shamash may have been a Sumerian corn goddess, though this latter supposition is not probable. However this may be, Shamash in later times was always a god. Perhaps the Semitic settlement at Agade was very old, or the foreign influence there was very strong. At all events, by the time of Sargon of Agade, about 3800 B.C., Shamash was a masculine deity. Although Ishtar appears by his side in some of the inscriptions of Sargon,[1] yet he could invoke Shamash without mentioning her. Probably, therefore, Shamash was a Semitic deity. The fact that we have found the worship of Shamash at Shirpurla, also a Semitic community, points in the same direction.[2]

At times his worship so overshadowed that of the goddess that Khammurabi as well as Sargon mentions Shamash alone,[3] but an old hymn, in which the goddess is called Malkatu,[4] shows us the worship of the two in con-

Col. III, 1. IIIMVIC E BABBAR LUǴ AB TAB BAR
2. IIIMVICL BURU KUR IR(?) DU(?) BAD
3. LIK-A GAR-A
4. GIR(?) ŠAG(?)

III, 1. "36,000 cubits (along) the temple of Shamash, the messenger of the father who pours forth brightness (*i.e.* Sin); ². 36,050 cubits below(?) the mountain where the abode(?) of Ishtar (??) is, ³. to the beginning; for making brick. ⁴. May he strengthen, may he bless!"

[1] Cf. *OBI.*, No. 1, and Radau, *op. cit.*, 168, 169.

[2] See, for example, Eannadu in De Sarzec's *Découvertes*, pl. 4, *bis*, col. VII, ll. 7, 8.

[3] See *KB.*, Vol. III¹, pp. 106–125, and Radau, *op. cit.*, p. 169 ff.

[4] See Haupt's *ASKT.*, p. 122 ff. For translations, Zimmern's *Babylonische Busspsalmen*, p. 51 ff., and *Hebraica*, Vol. X, p. 24 ff. On the application of the name Malkatu to the goddess, see Schrader's article in *ZA.*, Vol. III, p. 353 ff.

junction, and in the inscriptions of Nabonidos we see them at the close of Babylonian history reigning as a united pair.[1] Between these extremes various modifications may have taken place. One of them we can trace. In the inscription of Nabu-apal-iddin (about 880 B.C.), Malik and Bunini[2] appear to be the attendants of Shamash, who rules above and apart from them. Here Malik was no doubt originally an epithet of Shamash, while Bunini is perhaps another name for Ishtar.

Ishtar at Agade probably never quite lost her identity in Shamash,[3] although at times she could be ignored. It was perhaps this goddess to whom the name Nin-Akkad, or "Lady of Accad," is given in an old list of deities,[4] though it is possible that that title is a survival from the time when "Lady" was an epithet of Shamash.

Not far east of Babylon, where the modern mound of Tell-Ibrahim now is, lay the ancient city of Gudua or Kutu[5] (Kutha), of which the tutelary deity was Nergal.[6] His principal temple was called Eshidlam. How old the city was we have no means of knowing. The worship of Nergal first comes to light in the inscriptions of Dungi, king of Ur about 2450 B.C., who repaired his temple.[7] The god was then known as Shidlam-ta-e-a,[8] or "the god who goes forth from Eshidlam," a name which appears later in the *ašipu* texts published by Zimmern.[9] The

---

[1] Cf. V R., 65, col. i, l. 35 (also *KB.*, Vol. III², pp. 110, 111), and col. ii, l. 12 (*KB.* as above, pp. 112, 113); also V R. 61, col. i, ll. 7 and 46; col. ii, ll. 5 and 40 (cf. *Hebraica*, Vol. X, p. 25).

[2] Cf. V R., 60, *KB.*, Vol. III¹, pp. 174–183, and Jastrow's *Religion of Babylonia and Assyria*, p. 176 ff.

[3] See the evidence collected in *Hebraica*, Vol. X, pp. 24, 25.

[4] See III R., 66, col. iii, l. 26, rev. col. v, ll. 27, 35.

[5] See Delitzsch's *Wo lag das Paradies ?* p. 218.

[6] Cf. II R. 61, col. ii, l. 53, and 2 Kgs. 17³⁰.

[7] *CTBM.*, Pt. IX, No. 35389, and *KB.*, Vol. III¹, pp. 80, 81.

[8] Cf. Brünnow, *List*, No. 7873.

[9] Cf. his *Beiträge zur Kentniss der babylonischen Religion*, pp. 149, 151, 159, 165, 169, and the corresponding plates of cuneiform text.

temple was also repaired at another time by Sin-gamil, another king of Ur.[1]

When Nergal appears in the syncretistic pantheons of later times, he had been assigned the twofold function of god of the underworld and the god of death-bringing war and pestilence.[2] Jensen,[3] who is followed by Jastrow,[4] believes that Nergal was originally a god of the glowing flame of the sun, and that his destructive functions are to be attributed to that fact. As the god of destruction, they hold that he became the god of the underworld.

It may well be doubted whether this view will satisfactorily explain all the facts. The solar explanation of deities which are ancient are, I believe, never able to lead us to the most primitive character of the god. Men thought of objects on the earth, and identified their gods with them before they thought of identifying them with anything in the far-off sky. If Nergal was the deity of Kutha in that early time when each city was independent and had its own god, it is certainly unlikely that they then identified him with the glowing heat of the sun. It is much more probable that he was then an agricultural god, a deity of the soil and the giver of fertility. When the gods of the various cities were grouped in a pantheon, Enlil of Nippur, who was also a god of the soil, took precedence of Nergal, no doubt because Nippur was a more powerful city. Nergal could of course not be assigned the same functions, but was still connected with the earth, though limited in his sphere by being assigned to the underworld. As lord of the region of the dead he would naturally be conceived as eager to people his realm, and so become in time the god of war and pestilence — forces which cause death. This might naturally lead also to his identification with the glowing heat of the sun. We thus,

---

[1] *KB.*, Vol. III¹, pp. 84, 85.
[2] IV R. 26, No. 1.
[3] *Kosmologie*, pp. 476–487.
[4] *Religion of Babylonia and Assyria*, p. 66 ff.

I believe, have a genesis for Nergal more probable than that suggested by Jensen.

So far as appears Nergal was a Sumerian god. There is no trace, in the scanty information concerning him which has come down to us, of the peculiar characteristics of fertility which attach to all the chief Semitic deities. Delitzsch long ago called Kutha one of the oldest centres of Sumerian civilization,[1] and that still seems the more probable view. This old Sumerian agricultural god was adopted by the Semites and assigned a place in their pantheon as the god of the underworld.[2] The etymology of his name is uncertain.[3]

Another people whose home lay to the eastward of Babylon across the Tigris were the Guti, sometimes called the Suti.[4] A Semitic king of this country has left us an inscription which dates from 3800 B.C. or earlier.[5] In this inscription the monarch invokes the deities, Guti, Ishtar, and Sin. From what we have already learned of the god Sin and the religious syncretism of this period, it is clear that this deity was not native to the Guti. Of the other two, Ishtar is of course our old Semitic goddess. From a list of Babylonian deities which comes to us from the library of Assurbanipal,[6] we learn that the worship of Ishtar was maintained here in much of its primitive purity down to a much later time. In our extant inscriptions the god Guti does not, so far as I have observed, appear again. This one glimpse of him makes upon one the

[1] *Paradies*, p. 217.

[2] By the transportation of Kutheans to Palestine by Sargon (2 Kgs. 17$^{24\text{-}34}$), the worship of Nergal was introduced among the western Semites. It seems to have spread from Samaria to Sidon, and thence was carried by Sidonian emigrants to Athens. See *CIS.*, Pt. I, Vol. I, No. 119.

[3] See Jensen and Jastrow as cited above.

[4] Cf. Delitzsch, *Paradies*, pp. 233-237.

[5] Cf. Winckler, *ZA.*, Vol. IV, p. 406 ; Hilprecht, *OBI.*, p. 12 ff.; Radau, *Early Babylonian History*, p. 175 ff., and Rogers, *History of Babylonia and Assyria*, Vol. I, p. 359 ff.

[6] III R. 66, reverse col. vi, ll. 18-26. Cf. translation and comments in *Hebraica*, Vol. X, p. 26 ff.

impression that he was probably the pre-Semitic god of the country Guti, who had been adopted by the Semitic immigrants in accord with conceptions with which we are already familiar, and associated with their goddess.

Another of the petty states of ancient Babylonia of the god of which we get a glimpse in the inscriptions is Gishban, a place which as Thureau Dangin has shown lay just north of the Shatt-el-Khai.[1] We learn from the inscription of Lugalzaggisi that the chief god of this place was represented in writing by the two signs ŠI-ELTEG(?), which mean "the one who pours forth grain,"[2] but which a much later tablet defines as Nidaba.[3] The emblem of Nidaba was the waving grain; for in the Gilgamish epic, the unkempt hair of the wild man, Eabani, is said to have grown as luxuriously as Nidaba.[4] We know, therefore, that this deity was an agricultural deity, and a giver of fertility. Lugalzaggisi, whom Hilprecht believes to be a Semite because of Semitisms in his inscription,[5] calls himself a son brought up by this deity. There is no direct evidence in the inscription as to whether Nidaba was masculine or feminine, but grain deities are so often feminine, that whether Gishban was a Semitic settlement or not, it is probable that Nidaba was a goddess or developed out of a goddess. The culture either of Arabia or of Mesopotamia might, so far as we can tell, have produced this deity. We must leave the origin of this goddess, therefore, to be determined when further inscriptions have arisen from the dust to throw light on her character.

The origin of the god Anu is shrouded in great obscurity. From the time of Gudea[6] onward, and probably

---

[1] See *Comptes rendus de l'academie des inscriptions et belles-lettres*, Vol. XXIV, (1896), p. 593 ff. and *Revue d'assyriologie*, Vol. IV, p. 41.

[2] See Brünnow's *List*, Nos. 7433 and 4447.

[3] Brünnow, *op. cit.*, No. 7453.

[4] Haupt, *Nimrodepos*, p. 8, l. 37; cf. Jensen in *KB.*, Vol. VI, p. 121, who renders Nidaba by *Weizen* "Wheat."

[5] *OBI.*, Pt. II, p. 55.

[6] See Statute B (De Sarzec, *Découvertes*, pls. 16-20), col. viii, l. 45 ff., and *KB.*, Vol. III¹, p. 46, 47.

from the time of Anu-banini,[1] some eight hundred years before Gudea, Anu in theory stood at the head of the Babylonian pantheon. We are, however, unable to connect his name with any city the political importance of which would help to give him this commanding position. We learn from an inscription of Nebuchadnezzar I [2] (about 1130 B.C.) that the city Der, situated on the Tigris,[3] was a city of Anu; but this city plays no part, so far as we know, in early Babylonian history, and the god can hardly have been placed at the head of the pantheon in consequence of its importance. It is probable, as Jastrow has suggested,[4] that he was given this position as the result of those abstract and more scholastic conceptions which resulted in the formation of the first triad, Anu, Bel, and Ea, the gods of heaven, earth, and the deep, of which the god of heaven, Anu, naturally took the first place. Jastrow supports this view by the supposition that the heavens were not really personified as a god till about the time of Khammurabi. He reaches this conclusion in part because of the fact that in passages which are often interpreted as referring to Anu the determinative for god is not prefixed to the name of the deity.

This latter fact does not necessarily support the view in question, but is open to another explanation. The name Anu was written by the sign *an* with a phonetic complement. *An* had also as a determinative the value *dingir* (*ilu*), and was placed before the names of gods. When repeated it stood for the plural "gods." To write it twice for the name of Anu would suggest to the reader a plural, and tend to create confusion; it may have been omitted from the name of Anu for this reason. It is true

[1] See *Recueil de traveaux*, Vol. XIV, pp. 100-106, and Radau, *Early Babylonian History*, p. 177 ff.
[2] See Hilprecht's *Freibrief Nebuchadnezzars I*, l. 14, and Peiser in *KB.*, Vol. III[1], pp. 164, 165.
[3] Hilprecht, *OBI.*, No. 83, l. 2, *Assyriaca*, pp. 10, 11, and Peiser, *KB.*, Vol. IV, pp. 64, 65.
[4] *Religion of Babylonia and Assyria*, p. 89 ff.

that in a number of passages in Lugalzaggisi, Gudea, etc.,[1] it is possible to translate the sign as an adjective as Jastrow would, but in the inscription of the king of Lulubi, who, before 3800 B.C., erected an inscribed stele in the mountains near the modern town of Zohab,[2] such is not the case. Anu and Anat were then already deities at the head of Anu-banini's pantheon.[3] Not only so, but the king bears the name Anu-banini ("Anu is our begetter"), a name which suggests that some chthonic god of fertility — a god originally connected with some tribe or place — had been identified with the heavenly expanse, so that an earthly history really lay back of this celestial deity.

The name of the Semitic king, together with the fact that Anu and Anat stand at the head of his pantheon, suggests the view that this pair may have been developed out of an Ishtar at Lulubi, as Ea and Damkina were at Eridu. This hypothesis cannot, in consequence of the scantiness of our present information, be either proved or disproved. It is also possible that Anu may have been some pre-Semitic god of Lulubi, whose worship the Semites had adopted on coming to the country; but if so, they had probably merged the cult of their own goddess with him till she became Anat, so that by the time of Lulubi the history of Anu and Anat was parallel to that of Enlil and Ninlil at Nippur. It is at all events probable that Anu resulted from the identification of an earthly deity with the sky, and was at the first no more of an abstraction than Sin and Shamash were.

[1] See Hilprecht, *OBI.*, No. 87, col. i, l. 5; De Sarzec, *Découvertes*, pl. 13, Nos. 1, 2, col. i, l. 3; col. ii, l. 15; and pl. 13, No. 4, col. i, l. 3. See also Thureau Dangin in *Rev. semitique*, Vol. V, p. 269; Amiaud in *Rec. of Past*, New Series, Vol. II, pp. 92, 93, and 103; also Radau, *op. cit.*, pp. 152, 202, 204, 209, 257, 267, 280, and 281. The determinative is not infrequently omitted, however, before the names of deities, especially in the older inscriptions.

[2] Rogers, *History of Babylonia and Assyria*, Vol. I, p. 360 ff., and Radau, *op. cit.*, p. 177 ff.

[3] It is impossible in this inscription to translate in any other way than as the name of a god.

It seems clear from the preceding discussion that the application of our economic-religious test to the gods of Babylonia sheds a little light on what was Semitic in ancient Babylonia, and what may with plausibility be claimed as non-Semitic. The test cannot at present be applied throughout in consequence of the fragmentary character of the material, nor is it a test which will in all cases yield perfectly definite results. It is one, notwithstanding, which should be applied conjointly with linguistic tests, and in the mixed problem of Babylonian origins it proves its worth. If it leads us at times to determine the boundaries of nationality somewhat differently than we should from linguistic evidence alone, that is only a tribute to its value.

About the middle of the nineteenth century B.C. the written records of the Assyrian people whose home lay to the north of Babylon begin. This kingdom was primarily the dominion of the city of Ashur. The Assyrian empire, like the Roman, resulted from the dominion of a single city. This city was the city of the god Ashur, who thus became the national god of the Assyrians.[1] The Assyrian was even more than most of the empires of antiquity a well-organized fighting machine, and, as all the statements about Ashur occur in inscriptions written after the era of conquest began, they necessarily represent Ashur as a god of war.[2] As a local deity he must originally have possessed all the functions of a local god, among which would be in an agricultural community those of fertility. Some recollection of this has survived in the language of Assurbanipal, who calls himself the offspring of Ashur and

[1] The name of the city Ashur appears originally to have been derived from the name of the god. This is not so strange as Jastrow (*op. cit.*, p. 196) thinks. The same was true of Ninâ (see above, p. 155 ff.), and probably Nineveh (see below). Eridu, Ur, and Nippur are represented by the same ideograms as Ea, Sin, and Enlil, showing that at some time the names of these gods and their cities were the same.

[2] For a statement of this phase of Ashur, see Jastrow's *Religion of Babylonia and Assyria*, p. 193 ff.

Ishtar.¹ With him the expression was perhaps somewhat figurative, but it points to a primitive conception of these gods similar to that underlying Târab Riyam and Shams in south Arabia, whose worshippers regarded them as their parents.²

Ashur was, so far as appears, a purely Semitic town, and although there existed in it a temple of Anu and Ramman³ which was built before our written records begin, the worship of these gods must have been a later importation than the worship of that deity for whom the city was named. The god Ashur cannot be connected with either of these since he is never connected with any of the elemental powers of nature. Nineveh and Arbela were founded by Semites who brought with them the worship of some form of the goddess Ishtar,⁴ and while Ashur is probably older than either of them, it is probable that the immigrants who founded it did the same. Haupt suggested some years ago that the name Ishtar was derived from the name Ashur.⁵ This view we have found it impossible to accept, but it is possible that the reverse may be true, and the name Ashur be derived from Ishtar. In Assyrian the ʿAyin and ʾAleph were both so weakened as to be at times indistinguishable, so that it only remained to assimilate the *t* to the preceding *sh* to transform the name of the goddess into that of the god.⁶

---

¹ V R., 1, 1. Cf. *KB.*, Vol. II., pp. 152, 153.
² See above, p. 130.
³ I R., 15, 60 ff.; cf. *KB.*, Vol. I, pp. 42, 43.
⁴ See below, Chapter VI.   ⁵ See above, p. 103, n. 2.
⁶ Such assimilation of a *t* to a preceding *š* is not infrequent in the common speech of the Babylonians and Assyrians (cf. Delitzsch, *Assyr. Gram.* § 51, 2). The *š* was in such cases usually changed to *s*, but in the name Ishtar other phonetic laws of the Babylonians and Assyrians suffer variation, *e.g.*, *š* before a dental is usually changed to *l*, but in the name Ishtar the *š* always held its place. The *šš* in *Aššur*, if real, may be a similar exception. It is not certain that it is real, however. If the view of Tiele and Muss-Arnolt (p. 223, n. 1), represents as assumed below a folk interpretation of a later time, the writing of the name may have been changed from *Assur* to *Aššur* in the state inscriptions in accordance with

Tiele[1] and Muss-Arnolt would connect the name with the root *a-sh-r* which occurs both in Hebrew and Assyrian in the sense of "be gracious, bless, cause to prosper." Although this view is supported by the fact that the name of the god is written by an ideogram which means good, it is probable as Jastrow[2] suggests that he was called the "good" as a mere epithet. It is most probable that the epithet was applied to Ashur by a folk etymology, which made a play upon the name as is so often done with Old Testament names and as was done at Babylon in the case of Sarpanit. If so, this view is really an argument in favor of another origin of Ashur. Possible as I consider these etymologies to be, Hommel has suggested one[3] which must be regarded as far more probable. He takes the name like the Assyrio-Babylonian word for sanctuary (*ashirtu*), to be derived from the old '*asheras* or posts which marked the boundaries of Semitic sanctuaries. In several parts of the Semitic world the name of the post was transferred to the goddess,[4] and in one other case the goddess was in all probability transformed into a god. Such really seems to have been the course of events in Assyria. This view is supported by the fact that Khammurabi seems to have known such a goddess,[5] and it affords a simple and satisfactory etymology for Ashur.

The general development of purely Semitic deities from the primitive mother goddess as a starting-point establishes a strong probability that Ashur was a transformed Ishtar. In favor of this view is the fact that there is but

this interpretation. That the speech of the people was not always in similar cases represented in the writing Delitzsch admits (*Gram.* p. 119). I regard another origin, however, as far more probable. For another folk interpretation of the name see below, p. 224, n. 3.

[1] *Babylonisch-Assyrische Geschichte*, p. 533. So Muss-Arnolt *Handwörterbuch*, p. 118.

[2] *Religion of Babylonia and Assyria*, p. 196 ff.

[3] *Aufsätze und Abhandlungen*, Vol. II, p. 209.

[4] See below Chapter VI.

[5] Cf. King's *Letters and Inscriptions of Hammurabi*, No. 66.

one trace of an Ishtar of the city of Ashur, and that is a very late one, capable of another interpretation. Assurbanipal speaks of "Ishtar the Assyrian,"[1] but in reality he probably refers to the goddess of Nineveh, who had by his time long been associated with the god Ashur. Nineveh was a part of the Assyrian dominion long before the earliest of our extant inscriptions, and it is probable that the worship of its goddess had been united with that of Ashur, so that Raman-nirari I and Tiglath-pileser I, when they refer to Ishtar, mean the goddess of Nineveh.[2]

Probably, therefore, the original goddess of the city of Ashur was transformed into a god before the dawn of the historical period, and after Nineveh had been conquered its goddess became, through the operation of those laws of syncretism with which we are already so familiar, the spouse of the god Ashur.[3] The deity whose worship next to that of Ishtar was most widely extended over the Semitic world was the god known in Assyria as Ramman and among the Aramæans as Hadad (in cuneiform Addu), or Rimmon. The most widely recognized function of this god caused him to be regarded as the god of thunder, lightning, wind, and storm, though as we shall see other attributes were not lacking in the minds of some of his worshippers.

---

[1] V R., 1, 65 ff.; cf. *KB.*, Vol. II, pp. 158, 159, and *Hebraica*, Vol. IX, pp. 156, 157.

[2] This point was not clear to me when the article on the "Ishtar Cult" was written. The classification of the Assyrian material adopted in that article (*Hebraica*, Vol. IX, p. 131) was I now think a mistake. Its results were not very far-reaching, as it only led to the assignment of four or five allusions to the city of Assur which belonged to Nineveh.

[3] It seems probable as Jensen and others have suggested (see Jensen, *Kosmologie*, p. 275, and *ZA.*, Vol. I, p. 1 ff.; Delitzsch, *Weltschöpfungsepos*, p. 94; and Jastrow, *op. cit.*, p. 197), that the god *Anshar* who plays a prominent part in our present version of the Babylonian creation epic is intended for the god Ashur, and is introduced as a compliment to Assyria, *An-shar* being a dissimilation of *Aššur*. If this be true, however, it probably does not help us with the real etymology of the name *Ashur*, but is a folk etymology similar to the one discussed above, p. 223 and 222, n. 4.

The name by which this deity was known in the older Babylonian period is in dispute.¹ His name is written by the ideogram IM, and Thureau Dangin may be right in holding that in the oldest period it was pronounced "Immeru."² However this may be, he was certainly called by the Assyrians Ramman. Material recently made accessible to scholars makes it clear that the worship of this god is of great antiquity in Babylonia. We do not know in what locality his worship first originated, but he was invoked by Anu-banini before 3800 B.C.,³ and is coupled by that monarch with the goddess Ishtar. The same god also appears as a deity of popular worship on tablets of the time of Bur-Sin, king of Ur.⁴ He must therefore have had a long career in Babylonia before the time of Khammurabi, although the material so far recovered does not enable us to trace it. All that we know of his nature in this early time is that the ideogram IM, "wind," indicates that he was connected in some way with the weather. By Khammurabi he was worshipped, and was associated with Shamash.⁵ Shamsu-iluna built a fortress or town to him.⁶ Later in the Kassite period he became very popular, and several of the kings bore names which ascribed honor to him. At this time a second triad of gods appears, composed of Sin, Shamash, and Ramman.⁷

[1] That he was called by several names appears from the tablet published by Bezold, *PSBA.*, Vol. XI, pp. 173, 174, and pl. 1. For discussions as to the name, see Hilprecht, *Assyriaca*, p. 76 ff.; Oppert, *Comptes rendus de l'academie des inscriptions et belles-lettres*, June, 1893; *Jour. asiatique*, 1895, pp. 393–396, and *ZA.*, Vol. IX, pp. 310–314; Thureau Dangin, *Jour. asiatique*, 1895, pp. 385–393; Jastrow, *AJSL.*, Vol. XII, pp. 159–162; and *Religion of Babylonia and Assyria*, p. 156 ff.

[2] He was also called Mer in Babylonia and Bir in Syria. Cf. Hilprecht, *Assyriaca*, p. 77 ff.

[3] See *Recueil de traveaux*, Vol. XIV, pp. 100–106, and Radau, *Early Babylonian History*, p. 177.

[4] Cf. Radau, *op. cit.*, pp. 327, 353, l. 33 ; 427, l. 6, and 429.

[5] Cf. *KB.*, Vol. III¹, pp. 112, 113.

[6] *KB.*, Vol. III¹, pp. 132, 133.

[7] See any list of the kings of the third Babylonian dynasty, and Belser in *BA.*, Vol. II, p. 201, col. vi, l. 3.

In Assyria the worship of Ramman goes back to prehistoric times,[1] and he was very popular in the historic period as the god of storm, lightning, and thunder, who helped to overthrow the enemies of his worshippers.[2] Tiglath-pileser I once refers to him as the god of the "west country,"[3] which shows that he identified him with the Aramæan deity. It is hardly probable that Ramman was born on Assyrian soil. It is more probable that his worship was carried thither by Babylonian or Aramæan immigrants, preferably the former.

In the El-Amarna letters from Syria and Palestine the ideogram IM is used to represent the name of a Syrian god, which is at times spelled syllabically as *Ad-di*,[4] and once as *Ha-da-di*.[5] The same writing occurs centuries later in a contract written in Babylonia for an Aramæan immigrant.[6] These passages equate the Syrian god Hadad with the Babylonian-Assyrian god Ramman. The equation was a most natural one to make, as the names Ramman and Hadad both appear to have meant "Thunderer."[7]

The worship of this god in Damascus is known to us through the Old Testament, where his name usually appears as Hadad,[8] but once a corruption of the Assyrian form occurs as Rimmon.[9] It appears from the obelisk

---

[1] I R., 15, 71 ff. Cf. *KB.*, Vol. I, pp. 42, 43.

[2] Cf. Tiglath-pileser I in I R., 9, 9 ff. and 78 ff.; also *KB.*, Vol. I, pp. 16-19. Assurnasirpal exhibits the popularity of Ramman by calling him "The mightiest of the gods" (*KB.*, Vol. I, pp. 116-117).

[3] I R., 14, 87; *KB.*, Vol. I, pp. 38, 39.

[4] Cf. *KB.*, Vol. V, Nos. 33^3, 104^1, and 85^1. The name is written by Assurbanipal *Da-ad-da* (V R., 9, 2; cf. *KB.*, Vol. II, pp. 222, 223).

[5] *KB.*, Vol. V, No. 88^1.

[6] See *TSBA.*, Vol. VIII, p. 282 ff., and Sp. 41; also Strassmaier's *Nabonidos*, No. 356.

[7] For "Ramman" cf. Delitzsch, *HWB.*, p. 624, and Jastrow in *AJSL.*, p. 160 ff.; for "Hadad" cf. Buhl in Gesenius's *Handwörterbuch*, 13th ed., p. 191; the Brown-Robinson-Gesenius *Lexicon*, p. 212, and Hoffmann, *ZA.*, Vol. XI, p. 227.

[8] See 1 Kgs. $15^{18, 20}$, 20^{passim}, and 2 Kgs., $6^{24, etc.}$, where it appears as the divine element in the name of the king of Damascus.

[9] 2 Kgs. 5^{18}. Cf. Baudissin's discussion, *Studien zur semitischen Religionsgeschichte*, Vol. I, 308 ff.

inscription of Shalmeneser that he was also known as
"Bir."[1] He seems to have been the chief deity of Damascus, as well as of the Aramæans generally.[2] Two
passages in the El-Amarna letters prove that he was regarded in Assyria as the majestic thunderer who overwhelmed enemies.[3] His worship would seem to have been
carried in this period to several places in Palestine by
Aramæan immigrants, where in after centuries places
bearing the name of "Rimmon" attest the fact that the
worship of a deity bearing that name had once held sway.[4]

The excavations at Zendchirli, in the extreme north of
Syria, have brought to light the statue of the god Hadad,
together with an inscription partly in his praise written
by a king of the eighth century B.C. His worship would
seem to have extended wherever Aramæans went. In
their migrations they carried it to Babylonia, as already
noted, and the name of the god has been found in an Aramaic inscription as far south as Telloh.[5] In Egypt it has
been found in the vicinity of Memphis,[6] while the worship
penetrated north Arabia at Hegra,[7] and into south Arabia,[8] where the god was known as Rimmon; while as the
cult of Hadad it is also found in both the northern and
southern parts of that peninsula.[9]

To determine the origin of such a god from the general
point of view of our preceding discussion would seem at
first glance a difficult matter. The disciples of Max Müller, who take every deity for the personification of some

[1] See Abel and Winckler's *Keilschrifttexte*, p. 8, l. 59, and p. 9, l. 88;
also Hilprecht, *Assyriaca*, p. 77.
[2] See the name of the king of Zobah in 2 Sam. 8[3, etc.]
[3] *KB.*, Vol. V, Nos. 149[14] and 150[7].
[4] Josh. 15[32], Jud. 20[47], 21[18], and Zech. 12[11].
[5] *CIS.*, Pt. II, Vol. I, No. 72.
[6] *CIS.*, Pt. II, Vol. I, No. 124.
[7] *CIS.*, Pt. II, Vol. I, No. 117.
[8] Cf. Glaser's *Die Abessinier in Arabien und Afrika*, p. 105.
[9] See Halévy, *Melanges de critique*, p. 424; *Revue semitique*, Vol. II,
p. 21; Winckler, *Untersuchungen*, p. 69, n.; Nöldeke, *ZDMG.*, Vol. XLI,
p. 712; and Wellhausen, *Reste arab. Heidentums*, 2d ed., p. 55.

natural element, might be thought to have here a clear case of a pure and simple storm god.

There are not lacking, nevertheless, conceptions connected with this god which such a theory is powerless to explain. The name of an Old Testament city, Ain-Rimmon, or "Fountain of Rimmon,"[1] proves that the god was once connected with a spring, while the request which Naaman made of Elisha concerning Yahwe[2] suggests that he was accustomed to connect his own god, Rimmon, with the soil. Panamu of Zendchirli also calls Hadad "Baal of water,"[3] which shows that he regarded him as a Semitic Baal. The proper name, Ben-Hadad-nathan, or "Hadad has created a son,"[4] of which the Biblical name Ben-Hadad is an abbreviation,[5] proves him to have been connected with animal fertility as well as vegetable productiveness. It would thus seem that Hadad had been an earthly Baal before he became the god of storms and thunder. Jastrow has pointed out[6] that in Assyria Ramman was at times identified with Shamash, who was a god of fertility, so that it is probable that a similar earthly history lay back of him there.[7] This is rendered practically certain by an old Babylonian hymn, which calls Ramman "lord of wells."[8]

[1] Josh. 15^{32}. Cf. recent commentaries.
[2] 2 Kgs. 5^{17}.
[3] *Konigliche Museen zu Berlin,* — *Mittheilungen aus dem orientalischen Sammlungen,* Heft XI, Taf. vii, l. 1, or Lidzbarski's *Handbuch der nordsemitische Epigraphik,* Taf. xxii, l. 1. Cf. Cook's *Glossary of Aramaic Inscriptions,* p. 32.
[4] See references, p. 226, n. 6.
[5] This fact was not clear to me in 1895; cf. *JBL.,* Vol. XV, p. 175.
[6] *Religion of Babylonia and Assyria,* p. 211.
[7] This view receives some corroboration from the fact that in one of the old hymns published by Reisner (Berlin, *Mittheilungen,* Heft X, p. 23, l. 10; cf. Banks's *Sum.-Bab. Hymnen,* p. 25), Ramman is described as a wild ox. The bull as already noted is a symbol of the gods of fertility in agricultural communities, and if Ramman had once been such a god, it would be very natural when he had become the destructive god of storms to change the domestic ox which symbolized him into a wild ox.
[8] Translated by Sayce, *Hibbert Lectures,* p. 530 ff.

Indeed, the steps by which a god of the soil — a giver of grain — became a storm god are very clear. As the god of fertility he was naturally the giver of rain, and as the god of rain he would become the god of thunder and lightning. When, as in Babylonia and Assyria political union caused the formation of the gods into a pantheon, the more active functions of production were thought to be presided over by other gods, the rain god would in time be associated with the more violent manifestations of his power, and become the god of storm and destruction.

If then a god of fertility — a Baal — were a stage in the development of Ramman-Hadad, it is highly probable in view of the many cases of transformation which have been already traced that this Baal was in turn a metamorphosis of the primitive goddess of fertility. Thus the evolution of the storm god probably followed the same course as that taken by other Semitic deities.

This evolution probably went on independently in Babylonia and among the Aramæans.[1] The god worshipped by Anu-banini 3800 B.C. can hardly have been affected by Aramaic influence, and we have no reason to suppose that Babylonian influence seriously affected the development of Hadad. In Assyria two waves of his worship meet and unite, — one from Babylonia and one from the West.

The worship of the god Dagan like that of Ramman is found in both the East and the West, — in Babylonia and Assyria on the one hand and in Palestine on the other. It is found about 2500 B.C. in the name of a prince of Nippur,[2] and on a tablet from the time of the sovereignty of Ur which is perhaps earlier still.[3] It also appears in an inscription of Khammurabi.[4] In Assyria the cult

---

[1] Of course in Babylonia some Sumerian influences may have hastened the process of evolution.
[2] I R., 2, No. 5; *KB.*, Vol. III, pp. 86, 87.
[3] Radau, *Early Babylonian History*, p. 261.
[4] Schrader, *KAT.*², p. 181.

seems to have been established before the written records of that country begin, for we find it as an element in a proper name at the very dawn of history.[1] Dagan seems to have been worshipped in Assyria down to the eighth century B.C. as the inscriptions of Assurnasirpal, Shamshi-Ramman, and Sargon show.[2] According to the Hebrew version of Tobit it continued till the time of Sennacherib,[3] but this cannot be regarded as reliable evidence.

The El-Amarna letters attest the presence of Dagan in Palestine in the fifteenth century B.C.,[4] while we learn from the Old Testament that he was the god of Gaza[5] and Ashdod,[6] and the inscriptions of Sennacherib make it probable that he was the god of the Philistines generally.[7] He appears also to have been once worshipped near Nablus[8] and in the neighborhood of Jericho.[9]

Various theories of the origin and nature of Dagan have been propounded. Rashi advanced the idea that his name was derived from the Hebrew *dag*, fish, and that Dagon was a fish god.[10] In recent times attempts have been made to strengthen this view by comparing the Babylonian pictures of the fish god Ea, but the compari-

---

[1] *KB.*, Vol. I, pp. 42, 43; *ZA.*, Vol. V, p. 79, and *Hebraica*, Vol. IX, p. 132.

[2] See references in Jensen's *Kosmologie*, p. 452.

[3] See Neubauer's edition, p. 20.

[4] Cf. the name Dagan-takala in *KB.*, Vol. V, Nos. 215, 216.

[5] Jud. 16^{23}.

[6] 2 Sam. 5$^{2\,\text{ff.}}$; 1 Macc., 10$^{83.\,84}$, 11^4, and Josephus, *Antiquities*, xiii, 4^5.

[7] *KB.*, Vol. II, pp. 92, 93; cf. Schrader, *KAT.*^{2}, p. 181; and Delitzsch, *Paradies*, p. 289.

[8] See *Bait Dejan* on Pal. Expl. Funds, map seven miles east of Nablus, and G. A Smith's *Historical Geography*, p. 332, n.

[9] Josephus, *Antiquities*, xiii, 8^1, and *Jewish Wars*, i, 2^3.

[10] See Moore's article "Dagon" in *Encyc. Bib.*, and Jules Rouvier in *Jour. asiat.*, September, October, 1900, p. 347 ff. Ὠδάκων, who was according to Eusebius a Babylonian fish god, is also compared. Cf. Schrader, *KAT.*^{2}, p. 182; and Jensen, *Kosmologie*, p. 450. Eusebius is, however, too late to count for much when unsupported. His *Odakōn*, perhaps, is for a corruption of *Oannes*.

son is inapt, since the Dagan of the Babylonians was quite a different god from Ea.

Philo Biblos took the name from the Hebrew *dāgān* "grain" and regarded Dagon as an agricultural deity.[1] This view, though rejected by many modern scholars, probably comes nearer to the truth than the former one. The real nature of the god cannot be determined, however, without taking into account the evidence from both the East and the West.

In Babylonia Dagan was associated with Bel, the god of the earth, and his cult would seem ultimately to have been merged into that of Bel.[2] Dagan must therefore have been a god of the earth like Bel, or in other words he was a Baal[3] — a god of the soil. Jensen holds that he was a Semitic deity,[4] and believes with Jastrow[5] that the Babylonian god is closely related to the god of Philistia.

The course of evolution by which the great Semitic deities were produced leads us to suspect that the Semitic Baal called Dagon was, like the others of his kind, developed out of a still earlier mother goddess in some sheltered nook at a time when intercommunication had not produced religious syncretism. It is a difficult matter to determine where the sheltered nook which formed the earliest habitat of Dagon was situated. His worship may have originated in Babylonia, whence it was carried to Assyria in prehistoric days and to Palestine before the El-Amarna period. It can hardly have been the native religion of the Philistines before their coming to Palestine, but must have been adopted by them because Dagon was the god of their newly acquired home.[6]

---

[1] See *Sanchoniathontis Fragmenta*, ed. Orelli.
[2] III R., 68, 21 c, d, and Jensen, *Kosmologie*, p. 453.
[3] So Jensen, *op. cit.*, p. 456. [4] *Ibid.*, p. 455.
[5] *Religion of Babylonia and Assyria*, p. 208.
[6] Whence the Philistines came we do not know; perhaps from Asia Minor. Cf. the article of W. Max Müller, "Die Urheimat der Philister," in *Mitteilungen der vorderasiatischen Gesellschaft*, Vol. V, Heft 2, pp. 1–13.

Another view is that Dagon was an Aramæan god whose worship radiated from the highlands between Palestine and Mesopotamia to the countries on both sides.[1] In view of the early appearance of the name in Babylonia this theory encounters grave difficulties. We cannot at present pronounce definitely upon the matter, but must patiently wait for the appearance of further material. It seems probable, however, that Dagon was a Baal developed at some point on Babylonian soil out of the primitive Semitic cult, and that thence his worship was diffused by emigration to Assyria and Palestine.[2]

[1] So Jastrow, *op. cit.*, p. 208, and Sayce, *Hibbert Lectures*, p. 188. Sayce infers from Sargon's declaration that he had extended his protection over Harran and according to the ordinance of Anu and Dagon written down their laws, that Dagon was especially connected with Harran — a conclusion which seems no more necessary for Dagon than for Anu.

[2] The god Nusku was a fire god (cf. IV R., 26, No. 3, Sayce, *Hibbert Lectures*, p. 497). His origin is obscure. He was worshipped in the Assyrian period especially by Shalmeneser II and Assurbanipal.

Ninib (Adar?) was the same as or a development from Ningirsu, (cf. II R., 54, 74, and Brünnow, *List*, No. 10994), so that his origin has already been discussed.

In the oasis of Palmyra, some 150 miles northeast of Damascus, no special male deity seems, so far as the inscriptions indicate, to have been developed, but the inscriptions show that the worship of Babylonian and Syrian gods was brought here by immigrants from different directions. The Babylonian Bel (De Vogüe, *Syrie centrale* [Palmyre] Nos. 117, 140), Shamash (No. 8), and the Syrian Baal (Nos. 16, 73) all appear.

CHAPTER VI

SURVIVALS

Having briefly traced in the two preceding chapters the transformations of the primitive Semitic goddess in the different parts of the Semitic world, something should now be said of the survivals of her cult. These have incidentally been already introduced in part at various points of the argument as they were needed, but have not all of them been adequately treated. They merit a brief, connected discussion. We shall begin with Arabia, the primitive Semitic home.

A clear case of survival here, though under a different name from that of the primitive divine mother, is the goddess Al-Lat, whose worship can be traced in several parts of Arabia. At Taif, to the south of Mecca, it flourished among the Thaqif,[1] where an old stone *nosb* or *maṣṣeba* of her still remains, and was seen by Doughty.[2] At Salkhad her cult can be distinctly traced in the Nabathæan inscriptions.[3] We learn that a temple was built to her there at one time, and at others a candlestick and a *nosb* were consecrated to her. In these inscriptions she is called the "mother of the gods." The other gods of the place were Dhu-'l-Shara and Manutu.[4] The god of whom she was especially the mother appears from a passage in Epiphanius,[5] who vouches for the presence of her worship at Petra

---

[1] Cf. Ibn Kutaiba, p. 60, and Wellhausen, *Heidentum*, 2d ed., p. 30.
[2] Cf. his *Arabia Deserta*, Vol. II, pp. 511, 515, and 517.
[3] See *CIS.*, Pt. II, Vol. I, Nos. 182, 183, 185, and De Vogüe's *Syria centrale*, Vol. I, pp. 107 and 119.
[4] *CIS.*, Pt. II, Vol. I, No. 190, etc.   [5] *Panarion*, LI.

in Edom, and tells us that the heathen Arabs at that place drew a parallel between her and her son Dhu-'l-Shara on the one hand, and the Virgin Mary and the child Jesus on the other.[1] It appears, then, that Dhu-'l-Shara was her son, and that she was an unmarried goddess. Robertson Smith[2] is no doubt right in interpreting this to mean that she was originally a goddess of unwedded love, for an unmarried virgin goddess was an unheard-of anomaly among the ancient Semites.

Perhaps it was from Petra that some other ancient writers heard of this goddess. Thus Herodotus speaks of her[3] under the name Alilat, and calls her son Dionysos. Ephraem Syrus speaks of her and her companion goddess Al-Uzza, and tells how women sacrificed chastity in their honor.[4] Jerome also bears testimony to the same fact, and tells us further that the goddess was identified with the morning star.[5]

At Hegra she was also worshipped, but there the name of Dhu-'l-Shara was placed before that of Al-lat.[6] At the date from which the inscriptions from Hegra come the influence of the patriarchal form of society had been felt to such an extent that Dhu-'l-Shara had become superior to his mother; perhaps he had become her husband.

At Palmyra, in the second century A.D., the worship of Al-Lat was coupled with that of the god Shamash.[7] It is

---

[1] Wellhausen (*Heidentum*, 2d ed., pp. 48, 49) seeks to break the force of this because Epiphanius says the goddess was called *Qaaba* (χααβου). Wellhausen thinks the god was regarded as the offspring of the stone which represented him. Robertson Smith is, I think, right (*Religion of the Semites*, 2d ed., p. 56, n.) in giving the interpretation which I have adopted in the text. Semitic gods were frequently so identified with the object which represented them, that Epiphanius, no doubt, has put the name of the stone fetich which represented her for the goddess herself.

[2] See preceding note.//
[3] Book III, 8.//
[4] *Opera*, Vol. II, pp. 457 E ; 458, l. 1 ; 459 C.//
[5] Cf. Jerome's *Vita Hilarionis*, c. 25.//
[6] *CIS.*, Pt. II, Vol. I, No. 198.//
[7] De Vogüe, *Syria centrale*, No. 8.

probable that the worship of Shamash had at this northeastern Nabathæan outpost been introduced from Babylonia, and that it had been united with the Arabian cult by the marriage of Shamash and Al-Lat.

The connection of the Al-Lat cult with the primitive Semitic goddess is obvious. Al-Lat is but an epithet[1] and was applied to the goddess at various points until it superseded her real name. All the features of her worship of which we know are best accounted for in this way.[2]

Another Arabian goddess, who has been in recent years proven to be a survivor of the primitive Semitic cult, is Al-Uzza.[3] She was, as we learn from the quotation which Yaqut,[4] the Arabian geographer, makes from Ibn-al-Kalbi, especially worshipped by the Koraish, the prophet's tribe, whose headquarters were at Mecca. They honored her, he says, with sacrifices and pilgrimages. In another passage he says that the place where her victims were slaughtered was called the Ghabghab,[5] a name which seems to have been applied to a rivulet or trench, into which the blood of the victims drained,[6] and which emptied into the Zemzem. The latter was a well which seems to have been especially connected with her worship; into it images of sacred animals, such as the gazelle, which were offered in her worship or in that of Allah, with whom she was connected, were thrown.[7] In a similar way she, with Allah, was connected with the Ka'aba, into which her golden gazelles were afterward put.[8] This connection with Allah and the Ka'aba is established by the Qur'an, which makes her one of Allah's daughters.[9]

[1] The name seems to have been originally Al-Lahat, "the goddess," corresponding to Al-Lah; cf. Wellhausen, *Heidentum*, 2d ed., p. 33.

[2] Cf. *Hebraica*, Vol. X, pp. 58–66.

[3] See W. R. Smith's *Kinship*, pp. 294, 295, and *Hebraica*, Vol. X, pp. 58–59.

[4] Cf. ed. Wüstenfeld, Vol. III, p. 664.   [5] *Op. cit.*, Vol. III, p. 773.

[6] Cf. Wellhausen, *Heidentum*, 2d ed., p. 103, Smith, *Religion of the Semites*, 2d ed., pp. 198, 228, and 340.

[7] *Ibn Hisham*, Vol. I, pp. 93, 94.

[8] *Ibn Hisham*, Vol. I, p. 94.   [9] Sura, 53^{19}.

The connection of Al-Uzza with the Zemzem shows that before the time of the prophet she had been a goddess of wells or a *ba'alat*, and consequently a goddess of the soil and of fertility like the old mother Athtar. The fact that the dove was sacred to her, together with the nature of her festivals, connects her worship with that of the Ashtart of Phœnicia and its colonies, to whom the same bird was sacred.[1]

The most decisive indication of the direct descent of Al-Uzza from the old mother goddess is the character of the festivals celebrated in her honor. Isaac of Antioch testifies that these feasts were licentious,[2] that boys and maidens were sacrificed in them,[3] and that the goddess was identified with the planet Venus. This festival still survives at Mecca. It is celebrated in the sixth month and is still of a licentious character.[4] It is the lineal descendant of one of the festivals of the primitive goddess described above in Chapter III.[5]

At Nakhla, a valley southwestward from Mecca, which takes its name from its abundant palm trees, Al-Uzza was identified with a *samura* tree or group of *samura* trees,[6] which, as noted above, are declared in a scholion to Ibn Hisham to be palm trees.[7] The doubts of Wellhausen and Robertson Smith as to the correctness of this statement have already been discussed. The general course of the development of Semitic civilization and the agencies which acted as factors of progress tend, as we have traced them, to establish the veracity of this scholion. Some Arabic writers declare that there was a temple of Al-Uzza at Nakhla, but Wellhausen[8] is probably right in holding that the temple was at another place called Bass, and that the later Arabs confused this temple with Nakhla, where

[1] Smith, *Kinship*, p. 294.
[2] Ed. of Bickell, p. 244. Cf. Wellhausen, *op. cit.*, p. 39 ff.
[3] Ed. of Bickell, p. 220.
[4] See Snouck Hurgronje's *Mekka*, Vol. II, pp. 59–61.   [5] p. 94 ff.
[6] Wellhausen, *Heidentum*, 2d ed., p. 38.
[7] p. 145. Cf. above, p. 77 ff.   [8] *Op. cit.*, p. 38.

the goddess was supposed to dwell in the trees already mentioned.

It was probably a sacrifice in worship of Al-Uzza which Theodulus, son of Nilus, witnessed "to the morning star" among the Arabs of the Sinaitic peninsula. None of this sacrifice could remain till the morning.[1] The ritual of this offering resembles that which Bent found in Abyssinia, which has already been traced to the primitive Semitic cult.[2]

Wellhausen and Robertson Smith[3] have perceived that Al-Lat and Al-Uzza are in reality one, and that their names are but epithets for the same goddess. As Al-Lat is the feminine of Al-Lahu, so Al-Uzza, "the mighty," is an epithet applied in its masculine form to Allah also, and in south Arabia was applied to other deities.[4] There can be no doubt that both are survivals in slightly different forms of the primitive mother goddess of the Semites, who was in part transformed at Mecca into, and became the basis of, the Mohammedan Allah.

With the movement of the Semites northward from Arabia the worship of their mother goddess was, as we have seen, carried. In many places she was in prehistoric times transformed into a god; but in others she survived in her original character far down into historic times.

One of the places where such survival occurred was a city which occupied an important site on the plateau east of the Jordan, and which took its name from the goddess. It appears in the earliest extant documents which refer to that section of the country, the inscriptions of Thothmes III[5] and the El-Amarna[6] letters. It is called in these

---

[1] See Migne, *Patrologia Græca*, Vol. LXXIX (*Nili Opera*), p. 611 ff. Cf. Wellhausen, *op. cit.*, p. 42 ff., and Smith, *Religion of the Semites*, 2d ed., pp. 166, 227, 281, 338, 361, 363, 364.

[2] Above, p. 112.   [3] *Heidentum*, 2d ed., p. 44; *Kinship*, p. 295.

[4] See the name Il-'Azza, "God is mighty," which occurs as a Sabæan proper name in *CIS.*, Pt. IV, Vol. I, No. 118.

[5] Cf. W. Max Müller's *Asien und Europa*, p. 162.

[6] Cf. *KB.*, Vol. V, Nos. 142^{10} and 237^{21}.

documents Ashtart, and in the Old Testament Ashtaroth[1] and Ashtoreth Karnaim.[2] It was therefore a prehistoric sanctuary of the goddess. It continued to be an important centre of her worship down to the Maccabæan period.[3]

What the name Karnaim ("two-horned") signified has been a matter about which opinions have differed, some taking it to mean that she was a moon goddess,[4] others that she was worshipped in the form of a cow.[5] The real meaning is probably that suggested by Moore,[6] which makes Karnaim "the two-peaked mountain," and supposes that the city was situated in a valley between two hills. In later times the name was shortened to Karnaim,[7] and under this name maintained its existence down to the second century[8] and perhaps later. By the time of Eusebius its importance had apparently waned.[9] Although we have no details concerning the worship of the goddess in this city further than that she had a temple there, there is no reason to suppose that it differed in any material feature from the forms which it assumed elsewhere. The writer of 2 Maccabees has confused the Ashtart of Karnaim with the goddess Atargatis, a divinity whose

---

[1] Josh. 13.^{21} [2] Gen. 14^5.

[3] The Onomastica of Eusebius and Jerome give two places east of the Jordan named Astarte. Buhl, in his *Geographie*, p. 248 ff., follows this, but it is doubtful whether it is true. The names floated about somewhat in the later times (cf. G. A. Smith's "Ashtaroth" in *Encyc. Bib.*, and my "Ashtaroth" and "Ashtoreth Karnaim" in *Jewish Encyclopedia*). Tell Ashtarah, Tell Ash'ari, and Muzeirib are sites which have been identified with the name. Excavation of the sites will be necessary before their identity can be determined.

[4] See Stade in *ZAW.*, Vol. VI, p. 323 ff.

[5] That was my view in 1894. Cf. *Hebraica*, Vol. X, p. 40.

[6] *JBL.*, Vol. XVI, p. 156 ff. Moore bases his suggestion on a parallel name of Baal contained in some Latin inscriptions from North Africa.

[7] So Amos 6^{13}, 1 Mac. 5^{43}, and 2 Mac. 12^{26}. Cf. Wellhausen, *Skizzen und Vorarbeiten;* Heft V, p. 86; G. A. Smith, *Book of the Twelve Prophets*, Vol. I, p. 176, and Nowack, *Kleinen Propheten*, p. 147.

[8] 1 Mac. 5^{43}, and 2 Mac. 12^{26}.

[9] This is inferred in consequence of the probable confusion of names by Eusebius.

origin and nature are much debated. Baethgen has pointed out[1] that the name Athtar or Ashtar would in Aramaic become Atar. Such a goddess was found by Assurbanipal among the Aramæans, who were associated with the Nabathæans encountered in his Arabian campaign.[2] Her worshippers called her Atar-samain, *i.e.* "Atar of the heavens." This proves the presence among the Aramæans of the old Semitic mother goddess. A goddess who is in part at least the same appears in a bilingual inscription (Aramaic and Greek) from Palmyra under the name ʿAtar ʿatah, in Greek Atargatis.[3] Atargatis is also the name of a goddess who is mentioned by Greek and Roman writers.[4]

Since the second element of the name of the goddess in the Aramaic portion of the Palmyrene inscription appears as a component element of theophorous proper names,[5] Baethgen concludes that it, too, was originally the name of a deity. Since Lucian and Macrobius describe the temple and rites of Atargatis at Hierapolis-Bambyce (Mabug) in Syria, where she was worshipped as the consort of the god Hadad,[6] and since Melito of Sardis and some Greek inscriptions from Batanea couple a goddess ʿAti with Hadad, Baethgen also concludes that Atargatis is a name compounded of the Aramæan goddess Atar and that of the goddess ʿAti, and formed like the name Ashtar-

---

[1] *Beiträge zur semitischen Religionsgeschichte*, p. 69 ff. The š or ṯ would in Aramaic become *t*, and the two *t*'s would be assimilated or written with a *dagesh* understood.

[2] Cf. III R., 24, ll. 98 and 106, and George Smith's *Assurbanipal*, pp. 270, 271, 283, and 295.

[3] De Vogüe, *Syrie centrale*, No. 3. The name is spelled עתרעתו on a coin. Cf. *ZDMG.*, Vol. VI, p. 472 ff.

[4] Cf. Lucian, *De Syria Dea*, §§ 14, 15; Strabo, Book XVI, 1, 27, and Macrobius, *Saturnalia*, I, 22, 18.

[5] In addition to the names cited by Baethgen, *op. cit.*, cf. Cook, *Glossary of Aramaic Inscriptions*, p. 95; Lidzbarski, *Nordsemitische Epigraphik*, Vol. I, p. 347, and Gottheil in *JAOS.*, Vol. XXI, Pt. II, pp. 109–111.

[6] In addition to the references in n. 4, cf. Lucian, *op. cit.*, §§ 31, 32, and Pliny, *Nat. Hist.*, V, 23.

Chemosh. The Phrygians had a goddess Attis,[1] and
since the name Atargatis occurs only in late sources, it is
possible that a fusion of two goddesses, one Semitic and
one foreign, had taken place. Jensen,[2] on a far more
slender thread of evidence, explains the name as a corruption of that of the Hittite god or goddess Tarkhu, with
an 'Ayin prefixed and a feminine ending added to make it
analogous to Ashtart. Such an explanation seems far less
probable than Baethgen's.

Still another possibility should be considered. 'Ati or
'Athi, the second element in the name of the Palmyrene
goddess, may originally have been an epithet descriptive
of her as the defender of her people, and finally by a
fashion similar to that which attached the name Sebaoth
to the name Yahwe among certain Israelitish writers it
may have become a part of the name of the goddess. If
it were an epithet, it would naturally come in time to be
used for the goddess herself, and thus would enter as an
element into proper names as *Abu*, *Akhu*, and *Melek* have
entered. This explanation cannot be regarded as very
satisfactory, as no good Semitic etymology of 'Ati is
forthcoming.

On the whole the explanation of Baethgen seems most
probable. The late date of the sources in which the name
is found, the well-recognized syncretism which took place
in Syria after the days of Alexander the Great, as well
as the tendency of the Semites of the Greek and Persian
periods to form divine names by compounding the names
of two separate gods,[3] all point in this direction. If such
combination took place, it was after the time of Assurbanipal's campaign (cir. 640 B.C.), — and probably long after,

---

[1] Cf. Macrobius, *Saturnalia*, I, 21, 7, and 22, 4 ff., and Lucian, *op. cit.*,
§ 15. Attis and Atargatis are both said by these writers to ride upon
lions — another point in favor of the theory of fusion.

[2] *Hittiter und Armenier*, p. 157.

[3] See the article on "West Semitic Deities with Compound Names"
in *JBL.*, Vol. XX, p. 22 ff.

— for the Semitic goddess in her Aramaic form at that time was worshipped under her own name.

Atar, even when compounded with the Phrygian goddess, did not differ materially from Ashtart in character and functions, as Lucian and Macrobius testify. We are therefore justified in regarding her as practically the same as the Aramæan goddess Atar. Atar was as like to Ashtart as was Ashtart to Ishtar. All had sprung from the same root, but had developed in different branches of the great Semitic family. It is not strange therefore that the author of 2 Maccabees should identify the two and call the temple of Ashtart the temple of Atargatis. Considering the tendency to fusion in the later time, this seems more probable than the supposition that there was in Karnaim a temple of both goddesses.[1] The writer probably called the goddess by the name most familiar to him.

The Aramaic goddess Atar (Atargatis) was, like her sister goddesses in other countries, worshipped sometimes alone as among the Isammikhi[2] and at Palmyra, and sometimes as the consort of the closely related deity Hadad. At Palmyra, where the population was composed in part of Nabathæan Arabs and of Aramæans, both Al-Lat and Atargatis found worshippers. At Hierapolis-Bambyce she was worshipped in the temple of Hadad as his consort. Fishes and doves were sacred to her. Statues in the temple represented both her and Hadad, that of the god being supported by bulls, and that of the goddess by lions.[3]

Another city in which the worship of this goddess survived and where its history seems to have run a similar course was Ashkelon. This town, situated on or near the Mediterranean coast, was a fortress of some importance under the eighteenth Egyptian dynasty;[4] it joined in the

[1] So Cheyne, *Encyc. Bib.*, Vol. I, col. 379.

[2] III R., 24, ll. 98, 106, and George Smith's *Assurbanipal*, pp. 270, 271, 283, and 295.

[3] See Lucian, *De Syria Dea*, §§ 14, 15, 31, 32, and Macrobius, *Saturnalia*, I, 22, 17–22.

[4] Cf. *KB.*, Vol. V, No. 211 ff.

R

conspiracy against Jerusalem which Abdi-kheba's letters reflect;[1] and seems to have revolted from Rameses II[2]. In the early days of Israelitish history it was one of the five Philistine cities of importance.

The earliest mention which we have of the temple of the goddess at this place is probably the statement in 1 Sam. 31^9, that the Philistines after the battle of Gilboa hung the armor of Saul in the "house of the Ashtaroth." As we have positive evidence afterward of the worship of the goddess only at Ashkelon, the reference is probably to the temple of that place.[3] If this be true, the goddess of Ashkelon was to the Israelites indistinguishable from the Canaanitish goddesses.

We catch a glimpse of her cult again in Herodotus,[4] who calls her the Oriental Aphrodite, and who by reference to the disease which the Scythians took from thence bears witness to the survival of those rites which we have found to be so characteristic of the primitive Semitic mother goddess.

Later writers[5] call the name of the goddess Atargatis, identifying her with the Aramaic-Syrian deity which we have already traced. It is impossible from our present information to determine absolutely whether it was the Aramæans or the Canaanites who first planted the worship of the goddess at Ashkelon. It seems reasonable to conjecture, however, that it was of Canaanitish origin, and that the Aramaic element was afterward introduced into it.

It was probably at Ashkelon that the custom of representing the goddess as half woman and half fish originated, for at Ashkelon her temple stood near a lake filled with

---

[1] *KB.*, Vol. V, No. 180$^{14\,\text{ff}}$.

[2] W. Max Müller's *Asien und Europa*, p. 222.

[3] Of course it is possible that there may have been smaller temples of the goddess elsewhere, but on the whole the position taken in the text seems probable.

[4] Book I, 105.

[5] See Diodorus Siculus, Book II, ch. iv, and Ovid, *Metamorphoses*, Book IV, ll. 44–46.

fish,¹ and was also not far from the sea-coast. Fishing must have become one of the means of living at a very early time, and by the same processes of thought which led to the representation of Ea at Eridu as half man, half fish, the goddess of the fishermen of Ashkelon took on a similar form. At Hierapolis-Bambyce, situated between the ranges of Lebanon, she was represented under a similar form, but the custom may have been transferred thither from Ashkelon. It has been inferred² from this form that the goddess was the personification of the fructifying power of water. It seems clear from the wide survey of the cult which has been made in the preceding pages that such connection of the goddess with water far antedates the time when her worship was planted at Ashkelon. The fish form, though, may well have been born in that peculiar environment.

By Greek writers Atargatis was more often called Dekerto. The myth, that becoming enamoured of one of her worshippers, she became by him the mother of Semiramis, the queen of Babylon,³ is additional proof of her practical identity with the old polyandrous goddess which was worshipped among the Nabathæans as Al-lat and sometimes held in later centuries to be a virgin.

At Sidon the chief deity was, as already noted, Ashtart, but in this city her worship underwent a twofold development. On the one hand, the old mother goddess was retained in her primitive independence, so that when her cult was opposed by Israelitish prophets she was called "the abomination of the Sidonians."⁴ To her, king Tabnith tells us, both himself and his father were priests,⁵ and Eshmunazer II says that his mother was her priestess.⁶

[1] Diodorus Siculus, *ibid*.
[2] Legarde, *Mittheilungen*, Vol. I, p. 77, and White's article, "Atargatis" in Hastings's *Dictionary of the Bible*.
[3] Diodorus Siculus, Book II, ch. iv.
[4] 2 Kgs. 23^{13}.
[5] Cf. *Revue archeologique*, 1887, p. 2.
[6] *CIS.*, Vol. I, Pt. I, No. 3$^{14, 15}$.

Side by side with this primitive cult there was one somewhat modified. "Ashtart of the name of Baal," an Ashtart probably which had in part been metamorphosed into a god, was also worshipped. To each of these goddesses Eshmunazer built a temple,[1] perhaps the same which Lucian afterward saw there.[2]

Sidon was one of the headquarters of the Phœnician shipping trade, and its goddess became in consequence the patroness of mariners. She is often pictured on Sidonian coins as standing on the prow of a galley with one hand outstretched, holding a crown and pointing the ship on its way,[3] a device also adopted on the coins of other Phœnician cities. According to Lucian, Ashtart of Sidon was also identified with the moon.[4]

It is stated by Eusebius on the authority of a Phœnician writer that at Tyre, Ashtart was the chief deity with whom two others (probably Melqart and Eshmun)[5] were associated, and that the goddess here had the head of a bull. Josephus also states that Hiram, king of Tyre, built, at Tyre, in addition to the temple of Baal, a temple of Ashtart, in which Eth-Baal, the father of Jezebel, was priest. Josephus no doubt gives the correct view in saying that Melqart (Heracles) was at the head of the pantheon of Tyre, and that the worship of Ashtart was in historical times subordinate to his.

At Byblos, the ancient Gebal (the Gubla of the El-Amarna letters),[6] the cult of Ashtart survived in much of its original form. Yahumelek,[7] a king of Gebal in the

---

[1] *CIS.*, Pt. I, Vol. I, No. 3.
[2] *De Syria Dea*, § 4.
[3] Cf. Driver in Hastings's *Dictionary of the Bible*, Vol. I, p. 167.
[4] *Op. cit.*, § 4.
[5] Cf. my article "The Pantheon of Tyre," in *JAOS.*, Vol. XXII, p. 115 ff., and Herod., II, 49, who vouches for the Tyrian origin of Aphrodite at Thebes, with whom Adonis was connected. Cf. Paus., IX, 16, 3, and below, Chapter VIII.
[6] See *KB.*, Vol. V, Nos. 50, 53, 123, and 137.
[7] *CIS.*, Pt. I, Vol. I, No. 1.

fifth century B.C., venerates the goddess as the *Ba'alat* of Gebal, and makes it clear that she not only stood at the head of the pantheon, but that all other worship there was practically subordinate to hers. Her temple at Byblos is pictured on an old coin,[1] and is also mentioned by Lucian. It was here that Lucian found the rites of Tammuz surviving in connection with the worship of the mother goddess. He describes it as follows: —

"But I also saw in Byblos a great temple of Aphrodite of Byblos, in which also the rites to Adonis are performed. I also made inquiry concerning the rites; for they tell the deed which was done to Adonis by a boar in their own country, and in memory of his suffering they beat their breasts each year, and wail and celebrate these rites, and institute great lamentation throughout the country. But when they have bewailed and lamented, first they perform funeral rites to Adonis as if he were dead, but afterward upon another day they say he lives, and they cast (dust) into the air and shave their heads as the Egyptians do when Apis dies. But women such as do not wish to be shaven pay the following penalty: On a certain day they stand for prostitution at the proper time; and the market is open to strangers only, and the pay goes as a sacrifice to Aphrodite."[2] . . .

"But there is also another marvel in the country of Byblos: a river from Mount Libanos empties into the sea. The name of the river is Adonis. But the river each year becomes bloody, and having lost its own complexion, falls into the sea and reddens a large part of the sea, and gives the signal for the lamentations to the inhabitants of Byblos. They say that in these days Adonis is wounded on Libanos, and his blood going into the water changes the river, and gives to the stream its name. The majority tell this. But a certain man of Byblos, who seemed to

---

[1] See Pietschmann, *Geschichte der Phœnizier*, p. 200, and *Journal of Hellenic Studies*, Vol. IX, p. 215.

[2] Lucian, *op. cit.*, § 6.

me to tell the truth, adduced another cause of the suffering. He spoke as follows: 'The river Adonis, O stranger, comes through Libanos; but Libanos has a great deal of yellow soil. Therefore, the hard winds in these days setting upon the soil bear it into the river — the soil being of an especially red color; and the soil gives it its bloody tint; and the country is the cause of this suffering, and not the blood as they say.' The Byblite adduced such causes to me, and if he related these things to me accurately, the incident of the wind seems to me especially supernatural."[1]

It is clear from these passages that the myth of the death of the son of the old mother goddess survived at Gebal in much of its primitive form. True, the myth had taken on a local coloring, and connected itself with local circumstances; but the rites attached to the celebration of the god's resurrection are in many respects still primitive. Some progress has been made since women could be shorn in lieu of a more degrading sacrifice, if they desired, but this progress does not hide the features in the rites which have survived from the Semitic matriarchal past. The worship of Ashtart was no doubt prevalent at many points in Canaan, whence it was adopted at various times by the Israelites, but we have not now the means of tracing it in detail.[2]

Another goddess which sprang from the same root as those we have been considering, and which exercised the same functions, though called by a slightly different name, was the goddess Ashera. In the period represented by the El-Amarna tablets she was apparently the goddess of a tribe called the Bne-Ebed-Ashera.[3] From a Sumerian hymn published by Reisner[4] we learn that she

---

[1] Lucian, *op. cit.*, § 8.
[2] Cf. Jud. 2^{13}, 10^6, 1 Sam. 7^4, Jer. 7^{18}, and Eze. 8^{14}.
[3] See *KB.*, Vol. V, No. 53 ff., and cf. *JBL.*, Vol. X, p. 82 ff.
[4] See *Mittheilungen d. kgl. Museen zu Berlin*, Heft X, p. 92; also a hematite seal in *ZA.*, Vol. VI, p. 161, an astronomical text in *ZA.*, **Vol. VI**, p. 241, and the remarks of Jensen, *ZA.*, Vol. XI, p. 302 ff.

was the consort of the god of the Westland, *i.e.*, Hadad. The tablet from which the hymn is published dates from the Greek period. We do not know that the goddess was worshipped alone in the fifteenth century, though it seems probable that she was. If she was then an independent mother goddess, she might long before the third century have become in some localities the consort of Hadad. In this latter character she was practically identical with Atargatis. From this fact it follows that from the first she must have been the old mother goddess under another name. She was probably known among the Aramæans much earlier than this, for she seems to have been known to Khammurabi,[1] king of Babylon about 2300 B.C. The name of this goddess also appears according to our present text in three passages of the Old Testament,[2] but it is thought that in every case the text has been corrupted or glossed,[3] and that the original reading was Ashtoreth (Ashtart).

Hommel has pointed out that Athirat, the Arabic equivalent of Ashera, appears as the consort of the god Wadd in a Minæan inscription.[4] Since the worship of the god Hadad found its way into Arabia, both as Hadad and as Ramman,[5] it may be that the worship of Ashera found its way thither from Syria in the same way. This is not probable, however, since she appears as the consort of the native Arabian god Wadd. Athirat is therefore to be regarded as a native Arabian product, brought forth by forces analogous to those which produced her Syrian counterpart.

It is a well-known fact that Ashera was in the Old

[1] See King's *Letters and Inscriptions of Hammurabi*, No. 66, and Hommel's *Aufsätze und Abhandlungen*, Vol. II, p. 211 ff.

[2] Cf. Jud. 3⁷, 1 Kgs. 18¹⁹, and 2 Kgs. 23⁴.

[3] Cf. Moore's article "Asherah," § 2, in *Encyc. Bib.*, and Budde in *New World*, Vol. VIII, p. 734.

[4] Cf. *Expository Times*, Vol. XI, p. 190, and *Aufsätze und Abhandlungen*, Vol. II, p. 206 ff.

[5] See above, p. 227.

Testament period a post or pole which was planted by the altars of the different gods,[1] which was sometimes carved into revolting shapes,[2] and probably sometimes draped.[3] G. Hoffmann has shown[4] that these posts originally marked the limits of the sacred precincts of the shrine, and in the Ma'sub inscription the name is equivalent to "sacred enclosure." Moore finds[5] in this the explanation of the use of the word in Assyrian (*ashirtu, ashrâti, eshirtu, eshrâti*), in the sense of sanctuary.

It is probable that the application of the name to the goddess arose from the connection of these points with her sanctuary. If one or more of these were carved into a rude representation of the goddess, it would be very natural for the name to pass from the post to the deity.

This seems to have happened independently in three centres, — in Arabia, in Syria, and in Assyria.[6] This process did not in any way change the nature or the functions of the deity, but simply gave her a new name. As pointed out above, Ashera is in the El-Amarna tablets the goddess of a tribe, and, it may be added, of a sheik who was the head of a tribe. The suggestion made in 1895[7] that the Bne-Ebed-Ashera is the same clan, or the nucleus of it, which appears in the Old Testament as Asher, still seems most probable. The Egyptian monuments show that under Seti and Rameses II of the nineteenth Egyptian dynasty this tribe was still in Palestine.[8] The Israelitish traditions classed it with the children of Jacob's concubines, showing that they had a consciousness that it was among the latest to join the Israelitish confederacy. It is therefore probably a tribe of Aramaic extraction, which became amalgamated with the Israelites after their settlement in Canaan.

---

[1] Cf. Moore's article "Ashera" in *Encyc. Bib.*, and mine on same subject in *Jewish Encyclopedia*.

[2] 1 Kgs. 15^{13}.

[3] 2 Kgs. 23^7.

[4] *Ueber einige phoen. Inschriften*, p. 26 ff.

[5] *Encyc. Bib.*, as above.

[6] See above, p. 223.

[7] *JBL.*, Vol. XV, p. 174.

[8] See W. Max Müller's *Asien und Europa*, p. 236.

In all probability the goddess of the tribe became a god soon after the El-Amarna period, for the name appears on the Egyptian monuments in its masculine form, as it does in the tribal name in the Old Testament. As the Israelitish nation was welded into a confederacy, the various tribal gods were either identified with Yahwe or banished. While the latter seems to have been the fate of the god of the tribe of Gad,[1] the former was the fortune of the god of the tribe of Asher. This appears from the fact to which Hommel has called attention,[2] that in Deut. 33^{29} Asher is an alternative name of Yahwe.[3]

As the Phœnicians in their restless movements for trade and colonization progressed westward, they carried the worship of the goddess Ashtart with them, and scattered it all over the islands and shores of the Mediterranean. In many of the localities where it was thus planted it can afterward be traced. For the present we shall confine our attention to localities where the Semitic element continued to be tolerably distinct. There are several of the islands of the Mediterranean where this was the case. The sources of our information are Phœnician inscriptions, Greek inscriptions, and Greek and Roman writers. In the Greek sources the goddess is usually called Aphrodite, and in the Latin, Venus; but there can be no doubt of the identity of the divinity of whom they speak.

In the island of Cyprus, which lies nearest to the coast of Phœnicia, this Semitic worship was naturally planted at a very early time — how early we cannot tell. In the Homeric poems Aphrodite is already spoken of as Cyprian,[4] and her temple at Paphos is referred to.[5] It was then no

---

[1] See Isa. 65^{11}, and cf. *Oriental Studies of the Oriental Club of Philadelphia*, p. 108.

[2] *Aufsätz und Abhandlungen*, Vol. II, p. 209.

[3] The passage should be translated, "Happy art thou, O Israel, a people saved by Yahwe, the shield of thy help, and Asher, the sword of thy excellency."

[4] *Iliad*, V, 330.   [5] *Odyssey*, VIII, 362 ff.

doubt very old. Tradition assigned its foundation to one Cinyras,[1] who plays a considerable part in Cyprian mythology. The priests of the Paphian shrine were afterward supposed to be his descendants and bore his name.[2] Of the early history of this worship we have no real data. These Greek legends and myths can hardly be historical. A number of the German Assyriologists believe that the letters of the king of Alashia[3] to the king of Egypt, which were found in the El-Amarna correspondence, are really letters from Cyprus; but even if they are, they make no mention of religious matters, and so leave us as much in the dark with reference to the religious status of the island in the fifteenth century B.C. as though we did not possess them. The Greek inscriptions written in the Cypriotic syllabary testify to the existence of the goddess at Paphos, but do little more than that.[4] Monuments have been recovered which were dedicated to the goddess at Paphos on behalf of various Ptolemies from 164–88 B.C.,[5] as well as on behalf of the Roman Emperor Tiberius.[6] These attest that the worship was flourishing during those centuries. From Strabo[7] and Pausanias[8] we learn that the shrine at Paphos was still important in their days, while Johannes Lydus[9] in the sixth century A.D. implies that the worship had then ceased.

At Kition, in the southeastern part of the island, traces of a temple of Ashtart also appear.[10] We lack, however, the means of tracing its history. One fragmentary inscrip-

---

[1] *Iliad*, XI, 19–23, and Tacitus, *Hist.*, II, 2, 3.
[2] Tacitus, *Hist.*, II, 2, 3.
[3] Cf. *KB.*, Vol. V, Nos. 25–32.
[4] Cf. Collitz, *Sammlung der griechischen Dialekt-Inschriften*, Gottingen, 1884. Vol. I, p. 13, No. 1.
[5] Cf. *Journal of Hellenic Studies*, Vol. IX, pp. 229–231, No. 14; p. 232 ff., No. 21; p. 233 ff., No. 24; p. 240, No. 50.
[6] *Journal of Hellenic Studies*, Vol. IX, p. 227, No. 6.
[7] XIV, 6, 3 (683).
[8] VIII, 5, 2.
[9] *De Mensibus*, IV, 45.
[10] Cf. *CIS.*, Pt. I, Vol. I, Nos. 11 and 86.

tion¹ reveals the fact that a large temple retinue, consisting of sacred prostitutes² or priests, slaughterers, barbers, and slaves were maintained. These facts vouch for the identity of the worship at Kition with other phases of the primitive Semitic cult.

The temple of Ashtart at Paphos has been excavated and its form may be studied in considerable detail.³ It was evidently a Semitic temple, built on the same general plan as the temple of Solomon at Jerusalem, but with considerable variation in details. It was more than once in later times destroyed by earthquakes, and rebuilt by the Romans.⁴ In the temple there was no statue of the goddess, but she was represented by an old Semitic *maṣṣeba*.⁵ Doves were sacred to her⁶ and many images of them have been found in her temple. She was regarded as a mother goddess, and was addressed as "mother." The Semitic feast of the old mother goddess was kept to her in the springtime, when a lamb or sheep was sacrificed to her.⁷ Only male victims were sacrificed to her, and kids were regarded as the best for the purposes of divination,

---

[1] *CIS.*, Pt. I, Vol. I, No. 86.

[2] It is probably thus that the term, כלבים, "dogs," should be interpreted. The term occurs in Deut. 23¹⁷·¹⁸, where it seems to mean "male priestly prostitute" (cf. Driver's *Deuteronomy*, p. 264 ff., and Steuernagle's *Deuteronomium und Joshua*, p. 86 ff.). Clement of Alexandria so understood the term and rendered it "fornicator" (*Paidagogos*, III, 3). One consecrated to a god was perhaps so called because of his fidelity in following his god (cf. W. R. Smith, *Religion of the Semites*, 2d ed., p. 292). We have a Biblical instance in Caleb, *i.e.*, "the dog who followed Yahwe" in Num. 32¹². This usage probably extended to Babylonia, for the real names of the kings of Shirpurla, commonly called Ur-Nina and Ur-Bau, were probably Kalbi-Nina and Kalbi-Bau (cf. Radau, *Early Babylonian History*, p. 144) *i.e.* "Dog of Nina" and "Dog of Bau."

[3] Cf. *Journal of Hellenic Studies*, Vol. IX, pp. 193–215.

[4] Cf. *Journal of Hellenic Studies*, Vol. IX, p. 193.

[5] Tacitus, *Hist.*, II, 3 ; Serv. *Aen.*, I, 720. Cf. *Hebraica*, Vol. X, p. 46 ff.

[6] Antiphanes, *ap. Athen.*, VI, 71, p. 257 ; XIV, 70, p. 655, and the "Paphiæ columbæ" of Martial (VIII, 28).

[7] Johannes Lydus, *De Mensibus*, 45.

in which her priests were thought to be especially skilful.[1] No blood was shed upon her altar, and though the *maṣṣeba* stood in the open air it was thought that it was never rained upon.[2] The devotees of the goddess were initiated by impure rites,[3] and parents often dedicated their children to the goddess.[4] In later times there was much admixture of Greek elements into the Paphian worship, but nevertheless the Semitic type of goddess on the whole prevailed.[5] It was from Cyprus as the Greeks themselves believed that the worship of Aphrodite spread to the islands and coast lands of Greece.

In Crete the worship of this goddess was also established at an early time, and the Cretans themselves believed that their island was the original home of the cult.[6] In the island of Rhodes she was worshipped along with Apollo and Æsculapius,[7] who were no doubt originally Baal and Eshmun,[8] but who through Greek influence were transformed into Greek gods. Her worship was also planted in the island of Malta by a Phœnician colony,[9] though the traces of it which remain are slight. A very important and ancient seat of it was at Eryx in the island of Sicily, whence its influence spread through that island to Carthage, and into many parts of Italy, extending

---

[1] Tacitus, *Hist.*, II, 3.

[2] Tacitus, *Hist.*, II, 3.

[3] Clement of Alexandria, *Protreptikos pros Hellenes*, pp. 12, 13; Arnobius, *adv. Gentes*, V, 19; Justin, XVIII, 5. Herodotus, after describing the impure rites of this goddess at Babylon (I, 199), adds, "In some parts of Cyprus there is a custom very similar."

[4] Cf. *Journal of Hellenic Studies*, Vol. IX, p. 228, No. 8; p. 235, No. 33; p. 236, Nos. 35, 39; p. 237, Nos. 41, 42.

[5] Cf. Dyer, *The Gods of Greece*, ch. vii, and Driver in Hastings's *Dictionary of the Bible*, Vol. I, p. 170. That vegetation was thought to be connected with the goddess in Cyprus as in ancient Arabia is shown in Ohnefalsch-Richter's *Kypros*, pp. 118–126.

[6] Cf. Diodorus Siculus, V, 77, and Farnell, *Cults of the Greek States*, Vol. II, pp. 631–633.

[7] Cf. *Bull. de Corr. Hell.*, 1880, p. 139.

[8] See *CIS.*, Pt. I, Vol. I, No. 143; cf. also *JAOS.*, Vol. XXI^2, p. 188 ff.

[9] Cf. *CIS.*, Pt. I, Vol. I, No. 132.

especially to Rome.¹ In Sicily the goddess was as elsewhere served by a troop of female priestesses,² whose character and functions we can from our previous knowledge easily divine. Here the dove was also sacred to the goddess, and there were two feasts, in reality parts of the same festival, the dates of which were supposed to be connected with the flight of the doves.³ This cult may be traced further among the islands and into the mainland of Greece and Italy, but that task belongs rather to another part of the work,⁴ since the goddess there took on such a foreign character. It is clear from the evidence already cited that in the Phœnician colonies of the Mediterranean islands all the essential features of the old Semitic mother goddess were preserved. At each sanctuary a certain local coloring was given to her myths as was natural and as was the case in other places, nevertheless she remained the unmarried mother goddess, fostering sexual love, maintaining a retinue of priests and priestesses who kept the atmosphere of social life impure by perpetuating under the guise of religion the long outgrown customs of a barbarous civilization.

It has already been pointed out⁵ that the Semitic mother goddess, whose cult we can trace through so many countries, was also established in North Africa. There, in the period from which our Punic inscriptions come, she seems to have been in part subordinate to, and in part superior to, her masculine counterpart Baal-Hamman. The name by which she was known in Africa was Tanith, which was, perhaps, given her as the one who increased life and blessings.⁶

¹ Cf. Diodorus Siculus, IV, 83; Paus. VIII, 24, 6; Polybius, I, 55; Strabo, VI, 2, 5; and Virg. *Aen.*, I, 750.
² Strabo, VI, 2, 5. ⁴ Chapter VIII.
³ Ælian, *De Natura Anamalium*, IV, 2. ⁵ Above, p. 150.
⁶ Georg Hoffmann, *Ueber einige Phoen. Inschr.*, p. 32, holds that the name is a rebus, made from the final letters of עשתרת‎, בעל־חמן‎ and תֵן‎. He believes that the Greek Διδω, Δειδω came from a corrupt pronunciation, in which the *t*'s were hardened to *d*'s and then ן‎ assimilated as in תֵן‎. This is ingenious, but it is not convincing. I would, with all reserve, suggest

The superiority of Tanith to Baal is shown in the fact that in the votive inscriptions she is regularly addressed first;[1] her subordination to him, in the fact that officially he seems to have been the head of their pantheon.[2] That she held the chief place in the popular thought is shown by the fact that no prayer for life and blessings seems to have been complete which did not include an address to her.[3] As pointed out above, the goddess had at some time passed in part through the process of transformation from feminine to masculine, Baal-Hamman being in fact a differentiation from her.[4] She was still represented by an image, feminine in form but with a bearded face, and is, therefore, addressed continually as "Tanith with the face of Baal."[5]

Tanith was a mother goddess, and upon her feast days songs were sung and deeds were enacted which, according to Augustine, shocked all modesty.[6] Georg Hoffmann has pointed out[7] that Dido is but another form of the name Tanith, and the identification is accepted by others.[8] It is no doubt correct to see in Dido another form of

that possibly the name is a noun of the form of the infinitive from the stem ותן (cf. Arab. وثن, and Eth. *watan*). Such infinitives are formed by the elision of the ו and the addition of ת, and are not uncommon in all the great branches of Semitic speech (cf. Barth, *Nominalbildung in den semitischen Sprachen* [1889], p. 122). The fourth stem of this root means in Arabic "to multiply," "increase." The only place where it occurs in north Semitic so far as I have observed is in Phœnician, where it appears naturally as יתן, and is used as a synonym of נתן, "to give" (cf. the references in Bloch's *Phoenicsiches Glossar*, p. 33). If thus derived, the name would mean "the giver," "multiplier," or "increaser," and would be most fitting for a goddess of fertility.

[1] Cf. the hundreds of votive inscriptions from North Africa in *CIS.*, Pt. I, Vol. I, No. 180 ff., and those published by Berger in *Actes du onzième congrés international des orientalistes*, Pt. IV, p. 273 ff.
[2] Cf. *CIS.*, Pt. I, Vol. I, Nos. 165, 167.   [3] *Ibid.*
[4] Above, p. 150.
[5] See the references in n. 1, and also *JAOS.*, Vol. XXI[2], p. 187.
[6] *De Civitate Dei*, II, 4.
[7] See reference in p. 253, n. 6.
[8] Cf. W. R. Smith, *Religion of the Semites*, 2d ed., p. 374.

Tanith, whether the name be the same, or whether it be derived from another epithet.[1] This identification enables us to see in the tale of Dido's love for Æneas[2] told by Virgil, another evidence of the survival in Tanith of the peculiar characteristics of love which were embodied in the old Semitic deity. Indeed it is probable, as Farnell has pointed out,[3] that the whole Æneas story is but a translation into poetry of the myths of this cult.

In later times, as other Phœnicians came into North Africa, they brought with them anew the worship of Ashtart, so that at times Ashtart and Tanith appear side by side as different goddesses.[4] This is a late phenomenon, however, and by no means disproves the original identity of the two.

In course of time the cult of the Phrygian Cybele penetrated North Africa, and was probably fused with the cult of Tanith. The pressure also of the ascetic reaction against the gross practices of this cult led, as it had done at Petra,[5] to the representation of the goddess as a celestial virgin.[6] But we have Augustine's testimony that her virginity was not of a very pure type. It is she, no doubt, to whom Tertullian refers under the name of Ceres.[7]

The temple of Tanith-Dido was situated a little outside the old city of Carthage, and in the fourth century of our era was surrounded by a thorny jungle, which the popular imagination pictured as filled with asps and dragons, the guardians of her sanctuary.[8] Outside its walls a pyre

[1] It may be from the Semitic root דוד, "love," from which the name David comes. Winckler thinks that in old Hebrew and Phœnician דוד was the *genus loci*, Greek δαίμων. *Altorient. Forschungen*, pp. 339–342.

[2] *Ænid*, IV.

[3] *Cults of the Greek States*, Vol. II, pp. 638–642.

[4] Cf. Lidzbarski, *Ephemeris für semitische Epigraphik*, Vol. I, p. 24.

[5] Above, p. 233 ff.

[6] Augustine, *De Civitate Dei*, II, 4.

[7] Cf. Tertullian, *Ad Uxorem*, I, 6, and *De Exhor. Cast.*, 15.

[8] See the evidence cited in W. R. Smith's *Religion of the Semites*, 2d ed., p. 374, and especially Justin, XIX, 1.

was erected each year, and the goddess was thought to throw herself into the flames.[1] As Virgil represents this as done from love of Æneas, it was probably originally a part of the mourning for her beloved Adonis, who was evidently worshipped here.[2] This topic will be treated more fully below.

Passing now from the West to the East, we have some of the oldest historical traces of the survival of this cult at Erech, the ancient Uruk, modern Warka, in southern Babylonia. Possibly the goddesses which survived at Shirpurla are older, or equally old. These the exigencies of our argument led us to treat in a previous chapter,[3] so that no more need be said of them here. The first distinct mention of Ishtar of Erech is in the inscriptions of Lugalzaggisi, about 4000 B.C. If she is mentioned at all earlier than that, it is by the kings of Shirpurla, and they do not distinguish her from the Nana of their own city. Lugalzaggisi calls her by the epithets Umu and Nina-gidkhadu, calls her priestess and mistress of Erech.[4] Later, if I do not misinterpret him, he calls Erech the land of Ishtar.[5] Something like twelve or fifteen hundred years later Ur-Gur[6] and Dungi,[7] of the kingdom of Ur, repaired her temple. Ur-Ninib,[8] Libit-Ishtar,[9] and

[1] See references in preceding note.
[2] See the article "The Genesis of the God Eshmun," *JAOS.*, Vol. XXI², pp. 188–190.   [3] Above, p. 185 ff.
[4] *OBI.*, No. 87, col. i, ll. 30–34; cf. Radau, *Early Babylonian History*, p. 133.
[5] *Ibid.*, col. ii, l. 43 ff. It reads: KI NANA URUG-ki-i LU DAGAL GUR-A-KIM MUR MU-DA-GIL, *i.e.* "The land of Ishtar, Erech, like a sheep ready for shearing, I walled in with bricks." This reading presupposes that the determinative *dingir* has been omitted before Nana, and the *gunu* signs from the ideogram for Erech. Such mistakes are not impossible in this inscription. Cf. RU for NI, col. iii, l. 37, and the variant. Radau, *op. cit.*, reads KI NANA URUG as Ki-inanni-ab.
[6] I R., 1, No. 6. Cf. *KB.*, Vol. III¹, p. 79.
[7] I R., 1, No. 3. Cf. *KB.*, Vol. III¹, p. 81. Also *OBI.*, No. 15; cf. Radau, *op. cit.*, p. 226.
[8] IV R., 35, No. 5. Cf. *KB.*, Vol. III¹, p. 85. Cf. also *OBI.*, No. 18.
[9] I R., 3, No. 18. Cf. *KB.*, Vol. III¹, p. 87.

Ishmi-Dagan,[1] all of the dynasty of Isin, by repairing her temple, or in some other way indicate their reverence for her. About the year 2280 B.C. her temple at Erech was destroyed by the Elamites, who captured a statue of her and took it to Elam.[2] It was probably the warfare connected with this episode which has become the nucleus of the Gilgamish epic.[3]

In the middle Babylonian period Karaindash (about 1450 B.C.) consecrated to her an inscription.[4] Later, in the seventh century, Esarhaddon restored her temple and worshipped her,[5] and Assurbanipal brought back from Elam the idol which had been taken thither from Erech 1635 years before.[6] In the next century Nebuchadnezzar once more repaired her temple,[7] and after this time we lose sight of her history. The temple upon which so many kings had worked was called Ianna, a name which it kept from century to century.

These various sovereigns by their devotion attest the importance of the goddess of Erech, but our chief source of information concerning her is the Gilgamish epic. This epic is composed of different strata which had their origin in different periods and different centres, and which are collected about the struggles of the hero Gilgamish, against the Elamites, probably in the war of about 2280 B.C.[8] In one of the oldest strata of the poem, Ishtar, under the name Aruru,[9] is represented as making a man from a bit of clay as Yahwe does in the second chapter of

[1] I R., 2, No. 5, I and II. Cf. *KB.*, Vol. III¹, p. 87.
[2] V R., 6, 107 ff. Cf. *KB.*, Vol. II, p. 209 ff.
[3] Cf. Haupt, *Nimrodepos*, pp. 24, 57, and *KB.*, Vol. VI, p. 159 ff.
[4] IV R., 36, No. 3. Cf. *KB.*, Vol. III¹, p. 153.
[5] Cf. *PAOS.*, May, 1891, *Hebraica*, Vol. VIII, p. 113 ff., and Vol. X, p. 8 ff.
[6] See references under n. 2.
[7] Cf. I R., 65, col. II. 50 ff., *KB.*, Vol. III², pp. 36, 37, and V R., 34, col. II. 33, *KB.*, Vol. III², pp. 42, 43; also *Hebraica*, Vol. X, pp. 12, 13.
[8] Cf. Jastrow, *Religion of Babylonia and Assyria*, ch. xxiii.
[9] See Jastrow, *Religion of Babylonia and Assyria*, p. 448.

Genesis.[1] A little later this man, who is covered with hair and is thoroughly wild, consorting only with beasts, is enticed by intercourse with one of Ishtar's consecrated harlots [2] to abandon his animals and to enter upon civilized life. In this story, as already pointed out,[3] we have the survival of one of the primitive notions connected with the Semitic mother goddess, viz.: the fact that civilization arose from consciousness of sex. In appreciation of this fact there were maintained for Ishtar, at Erech, three classes of harlot priestesses.[4] Here, too, those rites which Herodotus calls shameful [5] were also cherished.

In another part of this epic, which is also old, Ishtar is represented as a deified woman of the early Semitic times, who changed her husbands at will.[6] Tammuz, the husband of her youth, she brought to mourning each year; various animals — for the myth originated in a totemistic age [7] — had been married by her, and through her had come to grief. She then desired to wed Gilgamish, but he, learning wisdom by what the others had suffered, declined the honor. Such conceptions of her are another proof of the character of the goddess which was fostered at Erech. In order that Gilgamish should not escape her, Ishtar had a bull created to torment him. These myths which represent the goddess as such a harmful being, probably embody in story the perception of the primitive Semite that the unrestrained service of this sexual goddess was fraught with physical peril.

---

[1] Cf. Haupt, *Nimrodepos*, p. 8, *KB.*, Vol. VI, p. 121. Cf. Jastrow's article "Adam and Eve in Babylonian Literature" in *AJSL.*, Vol. XV, pp. 193-214.

[2] Haupt, *op. cit.*, p. 11; cf. *KB.*, Vol. VI, p. 127. Cf. *Hebraica*, Vol. X, p. 3.

[3] Above, p. 84.

[4] Cf. *KB.*, Vol. VI, pp. 176, 177 ; Jastrow, *Religion of Babylonia and Assyria*, p. 475, and Haupt, *Nimrodepos*, p. 49, ll. 1, 2.

[5] Bk. I, 199.

[6] Haupt, *op. cit.*, p. 42 ff. ; *KB.*, Vol. VI, p. 171. Cf. *Hebraica*, Vol. X, p. 5 ff.

[7] Above, p. 37.

The eleventh tablet of the epic contains the account of the flood. This, as Jastrow has pointed out,[1] originated in connection with the city of Surippak, in quite a different environment from the portions of the story we have hitherto considered. As it now stands, however, it is probably in mythology assimilated to the rest; and in it Ishtar is the mother of mankind who mourns that her offspring is destroyed.[2]

It is clear from a passage in the sixth tablet of the epic already referred to,[3] that the custom of wailing for Tammuz was a part of the ritual of the Ishtar cult at Erech. It is possible that the myth embodied in the poem which celebrates Ishtar's descent to the lower world originated, or at least was cherished, at Erech. I formerly held on mythological grounds that it was probably connected especially with Nineveh,[4] but the same mythological data would lead us to connect it with Khallabi[5] and perhaps with Shirpurla.[6] As the Semitic settlements at these latter towns are older than the settlement at Nineveh, it can hardly have originated in the latter city. In the Gilgamish epic Ishtar is called daughter of Anu[7] instead of daughter of Sin as in Ishtar's descent.[8] The idea that she was daughter of Anu may not have been the primitive one, however, so that it is quite possible that the legend of her descent to the lower world belongs to Erech in spite of this. Jensen conjectured[9] that the idea which finds expression in the poem, that the underworld is surrounded by seven walls, was, in the first instance, suggested by the seven walls of Erech. Be this as it may, if the poem was known at Erech, which is very probable, the conception which it embodies that when Ishtar disappeared from the

---

[1] *Religion of Babylonia and Assyria*, p. 494 ff.
[2] See Haupt, *Nimrodepos*, p. 139, ll. 117–125, and *KB.*, Vol. VI, p. 239.
[3] Above, p. 258.   [5] See below.
[4] *Hebraica*, Vol. IX, p. 145, n.   [6] See above, p. 199.
[7] Cf. Haupt, *op cit.*, p. 46, l. 107, and *KB.*, Vol. VI, p. 173.
[8] Cf. IV R., 31, 2; cf. *KB.*, Vol. VI, p. 81.
[9] *Kosmologie*, p. 172 ff.

earth, all desire in man and beast ceased,¹ would be another evidence of the survival at Erech in almost their primitive purity of the earliest conceptions of Ishtar.

Another town where the cult of Ishtar flourished was Khallabi, though but few references to her worship there have as yet been recovered. From the fact that Khallabi is mentioned on a contract tablet of the reign of Cambyses, found at Abu-Habba, Jensen concludes that it was situated near Sippar.² We have but two glimpses of this worship,— one in the reign of Arad-Sin, king of Larsa,³ and the other in that of Khammurabi, king of Babylon.⁴ Beyond the fact that there was, in this city, a temple of the goddess in which one of these kings placed a votive offering, and which the other repaired, we are able to learn little of her worship.

The ideogram for Khallabi occurs without the determinative for place in one of the inscriptions of Gudea in a passage descriptive of one of the goddesses of Shirpurla.⁵ The passage is a difficult one as both Jensen and Amiaud recognize, but its meaning seems to be rendered clearer if we understand the ideogram as Khallabi.⁶ The fact that it lacks the determinative for place is not a serious objection to this interpretation, since Shirpurla itself is some-

---

¹ IV R., 31, 76 ff., and *KB.*, Vol. VI, p. 87.
² Cf. Strassmaier's *Cambyses*, No. 48, l. 2, and Jensen, *KB.*, Vol. III¹, p. 106, n. 6. Cf. also Zimmern, *ZA.*, Vol. III, p. 97.
³ *PSBA.*, Vol. XIII, pp. 158, 159.
⁴ *KB.*, Vol. III¹, p. 106 ff.
⁵ On statue F, De Sarzec, *Découvertes*, pl. 14, col. i, l. 16 ; cf. Amiaud, *Records of the Past*, New Ser., Vol. II, p. 98, and Jensen, *KB.*, Vol. III¹, pp. 54, 55.
⁶ The passage would then read: (l. 12) *Dingir*-GA-TUM-DUG (13) NIN-A-NI (14) SHIR-PUR-LA-*ki* (15) URU-KI-AG-GA-NI-TA (16) TE-UNU-USLANUGUNU-ZA-A (col. ii, l. 1) MU-NI-TU-DA-A (2) E-*dingir*-GA-TUM-DUG (3) NIN-A-NA (4) RU-NI, *i.e.* "To Gatumdug, his mistress for (the sake of) Shirpurla, the city which she loved (at) Khallabi, where she bore him, the temple of Gatumdug, his mistress, he built." On this view the ideogram for Khallabi has the sign TE in addition to those which appear in it later, but for TE-UNU = UNU cf. Brünnow, *List*, No. 7721. For the order and identity of the other signs

times thus defectively written.[1] This passage makes it probable that Khallabi was a colony or dependency of Shirpurla in the earlier time, and that the worship of the goddess reached this town through Shirpurla.

Passing northward from Babylonia to Assyria, the city of Nineveh seems to have been another town which regarded Ishtar as its tutelary divinity. Her connection with this capital of the Assyrian empire is indicated by the following facts: (1) The city was called in Assyrian *Ninua*, a name which we have already seen to be a Semitization through a folk etymology of the Sumerian *Ninâ*, which was a part of the city of Shirpurla.[2] The identity of the two names is shown by the fact that they are expressed by the same ideogram. (2) By the fact that Ishtar, the goddess of this capital city, is constantly associated with Ashur, the god of the older capital from which Assyria took its name, as one of the two leading deities of the country. The chief temple in Nineveh, Ibarbar, was a temple of Ishtar.[3]

The historical inscriptions of Assyria contain many references to this goddess,[4] but beyond the fact that she was considered to be "the firstborn of the gods" (*i.e.* as the source and author of all life), and the spouse of Ashur, these inscriptions contain little information concerning her. The fact that a king like Assurbanipal could import to Nineveh literature like the poem of Ishtar's descent, suggests that from his youth he had known like traditions and like practices

---

of the ideogram, cf. Thureau Dangin's *Recherches sur l'origine l'ecriture cuneiforme*, p. 48. Gatumdug was, as we saw above, sometimes an epithet of Bau, but here, of Nana.

[1] Cf. De Sarzec, *Découvertes*, pl. 31, No. 1, l. 2 and pl. 2ᵗᵉʳ, No. 2, col. i, l. 3.

[2] Cf. above, pp. 187 and 196 ff.

[3] Cf. *ZA.*, Vol. V, p. 79, l. 40, and II R., 66, No. 2, l. 9; Smith's *Assurbanipal*, p. 305, l. 9; also *Hebraica*, Vol. IX, p. 143.

[4] These are collected in *Hebraica*, Vol. IX, pp. 132–143 and 156, 157.

in connection with the worship of the goddess of his native city.¹

Arbela, a city of Assyria to the eastward of Nineveh, was also the seat of an old shrine of Ishtar. The beginnings of her worship there are shrouded in a darkness even more dense than that which covers the beginnings of most of the Mesopotamian cities. We cannot even guess from what part of southern Mesopotamia the immigrants who settled Arbela came. The honor in which the Ishtar of Arbela was held toward the end of the Assyrian empire seems to point to a considerable antiquity for her worship there, but we obtain historical glimpses of it only in the reigns of Sennacherib, Esarhaddon, and Assurbanipal.² By these kings the Ishtar of Arbela is distinguished from the Ishtar of Nineveh. In the earlier reigns, if such a distinction was made, it has not been reflected in the literature hitherto recovered.

At Arbela, Ishtar continued to the close of Assyrian history to be an unmarried mother goddess. As a mother she was anxious for the welfare of her people, and consequently ready to defend them against all their enemies. Thus she became the goddess of war, to whom appeal was naturally made in times of especial danger.³ In the reigns of Esarhaddon and Assurbanipal she seems to have been much sought after as the giver of oracles and the revealer of the future fortunes of her worshippers.⁴ Connected with her temple at Arbela there seems to have been an observatory from which astronomical reports were sent to the king.⁵

These numerous and multiform survivals of the Ishtar

---

¹ This view is confirmed by Macrobius (*Saturnalia*, I, 21), who speaks of the worship of Adonis among the Assyrians as well as among the Phœnicians.

² Cf. *Hebraica*, Vol. IX, pp. 158–163.

³ Cf. Smith's *Assurbanipal*, p. 119 ff.

⁴ Cf. IV R., 61, *AJSL.*, Vol. XIV, 267–277, and the references in *Hebraica*, Vol. IX, pp. 160, 161.

⁵ See, for example, the texts in III R., 51.

cult, which project themselves far into civilizations which could never have originated them, are, to him who has an eye to read, sufficient evidence of the existence among the primitive Semites of such a social order and such a religion as that which is outlined in the second and third chapters of this work.

It was suggested in a former chapter [1] that the primitive Arabic environment and the early Semitic social organization combined to create for the primitive Semitic pantheon a goddess and her son. The transformations and survivals of the goddess having now been traced, it remains to inquire to what extent the primitive god, her son, survived. In the course of the preceding argument it has been frequently pointed out that, where the goddess was transformed, the primitive god, her child, may have been merged into the resultant god. In many portions of the Semitic territory, however, his distinct survival can be clearly traced.

Among the Nabathæans he survived as Dhu-'l-Shara.[2] The polemics which, in this region as elsewhere, attended the propagation of early Christianity, caused the fact to be recorded that Dhu-'l-Shara was regarded as the son of the old mother goddess.[3] Of the cult of this god we have little further evidence. The inscriptions which make mention of him record the consecration of votive objects or invoke his curse upon the violators of tombs. From analogy we conclude that he was in character probably identical with Tammuz and Adonis, who were elsewhere sons of kindred goddesses. This conjecture receives some confirmation from the fact that Herodotus calls him Dionysos.[4]

In Babylonia this god seems to have survived under different forms. The Sumerian name by which he is most commonly known is Dumu-zi, or Tammuz, "child of life." Although this name is once applied to a goddess,[5] it ordi-

[1] Chapter III, p. 85 ff.   [3] Cf. Epiphanius, *Panarion*, LI.
[2] *CIS.*, Pt. II, Vol. I, No. 190–199.   [4] Bk. III, 8.   [5] Above, p. 211 ff.

narily refers to a god who is variously called the "offspring,"[1] "the son of Ishtar,"[2] and the "husband of her youth."[3] He was supposed to die periodically and was then bewailed. Ishtar, once at least, and, perhaps, regularly, was thought to go to the underworld for him and to bring him back to life.[4] He is generally recognized as a god of vegetation[5] and of the underworld.[6]

At Shirpurla there was a god called Ningishzida, who was associated with the goddess Bau,[7] and who seems to have possessed many of the characteristics of Tammuz. In the Adapa legend Ningishzida and Tammuz are classed together and play the same part; both are intercessors for the life of Adapa, and both are keepers of the gate of Anu.[8] As pointed out above,[9] Ningishzida seems to have been a transformed Ishtar, but if so, Tammuz has been swallowed up in him. The way in which, in Semitic antiquity, the name of a deity constituted that deity a separate personality is well illustrated by the way Tammuz and Ningishzida are in the Adapa story put side by side as two distinct gods.

Jensen regards Tammuz as chthonic;[10] Jastrow regards him as a solar deity.[11] Probably both are right. If, as we suppose,[12] he was associated by primitive Semites with objects in an oasis, he was a chthonic god connected with vegetation. The yearly death of vegetation and its subsequent resurrection would, since it corresponded to the movements of the sun, naturally lead in time to the identification of Tammuz with the sun. That would, however, be a later view. In primitive times the god was chthonic.

In Phœnicia and the West the same god survived under

---

[1] II R., 36, 54.
[2] II R., 59, col. ii, l. 9.
[3] IV R., 31, 47, and *Nimrodepos*, p. 44; cf. *KB.*, Vol. VI, pp. 168, 169.
[4] IV R., 31, and Jeremias's *Leben nach dem Tode.*
[5] Jensen, *Kosmologie*, p. 197 ff. [8] Cf. *KB.*, Vol. VI, pp. 96–99.
[6] Jensen, *op. cit.*, p. 225. [9] p. 190 ff.
[7] Above, p. 190 ff. [10] *Kosmologie*, p. 197 ff.
[11] *Religion of Babylonia and Assyria*, p. 547 ff.
[12] *Hebraica*, Vol. X, p. 74, and above, p. 85 ff.

other names. Although Ezekiel called him Tammuz,[1] Ezekiel lived in Babylonia and no doubt used the Babylonian name or a corrupted form of it,[2] — a name otherwise unknown in the West.[3] The clearest description of the god which we have for this part of the Semitic world is Lucian's account of the worship of Adonis at Biblos (Gebal).[4] Here the myth had it that the god was killed by the tusk of a boar, and the reddening of the river by the highly colored soil was held to be the result of shedding the blood of the god. The sexual rites connected with his worship at this place make it very clear that his cult was a survival from primitive Semitic times. Later, the myth was interpreted as a nature myth, the tusk of the boar being regarded as the inclement winter and the resurrection of the god as his victory over the first six signs of the zodiac.[5]

The name Adonis, by which Lucian designates this deity, is simply the Semitic epithet *Adon*, "Lord"; it was not the real name of the god. As I have pointed out elsewhere,[6] the real name of this deity was probably Eshmun. The reasons for considering Eshmun as a Tammuz are: 1. That the epithet *Adon* was frequently applied to Eshmun, as the name Eshmun-Adon, which was quite popular, shows. 2. Eshmun was a very popular god among the Phœnicians, — as popular as one would expect Tammuz to be. 3. Eshmun was a god of the healing art and was identified with the Greek Æsculapius.[7] Several scholars identify him also with Iolaos, who in a Semitic myth in Greek dress, saved the life of Heracles.[8] Similar charac-

---

[1] Ch. 8¹⁴. [2] Dumuzu or Duzu. Cf. above, p. 263.
[3] Cf. Baethgen, *Beiträge zur semitischen Religionsgeschichte*, p. 44. Cf. also *JAOS.*, Vol. XXI², p. 188.
[4] *De Syria Dea*, §§ 6, 8; quoted above, p. 245.
[5] Macrobius, *Saturnalia*, I, 21. [6] *JAOS.*, Vol. XXI², p. 188 ff.
[7] *CIS.*, Pt. I, Vol. I, No. 143. On Æsculapius, cf. Dyer's *Gods of Greece*, pp. 220–256.
[8] See W. R. Smith, *Religion of the Semites*, 2d ed., p. 469, and Pietschmann, *Phœnizier*, p. 181.

teristics seem to have pertained to Tammuz. If Jeremias is correct in his interpretation of the enigmatical lines at the end of the poem on Ishtar's descent to the lower world,[1] appeal could be made, on the day of Tammuz, for the restoration of the dead to life. Such restoration was but a heightened form of healing the sick. 4. As the worship of Tammuz was closely connected with the worship of Ishtar-Ashtart, so was the worship of Eshmun; and also as we should naturally expect with that of Baal, the transformed Ashtart. At Carthage, Tanith-Ashtart and Baal were worshipped in the temple of Eshmun;[2] while Hannibal in ratifying the treaty with Philip of Macedon, swore by Heracles (Baal) and Iolaos (Eshmun).[3] Once Eshmun and Ashtart are compounded into a single deity,[4] — a fact which points strongly to a consciousness of identity of function, — an identity which in turn points to kinship of origin. At Sidon his worship was very popular and took rank with that of Baal and Ashtart.[5] At Kition and Idalion in Cyprus, where there were important temples of Ashtart,[6] the worship of Eshmun also flourished. This is proven by the many proper names on the monuments from these places, into which the name Eshmun enters as an element. Eshmun was, in the same region, called "Melqart," as several inscriptions show.[7] This title, meaning "king of the city," applies usually to the Tyrian Baal, and its application to Eshmun probably indicates a conscious union of Eshmun with that Baal.[8] Such a union with Baal, like the union with Ashtart, points to a similarity of function, and consequently of origin, for the two gods. As Baal was a transformed Ashtart, this

---

[1] Cf. *Leben nach dem Tode*, p. 7.
[2] *CIS.*, Pt. I, Vol. I, No. 252.
[3] Polybius, vii, 9, 2.
[4] *CIS.*, Pt. I, Vol. I, No. 245.
[5] *Ibid.*, No. 3.
[6] Cf. *CIS.*, as above, No. 86, *Journal of Hellenic Studies*, 1888, pp. 175-206; Tacitus, *Historia*, II, 2, 3; Pausanias, viii, 5, 2, etc.
[7] *CIS.*, Pt. I, Vol. I, Nos. 24-28.
[8] See the article "West Semitic Deities with Compound Names" in *JBL.*, Vol. XX, p. 22 ff.

fact points ultimately to a primitive Semitic origin for both Ashtart and Eshmun, — or in other words to the fact that Eshmun was a Tammuz. 5. With Eshmun as Æsculapius there are associated two accounts[1] of exposure to death and deliverance from it which approximate the death and resurrection of Tammuz. These accounts are probably variant versions of the myth which Lucian tells of Adonis at Gebal. In all probability, therefore, the god who is called Tammuz in Babylonia, Dhu-'l-Shara in north Arabia, and was known to the Greeks at Gebal as Adonis, was known among the Phœnicians generally as Eshmun.[2] This variety of name is due to the fact that the primitive Semitic appellation did not survive.

The myth of the death of the deity sometimes attached to the primitive goddess rather than to the god. This was apparently the case at Carthage, where Dido, it was said, yearly threw herself to death.[3] Such a variation is another indication of the close connection between the primitive goddess and her son.

In primitive Arabia the conditions of the country would produce two kinds of clans. On the oases the communal clan, devoted to the worship of the mother goddess, would flourish.[4] The flocks and the caravan trade would lead to the organization of the republican clan, the more hazardous life of which would lead to the worship of the ideal masculine character. Such clans are found in Arabia to-day,[5] and doubtless were called into existence in prehistoric times by the peculiar economic character of Arabia.

---

[1] Cf. Pausanias, II, 26⁴⁻⁶.

[2] What the name of Eshmun means and how it originated, it is hard to say. It was probably originally some kind of an epithet. Of the suggestions made, the one most worthy of credence is, perhaps, that of Lagarde (*Gr. Uebers. der Provv.*, p. 81), and repeated by W. R. Smith (*Religion of the Semites*, 2d ed., p. 469), viz.: that the name is to be connected with the Arabic سُمَانَى, "quail," because in the myth Iolaos brought Heracles to life by giving him a quail to smell of.

[3] Cf. W. R. Smith, *Religion of the Semites*, 2d ed., pp. 374, 410, and above, p. 255 ff.   [4] See above, p. 30.   [5] Cf. above, p. 72, n. 1.

Among such clans the worship of Tammuz would be practised, and as they migrated it would be diffused. Dependent as these clans were upon the oases for much of their nourishment, they would long perpetuate the myth that their god was the son of the goddess of the oases. The survival of Tammuz, Dhu-'l-Shara, Adon, and Eshmun was most natural. The widespread cult is accounted for by primitive Semitic social conditions, and in turn is an important link in the chain of evidence which enables us to restore the outlines of that far-off social and religious organization.

CHRONOLOGICAL TABLE

El-Amarna tablets, cir. 1400 B.C.
Exodus from Egypt, cir. 1250.
Israel invaded Canaan, cir. 1200.
David became king, cir. 1000.
Kingdom divided, 937.
Ahab king of Israel, 876–854.
The Prophet Amos, cir. 760.
The Prophet Hosea, cir. 745.
The Prophet Isaiah, 740–700.
Fall of Northern Kingdom, 722.
Manasseh king of Judah, 696–641.
Josiah king of Judah, 639–608.
Jeremiah the Prophet, 627–cir. 580.
Josiah's reform, 621.
The Prophet Ezekiel, 593–570.
Destruction of Jerusalem, 586.

The second Isaiah, cir. 545.
Cyrus captured Babylon and permitted return of Jews, 538.
Second Temple completed, 516.
Nehemiah, governor of Jerusalem, 444.
Jews pass under Greek rule, 332.
Jews under Egyptian Ptolemies, 323–198.
Jews pass finally under Seleucids of Antioch, 198.
Earliest parts of Enoch, 200–170.
Maccabæan revolt, 168–165.
Jews independent under Simon and the Asmonæans, 143–63.
Judea passes under Roman sway, 63.

CHAPTER VII

YAHWE

IN sketching the transformations which the primitive Semitic goddess underwent[1] as the Semites wandered from their Arabian home into other environments, no mention was made of Yahwe, the God of Israel. This omission was not accidental. No deity of the old Semitic world compares in importance with Yahwe; the worshippers of no other god contributed to the sum of humanity's ethical ideas and spiritual conceptions a tithe of the value of that contributed by the worshippers of Yahwe. The importance of Yahwe, therefore, demands that a separate chapter should be devoted to him. It is evident to one who has followed with any sympathy the argument of the preceding pages that the religion of the Semites as a whole moved forward by a process of evolution in which it was subject to certain great principles of general application. Is the religion of Israel subject in any degree to these great principles? Is its God Yahwe connected at all with that primitive Semitic root from which we have found nearly all other Semitic gods to spring? If he is, can it be claimed that there is in the Old Testament any special revelation of permanent religious value? These are questions which we must now try to answer, and it is the writer's belief that to each one of these an affirmative reply can be given.

The critical study of the Old Testament, which has seemed to some to destroy the historical and religious value of the earlier books of the Bible altogether,[2] has

[1] Above, Chapters IV and V.
[2] The reader who may chance to be unfamiliar with the results of criticism will find compendious statements of it in Driver's *Introduction*

really opened a new historical vista to the student of any phase of Israelitish history. This is as true of Israel's religion as of any other phase of her life. While there are critics who can bring themselves to regard as historical scarcely any of the material which relates to the times before David and Solomon, most critics regard the broad outline of the traditions which relate to the sojourn in Egypt, the exodus, the wilderness sojourn, and the conquest of Canaan, as representing real facts of history. This does not imply that there is no need to apply critical methods to these traditions in order to ascertain the truth. Tradition has no doubt often destroyed the historical perspective; it has applied to the whole of the nation that which in reality belonged only to parts of it. A discriminating student can nevertheless still in good degree untangle the thread and restore the main features of the history. In this task much help is secured by the recognition of the simple fact that in the genealogies tribes are often personified as men.

The beginnings of the nation Israel may, by the aid of critical study, be broadly sketched as follows:[1] From time immemorial wave upon wave of Semites had overrun Palestine, and had by fusion with its aboriginal inhabitants, whatever they were,[2] gradually formed the

to the Literature of the Old Testament, or Cornill's Einleitung in das alte Testament. The best presentation of the criticism of the Pentateuch and Joshua is Carpenter and Harford-Battersby's Hexateuch.

[1] This sketch gives the outline which my own studies have led me to adopt as most probable. For sketches of other scholars, cf. Kuenen, Religion of Israel, pp. 109–115; Stade, Geschichte des Volkes Israel, Vol. I, p. 113 ff.; Wellhausen, Israelitische und judische Geschichte, ch. ii; Kent, History of the Hebrew People, Vol. I, ch. v; Cornill, History of the People of Israel, pp. 45–55; Guthe, Geschichte des Volkes Israel, pp. 12–28, and § 9 of his article "Israel," in Encyc. Bib.; Winckler, Geschichte Israels, Vol. I, pp. 12–24; and § 1 of Woods's article, "Israel," in Hastings's Dictionary of the Bible.

[2] Sergi (Mediterranean Race, pp. 150–156) believes that these aborigines were Hittites who had separated from the North African race. It must, if true, have been at a considerably earlier time, of course, than the Semitic migration from Africa.

Phœnician or Canaanitish peoples. It has been already pointed out[1] that from the time of Lugalzaggisi (about 4000 B.C.) onward, many successive expeditions of conquest and migration from Babylonia had also swept over the land. With these Babylonians there were mingled, from about 1500 B.C. onward (and for all we know, from a much earlier period), Aramæan tribes who had previously inhabited the highlands between the Mesopotamian valley and the Mediterranean. The presence of these tribes can be traced in the El-Amarna letters about 1400 B.C.[2] A number of the clans which were afterward united into the nation Israel belonged to this Aramaic group of nomads. This is proven by the persistent traditions which connected Hebrew ancestry with Aram,[3] and receives confirmation from phenomena in the El-Amarna letters, which will soon be noted.

Of these clans, the Reubenites may have been at first the chief,[4] but that leadership soon gave way to the powerful Joseph clan, later divided into the clans of Ephraim and Manasseh, and of which the clan of Benjamin was a later offshoot.[5] Closely allied to the Reubenites were the clans of Issachar and Zebulon, and less closely the clans of Gad and Asher, the last of which we have already traced in Palestine in the El-Amarna period.[6]

[1] See above, pp. 146 and 160.
[2] They are mentioned in the annals of Tiglath-pileser I, about 1110 B.C. Cf. *KB.*, Vol. I, p. 33, and "Aram," in *Encyc. Bib.* and *Jewish Encyclopedia*, and above, p. 226 ff.
[3] Cf. Gen. 12^4, 24, 28^1-32^2, and Deut. 26^5.
[4] Cf. the tradition that he was Jacob's firstborn, Gen. 29^{32}, 49^3, etc. Birthright implied hegemony and power.
[5] Cf. the tradition of Benjamin's late birth, Gen. 35$^{16-18}$. The name Benjamin is really Bne-Yamin, "sons of the south," *i.e* "southerners." The kinship to the Joseph tribes which the traditions assign means that the Benjaminites were the "southerners" of the Josephites. Cf. the Arabic Yemenites. A more remote kinship to these tribes is assigned by the traditions to the tribes of Dan and Naphtali. This means that they joined the confederacy later, perhaps after the emancipation from Egypt.
[6] The tribes of Judah, Simeon, and Levi are also assigned in the traditions to the Leah group. On Judah, see p. 272, n. 4. Simeon as a clan

The Joseph clans[1] wandered in time of famine to Egypt,[2] whither they were followed by others, probably some of the Leah tribes, of which the Reubenites were the most powerful. There, in course of time, these tribes found themselves in bondage. Meantime the Kenites, a clan whose origin was more directly Arabian, having been touched by the northern wave of Minæan influence from south Arabia,[3] and which afterward formed part of the tribe of Judah,[4] had occupied the Sinaitic peninsula and the region to the north of it, and had become a pastoral people. Moses, a man of one of the tribes which were in bondage, fled from Egypt, sojourned among the Kenites, became a devotee of the Kenite god, Yahwe, went back to Egypt, proclaimed Yahwe the deliverer of the oppressed clans, led his brethren to Sinai, and with the aid of Jethro, Yahwe's priest in Midian, bound them for the future in alliance with the Kenites and to the service of Yahwe.[5]

has in the historical period a most shadowy and problematical existence. Possibly it was an early clan which was overtaken by misfortune (Gen. 49⁵ ff.). The same may be said of the tribe of Levi, though it is possible, as Budde thinks (*Rel. of Israel to the Exile*, p. 80 ff.), that it was a priestly clan of later origin.

[1] Cf. Wildeboer, *Jahvedienst en Volksreligie in Israel*, p. 15.

[2] Winckler, *Altorientalische Forschungen*, p. 337 ff., has suggested on the basis of a Sabæan inscription that *Miṣraim* is in the Old Testament a later misunderstanding for *Miṣr*, a name which he believes was applied to the part of Arabia which included the Sinaitic peninsula, and that the Hebrews never were in Egypt proper. This view is accepted by Schmidt, *American Journal of Theology*, Vol. V, p. 136. This is, however, too slight a basis on which to cast away all the traditions of later time.

[3] Cf. Weber's article, "Studien zur südarabischen Altertumskunde," and the literature cited in it, published in *Mittheilungen der vorderasiat. Gesell.*, 1901, especially pp. 29 and 36 ff. Cf. also Lidzbarski's *Ephemeris für semitische Epigraphik*, Vol. I, p. 128.

[4] The traditional genealogies indicate that there was a close kinship between Judah and the Reubenites. This means that there was an Aramaic element in Judah, to which other elements, as pointed out below, were joined later. The possible mention of Judah in the El-Amarna tablets (cf. Jastrow, *JBL.*, Vol. XII, p. 61 ff.) would, if real, seem to confirm this view.

[5] Cf. Ex. 18¹² ff. and Budde, *Rel. of Israel to the Exile*, p. 22 ff.

After wandering for a time as nomads, these clans or a part of them conquered the east-Jordanic country, in which probably some of their kinsmen, the tribe of Gad, had remained from earlier times. After they became too numerous for this region, the Jordan was crossed and the heart of Palestine conquered. After their settlement there, tribes which had never left the country, such as Asher and perhaps Dan and Naphtali, were incorporated with them. It is perhaps true that an Aramaic element, kindred to the Reubenites, an element which formed the nucleus of the tribe of Judah, was concerned in this general movement to Egypt and back; but the Kenite clan, at least in part, and perhaps others who were afterward important elements of the tribe of Judah, moved from the south into the territory later occupied by them making their entrance at a time considerably subsequent to that of the Joseph tribes. Long after the time when the book of Judges takes up Israel's history, Judah was even less closely attached to the other tribes than they were to one another.

These Israelitish clans — always in the early days without fixed organization — became in time, by absorbing elements already in the land, the tribes of the book of Judges. Within each tribe there seems to have been no more organization than Arabic tribes in the desert show at the present time, and as regards one another they had no real governmental connection. A sense of kinship and of loose alliance was their only bond. The two most powerful of these were the clans of Joseph and Judah. These clans were never permanently united, and afterward formed the centres of the northern and southern kingdoms. Some of the features of this sketch will be enlarged upon below when some of the proof for it will be considered. At present we must turn to one or two matters which are thought to oppose difficulties to the course of events just outlined.

Among the El-Amarna letters, about 1400 B.C., there

are several from Abdikheba of Jerusalem[1] in which he complains that his government is being overthrown by a people called Khabiri, whom Zimmern and Winckler[2] have identified with the Hebrews. If this identification were correct, it would follow that the exodus should be dated considerably earlier than has of late been customary among scholars. That the Khabiri and the Hebrews are the same is, however, very improbable.[3] The suggestion of Jastrow[4] that the Khabiri were a clan afterward embodied in the tribe of Asher as Heber (Kheber) seems to me far more probable. If, as we have supposed,[5] the tribe of Asher was fused with the other tribes after the settlement in Canaan, the presence of the Khabiri about Jerusalem at a time when the bulk of the Hebrews were in Egypt would afford no difficulty.

Another fact which is supposed by some to present difficulty is the mention of Israel on a stele of Meren-Ptah (Menephtah), discovered by Petrie in 1896. The context places Israel among enemies whom the king destroyed in Palestine.[6] This implies that Israel was settled there in the reign of the Pharaoh under whom the exodus is usually supposed to have occurred. The force of this consideration some would break by the claim that the poetical and exaggerated language of the inscription of Menephtah cannot be sufficiently definite to be taken seriously. It seems clear, however, that if the inscription has any meaning at all, it implies that Israel was in Palestine when it was written. But it does not follow that the term "Israel" then connoted all that it signified at a later time. Jacob and Joseph in the reign of Thothmes III,[7] a

---

[1] Cf. *KB.*, Vol. V, Nos. 179–185.
[2] See his *Geschichte Israels*, Vol. I, pp. 17–20.
[3] Cf. Hommel's *Ancient Hebrew Tradition*, pp. 230 ff. and 258 ff.
[4] In *JBL.*, Vol. XI, p. 120.   [5] p. 273.
[6] Cf. Steindorf in *ZATW.*, Vol. XVI, p. 330 ff.; and Breasted in *Biblical World*, Vol. IX, p. 62 ff. For a summary of conflicting opinions cf. *ibid.*, Vol. VIII, p. 243 ff.
[7] W. Max Müller, *Asien und Europa*, p. 163.

little earlier, were the names of places, and Joseph at least underwent a change ; may not Israel have done the same ? The inscription makes it clear that Israel is used in the sense of a people ; but if our view of the gradual aggregation of the Israel of later times be correct, not all the clans which we know under that designation in the Old Testament need have been present among those whom Menephtah vanquished. If a small detachment were there, the conditions would be satisfied.[1] This difficulty therefore vanishes.[2]

On the view of the origin of the Israelites outlined above, Yahwe was the god of the Kenites before he became the God of Israel. This view was first suggested by Ghillany,[3] and afterward independently by Tiele,[4] more fully urged by Stade,[5] and has been thoroughly worked out by Budde.[6] It is now accepted by others, as Guthe,[7] Wildeboer,[8] and H. P. Smith.[9] It is naturally rejected by Dillmann,[10] and his school,[11] as well as by writers like Robertson,[12] who contend against all critical theories of the origin of Israel's religion. The reasons for accepting the view that Yahwe was the god of the Kenites before Moses mediated a covenant whereby he became the god of

[1] Cf. Budde, *Rel. of Israel*, p. 7.

[2] The indefiniteness of Menephtah's use of the word " Israel " is shown by the contradictory theories built upon it ; cf. *Biblical World*, Vol. VIII, p. 243 ff.

[3] In 1862, writing under the pseudonym of Richard von der Alm. Cf. Holzinger in *Exodus* in Marti's *Kurzer Hand-Com.*, p. 13.

[4] *Manuel de l'histoire des religions*, 1880, p. 84 ; *Histoire comparée des anciennes religions*, 1882, ch. ix ; and *Outline of the History of Ancient Religions*, 1888, p. 85.

[5] *Geschichte des Volkes Israel*, Vol. I, p. 130 ff.

[6] *New World*, 1895, pp. 726–746 ; and *Religion of Israel to the Exile*.

[7] *Geschichte des Volkes Israel*, p. 21.

[8] *Jahvedienst en Volksreligie in Israel*, p. 15 ff.

[9] *American Journal of Theology*, Vol. IV, p. 549 ff.

[10] *Com. on Exodus* (ch. 3^{14}) ; and *Alttestamentliche Theologie*, p. 103, n.

[11] Cf. *e.g.* Kittel, *History of Israel*, Vol. I, p. 250 ; and Strack, *Com. on Exodus* (ch. 3^{14}).

[12] See his *Early Religion of Israel*.

the Joseph tribes and ultimately of Israel are, in brief, as follows: —

1. Of the three documents, J, E, and P, which narrate the exodus, two, E and P, relate that the name Yahwe was quite unknown until the time of Moses,[1] and that it was revealed to him while tending the flock at Yahwe's mount of Horeb or Sinai. Moses was told that he was treading on holy ground, *i.e.* that the mountain where he was was the sacred dwelling of Yahwe. P declares that the patriarchs had worshipped Yahwe under the name El-Shaddai, but that he was unknown to them by his name Yahwe. It was thus by the late date at which P wrote that the identity of two gods could be asserted, but in the earlier time of Moses such was not the case. A different name soon came to mean a different deity, even when it had been at first a mere epithet of a god already well known. E, on the other hand, declares[2] that up to the time of the exodus the ancestors of Israel had been idolators. True, he seems to make an exception in the case of Abraham, Isaac, and Jacob,[3] but the exception is more in seeming than in reality. E, as critics agree,[4] was an Ephraimite. In him the traditions as they were current among the Joseph tribes find expression; and those traditions had preserved the definite recollection that the knowledge of Yahwe was not original in Israel, but came in at the time of Moses. P was dependent for his knowledge of the subject upon E, and simply retold the story in his own way.

2. That Yahwe was the god of the Kenites is further shown by the nature of the sacrificial covenant which, according to E,[5] preceded the giving of the law. At that sacrifice to Yahwe it was not Moses or Aaron who officiated as though initiating Jethro into a new worship, but

---

[1] E, in Ex. 3^{13} ff.; P, in Ex. 6^{2} ff. [2] Josh. 24^{14}. [3] Ex. 3^{15}.
[4] Cf. Kuenen, *Hexateuch*, p. 248 ff.; Driver, *Introduction*, p. 115 ff.; and Carpenter and Harford-Battersby's *Hexateuch*, Vol. I, p. 116.
[5] Ex. 18^{12} ff. Cf. Budde, *Religion of Israel*, p. 22.

Jethro, the Kenite,[1] officiated as though introducing Moses into a new cult.

3. For centuries after Moses Sinai was regarded as the home of Yahwe, even when it lay beyond Israel's borders. From Sinai Yahwe came to give victory to his people in the days of Deborah;[2] to Sinai Elijah made a pilgrimage in order to seek Yahwe in his home;[3] and the prophetic writer who shaped the blessing of Moses echoed the same conception.[4] So deeply was the idea fixed in the religious thought that it survived in poetry in post-exilic times after the sanctity of the temple at Jerusalem had caused that structure to supplant Sinai in the popular thought as the abode of Yahwe.[5]

4. The Kenites were during several succeeding centuries the champions of the pure worship of Yahwe, even among the Hebrews themselves. Thus Jael, the wife of Heber, the Kenite, was the slaughterer of Sisera and the champion of Yahwe;[6] Jonadab, the son of Rechab, who was a Kenite,[7] and who maintained the nomadic ideals of the worship of Yahwe as they had existed in the steppe, aided Jehu in the eradication of Baal-worship in Israel, and in the establishment of the worship of Yahwe;[8] and centuries later the fidelity of these Kenitic Rechabites to Yahwe was such that it served admirably in the hands of Jeremiah to point a moral to his degenerate fellow-citizens.[9]

5. These Kenites (sometimes called Midianites[10]) seem, a part of them, to have joined Israel in their migrations,[11] becoming mingled with the people at various points, both in the North[12] and the South,[13] and in part they remained in their old habitat on the southern borders of Judah as a separate though friendly clan in the days of Saul;[14] finally,

---

[1] Cf. Jud. 1^{16} and 4^{11}.   [4] Deut. 33^2.   [7] Cf. 1 Chr. 2^{55}.
[2] Jud. $5^{4\,\text{ff.}}$.   [5] Cf. Hab. 3^1 and Ps. $68^{5\,[4]}$.   [8] 2 Kgs. 10^{15}.
[3] 1 Kgs. 19.   [6] Jud. $5^{24\,\text{ff.}}$ and $4^{17\,\text{ff.}}$.   [9] Jer. 35.

[10] The Kenites seem to have been a part of the Midianites. The latter was the broader term. Cf. Budde, *Rel. of Israel*, p. 19.

[11] Num. $10^{29\,\text{ff.}}$.   [12] Jud. $4^{17\,\text{ff.}}$; $5^{24\,\text{ff.}}$.   [13] Jud. 1^{16}.   [14] 1 Sam. 15^6.

in the days of David, they were incorporated into the tribe of Judah,[1] with which they were afterward counted.[2]

6. Now it was in the tribe of Judah, into which these Kenites had been incorporated, that, as most recent critics believe,[3] the J document was composed, — that document which betrays no consciousness that there had ever been a time in Israel when the worship of Yahwe was unknown, and which makes that worship almost coeval with man.[4] This fact is all the more striking when it is remembered that J had accepted so many of the Aramaic traditions[5] which were in all probability originally the possessions of the tribes farther to the north; and it is best accounted for by the supposition that the Kenites, whose god Yahwe originally was, had been fused with the tribe of Judah and had thus infused into Judæan tradition a strong semi-Arabian current of thought, on which was borne the consciousness of the immemorial knowledge of Yahwe. The perpetual separateness of Judah from the other tribes would help to maintain this tradition in spite of antagonistic currents from other quarters.

We conclude, therefore, that the result of the application of critical methods to the history of Israel is to make it clear that Yahwe was the god of the Kenites before the days of Moses.

Can we now go farther and determine anything of the nature of Yahwe or of his history before he became the God of Israel? Our investigation has, I think, placed us in a position to do this. But before proceeding to the task we must first notice a view which has sometimes been ad-

---

[1] 1 Sam. $30^{26\text{ ff.}}$, esp. 29.

[2] Cf. the genealogy of the Calebites and Bethlehemites in 1 Chr. 2, ending with v. 55, according to which David himself came from a family of Kenites. For a comprehensive statement of the Biblical data concerning the Kenites see Kuenen's *Religion of Israel*, pp. 179–182. The statement is condensed from an earlier article of Nöldeke.

[3] See discussions in Driver's *Introduction*, p. 115 ff., and Carpenter and Harford-Battersby's *Hexateuch*, Vol. I, pp. 104–106.

[4] Gen 4^{26}.   [5] Cf. Gen. 24 and the J element in Gen. 28–31.

vocated,[1] and which I formerly held,[2] that Yahwe in his primitive character was a storm god. In favor of this theory it may be urged that in the theophanies he is usually represented as coming in a thunder-storm;[3] that he is said to have led his people in a cloud;[4] that he appeared on Mount Sinai and in the temple as a cloud;[5] that in the middle books of the Pentateuch the cloud is used as a token of Yahwe's presence more than forty times; that the thunder was the "voice of Yahwe";[6] and that Yahwe controlled the stormy movements of nature.[7] These facts, which are beyond dispute, have led Winckler to regard Yahwe as a Hadad or a Ramman.[8]

There can be no doubt but that in the case of Yahwe, as in that of Hadad and Ramman, the god was conceived as controlling the phenomena of the weather and of the heavens, and of manifesting himself through them. Such conceptions may well have been entertained by residents in the Sinaitic region as well as by the Aramæans, resident in the various parts of Syria, and by the ancient Assyrians and Babylonians. Robertson Smith has, however, wisely warned us against finding the origin of any Semitic god in the personification of any one power of nature;[9] the primitive Semite looked to his god to perform for him the whole circle of divine activities, and the theory that Yahwe was primarily the personification of the storm is as inadequate as the theory that Hadad or Ramman was.[10] Indeed, we are now in a position to show that in all probability the Yahwe of the Kenites was developed like

[1] Cf. Stade, *Geschichte des Volkes Israel*, Vol. I, p. 429 ff.
[2] Cf. *Oriental Studies of the Oriental Club of Philadelphia*, p. 86 ff.
[3] Cf. Ps. 18, Ez. 1, Hab. 3, Isa. 19^1, and Job 38^1.
[4] Ex. 13 and 14.
[5] Ex. 19 and 1 Kgs. $8^{10.\,11}$.
[6] Ps. $29^{3\,\text{ff.}}$, Job 37^4, and Ps. 68^{33}.
[7] Ps. $104^{13.\,14}$, and Ps. $147^{8.\,16\text{-}18}$.
[8] *Geschichte Israels*, Vol. I, p. 37 ff.
[9] *Religion of the Semites*, 2d ed., p. 81 ff. Cf. Budde, *Rel. of Israel*, p. 57, n.
[10] See above, p. 227 ff.

Ramman, Hadad, and most other Semitic deities, by the same processes which we have traced elsewhere, out of the primitive mother goddess. The reasons for this view are as follows: —

1. The Kenites were a Semitic tribe resident upon the confines of Arabia itself, and it is to be presumed that their religious life had been continuous and subject to the ordinary laws of Semitic development. 2. They were a pastoral people,[1] who, according to the general laws of clan organization as outlined by Professor Keasbey,[2] must have developed the patriarchal clan. Like the Moabites,[3] their neighbors, then, the primitive goddess which was their common Semitic inheritance had among them been transformed into a corresponding masculine deity. 3. That Yahwe had some genetic connection with the primitive goddess is shown by the emphasis which his cult laid upon circumcision. We are told by J[4] that Yahwe sought to kill Moses till his son was circumcised, when the god became friendly.[5] The same writer tells us that after their entrance into Canaan[6] the marriageable young men were circumcised to complete their consecration to Yahwe. The Priestly writer represents circumcision as instituted in the time of Abraham as a token of Yahwe's covenant with him,[7] and informs us that no uncircumcised person could keep Yahwe's passover.[8] Such was the stress laid upon circumcision that in later times it became a synonym for Israelite, and uncircumcised a synonym for foreigner.[9] Circumcision became also a synonym for all the spiritua˙ and ethical qualities for which the Yahwe cult had then

---

[1] Ex. 2^{16} ff., 3^1 ff.   [2] Above, p. 30.   [3] Above, p. 140 ff.   [4] Ex. $4^{24, 25}$.

[5] The real meaning of the passage seems to be that Moses himself was uncircumcised, and that, therefore, Yahwe tried to kill him; that Moses's wife circumcised her son and smeared the blood upon Moses, so as to make it appear that the blood proceeded from an incision in him, and that then Yahwe was appeased. Cf. Wellhausen, *Heidentum*, 2d ed., p. 175.

[6] Josh. $5^{3, 9}$.   [7] Gen. 17.   [8] Ex. 12^{48}.

[9] Cf. 1 Sam. 31^4, 2 Sam. 1^{20}, 1 Chr. 10^4, and Rom. 3^{30}.

come to stand.[1] Abraham, it was thought, would save from the pit all who bore the mark of circumcision.[2] How deeply fixed this rite became is indicated by the struggle which Paul and others had to undergo in order to throw it off. The fixed and important character which it had at all periods indicates that from the very beginning it must have been considered a vital part of the religion of Yahwe, and must have had its motive in a conception which identified the rite with some of Yahwe's most important functions. Now, at the first, circumcision seems to have been in Israel itself a preparation for connubium.[3] The same rite with the same meaning we have previously found to be a part of the cult of the primitive mother goddess.[4] The existence of circumcision in the cult of Yahwe is therefore a strong argument for the theory that the cult of Yahwe was a direct development from that primitive Semitic worship.

4. Another indication that Yahwe was originally developed out of the mother goddess is the old Hebrew custom of swearing by Yahwe with the hand "under the thigh," *i.e.* upon the organs of reproduction.[5] This custom shows that in early times this part of the body must have been especially sacred to Yahwe. That would naturally be the case if he were developed from an Ashtart. 5. All critics agree that the passover was the feast of Yahwe which without question antedates the settlement in Canaan.[6] This festival, with its sacrifice of a sheep, we have already traced[7] in its beginnings to the feast of the primitive

[1] Cf. Rom. 2^{28} ff.

[2] Cf. Weber's *Judische Theologie*, 2d ed., pp. 342, 343.

[3] Cf. Gen. 34 and Ex. 4^{25}. In the latter passage the phrase "bridegroom of blood" connects it with connubium.

[4] See above, pp. 98 ff. and 110 ff.

[5] Cf. Gen. 24$^{2, 9}$, and 47^{29}.

[5] Cf. *e.g.* Wellhausen, *Prolegomena*, 5th ed., ch. iii; W. R. Smith, *Rel. of Sem.*, 2d ed., 227 ff., 445 ff.; Piepenbring, *Theology of the Old Testament*, p. 50; Budde, *Rel. of Israel*, p. 73 ff., and Moulton's article "Passover" in Hastings's *Dict. of the Bible*.

[7] Above, p. 109 ff.

Semitic goddess. If, therefore, it was a festival of Yahwe in the steppe, it is another link connecting him with that primitive cult. This inference receives confirmation from another quarter. Three times in the book of Deuteronomy are lambs — the characteristic offerings of the passover — called the "'*ashtaroth* of the flock,"[1] a phrase which probably had survived from primitive usage, when the connection of the offering with a deity bearing this name had been obscured by the introduction of no other epithet. Further confirmation of this view may be found in the fact of the sanctity of the threshold which is prominently recognized in the ritual of the passover.[2] Trumbull[3] traces this sanctity back to a recognition of the relation of the sexes to one another, and, although my own studies would lead me to think that the direct application which he makes of it to the passover leaves out of account some other important elements, yet his explanation of the fact harmonizes with the general explanation of this cult which we have reached. All these phenomena connected with the passover, therefore, confirm the view that that festival, even in the worship of Yahwe, goes back to a primitive Semitic root.

6. The origin of Yahwe for which we contend is confirmed by the most probable etymology of his name — that proposed long ago by Le Clerc[4] and accepted by many modern scholars — viz.: that the name Yahwe is a Hiphil form meaning, "He who causes to be," *i.e.* "gives life."[5]

[1] Deut. 7¹³, 28⁴·¹⁸.

[2] The name פסח probably has nothing to do with leaping over the threshold, but seems to mean a "dance." Cf. Toy, in *JBL.*, Vol. XVI, p. 178 ff., and Buhl, *Gesenius' Handwörterbuch*, 13th ed.

[3] *The Threshold Covenant*, ch. v.

[4] In his Commentary, on Ex. 6³, published in 1696. Cf. Driver in the Oxford *Studia Biblia*, Vol. I, p. 13. Le Clerc made a somewhat different application of it from that advocated here.

[5] The name occurs in the Old Testament in four forms, Yahwe, Yah, Yô, and Yehô. The second form occurs in proper names and in late poetry, and the third and fourth in proper names (cf. Gray, *Hebrew Proper Names*, p. 149 ff., and Bonk, *ZATW.*, Vol. XI, p. 125 ff.).

The explanation given in Exodus 3¹⁴ ff. no doubt represents the understanding of the name prevalent in Israel

The prevailing opinion among scholars is that the shorter forms are derived from the longer form, Yahwe. Friedrich Delitzsch, however, *Wo Lag das Paradies*, pp. 158-164, held that the shorter forms were the earlier, that they were derived from the name of the Babylonian god Ea or Ya, and that the longer form was developed from this by the Hebrews, a view which has not met with general acceptance (cf. Driver in *Studia Biblia*, Vol. I, pp. 4-6, and 10 ff.), although Hommel holds it (*Anc. Heb. Trad.*, p. 114). Margoliouth has more recently revived it in a crude form which has, so far as I know, convinced no one (cf. *Contemporary Review*, October, 1898, p. 581 ff.). The Babylonian origin is not made out (cf. Sayce, *Higher Criticism and the Verdict of the Monuments*, p. 87 ff., and *Early History of the Hebrews*, p. 164 ff.), and it is hardly possible philologically to derive a long form like Yahwe from a short form like Yah. Words everywhere wear down, but are not lengthened. More recently Spiegelberg (*ZDMG.*, Vol. LIII, p. 633 ff.) has proposed an Egyptian origin for the name Yahwe. It can, however, hardly be supposed that a people whose religious ideas hardly influenced those of Israel at all furnished them the name of their God.

Most scholars have sought a meaning for it in Hebrew and have explained it as follows:—

1. As a Qal of הוה an old form equivalent to היה in the sense of "He who is," *i.e.* "the self-existent" or "unchangeable one," following Ex. 3¹⁴; so Dillmann, *Com. üb. Ex.*, *in loc.*, Franz Delitzsch *Com. üb. Gen.* (1872) p. 26, 60, and Oehler (*Theol. of O. T.*, § 39). This form is, as has been remarked in the text, too abstract to be primitive.

2. As a Qal in the sense of "He will be," also based on Ex. 3¹⁴, and Hos. 2⁹. This theory of the name has given rise to several different interpretations: Robertson Smith (*British and Foreign Evangelical Review*, 1876) explained it as "He will be it," *i.e.* all that his servants look for; Driver (*Studia Biblia*, Vol. I, p. 17), Hommel (*Anc. Heb. Trad.*, p. 114), Marti, *Theologie* (3d ed., p. 61, n. 20): "He will approve himself," *i.e.* give evidence of his being, or assert his being, will reveal himself, or enact history; Skipwith: "He will be with us," *i.e.* in battle (in *Jewish Quarterly Review*, July, 1898). Of the applications of this explanation, the first and second are too abstract to be primitive. The third would do very well if we could be sure that the god who first bore the name was conceived chiefly as a god of war. Such a supposition is precarious, for as we have seen the early Semite looked to his god to do whatever he needed, and the war function was only one of many.

3. As a Hiphil from הוה (cf. Arab هوى and Job 38⁶) in the sense of "cause to fall," *i.e.* to send down. This explanation has received various applications, as follows: Robertson Smith (*Old Test. in Jewish Church*, 1st ed., p. 423) and Barton (*Oriental Studies of Or. C. of Phila.*, p. 87):

in the prophetic period, but, as many scholars have felt, it is too abstract to be primitive. Smend and Piepen-

"He who sends down rain"; Wellhausen (*Heidentum*, 1st ed., p. 175) and Stade (*Geschichte*, Vol. I, p. 429): "He who causes enemies to fall"; Margoliouth (*PSBA.*, Vol. XVII, p. 57 ff.): "He who sends down law"; and Holzinger (*Ein. in das Hexateuch*, p. 204, and *Com. üb. Exodus*, p. 13): "He who causes to fall," *i.e.* the destroying demon or destroyer. For reasons already explained this etymology now seems unsatisfactory.

4. The etymology suggested by Le Clerc has been adopted by several modern scholars, taking the name as a Hiphil of היה=הוה. Not all, however, take it in the same sense. Gesenius (*Thesaurus*, 1839, p. 577, n.), Baudessin (*Studien*, Vol. I, p. 229), Schrader (in Schenkel's *Bibel-Lexicon*), and Schultz (*Theologie*, 2d ed., p. 487 ff.) take it in the sense of "He who causes being" or "life"; Kuenen (*Religion of Israel*, pp. 279, 398), "He who gives existence"; and Lagarde (*ZDMG.*, Vol. XXII, p. 331, *Symmicta*, Vol. I, p. 104, *Psalterium juxta Hebræos Hieronymi*, p. 153 ff., *Orientalia*, Vol. II, pp. 27–30, and *Gött. Gel. Anzeigen*, 1885, p. 91) and Nestle (*Isr. Eigennamen*, p. 88 ff.) take it as "He who brings to pass," *i.e.* the performer of his promises. Of these the general nature of Yahwe, which a broad view of Semitic development leads us to take, makes "He who gives life" the most probable original meaning.

There are some traces of the name Yahwe among non-Israelites which are interesting. Among these I do not count names ending in Ya, for as Jastrow has shown (*JBL.*, Vol. XIII, p. 101 ff.), such names do not necessarily contain a divine element. This applies even to *Bit-ya*, which W. Max Müller (*Asien und Europa*, p. 312 ff.) finds in a list of Thothmes III. *Ya-u-bi-'i-di*, a king of Hamath in the days of Sargon (see Schrader, *KAT.*[2], p. 23, and *KB.*, Vol. II, p. 57), in whose name *Yahu* appears as a divine element, is very interesting. It suggests the possibility that the Kenites who in earlier days settled in the north had extended their influence to Hamath, so that the epithet by which they called their god had been applied by the Hamathites to their Hadad. It is possible, of course, that the Aramæans developed the name independently. Baudessin has shown (*Studien*, Vol. I, p. 180 ff.) how the name Yahwe passed to Greek writers from the Jews as 'Ιάω. Macrobius (*Saturnalia*, I, 18, 19 ff.), connects the name 'Ιάω with the Clarian Apollo. There is also considerable evidence which was collected by Movers (see *Phœnizier*, Vol. I, pp. 542–547), which connects 'Ιάω with the Phœnician Ἄδωνις. Lenormant thought (*Lettres assyriologique*, 1st ser., Vol. II, pp. 196–201), that the Phœnicians also had the name as applied to this god in the sense of the "self-existent one." Driver (*Studia Biblia*, Vol. I, p. 3) claims with considerable force that the name, if derived from הוה can hardly have been of general Canaanitish usage, because in Phœnician as in Arabic and Ethiopic the substantive verb in כן. It is possible that they used הוה also as well as their Hebrew and Aramaic neighbors, only

bring's[1] objection that Israel did not in the Old Testament period look upon Yahwe as especially the creator is wide of the mark, if Yahwe was his name first among the Kenites. To find its meaning we must look at the religious conceptions of the Kenites, and not those of later Israel. The Kenites were without doubt in their general religious conceptions practically on a level with their Semitic neighbors of the period, and among such peoples nothing would be more natural, as the preceding pages have shown, than to call one of their gods of fertility the giver of life.

Indeed, there is some evidence to show that the name was actually employed far beyond the bounds of the Kenites, and that it has entered as an element into at least one Aramaic proper name.[2] Yahwe seems, therefore, to have been an epithet applied by more than one family of western Semites to gods of the Semitic life-giving type.

7. Another fact which indicates the connection of Yahwe with the primitive Semitic cult is the connection of the Kenites with palm trees. The city of Jericho was at one time one of their seats,[3] and Jericho was a city of palm trees.[4] Elim, which was apparently a sacred oasis in the neighborhood of Sinai, contained its twelve sacred wells and its seventy palm trees.[5] About Sinai itself, in ancient as in modern[6] times, the culture of the palm tree

the word has not chanced to survive in any extant inscriptions. At all events, the view which we are led to take of the meaning of Yahwe makes it a tempting hypothesis to suppose that either as a native Phœnician epithet, or as one borrowed from their Hebrew and Kenite neighbors, the Phœnicians applied the name Yahwe, "the life-giver," to their god of healing, Eshmun-Adonis, though it may well be that the 'Ιάω which was applied to Adonis was of different origin from the 'Ιάω which was borrowed from the Jews. For a recent account of the occurrence of this name in Greek sources, cf. Deissmann, *Bible Studies*, 1901, pp. 321-336.

[1] Piepenbring, *Theology of the Old Testament*, p. 100 ff., and Smend, *Lehrbuch*, p. 21, n. 1.
[2] Yahu-bidi, cf. Schrader, *KAT*.[2], p. 23. Cf. *KB.*, Vol. II, p. 57.
[3] Jud. 1^{16}.   [4] Deut. 34^3.   [5] Ex. 15^{27}.
[6] Cf. Wellsted's *Travels in Arabia*, Vol. II, p. 12.

must have been known; and, no doubt, its culture helped to keep alive among the Kenites the religious conceptions and practices which their primitive forefathers had connected with that tree. Perhaps the recollection of the connection of the Kenites with the palm is found in the story of the union of Tamar[1] (Palm) with Judah. If not the Kenites, the tale at least is evidence for the absorption in Judah of some clan to which the palm was sacred, — a clan which seems to have made the palm its totem.[2] Afterward there was on the border of Judah and Benjamin a place known as Baal-Tamar, — a name which bears witness to the worship of a god of the primitive Semitic type. There seems to be some evidence that the place was once named for the old Semitic goddess;[3] there can, therefore, be little doubt that the characteristic Semitic cult was known among the early clans which afterward were fused in the tribe of Judah. These clans may not all have been Kenites, but the union of the Kenites with such clans, so as to form the tribe of Judah, is itself proof of affinity between them, and an argument in favor of the similarity of their conceptions and institutions.

The original connection of Yahwe with the palm tree also receives some confirmation from the fact that palm trees formed a part of the ornamentation of his temple as conceived by Ezekiel[4]; and, as Ezekiel is thought to have had as his model the temple of Solomon, it is probable that they had a place in that temple also. The place of the palm tree in the book of Enoch[5] may be due to Babylonian influences; but, even then, such influences would be much more readily assimilated if there was a lingering conception that such a tree was fundamentally connected with Yahwe.

[1] Gen. 38.
[2] Winckler, *Geschichte Israels*, Vol. II, p. 104, would interpret this story as the conquest of Judah over the place, Baal-Tamar.
[3] Cf. 1 Kgs. 9^8. Winckler (*op cit.*, p. 97 ff.) is probably right in omitting the conjunction of the Massoretic text, and reading "Baalat-Tamar."
[4] Ez. 41^{18}.   [5] Eth. Enoch, 24.

Our studies, therefore, taken in connection with the work of critical students of the Old Testament, enable us to trace the ancestry of Yahwe back to primitive Semitic times. Primarily Yahwe was not radically different from other deities of the steppe and the oasis; and in its earliest form the religion to which Moses introduced Israel cannot have differed radically from other Semitic cults. An endeavor will be made a little later to estimate the content of Mosaism, and to trace the process by which the distinctly moral elements of the Yahweism of the prophets were introduced; but, for a clear understanding of our subject, it is necessary first to determine something of the ritual and the religious conceptions which belonged to Yahwe in common with other Semitic gods, and which passed with him from the Kenites to the Israelites.

Critics are agreed[1] that the passover, as distinct from the feast of unleavened bread, belongs to primitive Yahweism.

It is described even by P (Ex. 12^{1-14}) as practically a nomadic festival, — a commensal meal, not unlike those of Arabic paganism. If, however, our previous investigation has any bearing on the primitive nature of Yahwe and his worship, there must have been some sexual conceptions, and probably in the earlier days some similar rites, connected with the passover, which in P's account have been eliminated. It is, of course, possible that among the Kenites less stress may have been laid upon these elements than among the Semitic peoples generally, but such a supposition is hazardous and cannot be accepted without clear proof. In later times we find Hannah at the time of Yahwe's festival — probably the passover — praying for offspring and gaining the answer to her prayer,[2] a fact which shows that there still survived in connection with Yahwe's feast some of those conceptions of fertility which

[1] Cf. *e.g.* W. R. Smith, *Rel. of Sem.*, 2d ed., pp. 333 ff., 346 ff.; Wellhausen, *Prolegomena*, 5th ed., ch. iii; Budde, *Rel. of Israel*, p. 73 ff.
[2] 1 Sam. 1.

pertained to the primitive goddess.[1] Later Hebrew sentiment explained the misfortunes of the house of Eli[2] on the ground that he did not restrain the loose conduct of his sons upon such occasions, but it is not impossible that in Eli's time such license may not under the excitement of Yahwe's festival have been considered wrong. The analogy of other Semitic deities would lead us to expect that in their worship of the giver of life and fertility the Semitic tendency to license, of which the Hebrews had their part, would find expression among them similar to that which it found elsewhere.

Budde,[3] though remarking that he can not and would not assert that the worship of Yahwe in ancient times was restricted to this simple annual festival, makes no attempt to determine what other features it contained. Beyond the supposition that victories in war were celebrated by especial worship of the god, he contents himself with the supposition that the worship of Yahwe was of an extremely simple nature. We are, however, now in a position to point out that the god of the Kenites, who inhabited oases like Elim and Jericho,[4] and who roamed over the steppe, would be celebrated in a second festival in the autumn at the gathering of the date harvest.[5] This festival, after the settlement in Canaan and the acquirement of agricultural habits of life, was naturally interpreted as the festival of the grape gathering,[6] but in the book of Leviticus, where archaic practices are frequently preserved, the memory that the feast had a nomadic origin is perpetuated in the name "Feast of Booths,"[7] — a name which is rightly interpreted as a survival of nomadic life.[8] At the time of the date harvest the nomads gather about the oases to lay in a supply of dates and to worship the god of the date tree; their tents would dot the outskirts of the oasis and form a striking feature of the landscape. The book of

[1] See above, p. 110.
[2] 1 Sam. 2.
[3] *Rel. of Israel*, p. 75.
[4] Jud. 1^{16}.
[5] Above, p. 111 ff.
[6] Ex. 34^{22}; 23^{16}.
[7] Lev. 23^{34}.
[8] Lev. 23$^{40-43}$.

Leviticus comes to the aid of analogy, therefore, to prove a second primitive festival of Yahwe. No doubt in later times the good things, which the grape harvest with its quickly fermenting grape juice afforded, gave to the agricultural festival a more luxurious and boisterous character than attached to the nomadic feast which it displaced, but that the one was merged into the other there can be no doubt.

This autumn festival was, as we have seen above,[1] preceded by the rite of wailing for Tammuz, — a custom which, as Robertson Smith pointed out,[2] has survived in the fasting and humiliation which preceded the Hebrew Day of Atonement, — a day which itself preceded this autumn festival. The ritual of the Day of Atonement is probably a survival under a new interpretation of the worship of Tammuz, or equivalent god, in connection with the worship of Yahwe, for there is no more reason to suppose that this was borrowed from the customs of the Canaanitish Baalim than that the date feast itself was. If, then, the worship of Tammuz was a part of the primitive cult of Yahwe, as it was of other Semitic cults, one may naturally ask if the primitive goddess Ashtart was not also originally connected with Yahwe. On this point we have no direct evidence. A number of scholars[3] recognize in the wailing for Jephthah's daughter[4] a survival of the Tammuz wailing. The story as it has been preserved to us makes it clear that the wailing was performed, not for a deceased god as at Gebal,[5] but for a goddess as at Carthage.[6] Whether this cult in Gilead was directly connected with the Yahwe cult in early times is exceedingly problematical. It was probably connected with some local clan cult of the tribe of Gad or Manasseh. Winckler has with much acuteness shown[7]

---

[1] p. 100.   [2] *Rel. of Sem.*, 2d ed., p. 411 ff., especially p. 414.
[3] W. R. Smith, *op. cit.*, p. 416; Moore, "Judges," in *Inter. Crit. Com.*, p. 305; and Winckler, *Geschichte Israels*, Vol. II, p. 140 ff.
[4] Jud. 11⁴⁰.   [5] Above, p. 245.   [6] Above, p. 255 ff.
[7] *Geschichte Israels*, Vol. II.

that many of the traditions of patriarchal Israel go back to myths of Tammuz and Ashtoreth. No doubt in his application of this solution to the period of David and after, he has applied his key where it is unnecessary, but many of his suggestions seem exceedingly plausible. If they are true, this common Semitic mythology was well known in ancient Israel, and it is surely a gratuitous supposition to claim that it was all borrowed from other sources than the Kenites. Analogy thus leads us to believe that probably the Yahwe worship of the Kenites contained an Ashtart. If such was the case, some will be ready to urge that that is no evidence that such worship was adopted by Moses. It must be admitted, however, that if the Kenites associated an Ashtart with Yahwe, Moses and the Hebrews would inevitably worship her too. Converts to a new religion are not its reformers, but its blindest devotees. Gratitude to the deity who had delivered them from Egypt would compel the early Israelites to take the cult of that god over *in toto*. For reasons, however, which will be adduced a little later such a goddess, if connected with Yahwe, must as a goddess of the steppe have had a character comparatively mild and consequently innocent as compared with the Ashtaroth of more bountiful and luxurious Canaan, or the Ashtart of the mercantile, rich, and luxurious Sidon. Increasing wealth increased the evil tendencies of this cult; thus Ashtart, "the abomination of the Sidonians," became a byword even among her Semitic kinsmen.

Along with the two feasts which can be traced to primitive Yahweism, and along with Tammuz and Ashtart, we must place the pillar (*masseba*), common to Yahwe with other Semitic deities, and which continued to represent him down to the time of Hosea,[1] and probably till the reform of Josiah. Here too must be placed the 'ashera, which marked the limits of primitive Semitic shrines, and which were not eliminated from Yahwe's temple till the

[1] Gen. 28^{22}, Hos. 3^4, Deut. 7^5, and 2 Kgs. 23^{14}.

time of Josiah.[1] If the foregoing argument be valid, these objects must have been as much a part of the Yahwe ritual of early days as of that of any Semitic god.

Yahwe, the god of the Kenites, then,—probably Yahwe as Moses knew him,—was a Semitic god of the oasis and the wilderness, of the type found in the Arabian environment. He was a god of life in the broad sense of that term; the Tammuz wailing was a part of his ritual; probably to his myths were attached all those feminine associations which are implied in the wailing for Tammuz. This god, because of the nature of the weather in the region where his people lived, had become associated in their minds with clouds, storms, and thunder; because of their warlike struggles with their neighbors, he was also regarded as the giver of victory in war. The new cult, to which Moses introduced Israel, did not, therefore, differ as much from the worship of their neighbors, or even from their own former clan cults, as even critical scholars are wont to suppose.[2] The chief and significant difference, as has often been said, lay in the fact that the worshippers were bound to the god by covenant and not by kinship;[3] but in this difference, as will be pointed out in more detail below, lay the possibility of all spiritual progress.

Israel, with her new faith, entered soon into a new land — a land where nature was more benignant than on the steppe; where human effort was rewarded with more abundant harvests, so that to those accustomed to the poorer life of the wilderness it seemed a "land flowing with milk and honey." In this land they found Canaanitish tribes dwelling, whose gods had originally been gods of the wilderness, like Yahwe, with a comparatively simple ritual, but who in their more luxurious environment had become considerably transformed. The revolt-

[1] 2 Kgs. 23[4, 14].   [2] Cf. Budde, *Rel. of Israel*, p. 73 ff.
[3] Cf. W. R. Smith, *Rel. of Sem.*, 2d ed., p. 318 ff.; Piepenbring, *Theology of the Old Testament*, p. 30; and Budde, *op cit.*, p. 35 ff., esp. p. 38.

ing aspects of their worship had become more revolting, the inequalities among their worshippers much greater. How inevitable it was that Israel should worship these deities Budde has depicted with great clearness and force.[1] It was the commingling of their worship with that of Yahwe which introduced into the latter some elements of civilization which were much needed, but which had been lacking in the Yahweism of the desert. Ultimately, too, these Canaanitish cults proved not only as reagents for the purification of Israel from the old clan cults, as Budde supposes,[2] but from the baser and grosser elements inherent in itself. How this came about we shall try to sketch presently; but, for the sake of clearness of thought, it will first be necessary to consider a little more fully what the moral contents of Mosaism were.

Much effort has been made to maintain the position which criticism had reached in the time of Ewald, that the kernel of the Elohistic decalogue,[3] which is repeated in Deuteronomy,[4] is of Mosaic origin.[5] It is of little avail to point out that the Egyptian book of the dead, which is older than Moses, contains nearly all the moral requirements of the decalogue.[6] Possibility of existence does not demonstrate actual existence; and the actual existence of the moral decalogue in the time of Moses seems to be made practically impossible by the existence of a ritualistic decalogue in J[7] which is evidently older than the moral decalogue of E.[8] If the Pentateuch contains any

---

[1] *Op cit.*, pp. 42-60.   [2] *Ibid.*, p. 71.   [3] Ex. 20.   [4] Ch. 5.

[5] Cf. Dillman, *Alttestamentliche Theologie*, pp. 58, 105, 228, and 426 ff.; Kittel, *History of Israel*, Vol. I, p. 198; Robertson, *Early Religion of Israel*, p. 70, n.; Bruce, *Apologetics*, p. 209; and Peters, President's address before the Society of Biblical Literature and Exegesis, December, 1900. The argument that the author of Deut. 10 must have known the moral decalogue in J is not convincing.

[6] See ch. cxxv of the Book of the Dead in *PSBA.*, Vol. XVII, p. 216 ff.

[7] Ex. 34.

[8] Cf. Wellhausen, *History of Israel*, p. 392 ff.; *Prolegomena*, 5th ed., p. 400 ff.; Kuenen, *Religion of Israel*, p. 244 ff.; Briggs, *Hexateuch*, p. 189 ff.; and Budde, *Rel. of Israel*, p. 172, n.

decalogue which dates from the time of Moses it must, accordingly, be the decalogue of J, which reads as follows : —
1. Thou shalt worship no other god.
2. Thou shalt make thee no molten gods.
3. The feast of unleavened bread thou shalt keep.
4. The firstling of an ass thou shalt redeem with a lamb. All the firstborn of thy sons thou shalt redeem.
5. None shall appear before me empty.
6. Six days thou shalt work, but on the seventh thou shalt rest.
7. Thou shalt observe the feast of weeks and of ingathering at the year's end.
8. Thou shalt not offer the blood of my sacrifice with leavened bread, neither shall the sacrifice of the passover be left until the morning.
9. The first fruits of thy ground thou shalt bring unto the house of Yahwe, thy God.
10. Thou shalt not seethe a kid in its mother's milk.

These commands are almost purely ritualistic, and at first glance betray, perhaps, to the unpractised eye nothing which might not be Mosaic. True, the command to worship no other god was not kept ; but it is nevertheless possible that it may have existed as a prohibition of the introduction of other gods into Yahwe's proper domain. The second command of this decalogue is really not a prohibition of idols, but only of expensive idols. In the nomadic life and among the poorer after the settlement in Canaan there were two kinds of idols : "graven images," made of wood, and "molten gods," cast of silver and gold.[1] Sometimes the latter were of wood overlaid with gold. What the decalogue of J really prohibits is the making of these molten gods, *i.e.* the carrying of luxury and extravagance into the worship of Yahwe. It is the protest of Spartan simplicity and religious conserva-

---

[1] Cf. Moore, "Judges," in *Inter. Crit. Com.*, p. 375.

tism against wealth and innovations. This command might, therefore, well be nomadic. The same may be said of the redemption of the firstlings of men and of asses; it is likely that human sacrifices were outgrown, except upon extraordinary occasions, before the settlement in Canaan, and other reasons may have led to the exemption of the firstborn of the ass. The command that none should appear before Yahwe empty, *i.e.* each should bring a gift or sacrifice of some kind, is as appropriate to the life of the wilderness as to that of settled Canaan. The exclusion of leaven from Yahwe's sacrifices, and the obligation to consume the passover victim before morning, are both obligations which were felt in the nomadic form of life.[1] The same is true of the prohibition to seethe a kid in its mother's milk.

A careful examination of some of the remaining commands produces, however, a different impression. The keeping of the feast of unleavened bread is an agricultural and not a nomadic regulation. It must have been introduced into the present decalogue after the settlement in Canaan; but it is quite possible that it displaced a command to keep the passover which stood in an earlier nomadic decalogue. As the feast of unleavened bread and the passover were merged into one, it would be very easy for the agricultural name in course of time to displace the nomadic. Similarly, the command to observe the feast of weeks is an obligation of agricultural and not of nomadic life. As it stands it is coupled with a command to observe the feast of "ingathering," or of "tabernacles." In the later Hebrew calendar these two feasts occurred some months apart; why, then, should they be here united in one command? Is it because the command is but a rewording of an earlier nomadic law expressive of the obligation to observe the Tammuz wailing and

---

[1] Cf. the sacrifice of the Arabs, witnessed by the son of Nilus, which was consumed before the sun obscured the morning star. See W. R. Smith, *Rel. of Sem.*, 2d ed., p. 338.

keep the date harvest festival? Such a theory is not impossible and it is certainly attractive. If we take this view, the substance of nine of these commands may with plausibility be attributed to Moses.

Of the tenth, the command to keep the seventh day, the same in the opinion of some scholars cannot be said. The sabbath seems to Jastrow and Budde to have been of Babylonian origin, and not a part of the religion of the steppe.[1] Budde thinks it became an institution of Yahweism during those years when Israel was making the transition from nomadic to agricultural life, and when Yahwe was being transformed from a god of the oasis and the steppe to a Palestinian Baal. Perhaps it was then organized into the form in which we now have it, but as Toy[2] has shown, it probably goes back to a taboo which is considerably older. Probably, then, this command has displaced the expression of this early taboo in an earlier nomadic decalogue. We have now no means of proving this, though from what has been said of the other commands, it does not seem improbable.

We conclude, then, that Moses probably summed up the precepts of the worship of Yahwe in ten "words"; that if he did so, the decalogue of J has more nearly preserved them than any other part of the Pentateuch, but that even the decalogue of J as it now stands has undergone some changes since the time of Moses.

In close connection with the decalogue there stands in the Old Testament the ark, called variously "the ark," "the ark of Yahwe,"[3] "the ark of the covenant of Yahwe,"[4] and "the ark of the testimony,"[5] which, according to a late tradition,[6] contained the decalogue written on tables of stone. This ark seems to have been a box similar to those which the Egyptians and Babylonians used

---

[1] Cf. Jastrow in *American Journal of Theology*, Vol. II, pp. 312–352, and Budde, *Rel. of Israel*, p. 66 ff.
[2] Cf. *JBL.*, Vol. XVIII, pp. 190–195.
[3] In J, E, and Samuel. [4] In D. [5] In P. [6] 1 Kgs. $8^{9, 21}$.

for carrying their gods from place to place.¹ Among the Hebrews the ark probably formed a kind of nomadic temple.² The fact that in the Judæan source, J, the ark plays no prominent part, but Yahwe is represented as dwelling at Sinai, while his angel goes before Israel,³ and in E, the Ephraimite source, the ark plays a much more prominent part,⁴ led Wellhausen and Stade to believe ⁵ that the ark was originally the movable sanctuary of the Joseph tribes from whence, after the union of the tribes, it was adopted by the nation. This view has been adopted by many others.² As Moses was the deliverer of the Joseph tribes, it is altogether probable that the ark was of Mosaic origin, and was a part of the Yahwe ritual of the time of the wilderness sojourn.

The difficulties with reference to the decalogue and the several versions in which it exists, have led these scholars to doubt the accuracy of the tradition that the ark contained a copy of the table of ten words. They have supposed that it contained a sacred stone or aerolite, similar to the sacred stone in the Qa'aba at Mecca, which was a kind of fetich. This may be true, but our analysis of the decalogue of J has shown us how possible it is that a nomadic decalogue of ritual lay back of J's ten words. It would be most natural for such a decalogue to be inscribed on such a sacred stone. The tradition, therefore, seems worthy of credence.

---

¹ Wilkinson, *Ancient Egyptians*, Vol. III, p. 289; Delitzsch, *Assyrisches Handwörterbuch*, under *elippu*, and "Isaiah" in *SBOT.*, p. 78.

² Cf. Wellhausen, *Prolegomena*, 5th ed., p. 46, n., and *Heidentum*, 2d ed., p. 215; Stade, *Geschichte*, Vol. I, p. 457; Nowack, *Archæologie*, Vol. II, p. 3 ff.; Benzinger, *Archæologie*, p. 367 ff.; Winckler, *Geschichte Israels*, Vol. I, p. 70 ff.; Couard in *ZATW.*, Vol. XII, p. 53 ff.; and Hopkins in *JAOS.*, Vol. XX, pp. 303–308.

³ Ex. 32².

⁴ Even if it be true, as Driver supposes ("Deuteronomy" in *Inter. Crit. Com.*, p. 118), that J originally described how Moses made the ark, that would not affect this conclusion, for by the time of J, as we have pointed out above, many of the Ephraimitic traditions had become current in Judah and are mingled with the Judæan in J's writing.

⁵ See references in n. 2, above.

Couard believes[1] that the ark was carried from Jerusalem by the Egyptian king, Shishak, in the time of Rehoboam. That would adequately explain its disappearance from the later history. That disappearance would also give scope to the traditions to substitute without conscious violence the ethical decalogue of later times for the ritualistic decalogue of earlier days, in response to the advance of the moral consciousness.

Moses then, we may suppose, gave Israel its Yahwe worship, its ark as a movable temple, and a ritualistic decalogue. In course of time the nation passed on from the steppe, and, attracted by the more fertile fields of Palestine, won its way into Canaan. It was then most natural for them to give some worship to the Baals. Later, in the time of David, it was thought that when one entered upon a new land it was necessary to worship the god of that land,[2] and centuries later than this the Babylonians whom Sargon imported into Samaria found it necessary to propitiate the god of the new land in which they found themselves.[3] That the Israelites actually worshipped the Baalim Hosea directly testifies.[4] The worship of Yahwe as their own tribal god was also maintained, and in process of time, as Budde has so well depicted,[5] Yahwe became a Baal, — a god of the land. Agricultural festivals, once celebrated to the Baalim, became festivals of Yahwe, and agricultural functions, once foreign to him, were now thought to be his.

The proof that Yahwe became a Baal is of various kinds, as follows:[6] 1. Saul and David, both champions of the worship of Yahwe, gave names to their sons into which Baal enters as a constituent element, as Ish-Baal, Meri-Baal, and Baalyada, — names in which critics generally agree that Baal is an epithet of Yahwe. 2. The shrines of Baal became in many places, as Bethel,

---

[1] *ZATW.*, Vol. XII, p. 84.
[2] 1 Sam. 26^{19}.
[3] 2 Kgs. 17$^{24-34}$.
[4] Hos. 2^5.
[5] *Rel. of Israel*, ch. ii.
[6] Cf. Budde, *op cit.*, p. 106 ff.

Schechem, and Hebron, shrines of Yahwe. The processes by which this was accomplished are described to us in Jud. 6. It resulted from the conquest of Yahwe and Israel over the Canaanites and the local Baalim.[1] Yahwe had proven himself stronger than these gods by conquering their land and their shrines. Gradually, as he became associated with their shrines, traditions arose to explain how he had consecrated them in former days by revealing himself to patriarchs or heroes there, so that Israel came to believe that Yahwe was only conquering back that which had been his own. The old rites continued, but now they were rites of Yahwe. 3. The transformation of Yahwe's ritual from the simple nomadic to the rich agricultural type, and its fusion with previously existing Canaanitish ritual, is another proof that Yahwe became a Baal. To this transformation the prophets bear direct witness, — Amos declaring that such ritual formed no part of the wilderness religion,[2] and Hosea that Yahwe was the giver of plenty.[3] 4. Another proof that Yahwe became a Baal, is the fact that the bull became his symbol. It has been pointed out already[4] that in agricultural communities the bull frequently became the symbol of the deity, who was regarded as the giver of agricultural plenty. This became true also of Yahwe in Israel. Jeroboam could say of the bull images at Bethel and Dan, which from their diminutive size were called "calves," "Behold thy god, O Israel, which brought thee up from the land of Egypt,"[5] *i.e.* "behold Yahwe." Probably similar images were in the temple of Yahwe at Gilgal.[6] In the temple at Jerusalem the bull symbols appeared in another form; they there supported the great laver. From such facts as these it is clear that when Israel conquered Canaan, Yahwe became a Baal, — a god of the land. This accounts for the fact that Naaman took Pales-

---

[1] Budde, *op. cit.*, p. 103 ff.
[2] Amos 5^{21} ff.
[3] Hos. 2^8.
[4] Above, p. 201 ff.
[5] 1 Kgs. 12^{28}.
[6] Amos 5^{4} ff., Hos. 4^{15}, 9^{15}, 12^{11}.

tinian soil to Damascus in order that he might worship Yahwe there.¹ By the time of Elisha, Yahwe was so much a Baal that he could be worshipped only on Palestinian soil. For the same reason at a later time the Babylonians, resident in Samaria, learned the worship of Yahwe, so that as god of the land he might not send lions upon them.²

In the development of Yahwe into a Baal, his cult, or rather the conception of him held by his worshippers, gained something which was necessary before Yahwe could perform for the world the lofty service which lay before him, for it passed from the narrow, tribal type of religion, hostile to culture and civilization into the broader sphere of a national religion, capable of adapting itself to the purposes of a finer and more civilized life. This transformation was accomplished, as Budde has pointed out,³ by the achievement of Israelitish mastery over Palestine and the united efforts of prophets, priests, and kings. Meantime, on the outskirts of the nation lingered the Rechabites, a conservative force, maintaining the nomadic ideal, and presenting a continual protest against what they regarded as the degenerate tendency which was Baalizing Yahwe. The part performed by this element of the nation was in the end quite as necessary as that of their opponents for the preparation of the Yahwe cult for its high service to mankind.

This transformation of the god of the steppe into the Baal of a settled community was by no means an experience peculiar to Yahwe; it occurred wherever the nomads of the oasis and the desert passed over into settled agricultural communities. The Baals of Canaan were, as we have seen,⁴ themselves only gods who, like Yahwe, had sprung from Semitic nomadic society and had been Baalized a little in advance of him. Yahwe's kinship to them hastened in his case the Baalizing process.

While this Baalizing of Yahwe was a necessary part of

[1] 2 Kgs. 5¹⁷.
[2] 2 Kgs. 17²⁷,²⁸.
[3] *Rel. of Israel*, p. 77 ff.
[4] Above, pp. 147-150.

the preparation for the place he was to hold in the religion of the human race, for that place he would have been no more fitted than any other Semitic Baal, if providentially the Baalizing process had not been checked at the proper point, and Yahwe forever differentiated in the minds of his worshippers from these gods. The outward events which were the occasion of this differentiation were as follows: In the reign of Ahab the natural assimilation of Yahwe to Baal was interrupted by the violent introduction of a foreign influence. Ahab had married a Tyrian princess, who was of course allowed to bring the worship of her native gods with her. Being of an ambitious nature, she prompted her husband to trample upon the popular rights,[1] and thereby aroused the sentiment of the people against her. She seems to have looked with disdain upon the simpler religious rites of her new and comparatively rustic home, and to have endeavored to introduce the more ornate and voluptuous cult of Tyre. Tyre was at the time one of the world's great emporia ; through its sea-faring merchants the wealth of the nations flowed into it.[2] Its riches had pampered the lusts of its citizens, and had made the excesses of that Semitic worship, the rites of which appealed so strongly to the passions of men, as much worse than the rites of that worship at Samaria as those of Samaria were worse than those of the wandering tribes of the steppe. It was this new and sudden excess of wantonness combined with oppression which aroused the opposition of the conservatives in Israel. This opposition was headed by Elijah the Tishbite, from Gilead, a country of pasture lands where the forms of nomadic life and the original ritual of the worship of Yahwe were probably less disturbed by the settled life of Israel than in the more productive regions west of the Jordan. Accompanying this new assertion of popular rights and of Yahwe's abhorrence of foreign gods and oppressive, debased morals, there was manifested a new and unique conception of God and

[1] 1 Kgs. 2   [2] Ez. 27, 28.

of ethical standards. How far these were manifested in Elijah himself it is impossible to say ; but his work was in successive generations taken up by Elisha, Amos, Hosea, Isaiah, and the great succession of literary prophets down to the close of the Babylonian exile, and from Amos onward the new moral and monotheistic conception of Yahwe can be traced. This is not the place in which to sketch in detail this prophetic struggle ; those who wish to read it may easily do so in the masterly little treatise of Budde [1] so frequently mentioned already.

So far as the outward features of this struggle were concerned, it seemed at the start to be a battle between the nomadic ideal of Yahwe and the excessively voluptuous Baal of a wealthy Semitic city, — a struggle which appears perfectly natural, and indeed inevitable. We cannot, however, follow the story of the conflict far without perceiving that there were unexpected issues involved in it, — that unique ethical standards and conceptions of God were here struggling for expression, standards which are quite unaccounted for by their environment. From Amos onward practical monotheism, social justice, and purity — a justice and purity which are thought to have their root in the very nature of Yahwe — are proclaimed.

The way for this proclamation had been prepared by the covenant which Moses had mediated between Yahwe and his people. A god bound to his people by kinship could never exert upon his worshippers an influence for moral elevation which should transcend their inclinations. Like an Arabic sheik, he might be angry and neglect his people for a time, but in the last extremity he must help them, for his position, nay, his very existence, depended upon that of his kinsmen. With a covenant god all this was changed. Bound to his people by contract only, with an independent existence quite apart from them, he could easily cast off an unfaithful people who refused to fulfil their part of the covenant. Upon this fact the

[1] *Religion of Israel to the Exile.*

prophets seized, and from generation to generation urged it with persistence and force.[1]

This fact would have had little significance, however, but for the new moral and spiritual conception of Yahwe which they taught along with it. Never in the Semitic world before had such lofty conceptions of God been proclaimed; never had such ideals of life been urged upon a people. While these ideals form the burden of the utterance of all the literary prophets, they did not begin with them; they had been felt in part for some time in those prophetic circles in which the J and E documents were composed, and probably in germ were harbored in the breast of Elijah. This prophetic conception of Yahwe aimed to bring back his cult to what the prophets conceived to be its primitive purity. Such in every age has been the goal of reform, — to establish Mosaism, or apostolic Christianity, or whatever the primitive form of the religion in which the reform is working may have been. We have not yet reached a point of religious culture, where men generally are willing to work for, or to accept, a religious ideal which they are not persuaded is primitive. To consciously strive for an entirely new ideal is even now a rare phenomenon in religious activity. So the prophets labored and struggled, — Amos, to get rid of feasts which he declared formed no part of the wilderness religion;[2] Hosea, to take Israel away from her Baal lovers back to the wilderness ideal as he conceived it, of conjugal fidelity to Yahwe;[3] and subsequent prophets take up similar plaints and labor for similar ends.[4]

In this connection it will be of help to a clear understanding of the work of the prophets and the outward aids to their success to note four facts: 1. In this long battle Yahwe was not only differentiated from the Baals and the

---

[1] See *e.g.* Amos $3^{2,3}$; Hos. 2; Isa. 5^{1-7}; Jer. $31^{\text{ff.}}$; Ez. 20; and Isa. $50^{1\,\text{ff.}}$.

[2] Ch. $5^{24,25}$.   [3] Hos. 2.   [4] Cf. *e.g.* Isa. 1^{13-15} and Jer. 3.

clan cults of the various Israelitish tribes,[1] but from his own original nature. The Yahwe whose ancestry we have been tracing was, as Paul would say, the Yahwe according to the flesh; in the age of the prophets the Yahwe according to the Spirit appeared in the world. Yahwe at the close of the prophetic period — Yahwe, the one God of the world — was as conceived by his followers a very different being from Yahwe as worshipped by the Kenites and by Moses.[2] The latter was, as we have seen, a god of fertility, pleased with such rites as similar gods of fertility among Semites of a like degree of civilization were supposed to sanction. He was less gross than Baal only because the nomadic environment imposed greater simplicity of life upon his followers. Yahwe as conceived by the faithful in Israel at the end of the exile was the God of the world, just and righteous himself, and satisfied with nothing less in his followers. The conception of him then held needed but the broadening and deepening which was to come in part through the contact of his followers with a larger world in the succeeding centuries, and in part through the teaching of Jesus Christ, to become the ultimate conception of God for the ages, — metaphysically perfect,[3] morally perfect,[4] religiously perfect.[5]

2. In this transformation of Yahwe the absence of written religious records of the earlier time was a positive help. If there were written tables of law in the ark, as we have seen, they probably disappeared in the time of

---

[1] Budde, *Rel. of Israel*, p. 71 ff.

[2] If, as we have supposed, Moses conveyed to Israel a brief summary of ritual, and as many critics have also supposed, as the leader of Israel he judged causes (or brought them to the sacred lot of Yahwe for adjudication), it would be most natural for the successive legislation, each code of which was designed by its promoters to revive what they conceived to be primitive Mosaism, to be all ascribed to him.

[3] "God is Spirit," John 4^{24}.

[4] "God is light," 1 John 1^5. Light is used by this writer as equivalent to moral purity; darkness is his synonym for evil.

[5] "God is love," 1 John $4^{8,16}$. Love here has lost its old Semitic physical meaning. It is love as defined in 1 Cor. 13.

Rehoboam. The whole fate of the ritual and the conception of what Yahwe required were thereafter committed to tradition. If one came forward from Judah claiming one ideal as Mosaic, Ephraim, if she possessed a higher ideal, could claim the authority of her own traditions as proof of the Mosaic authority of the loftier conception. When the Deuteronomic law was afterward found in the temple, there was no authoritative written bar to its reception, and as that law appealed to the religious consciousness of the prophets of the time,[1] it too could be freely adopted. Thus freedom for advance without unnecessary friction was afforded. The ghost of the natural Yahwe could not rise to successfully contest the rights of the spiritual Yahwe.

3. The endeavor of the prophets to gain a hearing for their spiritual conceptions of God and their ethical conceptions of life were greatly aided by the outward events of Israel's history. A series of national disasters, resulting in the overthrow of the northern kingdom in 722 B.C. and of the kingdom of Judah in 586 B.C., gave especial point to the teachings of the prophets. The better minds among the people were thus aroused to listen and obey; while the obstinate were absorbed, either among the nations whither they were carried captive, or among the mongrel Samaritans where they were left.

4. It should be borne in mind that the prophetic endeavor of those centuries did not, in one sense, accomplish the ideal which at the beginning (or at least early in the conflict) it had set before itself. In the eighth century it had high hopes of sweeping away the ritual altogether;[2] but the reaction under Manasseh seems to have convinced the prophetic leaders that the time was not yet ripe for trusting their spiritual conceptions to the stormy voyage of the centuries, unprotected by some ark of legal forms. The Deuteronomic law was then formulated to embody the new conception of the fundamental

---

[1] 2 Kings 22^{13} ff.   [2] Cf. Amos 5$^{21-25}$; Hos. 6^6; Isa. 1^{13} ff.

principles of Yahweism in a practical working form. In this law all sanctuaries but one were abolished; all outward paraphernalia which might tend in the popular mind to associate Yahwe with Baal, or even with the common root from which both had sprung, were rigidly excluded. Ritual there was to be sure, but ritual robbed, in so far as it could be, of power to degrade the worshipper. *Maṣṣebas* and *'asheras* were swept away, and all sexual ritual was absolutely prohibited. In the adoption of this law, however, the older ideal was in some degree abandoned, and concession made to practical conditions. In the earlier days the prophets and the priesthood — at least in the northern kingdom — appear in strong antagonism to one another, but in the Deuteronomic reform they joined hands. A little later, in Jeremiah and Ezekiel, members of the Levitical and priestly circles became prophets. Ezekiel proposed for the post-exilic days a modification of the Deuteronomic law; others of the priestly circles followed in his steps, till by the time of Ezra and Nehemiah the earlier prophetic standards were quite reversed, and legal morality had become the ideal — instead of the free, spiritual morality of the earlier prophets.

This change seems to have been in its turn providential. The joyous period, when the inspiring voice of contemporary faith could nerve to noble endeavor, had passed away; times were at hand which would try men's souls, — times when an objective ritual for which Israel could struggle was a necessity, if she were to survive for the high service which awaited her. This ritual was codified and accepted, moreover, at a time when the prophetic ideals of Yahwe had deeply penetrated both people and priests, so that the new Levitical law, though compiled from the ancient and sometimes superstitious [1] usages of the old local sanctuaries, was so purified of most of its dross that it reflected the new conception of God.

The outline of the genesis and development of Yahwe

[1] Cf. Nu. 5$^{11-21}$ and the sacrifice to Azazel in Lev. 16.

given above may not be attested by evidence sufficient to commend it to those who are averse to critical study, or are unaccustomed to the reconstruction of the origins of civilization by the restoration to their original environment of fossil customs, born in barbarism, which survive long after their origin is forgotten. The evidence is, however, sufficient, I believe, to carry weight with those who have some familiarity with investigations in primitive religion and of the nature of the evidence which we have a right to expect.

The results which our discussions have reached are also most reassuring to the lover of the Old Testament. Nothing could show more conclusively than the above investigation does that the moral standards of the prophets and their conception of God are utterly unaccounted for by their environment. The tendency, shared by the ancestors of the Hebrews in common with other Semites, to deify the functions whereby physical life was produced, could give no promise, when judged by the fruits it produced in other places, of the rich and pure ethical and religious harvest which it bore in Israel. The primitive conception of physical fatherhood became after Hosea[1] the conception of a moral father with all the high qualities of an unselfish parent raised to an infinite power. The early conception of a deity who gloried in the processes of reproduction, however savagely they were indulged in, was replaced by the conception of Yahwe as a tender and affectionate Husband who grieved over the incontinent pollution of Israel, the bride of his choice, — a Husband whose love was the embodiment of all purity, whose rule demanded perfect ethical relations between his sons, and especially between his sons and daughters. If critical study makes it impossible for us to trace the birth of these conceptions back to Abraham or Moses, or to account for them by the supposition that they descended from heaven amidst the thunders of Sinai, it nevertheless

[1] Hos. 11^1.

emphasizes their real inspiration, for it demonstrates on the one hand that they first took their shape on earth in human minds, as all spiritual conceptions must, and on the other that there was nothing in their physical and social environment which adequately explains them, — that, after all, the inspiring touch of these prophetic hearts by the divine Spirit is their only real explanation. We go back to the rise of Semitic life, we test its nature at the root, we trace its many-branched trunk through the various civilizations; but we find in none of them except this little Hebrew branch [1] any potency or promise of spiritual flower or ethical fruit so rich and fair ; we trace the outward events of the appearance and growth of this little branch, we find here a favorable condition, there a providential adversity, but none of these fully account for the beauty of the branch or the purity of its flower and fruit. Nothing approaching it in sublimity [2] has without its help been produced in other parts of the world. We are compelled at the end of our study to confess that "men from God spake, being moved by the Holy Spirit." [3]

It must be remembered, however, that it is not as strange as it might at first appear to be, that such spiritual conceptions should have been grafted upon the Semitic stock, which has often seemed so sensual; for as was pointed out above,[4] recent investigation is opening our eyes to the fact that the religious and moral development of the race has been closely bound up with fatherhood and motherhood, and that the periods of religious

---

[1] I do not forget the good points of Mohammedanism, but Mohammed was clearly indebted to Judaism and Christianity for much of his conception of God.

[2] Single thinkers in Egypt, Greece, India, and China may have reached thoughts similar to these, but the sublimity which appears in Israel is that of a practical monotheism accepted by the whole nation, — men, women, and children ; the loftiest thoughts of God applied to daily duties by all.

[3] 2 Pet. 1^{21}.   [4] See above, p. 107.

growth in the individual coincide with the periods of physical preparation for these functions. Religious progress has always been most marked where the rational and mystical elements appear in the happiest combination. Where the rational element predominates, religion becomes a cold formality; where the mystical is in excess, it becomes fanciful and extravagant, losing real touch with life. But the mystical has always delighted to express itself in terms of spiritual matrimony, and is the purified form of that which the early Semites far back in the evolution of civilization so grossly expressed.[1] With all its excesses, therefore, we must consider the widespread Semitic cult as the preparation of a religious soil, in which the lofty conceptions of God and duty, which appear so unique in Israel, could take root and produce their fruit.

[1] See the paper of de la Grassarie, read in 1900 at the Paris Congress of Religion. Cf. *Revue de l'histoire de religion*, Vol. XLII, p. 158.

CHAPTER VIII

BRIEF ESTIMATE OF SEMITIC SOCIAL AND RELIGIOUS INFLUENCE ON THE NON-SEMITIC WORLD

WE have now concluded our brief survey of the birth of Semitic social and religious life, and its various developments among the Semitic peoples. Before concluding this imperfect sketch, it will be helpful to briefly indicate the various points at which the institutions studied in the preceding pages have touched and influenced the non-Semitic world. No extended discussion can be attempted here; we shall content ourselves with indicating what the influences have been, and the points at which they have been felt. To attempt to follow them out in detail would require the services of many specialists in several different fields; but to ignore them entirely would leave upon the reader an unjust estimate of the value of the institutions we have been studying as contributors to modern civilization.

From institutions such as these it is obvious that two circles of influence would radiate. From the barbarous Semitic institutions, perpetuated by religious conservatism far into a succeeding and higher civilization, corrupting and disintegrating influences would surely radiate. From the lofty and austere morality of the Hebrews of later times, from the lofty spiritual vision of the prophets, there have come, on the other hand, some of the best elements of subsequent civilization.

In attempting this brief estimate, we shall, for obvious reasons, confine our attention mainly to the world which lay west of the Semitic territory. The Semites of the ancient Babylonian kingdom of Kish must, through their colonies in Elam,[1] have exerted an important influence upon the kingdom of Elam and upon all the neighboring states which Elam could influence ; but until more of the inscriptions of Elam have been discovered and we are able to read the Elamitic language,[2] we cannot even reconstruct the Elamitic civilization, much less tell the influences which moulded it.

Similarly we might inquire whether after the time of Cyrus the institutions of the Persian conquerors of Babylon were affected by their contact with the older Semitic civilization, but no very positive results can at present be obtained. Cyrus himself speaks, in his well-known cylinder inscription,[3] as though he had become a worshipper of Babylonian gods, or at least of Marduk, but it is probable that in this respect he was simply a statesman who, as a matter of fact, kept his own native creed.[4] At all events, his immediate successors appear by their religious expressions[5] to be practically untouched by Semitic influences, and to have maintained the worship of Ahuramazda in tolerable purity. Whether Babylonian architecture influenced Persian architecture, or the Babylonian religious hymns the later Persian religious literature, are problems for the Iranian scholar rather than the present writer. They would not, even if we had their solution, give much help in the pursuit of the influences we are now trying to trace.

If now we turn to the other extremity of the Babylonian and Assyrian world, we come upon a territory where our problem, though far from soluble, presents us, even in

---

[1] Cf. *Delegation en Perse. Mémoires publiés sous la direction de M. J. de Morgan*, Tom. II, *Textes élamites-sémitiques*, par V. Scheil, Paris, 1900.

[2] For an attempt to read certain Elamitic words, cf. Jensen's "Alt- und Neuelamitisches" in *ZDMG.*, Vol. LV (1901), p. 223 ff.

[3] *KB.*, Vol. III², p. 120 ff.

[4] Cf. Gray in *JAOS.*, Vol. XXI², p. 179.

[5] Cf. Bezold's *Achimeniden Inschriften ; Assyrian and Babylonian Literature*, Aldine ed., N. Y., 1901, pp. 171-194, and Jackson in *JAOS.*, Vol. XXI², p. 160 ff.

the imperfect state of our present knowledge, with an answer which, though somewhat dim in outline, is probably in general correct. A group of contract tablets from Cappadocia, in the eastern part of Asia Minor, written somewhere between 1300 and 1100 B.C.,[1] attest the presence of a strong Assyrian influence in this part of Asia Minor at that period. These tablets contain proper names into which the names of the deities Assur and Ishtar enter as compounds, and make it probable that the Assyrian religion, as well as Assyrian culture, made itself felt in this region at that time.[2] It is hardly probable that the wave of Semitic migration represented by these tablets stands alone. If the Assyrians had not penetrated into this region at an earlier time than that just indicated, it is probable that the Aramæans had done so. At least, a little later their influence, Jensen thinks, can be distinctly traced.[3] Thus they had given the region a touch of Semitic influence. How far Semitic influences coming in this way penetrated the life and moulded the institutions of the country, it is impossible now to say. It was evidently considerable. A little later, and possibly at the time of which we speak, Cilicia and the regions to the westward seem to have been occupied by the Hittites, whose monuments indicate that they penetrated to the neighborhood of Cappadocia.[4] Hittite monuments are found in many parts of Asia Minor, and Hittite civilization must have penetrated the country deeply.[5] Not until the Hittite inscriptions are deciphered can we justly estimate how far Hittite civilization has been influenced by Semitic.

Jensen, who has struck out a new path for the decipherment of Hittite and has probably rightly identified some

[1] Cf. Peiser in *KB.*, Vol. IV, p. viii.
[2] For the contents of some of them cf. *KB.*, Vol. IV, pp. 50–57.
[3] *Hittiter und Armenier*, pp. 170–177.
[4] See Messerschmidt's "Corpus Inscriptionum Hettiticarum," in the *Mitteilungen der vorderasiatischen Gesellschaft*, 1900, I, p. 21, and II, Tafeln XXVII, XXVIII, and XXIX.
[5] See the work of Messerschmidt just cited, *passim*.

of the signs,¹ has shown that these inscriptions probably date from 1200 to 800 B.C. While it is probable that the Hittites were in this region considerably earlier than the time when their written monuments begin, it is also probable that they had felt the influence of the Semitic contact long before Tiglath-pileser I encountered them about 1100 B.C. in the region of Carchemish.² Probability receives in this case some slight confirmation from other sources. Some of the specimens of their art, like the statue, discovered by Koldeway,³ of the weather god, shows positive evidence of the influence of Babylonian and Assyrian art.⁴

It is not certain, however, that Hittite civilization was altogether dissimilar to the Semitic. It is true that many scholars have regarded the Hittites as belonging to the Turanian or Mongolian family of peoples,⁵ while Jensen believes them to be Aryans,⁶ and the ancestors of the modern Armenians. Jensen's arguments on this point are, however, too slender to be convincing. Jensen himself has pointed out that many of their characters resemble in certain characteristics⁷ Egyptian hieroglyphs, while Jastrow claims that many of their proper names found in Assyrian and Egyptian inscriptions are of the Semitic type.⁸ Sergi,⁹ from anthropological evidence, be-

[1] In two articles in *ZDMG.*, Vol. XLVIII, and his *Hittiter und Armenier*, 1898. For dates see the latter work, pp. 189–216.

[2] *KB.*, Vol. I, p. 33.

[3] Cf. Messerschmidt, *op. cit.*, Tafel I, Nos. 5, 6.

[4] Possibly too at a later time Semitic influences directly from Arabia were felt here. Ramsay (*Cities and Bishoprics of Phrygia*, p. 91, n. 2) inclines to accept a suggestion of Robertson Smith's that Leto, the name of a goddess of this region, is a corruption of Al-Lat.

[5] Cf. Wright, *The Empire of the Hittites;* Sayce, *Races of the Old Testament;* Conder, *The Hittites.*

[6] *Op. cit.*   [7] Cf. *Hittiter und Armenier*, p. 63.

[8] Cf. his article "Hittites," § 12, in *Encycl. Bib.* The point is of comparatively small value because the inscriptions use the term *Hittite* so loosely that they frequently refer to Semites under this name. Thus Sargon (*KB.*, Vol. II, p. 57) calls an Aramæan king of Hamath a Hittite.

[9] *Mediterranean Race*, p. 144.

lieves that the Hittites were an African race of the same stock as the Libyans or Berbers, and that all Asia Minor was peopled by this same stock, which he believes were one in race with the Pelasgians. In the midst of so many conflicting views one cannot hold any positive opinion with reference to the origin of the Hittites, though it may be pardonable to take the opinion of Sergi as a working hypothesis. If they are a branch of the great North African race, it is quite possible that the same oasis influence which produced the Egyptian Isis and the Semitic Ishtar may have given them a similar goddess. At all events, whether from native Hittite conceptions, or Semitic influences, or from both,[1] the Hittites possessed such a goddess.[2] The evidence of this comes not only from their monuments, but from the evidences of their influence on Asia Minor. Hittite civilization spread over all Asia Minor,[3] and it is altogether probable that the Phrygian goddess, known variously as Rhea, Attis, Cybele,[4] Leto, and Artemis, is but a later form of this Hittite divinity, who, whatever her home-born inheritance may have been, probably had a considerable element of Semitic conception about her. She dates from a time when the inhabitants of the country were totemistic and lived in caves, as many of her shrines were grottos.[5] That this goddess was in nature the same as Ashtart is clear from the fact that she was an earth goddess of fertility and love, that a feast was celebrated to her at the time of the vernal equinox, that the swine was sacred to her, that ceremonies practically identical with the Tammuz wailing were yearly celebrated

---

[1] Cults of similar nature would assimilate the more readily.

[2] Cf. Jensen, *Hittiter und Armenier*, pp. 157 ff., 166 ff., and Messerschmidt, *op. cit.*, Tafel XXVII, B.

[3] Cf. Jastrow, "Hittites," § 11, in *Encyc. Bib.*, and the evidence of the widely scattered inscriptions in Messerschmidt, *op. cit.*

[4] Cf. Strabo, X, 3, 12.

[5] Cf. Pausanias, X, 32, 3, and Ramsay, *Cities and Bishoprics of Phrygia*, pp. 89 ff., 138 ff.

to her,[1] and that she is often described by Greek writers as androgynous,[2] as we have seen the Semitic goddess in various places to be,[3] and that like the Semitic goddess, a god is in many places represented as her son.[4] The androgynous character indicates what we also learn elsewhere, that this goddess of Asia Minor, like the great Semitic deity, had a long career as a goddess in a matriarchal community,[5] before the changing conditions of civilization transformed her in some places to a male,[6] and that at some points religious sentiment crystallized (or was embalmed in literature) while popular conceptions were in a confused state with reference to her sex. This cult as has been said, was widely disseminated in Asia Minor.[7]

While we cannot claim that this cult in Asia Minor was solely of Semitic origin, it is probable that it was not only of kindred origin, but also deeply penetrated by Semitic influences. The cult of Aphrodite-Æneas, which flourished in the Troad, was, as Farnell has pointed out,[8] an offshoot of the cult of this old Phrygian-Hittite goddess. Much obscurity attaches to the person of Æneas, but Farnell's conjecture[9] that he was the mythical founder of a house of priestly kings who maintained the worship of the goddess seems the most satisfactory explanation of it. The

---

[1] Cf. Baudessin, *Studien zur semitischen Religionsgeschichte*, Vol. II, pp. 188 and 203–207; also P. Decharme's article "Cybele," in Darmberge and Saglio's *Dict. des ant. grec. et rom.*, p. 1682.

[2] Cf. Pindar, *Pyth.*, II, 127; Pausanias, VII, 17, 10; and Lucian, *de Syria Dea*, § 15.

[3] Cf. above, pp. 148 ff., 181 ff., 244, and 254; also *JAOS.*, Vol. XXI^2, p. 185 ff.

[4] Cf. Ramsay, *Cities and Bishoprics of Phrygia*, pp. 130 ff., 133 ff., 167 ff., 169 ff.

[5] Cf. Ramsay, *op cit.*, pp. 7 ff. and 94 ff.

[6] Cf. Ramsay, *op cit.*, pp. 7 ff., 52 ff., 167 ff.

[7] In addition to references given above cf. Herodotus, V, 102, Pausanias, III, 22, 4; Messerschmidt, *op cit.*, I, p. 33; and Ramsay's *Cities and Bishoprics of Phrygia*, pp. 51 ff., 89 ff., 130 ff., 133 ff., 138 ff. For Artemis at Ephesus, cf. Acts 19.

[8] *Cults of the Greek States*, p. 641.

[9] *Ibid.*, p. 638. Cf. Strabo, XIII, 1, 53.

myths of the wanderings of Æneas are the story of the diffusion of this cult.[1] By means of these myths we may trace it to Thrace, to Zacynthos, to Buthrotum, to the southeast coast of Italy, and to Eryx in the Island of Sicily,[2] where it met and mingled with waves of influence direct from Phœnicia.[3] On the way to these points it had planted itself in southern Laconia,[4] Arcadia,[5] and Argos.[6] All forms of the myth, however, represent the goal of Æneas as Italy, and it is certain that the cult was established at various points along the Italian shore of the Adriatic,[7] at Naples,[8] and also at Rome.[9] At the latter city it seems to have been unknown in the days of the kings, but was afterward introduced from the South. In later times it became a powerful influence, reënforced as it was by more recently imported influences from the East, for the corruption of Roman society and the destruction of the austere morals of the earlier Roman period.

From Phœnicia waves of migration to the westward began at an early date, — probably by 1400 B.C. or earlier, — and wherever the emigrants went, they carried with them the cult of their native goddess. We have already followed in part their course through the islands of the Mediterranean,[10] but they also made their way to the mainland of Greece, where settlements were made at several points, and Phœnician influence was accordingly a factor in the resulting religion and mythology.[11] Thus in Greece two waves of this cult met and mingled, one from Asia Minor and the region of Semitized Hittite influence, and

[1] Cf. the references in Farnell, *op cit.*, p. 737 ff. I am indebted to this work for a number of the references given below.
[2] For these places cf. Dion. Halic., I, 39-50.
[3] See above, p. 252 ff. [7] Catullus, XXXVI, 11.
[4] Pausanias, III, 22, 11. [8] *C. I. Gr.*, No. 5796.
[5] *Ibid.*, VIII, 12, 9. [9] Strabo, V, 2, 6.
[6] *Ibid.*, II, 21, 1. [10] Above, p. 252 ff.
[11] Cf. Farnell, *op. cit.*, p. 618 ff., especially, p. 624; Robert Brown, Jr., *Semitic Influence in Hellenic Mythology;* and Dyer, *The Gods of Greece*, pp. 163-173.

the other from Semitic Phœnicia. One of the places where Phœnician influence was most directly felt was at Thebes, in Bœotia. The Phœnician influence is not only attested by the name, Kadmos,[1] but Herodotus was acquainted with a tradition that Kadmos was a Tyrian.[2] The traditional origin of this worship at Thebes is confirmed by the functions of the Aphrodite worshipped there. She was a goddess of fertility, who presided over the relations of the sexes to one another, and was also regarded as the mother of Adonis, the wailing for whom formed a part of her ritual.[3]

The cult which thus penetrated Greece from two directions was spread pretty generally over it.[4] That it was not native to the Greeks is very clear.[5] Perhaps the cult found its way into Greece at a time before the development of wealth and luxury in Hittite and Semitic lands had removed from its peculiar rites the simple innocence of early days; or perhaps early Greek morals were too pure to be seriously corrupted by these streams from abroad. However this may be, if Farnell is to be believed,[6] Aphrodite in the early years of Greek history was little more than the personification of the power of fertility and love in life, and neither moral nor immoral. In later times — after the fourth century B.C. — this was considerably changed. The influence of the hetæræ spread in social life; national pride sank, and the temples of Aphrodite, as the restraints of the earlier time were thrown aside, became more and more what they had been in Phœnician cities like Tyre and Sidon, and from many centres debased Greek life.

By the beginning of the Christian era, then, this cult, which in one way or another had come to be widely scattered in the Mediterranean countries, had produced in the society of the Roman Empire, especially in the eastern

---

[1] From קדם, "the east."   [2] Bk. II, 49.   [3] Pausanias, IX, 16, 3.
[4] Farnell, *Cults of the Greek States*, p. 618 ff.
[5] Farnell, *ibid.*, p. 619 ff.   [6] *Ibid.*, p. 664 ff.

portion of it, a condition of social and domestic laxity analogous to that in ancient Israel against which Elijah and his successors had protested. At Corinth, for example, the sensuality so strongly rebuked by the apostle Paul[1] is directly traceable to the corrupting influences of the temple of Aphrodite which overlooked the city.[2] The corruption thus produced by the religious sanction, which was thrown over practices which were no longer *naïf* and innocent, must be set down to the disadvantage of the old Semitic cult. To that extent it is chargeable for human degradation.

Out of the society of these times there came, however, an institution for the birth of which the laxity in social life, produced by the worship described above, is in large part responsible, concerning which different individuals will make widely different estimates. Whether monasticism — for it is this to which I refer — has been on the whole a blessing to the world depends upon the point of view from which one looks at it. No doubt there were many forces at work in the society and theology of the early Church to produce that exaltation of virginity and celibacy in the first century which culminated in the formation of the monastic orders of the fourth and subsequent centuries;[3] but one of those forces—and one which, I am convinced, was more potent than has often been supposed — was a reaction from that sensuality, consecrated under the name of religion, which was destroying the society of the civilized world. It is little wonder that for a time earnest souls should almost couple the matrimonial state, even in its purity, with heathenism, and extol celibacy as the only pure and Christian life.

[1] 1 Cor. 5, 6. [2] Pausanias, II, 5, 1.
[3] Cf. *Kirchengeschichte*, von K. Müller, Vol. I, pp. 208-216, *Monasticism, its Ideals and History*, by Adolf Harnach, translated by C. R. Gillett, N.Y., 1895, pp. 5-44, *The Monastic Life*, by T. N. Allies, London, 1896, chs. i-iii, *Christian Monasticism*, by I. G. Smith, London, 1892, ch. v, *Monasticism, Ancient and Modern*, by F. C. Woodhouse, London, 1896, chs. i, ii, and Schaff's *History of the Christian Church*, Vol. III, p. 158 ff.

Doubtless in the centuries which have since elapsed other causes have perpetuated the monastic orders. As a means of consecrating life to contemplation and service they have appealed to ardent individuals; because armies of men and women, thus unencumbered by the ordinary ties of domestic life, have been useful to the rulers of the church for the accomplishment of their various ends, they have appealed to the hierarchy; but in them we have with us to the present hour an institution which is, in part at least, a monument to the reaction from the influences for evil of the worst elements of the old Semitic cult.

In the last analysis, however, the powers for good which the world has derived from Semitic influence outweigh those which have made for evil. We should never forget that the three great monotheistic religions of the world, Judaism, Christianity, and Mohammedanism, have all sprung from the religious soil which was prepared by the primitive cult, the origin and history of which we have been tracing.

The rise in Israel of the sublime conceptions of God and duty which created Judaism we have already sketched,[1] but we have not hitherto noted the beneficent influence which Judaism exerted, in the centuries immediately preceding the beginning of our era, upon the Græco-Roman world. Dispersed as the Jews had been after the time of Alexander the Great, by contact with the world their conception of their mission was greatly broadened and exalted. Formerly they had thought that for the sake of themselves alone they were the favorites of heaven; now they regarded themselves as divinely sent missionaries to the world. A propaganda was accordingly inaugurated, equipped with an extensive literature,[2] to win the world to Judaism. At the time old national faiths were worn

---

[1] Above, pp. 300-305.

[2] Cf. Schürer's *History of the Jewish People in the Time of Jesus Christ*, Div. II, Vol. II, p. 220 ff. For a briefer sketch, Thatcher's *Apostolic Church*, ch. ii.

out; philosophy had taught many the irrationality of former cults; the moral sense of numbers was turning in disgust from social corruption protected under the name of religion. To these Judaism, with its lofty conception of God and its austere morals, came as a refuge and an inspiration, and at this distance we can only guess at its power for good; it must have been immense.

Judaism had, nevertheless, its limitations; it was after all a national faith. Men could obtain its benefits only by becoming by adoption members of the Jewish race; therefore, soon after the beginning of our era, Christianity easily succeeded to its mission. The old Semitic cult had prepared the soil for Judaism; both had prepared the soil for the teaching of Jesus Christ. The matchless figure of the Master is much less explained by his environment than the monotheism of the Old Testament prophets; and yet it was no accident that the seed of his teaching was sown on a warm, religious, Semitic soil. Nowhere else in the world had such a soil been so remarkably prepared. Christianity, freed through the labors of Paul and such as he from the trammels of Jewish particularism, with the prophetic idea of God completed and perfected, with its consciousness of human brotherhood and the absolute worth of every individual, went forth to conquer, leaven,[1] and renovate the ancient world. Such is the imperfection of human nature that no ideals, when embodied in human institutions, are always perfectly expressed or altogether unmingled with baser metal. It has therefore happened to Christianity, as to every other religion, that much that should never have been connected with the name of religion at all has masqueraded under its garb. Notwithstanding this, the religion of Jesus Christ has exerted influences for the moral and spiritual elevation of the world such as have radiated from no other centre, and which are simply immeasurable. It is the religion of the

[1] See *e.g.* the beautiful description of the effects of early Christianity in the *Epistle to Diognetus*, ch. v.

best civilization; it is capable of becoming the religion of mankind; its dross is not inherent in it and may be purged away; its spirit, its ethics, and its ideals are the hope of the world. Yet Christianity, with all that it has been, is, and promises to be, traces its ancestry "according to the flesh" back to the primitive Semitic cult.

Mohammedanism must not be omitted from this estimate. Though born later than Christianity, and deriving its monotheism from the same source, its birth in the Arabian peninsula, where civilization had reached a less elevated plane, placed it at a great disadvantage, if judged from the point of view of an ethical civilization. Its prophet during the earlier years of his career was earnest and sincere, and the recipient of a genuine inspiration; but in later life he departed from this lofty plane, and lived for ends which were not entirely unselfish and are not above the suspicion of sensuality. Its book, the Qur'an, legislates on the plane of the simple and half-barbarous life of the Arabian desert for the civil and religious polity of the world for all time.

No doubt Mohammedanism has in many parts exerted an influence for good. Where its sway has extended over races of a lower order of civilization than that of Arabia, it has tended to elevate them; but it stunts and blasts higher civilizations wherever it comes in contact with them. Perhaps when at its best, in the Middle Ages, it was nearly on a par with the Christianity it opposed; but when its best products in the way of civilization to-day are placed by the best products of Christian civilization, the verdict of superiority does not fall in favor of Mohammedanism. Traditions have done much to modify the application of the teachings of its sacred book; differences of temperament and casuistry have produced almost as many sects and varieties of thought as those which have sought to express Christianity, varying from the literalism of the Wahabites to the mysticism of the Fatimites and the Persian sects, but wherever it is found its spirit and ideals fall so far short of the highest that the best civilization seems impossible under its rule. Its evil and its good alike possess elements in common with all human good and all human imperfection, but it has some imperfections which are peculiarly Semitic. It is a crude product of the Semitic religious soil; it is not wanting in noble elements, but the acids of the earlier stages of the growth of Semitic religious fruit have not been, as in Christianity, ripened out of it. However necessary these acids may be to the flavor of the ripened fruit, it is fatal to the flavor of that which wilts before it ripens.

An investigation such as that we have been pursuing makes it very clear that Renan's[1] hypothesis of a primitive Semitic tendency to monotheism (at least as at first presented) can no longer be maintained. If in the religious sphere the Semites have anywhere proven themselves worthy teachers of the race, it has not been because they had at the first a clearer conception of monotheism than others, but because the circumstances of their desert and oasis environment led them in their religion to emphasize those functions of life which are most closely connected with the growth of moral and religious feeling in the individual and in the race.[2] This emphasis led them to practices which were in the early time comparatively innocent, and which embodied in gross forms concepts of God which in spiritual form are now the best religious possessions of our humanity.[3] It was thus slowly, through long ages, as the strata of the earth are

[1] Cf. Renan's "De la part des peuples sémitiques" in the *Journal asiatique*, 1859, *L'histoire générale, des langues sémitique*, 3d ed., 1863, p. 5 ff., and *History of the People of Israel*, Vol. I, chs. iii, iv. What Renan really claims in the later work is not monotheism, but henotheism, — that each tribe had its own god, but did not deny the reality of the gods of other tribes. This position is a true one; but the road from it to monotheism lay through a long development in which tribes were welded into nations and the tribal deities were formed into polytheistic pantheons.

[2] Cf. above, p. 107 ff.

[3] *I.e.* "God is love," cf. p. 107.

formed, that by means of this Semitic life and worship a religious national character was created to which the highest conceptions could be intrusted for embodiment in human life, — in which "the Word could become flesh and dwell among us." We need here, as always, to remember that "that is not first which is spiritual, but that which is natural, and afterward that which is spiritual."

Matriarchates and polyandry have been developed in many parts of the world,[1] but nowhere on such a gigantic scale as among the Semites; nowhere else did environment so long protect the institution and render its effects so permanent; no other institution of the kind became the stock to produce such a noble fruitage; nor was any other so situated geographically as to discharge both its sewage and its nectar into the springs from which the civilization of our modern life drew its early draughts of inspiration. All this seems to have been permitted in the case of the Semites by a wise Providence, who thus prepared a soil in which the best religious and ethical ideals could flourish, and who thus brought out of this cult in the end more of good than of evil.

[1] See above, p. 59 ff.

GENERAL INDEX

Abdi-kheba, wrote letters from Jerusalem, cir. 1400 B.C., 242; complains government is being overthrown, 274.
Abel, Ludwig, 227.
Abu, meaning both "father" and "husband," 68; an early epithet of Sin, 201.
Abyssinia, 8, 25, 29; marriage in, 48 ff., 66; sycamore sacred in, 89; Semitic religion in, 135 ff.; agricultural nature of, 138.
Adapa myth, 264.
Adar, possibly a name of Ninib, *q.v.*
Adonis, Greek name of Tammuz-Eshmun, an epithet, 86, 263; worship of, at Gebal, 245 ff., 265; in North Africa, 256.
Ælian, 37, 253.
Æneas, story, a myth of Ashtart cult, 255, 314 ff.
Æsculapius, a Greek name for Eshmun, 252, 265, 267.
Afar or Dankali, 10, 25.
Africa, held to be home of Semites, 6; of Caucasic race, 7; northern part separated from southern, 18; from Europe by end of last glacial epoch, 19; home of Hamito-Semitic stock in north of, 23; Semites crossed into, 29; Baal worship in, 150 ff.; Ashtart worship in, 253 ff.
Agade, a city of Babylonia, 162; noted for its grain, 158; for its dates, 159; held hegemony for a time, 163; seat of worship of Shamash, 212; older than Larsa, 213.
Agriculture, beginnings of, in Palestine, 146; in Babylonia, 156 ff., 171 ff.; individual property in land in Babylonia, cir. 6000 B.C., 158 ff.; connection with growth of cities, 162, 171 ff.; effect of, on decalogue, 294 ff.
Aksum, capital of Semitic kingdom in Abyssinia, 135.

Alashia, El-Amarna letters from, thought to be Cyprus, 250.
Al-Fals, an Arabic god derived by epithet from Athtar, 134.
Al-Galsad, an Arabic god developed from Athtar, 134.
Alilat, Greek name of Al-Lat, 234.
Allah, God of Islam, developed from Semitic mother goddess, 131; said to have daughters, 235.
Al-Lat, daughter of Allah, 133; mother of Dhu-'l-Shara, 133; worship at Taif, Petra, and Palmyra, etc., 233 ff.; goddess of unwedded love, 234; name an epithet, 235.
Allies, T.N., 317.
Al-Uqaiṣir, an Arabic god developed from Athtar, 134.
Al-Uzza, lived in *samura* trees at Nakhla, 88; connected with Meccan sanctuary, 133, 235 ff.; daughter of Allah, *ibid.*; companion of Al-Lat, 234; nature and worship of, 235 ff.; an Ishtar (Athtar), 236 ff.; meaning of name, 237.
Amiaud, Arthur, 185, 186, 187, 189, 190, 191, 197, 200, 207, 210, 220, 260.
Ammianus Marcellinus, 47, 56, 61.
Amorites, old inhabitants of Canaan, 147.
Amr b. Kulthum, an Arabian poet, 62.
Antarah, an Arabian poet, 56.
Antiphanes, 251.
Anu, father of Bau, 191, 196; locality of, not known, 195; in oldest triad, 206; origin obscure, 218; head of pantheon after Gudea, 219; god of Der, *ibid.*; partly an abstraction, *ibid.*; originally a chthonic god of fertility, 220; temple of, in Ashur, 222.
Anu-banini, king of Lulubi, 200; worshipped Enlil and Ninlil, 203; significance of name, 220; worshipped Ramman, 225, 229.

323

Aphrodite, Greek name of Ashtart, 249.
Apollo, a name for Baal in Rhodes, 252.
Arabia, cradle of Semites, 4, 24 ff., 28 ff.; why Semites entered, 26, 119; had it forests once? 26; date of Semitic occupation, 27; physical character, 28; low civilization, 32; oasis life, 33; poor outside oases, 71; no fishing in, 74; some hunting, *ibid.*; once better watered? *ibid.*; produced early civilization, 76; early religion of, ch. iii.; Arabia Felix, 124; later religion of, 125 ff.; survivals of primitive goddess in, 233–237.
Arad-Sin, king of Larsa, 199; worshipped Ishtar of Khallabi, 260.
Aramæans, their god, 224 ff.; their goddess, 239 ff.; in Palestine, 271.
Arbela, a Semitic city in Assyria, 222; worship of Ishtar in, 262.
Ark of Yahwe, 295 ff.
Arnold, Friedrich August, 62.
Arnold, William Muss-, 84, 111, 113, 209, 222, 223.
Artemis, an earth goddess, 178; of Hittito-Semitic origin, 313.
Aruru, a name of Ishtar, 257.
Asher, a clan, 31, 32; tribe of the goddess Ashera, 248 ff.; a god Asher, 249; equated with Yahwe, *ibid.*; an Israelitish tribe, 271.
Ashera, a post, 106; a goddess, 246 ff.; consort of Hadad, 247; in Mesopotamia, *ibid.*; name derived from pole, 248; pole at Yahwe shrines, 290 ff; goddess changed to a god, 249.
Ashtar-Chemosh, god of Moab, developed from Athtar, 141 ff.
Ashtart, Ashtoreth, Ashtaroth Karnaim, a trans-Jordanic town, 238.
Ashtart, totemism of, 37; associated with water god, 87; goddess at Sidon, Tyre, etc., 148 ff.; symbolized by cow, 201; worshipped at Ashtaroth Karnaim, 241 ff.; at Sidon, 243 ff.; "name of Baal," 244; patroness of mariners, *ibid.*; identified with moon, *ibid.*; at Tyre, *ibid.*; at Byblos (Gebal), 244 ff.; carried to Mediterranean countries, 249 ff.
Ashtoreth, O.T. name of Ashtart, 148.

Ashkelon, seat of worship of Ashtart and Atargatis, 241 ff.
Ashur, chief god of the Assyrians, 221 ff.; a transformed Ishtar, 222 ff.; derivation of name, 223; folk etymology of, 224, n. 3.
Ashur, the old capital of Assyria, 221; a Semitic town, 222.
Asia Minor, Semitic influence in 311.
Assurbanipal, king of Assyria, 154, 217; repaired temple of Ishtar at Erech, 257; worshipped Ishtar at Nineveh, 261; at Arbela, 262.
Assurnasirpal, king of Assyria, 154; exhibits popularity of Ramman, 226, n. 2.
Assyria, dominion of the city Ashur, 221.
Astar, chief Semitic deity of Abyssinia, 135; worship carried from Arabia, 136 ff.
Atar, Aramaic name of Ishtar, 239 ff.; nature of, 241.
Atargatis, origin debated, 238, ff.; in Aramaic, "Atar-'atah," 239; associated with Hadad, 239, ff.; Jensen's theory of, 240; a composite deity, 240, ff.; nature of, 241, ff; fish form of, 242 ff.
Athirat, a Minæan goddess, derived from '*ashera*, 131, 247.
Athtar, Sabæan god of fertility, 86, 87; transformed from mother goddess, 87; called "mother" and "he," 125 ff; retained features of mother goddess, 126 ff.; localized in different places, 127 ff.; developed by epithets into other gods, 128 ff.
'Ati, name of a goddess, probably Attis, 239 ff.
Atonement, Day of, connected with Tammuz wailing, 114, 289.
Attis, a Phrygian goddess, 240; compounded with Atar in Atargatis, 240 ff., 313.
Augustine, 42, 100, 110, 254, 255.
Ava or Awa, ancient name of Yeha in Abyssinia, 135.
Baal, name applied to well-watered land, 105, 127; god of each Palestinian, Phœnician, and North African locality, 148 ff.; Baal-Hamman, Baal-Barith, etc., 148: worshipped on hilltops, 151; in Rhodes, 252; Baal-

Hamman in North Africa, 253 ff.; in Cyprus, 266.
Babylon, gained hegemony of Babylonia, cir. 2300 B.C., 163; connection with Gishgalla, 207 ff.
Babylonia held to be home of Semites, 1 ff.; wrongly, 22; civilization of, 155 ff.; nature of religion of, 171 ff.
Baethgen, Friedrich, 141, 144, 239, 240, 265.
Ball, C. J., 86, 160, 185, 207.
Bambyce, also called Hierapolis and Mabug, 239, 241, 243.
Banks, Edgar James, 205, 228.
Bantu language, not related to Semitic, 17; polyandry of Bantu race, 60.
Barras, an Abyssinian god, 138 ff.
Barth, J., 254.
Basques, 18; not related in language to Berbers, 19.
Battersby, G. Harford-, 270, 276, 278.
Bau, goddess of Uruazagga, 185; cult of, 189 ff.; a Semitic goddess, 190 ff.; meaning of name, ibid.; daughter of Anu, 191, 196.
Baudissin, Graf von, 226, 284, 314.
Baudoin, Jean, 177.
Bedža language, 10.
Belin language, 10.
Belkassen ben Sedira, 10.
Belser, C., 225.
Benjamin, a clan, an offshoot of Josephites, 271; meaning of name, ibid., n. 5.
Bent, J. Theodore, 25, 49, 89, 112, 135, 136, 137, 138, 237.
Benzinger, Immanuel, 68, 99, 115, 296.
Berbers, a white race, 16; identical with Iberian race, etc., 18 ff.; language of, kindred to Egyptian, 20; their independent system of writing, 20 ff.; polyandry and date culture among, 117.
Berger, Philippe, 150, 254.
Berossos, 91.
Bertholet, A., 85.
Bertin, G., 6, 22, 76.
Bezold, Carl, 225, 310.
Bickell, E., 236.
Blandford, W. T., 138.
Bliss, F. J., 137.
Bloch, A., 254.
Blunt, Lady Anne, 55, 71, 75.
Bne-Ebed-Ashera, a clan in the El-Amarna period, perhaps same as Asher, 32, 246 ff., 248.

Bokhari, 65, 105.
Bonavia, E., 90, 93.
Bonk, Hugo, 282.
Borelli, Jules, 25.
Borsippa, suburb of Babylon colonized from Shirpurla, 210 ff.
Breasted, J. H., 274.
Briggs, Charles A., 292.
Brinton, Daniel G., 6, 7, 13, 16, 18, 23, 24, 25.
British polyandry, 61; possibility of, among Semites, 69.
Brockelmann, C., 78.
Brown, Francis, 226.
Brown, Robert, Jr., 37, 116, 315.
Bruce, A. B., 292.
Brugsch, Heinrich, 10.
Brünnow, R. E., 113, 160, 182, 192, 193, 194, 196, 201, 207, 211, 215, 218.
Budde, Karl, 89, 95, 108, 148, 149, 203, 272, 275, 276, 277, 279, 281, 287, 288, 291, 292, 295, 297, 298, 299, 301, 303.
Bühler, Georg, 59.
Buhl, Franz, 68, 226, 238, 282.
Bull, as symbol of Athtar and other gods, 201; of Yahwe, 298.
Bunini, an attendant of the god Shamash, 215.
Bur-Sin, king of Ur, 159; worshipped Ramman, 225.
Byblos, or Gebal, worship of Ashtart in, 244 ff.

Cæsar, Julius, 60.
Camel, helped to destroy the vegetation of Arabia, 74; domesticated early, 75.
Cappadocia, Semitic influence in, 311.
Carpenter, J. Estlin, 270, 276, 278.
Carthage, chronology of, 122; Ashtart worship in, 255 ff.; temple of Eshmun in, 266, 267.
Catullus, 315.
Ceres, a North African name of Ashtart, 255.
Chamir language, 10.
Charles, R. H., 89, 95, 121.
Chemosh, chief god of Moab, 141 ff.
Cherubim, personification of winds, 91, 94.
Cheyne, T. K., 36, 241.
Christianity, influence and power of, 319 ff.
Chronology, of southern and western Semites, 122; of Babylonia and Assyria, 153, 154; grounds of Baby-

Ionian chronology, 155 n.; of Hebrews, 268.
Circumcision, originated in primitive Ishtar worship, 98 ff.; among Hebrews, 99; among Arabs, *ibid.*; Arabian ceremony of, 100; a preparation for marriage, 100 ff.; connected with spring festival, 110; among Hamites, 115; native Hamitic practice, 117; in Yahwe worship, 280 ff.
Cities, origin of, in Babylonia, 162.
Civilization, developed in river valleys, 155.
Clan, organization, 30; among Semites, 30 ff.; genesis of, 34; economic purpose of, 38 ff.; age of republican clans in Arabia, 71 ff.; two types of Arabian clan, 267 ff.
Clarke, W. N., 82.
Clay, A. T., 162.
Clement of Alexandria, 251, 252.
Coe, G. A., 107.
Collitz, Hermann, 250.
Collizza, Giovanni, 10.
Compound deities, late date of, 141, 151, 240 ff.
Conder, C. R., 312.
Cook, Stanley A., 228.
Cope, Edward, 170, 204.
Coptic language, 10.
Cornill, Carl Heinrich, 270.
Couard, Ludwig, 296, 297.
Covenant, religious consequence of Yahwe's, 291, 301.
Cow, significance of, as symbol of Ishtar and Ashtart, 201.
Cradle of Semites, theories of, 1 ff.; Arabia, 24 ff.
Crete, Ashtart worship in, 252.
Croll, James, 14, 15, 19.
Crum, W. E., 10.
Cybele, known in North Africa, 255; in Phrygia, 313.
Cyprus, Semitic Baal in, 151 ff.; worship of Ashtart in, 249 ff.; influence of Cypriotic worship on Greece, 252.
Cyrus, conquered Babylon, 154; did he worship Semitic gods? 310.

Dagon, a Semitic god in East and West, 229; in Assyria and Palestine, 230; theories as to origin of, 230 ff.; a transformed goddess, 231; probably not Aramæan, 232.
Damkina, goddess, spouse of Ea, 198.

Dan, Israelitish tribe, 273.
Dangin, François Thureau, 106, 146, 158, 159, 160, 161, 164, 169, 182, 187, 198, 199, 207, 218, 220, 225, 261.
Dankali or Afar, 10, 20, 25.
Dates, a fruit, 75; gathered in Sept.-Oct., 111 ff.; those of Agade famed, 159; house for storage of, 160.
Davis, John D., 185, 186, 190, 191, 195, 199.
Dawkins, Boyd, 18.
Death, conception of life after, 95 ff.
Decalogue, the Yahwistic, 110; the Mosaic, 292 ff.
Decharme, P., 314.
De Goeje, M. J., 5, 24, 88.
Deissmann, G. Adolf, 285.
Dekerto, Greek name of Atargatis, 243.
Delitzsch, Franz, 283.
Delitzsch, Friedrich, 97, 103, 160, 163, 164, 165, 166, 205, 209, 215, 217, 222, 223, 224, 226, 230, 283, 296.
Deniker, J., 20.
Derenbourg, Hartwig and Joseph, 124. 125, 126.
Descent, counted through mother, 51 ff.; transfer of, to paternal line, 66; from gods, 130; Ishtar's, to lower world, 259.
Dhu-'l-Khalasa, Arabic god, 134.
Dhu-'l-Shara, god worshipped with Al-Lat by Nabathæans, 233; son of Al-Lat, 234; his worship, 263; a Tammuz or Adonis, 267.
Dido, a name of Tanith, 254 ff.
Dillmann, August, 275, 283, 292.
Dilmun, an island in Persian Gulf, 211.
Diodorus Siculus, 242, 243, 252, 253.
Diognetus, Epistle to, 319.
Dionysios Halic., 315.
Divorce, among Semites, 45 ff.; among Hebrews, 45; Babylonians, 45 ff.; Arabs, 46 ff.
Dog, as name of a sacred prostitute, 188, 251, n. 2.
Doughty, C. M., 17, 28, 32, 39, 47, 51, 72, 74, 75, 77, 87, 88, 99, 100, 101, 109, 110, 111, 114, 136, 233.
Dozy, R., 69.
Driver, S. R., 3, 102, 103, 104, 141, 146, 244, 251, 252, 269, 276, 278, 282, 283, 284, 296.
Drummond, Henry, 107.
Dumuzi, same as Tammuz, 263.

Dumuzizuab, goddess of Kinunir, 211; precursor of Nabu, 212.
Dungi, king of Ur, 153; mentions Ninâ, 188; Ea, 198; Sin, 200; Nergal, 215; worshipped Ishtar of Erech, 256.
Dyer, Louis, 252, 265, 315.

Ea, a god, pictured as a fish, 91, 196 ff; one of Babylonia's principal deities, 195; god of Eridu, 196; a transformed Ishtar, 196 ff.; god of wisdom, 198; member of oldest triad, 206; said to be Marduk's father, 209.
Eabani, story of, 43 ff., 83 ff., 93 ff., 96 ff.; date of, 44; hair like grain, 218.
Eannadu I, (Eannatum), king of Shirpurla, 153; Eannadu II, Patesi of Shirpurla, *ibid.*, and 161; conquered Elam, 180; mentions Ishtar, 182; Nana, 186; Ninâ, 188; Ea, 198; ascribes his victory to Enlil, 206; conquered Gishgalla, 207; worshipped Shamash, 214.
Ebers, Georg, 101.
Economy, cause of paternal kinship, 72; effect on religious conceptions, 82; causes transformation of social structure, 120; economic condition of south Arabia, 124; economic test of deities, 179 ff; its value, 221; economic transformation of Yahwe worship, 291 ff.
Eden, meaning of Biblical narrative of, 43 ff., 93 ff.; origin and development of idea, 96 n.; meaning of expulsion from, 97 ff.
Edom, the country, 32; name of Baal among Edomites, 152; Al-Lat worshipped in, 233 ff.
Egypt, language of, 10; did not conquer Berbers, 20; nor influence Babylonian religious conceptions, 169.
Elam, conquered by Eannadu, 180; conquered south Babylonia, 257; Semitic influence on, 310.
Elijah, work of, 300.
Enki (Ea), a principal Babylonian god, 195.
Enlil (Bel), god of Nippur and chief deity of Babylonia, 163, 195; called king of countries, 183; superior to gods of Shirpurla, 185; father of Sin, 202; originally a Sumerian god, 204; Semitic element in, 204 ff.; member of oldest triad, 206.
Enshagkushanna, lord of Sumir, 153; devoted spoil to Enlil, 202, 206.
Entemena, Patesi of Shirpurla, 153, 160; built house for storage of dates, 160; mentions Nana, 186; Ninâ, 188; Ea, 198.
Enzu, a name of the god Sin, 199; meaning of, 201.
Ephraem, the Syrian, 42, 100, 110, 234.
Ephraim, a Josephite clan, 271.
Epiphanius, 233, 234, 263.
Epping, J., 106.
Erech, a city of Babylonia, 162; Lugalzaggisi, its king, 146, 153; held Babylonian hegemony at various times, 163; Ishtar cult in, 256 ff.; form of, 259.
Eridu, one of the oldest Babylonian cities, 162; held hegemony in Babylonia at various times, 163; oldest Semitic settlement, 196 ff.; seat of a prehistoric empire, 198.
Erim, a section of Shirpurla, 183, 185; wrongly called Gishgalla, 185, 207; shown by its goddess to be Semitic, 186 ff., 192; a colony of Ur, 200.
Erman, Adolf, 8, 9, 10, 20, 25, 26.
Erua, another name of Dumuzizuab or Tashmit, 212, n. 4.
Eryx, seat of Ashtart worship in Sicily, 252.
Eshmun, a name of Tammuz, 92; at Tyre, 244; reasons for identification with Tammuz, 265 ff.; possible etymology of, 267, n. 2.
Eshmunazer II, king of Sidon, 122; priest of Ashtart, 243; built her temple, 244 n.
Eth-Baal, king of Tyre and priest of Ashtart, 244.
Ethiopic language, 10.
Euphrates, overflow of, 156 ff.
Eusebius, 37, 150, 230, 238, 244.
Euting, J., 69, 70, 75, 77.
Ezana, royal author of inscription from Aksum, 138.

Family, Semitic, 39 ff.; of primitive man, 41 ff.; effect of temporary marriage upon, 49 ff.
Farnell, Lewis Richard, 178, 255, 314, 315, 316.
Father, not known in Thibetan poly-

andry, 68; head of Arabian family by time of prophet, 123; Athtar a father, 124; father and mother combined in one deity, 205; spiritual conception of fatherhood of Yahwe, 306 ff.

Feasts, number and character of, 108 ff.; in Nisan, 108 ff.; sacrifices and lewd ceremonies at, 110; date festival in autumn, 111; feast of *Mascal* in Abyssinia, 112, 137; feast of Tammuz, 112 ff.; agricultural feasts in Babylonia and Palestine, 114, 288 ff.; two feasts primitive, 115; feast of Bau, 190; of Adonis at Gebal, 245 ff.; spring feast at Paphos, 251; of Tanith in North Africa, 254; of Yahwe, 281 ff., 287 ff.

Fell, W., 86, 87, 128, 129.

Fischer, Theobald, 75, 76, 79, 98, 161, 171.

Fishing, no important part of Arabian life, 74; at Eridu, 196 ff.; at Ashkelon, 242 ff.

Fiske, John, 14, 18, 107.

Frazer, J. G., 85, 114, 179.

Frey, J., 120.

Frost, John, 173, 175.

Gabelenz, Graf von der, 18, 19.

Gad, a clan, 271; in east-Jordanic country, 273.

Gad, god of the tribe Gad, 249; Tammuz wailing in cult of, 289.

Galalama, Patesi of Shirpurla, 190.

Galla language, 10.

Gallas, the, 25, 115.

Game, in Arabia, 74.

Gamil-Sin, king of Ur, 159.

Gatumdug, an epithet of Bau, sometimes treated as a separate goddess, 191; once an epithet of Nana, 191, n. 6 and 260.

Gebal, a Phœnician city and seat of Ashtart worship, 244.

Geiger, Abraham, 132.

Gerland, A. A., 6, 12, 13, 15, 16, 25.

Gesenius, Wilhelm, 36, 226, 282, 284.

Ghabghab, a rivulet or trench at Mecca, 235.

Ghillany, R., 275.

Giddings, Franklin H., 13, 14, 33, 34, 40, 41, 49, 50, 53, 55, 60, 63, 73, 77.

Gillett, C. R., 317.

Girsu, one of the districts of Shirpurla, 185; a Semitic settlement, 192, 194; name interpreted as "body lance," 192, n. 1; oldest settlement of Shirpurla, 194; seat of original kingdom, *ibid.;* contained a district Kinunir, 210 ff.

Gishban, an old Babylonian town conquered by Eannadu, 206; situation and religion of, 218.

Gishgalla, a south Babylonian town of which Babylon was possibly a colony, 207 ff.

Glacial epoch, causes of, 14.

Glaser, Eduard, 64, 124, 125, 135, 136, 227.

Goat, destructive of Arabian vegetation, 74; domesticated early, 75.

Goddesses, the earliest Semitic deities, 120, 179 ff.; natural agricultural deities, 199; transformed by war, 180 ff.

Golenischeff, M., 124.

Gottheil, Richard, J. H., 239.

Grassarie, M. de la, 308.

Gray, G. Buchanan, 282.

Gray, Louis, 310.

Greece, goddesses of, 178; Semitic influence upon, 315 ff.; corruption of society in, 316.

Grüneisen, Carl, 95, 121.

Gudea, Patesi of Shirpurla, 153; sacrifices offered to his statue, 168; worshipped Nana, 183, 184, 186; Ninâ, 188; Bau, 189, 190, 192, 199; called Shirpurla a city, 207; mentions Khallabi, 260.

Gudua, another name for Kutu (Kutha), 215.

Guidi, Ignazio, 1, 2, 22, 75, n. 4.

Gula, an epithet of Bau, became goddess of healing, 191.

Gummere, F. B., 179.

Gunkel, Hermann, 98.

Guthe, Hermann, 270, 275.

Guti, a god of the Guti, 217 ff.

Guti or Suti, a people, 37, 199; their religion, 217.

Guyard, Stanislaus, 164.

Haarbrücker, Theodor, 99.

Hadad, Aramæan equivalent of Ramman, 224; equated with R., 226; worshipped in Damascus, *ibid.;* name means "thunderer," *ibid.;* called Rimmon, 227; diffusion of worship, *ibid.;* a god of fertility, 228; a

GENERAL INDEX 329

transformed Ishtar, 229; Atargatis worshipped with him, 239 ff.
Haeckel, Ernst, 13, 16.
Halévy, Joseph, 31, 64, 86, 130, 131, 135, 164, 165, 209, 227.
Hamilton, an English traveller, 48.
Hamites, language of, kindred to Semitic, 9 ff.; blonds among, 17; form one stock with Semites, 20; records of, go back to dawn of history, *ibid.*; home in North Africa, 21; totemistic, 37; passed savagery when Semites separated from, 73; polyandrous, 74; institutions of, 115 ff.; civilization derived from oases, 118.
Harding, E. E., 108.
Harith, an Arabian poet, 56.
Harnack, Adolf, 317.
Harran, a seat of the worship of the moon god, 202.
Hasa, a region in Arabia, 57.
Haupt, Paul, 36, 43, 83, 85, 91, 96, 97, 103, 113, 165, 168, 183, 184, 200, 214, 218, 257, 258, 259.
Heber, a clan of Asher, 31, 274.
Hebrews, beginnings of the nation, 270 ff.; proposed identification with the Khabiri, 274.
Hegra, an Arabian seat of the worship of Al-Lat, 234.
Hehn, Victor, 75, 76, 161.
Heracles, a Greek name of Baal, 265 ff.
Herodotus, 42, 43, 99, 100, 101, 117, 210, 234, 242, 252, 258, 263, 314, 316.
Heuzey, Leon, editor of De Sarzec's *Découvertes en Chaldée*, see De Sarzec.
Hierapolis, also called Bambyce and Mabug, 239, 241, 243.
Hilderbrand, Richard, 59, 60, 72, 73, 77, 119, 146.
Hilprecht, Hermann, V., 146, 162, 166, 180, 181, 197, 198, 200, 202, 203, 204, 213, 217, 219, 220, 225.
Hiram, king of Tyre, 122, 244.
Hittites, in northern Syria before Egyptian conquest, 147; civilization and language of, 311 ff.; Semitic influence on, 312 ff.; supposed origin, 313.
Hoffman, E. A., archaic tablet of, 158 ff.; 161, 213; translation of, 213, n. 5.
Hoffmann, Georg, 104, 141, 226, 248, 253, 254.

Holmes, William H., 14.
Holzinger, H., 275, 285.
Hommel, Fritz, 1, 3, 21, 22, 76, 106, 124, 131, 185, 207, 208, 211, 223, 247, 249, 274, 283.
Hopkins, E. Washburn, 59, 296.
Hubal, a pre-Islamic name of Allah, 134.
Hull, Edward, 139.
Human life, where first appeared, 12 ff.
Hunting in Arabia, 74.
Hurgronje, C. Snouck, 48, 100, 236.
Husband, living in wife's tribe, 54 ff.

Ibn-al-Kalbi, 235.
Ibn-Hisham, 88, 235, 236.
Ibn-Kutaiba, 233.
Idalion, a seat of Ashtart worship in Cyprus, 266.
Ihering, Rudolf von, 171.
Il-Azza, a Sabbæan god, 237, n. 4.
Iliad, 249, 250.
Ilmaqqâhu, a form of Athtar, 87, 128 ff.; god of 'Amrân, 128.
Immeru, a name of Ramman, 225.
Immortality, Semitic ideas of, 95 ff.
Imr-ul-Kais, 62.
Iolaos, a Greek name of Eshmun, 265 ff.
Isaac of Antioch, 236.
Isâf, a Meccan god, absorbed in Allah, 133.
Ishmi-Dagan, a king of Isin, 257.
Ishtar, totemism of, 37; cult of, in Semitic world, 42; connection with Eabani, 43; cult found, 83; a survival from primitive conditions, 84; impure priestesses of, *ibid.*; connection with desire, *ibid.*; a water goddess, 86, 92 ff.; connected with the palm, 92 ff., 98; with circumcision, 98; etymology of, 102 ff.; goddess of oases, 105 ff.; at Kish, 181 ff.; at Susa, 184 ff.; goddess of Erim, 185 ff.; of Khallabi, 190, 260 ff.; symbolized by cow, 201; at Agade, 213; maintained identity there, 215; among the Guti, 217 ff.; coupled with Ashur in Assyria, 221 ff., 224; survivals of, chap. vi; at Erech, 256 ff.; daughter of Anu, 259.
Isin, a Babylonian city which for a time held the hegemony, 163, 257.
Isis, Egyptian earth goddess, 116.

GENERAL INDEX

Islam, heathen basis of, 131 ff.; influence of, 320 ff.
Israel, beginnings of the nation, 270 ff.,; early disorganized condition, 273; stele of, 274 ff.
Issachar, a clan, 271.

Jackson, A. V. W., 310.
Jacob-el, a place in Palestine, 274 ff.
Jacobs, Mr., 35, 36.
Jacut, see Yaqut.
Jastrow, Morris, 7, 23, 37, 43, 44, 83, 86, 91, 93, 97, 98, 109, 111, 112, 156, 163, 190, 191, 195, 199, 200, 203, 209, 212, 213, 215, 216, 217, 219, 220, 223, 224, 225, 226, 228, 231, 232, 257, 258, 259, 264, 272, 274, 284, 295, 312, 313.
Jehovah, see Yahwe.
Jensen, Peter, 43, 83 ff., 85, 103, 106, 183, 185, 187, 197, 209, 210, 211, 212, 216, 217, 224, 230, 231, 240, 246, 259, 260, 264, 310, 311, 312, 313.
Jeremias, Alfred, 43, 84, 85, 95, 112, 164, 195, 264, 266.
Jerome, 144, 234, 238.
Jesus Christ, effect of His teaching on the conception of God, 303.
Jethro, priest of Yahwe in Midian, 272; initiated Moses into Yahwe cult, 276 ff.
Jinn, as partners with God, 36.
Johnson, F. E., 62.
Jolly, Julius, 59.
Joseph, a clan, 271; in Egypt, 272; delivered by Yahwe, *ibid.;* entered Palestine, 273; name as name of Palestinian place, 274 ff.; Moses mediated covenant for, 276.
Josephus, Flavius, 37, 99, 230, 244.
Judah, a tribe, 271; Aramaic element in, 272, n. 4, 273; absorbed the Kenites, 277 ff.; knowledge of Yahwe immemorial among, 278; union of Tamar with, 286.
Judaism, influence of, 318.
Justin, 255.

Kabyle language, 10.
Karaindash, king of Babylon, 257.
Karnaim, shortened name of Ashtaroth Karnaim, 238.
Keane, A. H., 7, 13, 15, 16, 18.
Keasbey, Lindley M., 30, 33, 39, 280.
Kengi, a name of Sumir, 202.
Kenites, a Sinaitic clan, 272; incorporated in Judah, 273, 277 ff.; champions of Yahwe, 277; connected with Midianites, 277; David said to be descended from, 278, n. 2; perhaps extended influence to Hamath, 284.
Kent, Charles Foster, 270.
Khabiri in the El-Amarna letters, 274.
Khallabi, a colony of Erim, 199; seat of the worship of Ishtar, 260 ff.
Khammurabi, king of Babylon, 153, 165, 198; worshipper of Marduk, 209; suppressed worship of Nabu, 212; repaired temple of Shamash at Larsa, 212; at Agade, 214; worshipped Ramman, 225; Dagon, 229; knew goddess Ashera, 247; worshipped Ishtar of Khallabi, 260.
Khumbaba, god of Elam, genesis of, 184, n. 3.
King, L. W., 202, 209, 212, 213, 223, 247.
Kinnir or Kinnunir, a part of Girsu and an old name of Borsippa, 210 ff.
Kinship, method of reckoning, 50 ff.; through females, 51 ff.; of Joseph's sons, 52; of Abraham and Sarah, *ibid.*; among Mandæans, Babylonians, and Hebrews, 53; of Jacob's children, 54; through father, 71 ff.; in Moab, 140 ff.; in Palestine, 146; in Babylonia, 159.
Kish, a Babylonian kingdom, 180; religion of, 181 ff.; conquered by Eannadu, 186 ff.; by Enshagkushanna, 202; colonies in Elam, 310.
Kition, seat of worship of Ashtart in Cyprus, 250 ff.; Eshmun worshipped at, 266.
Kittel, Rudolf, 93, 275, 292.
Koraish, a Meccan tribe to which Mohammed belonged, 235.
Kremer, von, 1, 2, 22, 75, n. 4.
Kuenen, Abraham, 270, 276, 278, 284, 292.
Kutha (Kutu), an old Babylonian city, 162; Nergal, deity of, 215.

Labîd, an Arabian poet, 56.
Lagash, a name of Shirpurla, 184.
Lake dwellers of Switzerland, 16, 17.
Lane, Edward William, 47, 104, 105.
Larsa, a Babylonian city, held hegemony for a time, 163, 199; a seat of Shamash worship, 212 ff.
Lasirab, king of Guti, 199.
Law, genesis of Pentateuchal, 303 ff.
Le Clerc, 282, 284.
Legarde, Paul de la, 104, 243, 267, 284.

GENERAL INDEX 331

Lehmann, C. F., 155, 156, 165, 168.
Lenormant, François, 86, 92, 196, 197, 284.
Lepsius, the Egyptologist, 25.
Leto, a name of Attis, 313.
Letourneau, Ch., 66, 67.
Leuba, James H., 107.
Levi, a tribe, 271; theory of origin, 272.
Levirate, connection with polyandry, 66 ff.
Libit-Ishtar, king of Isin, 256.
Lidzbarski, Mark, 203, 228, 239, 255, 272.
Lubbock, Sir John, 15, 40.
Lucian, 43, 85, 86, 100, 112, 113, 239, 240, 241, 244, 245, 265, 314.
Lugal-Erim, name of a masculinized Ishtar at Shirpurla, 183, 187.
Lugaltarsi, a king of Kish, 153; inscription of, 181, 187, n. 2, 205.
Lugalzaggisi, king of Erech, 153; reached Mediterranean, 146, 271; tendency to deification of, 168; mentioned Nana, 186; Ea, 198; son reared by Nidaba, 218; worshipped Ishtar, 256 ff.
Lulubi, an old Babylonian state, 200, 203, 220.
Lydus, Johannes, 109, 250, 251.

Mabug, a town in Lebanon otherwise called Hierapolis and Bambyce, *q.v.*
McAllister, Alexander, 99, 101.
McCurdy, J. F., 163, 164, 165.
McGee, W. J., 170, n 4.
McLennan, John F., 39, 40, 41, 59, 60, 66, 67.
Macrobius, 178, 239, 240, 241, 262, 265, 284.
Ma'in, an ancient city and kingdon in south Arabia, 124; gods of, 130 ff.; influence on Kenites, 272.
Malik, an attendant of the god Shamash, 215.
Malkatu, consort of Shamash of Agade, 214.
Malkiel, a clan, 31.
Mama, an epithet of Bau, 191, n. 1.
Man, first habitat of, 12 ff.; antiquity of, 14 ff.; effect of natural selection on mind of, 15 ff.
Manasseh, a Josephite clan, 271.
Manishtu-irba, king of Kish, 184.
Manutu, a Nabathæan god, 233.
Marduk, god of Babylon who displaced Enlil, 163, 207, 209; a Semitic god, 208 ff.; absorbed myths of Nabu, 209; name derived from sun, 209.
Margoliouth, G., 283, 284.
Marriage, Semitic, 41 ff.; temporary, 45 ff; in Sunan, 48; in Mecca, 48; in Abyssinia, 48 ff.; residence of wife during, 50 ff.; of Abraham, 52; of Amnon and Tamar, 52; of Tabnith, 52; interruption of, 55; *beena* marriage, 55; in Mu'allakât poems, 56; of Samson, 56; *mot'a* marriage, 61; rise of endogamy, 62 ff.; for certain days of the week, 63; by capture, 71 ff.
Marti, Karl, 283.
Martial, 251.
Maspéro, G., 38, 74, 115, 116, 117.
Massaba, phallic symbol of deity, 102; found in Abyssinia, 136; altars at bases of, 137; a part of Yahwe cult, 290 ff.
Mayer, Brantz, 173, 175.
Mecca, marriage in, 48; change of heathenism to Islam at, 132 ff.
Mediterranean, changes in level of, 17; race of, 18; shore of, home of Semitic stock, 21, 24.
Medr, an Abyssinian god, 138 ff.
Meissner, Bruno, 68, 158.
Melqart, god of Tyre, 149; developed from Ashtart, 150, 244; Eshmun called, 267.
Menephtah, stele of, 274 ff.
Merx, Victor, 58.
Mesha, king of Moab, 140, 143.
Mesopotamia, held to be cradle of Semites, 3 ff.; civilization of, 155 ff.
Messerschmidt, L., 311, 312, 313, 314.
Mexico, civilization and religion of, 172 ff.
Meyer, Ed., 147, 163.
Midianites, connected with Kenites, 277.
Migne, Jacques Paul, 237.
Mill, Hugh Robert, 118, 155.
Moab, physical conditions of, 139; a land of pastures, 139 ff.; language of kindred to Hebrew, 140; society of patriarchal, 140 ff.; religion of, 141 ff.
Mohammed, introduced into Islam many spiritual elements, 131; erected them on substratum of heathenism, 132 ff.
Mohammedanism, influence of, 320 ff.

Monasticism, a reaction from Semitic corruption, 317 ff.
Monogamy, temporary, in early times, 45 ff.
Monotheism, development of, 307 ff.; not primitive, 321.
Monro, Robert, 16.
Moore, George F., 89, 103, 141, 143, 148, 230, 238, 247, 248, 289, 293.
Mordtmann, J. H., 124, 126, 127, 128, 130, 138.
Morgan, J. de, 8, 20, 26, 310.
Mosaism, moral content of, 292 ff.
Moses, circumcision of, 99, 280; flight from Egypt, 272; mediated covenant with Yahwe, 275; a zealot for primitive Yahwe worship, 290; connection with Jewish law, 303 ff.
Mother, descent reckoned through, 51 ff.; mother goddess the primitive Semitic deity, ch. iii; transformed into masculine deities, chs. iv, v; in Arabia, Palestine and Africa, ch. iv; in Babylonia and Assyria, ch. v; not lost in transformation, 129 ff. and ch. vi; mother and father combined in one deity, 205.
Moulton, W. J., 281.
Movers, F. C., 284.
Mugheir, modern name of Ur, 199, 201.
Müller, D. H., 124, 129, 135, 136, 138, 139.
Müller, F. Max, 116, 227.
Müller, Friedrich, 10, 11, 12, 17, 24.
Müller, Karl, 317.
Müller, W. Max, 8, 9, 118, 146, 231, 237, 242, 248, 274, 284.
Mysticism, sexual aspects of, 308.
Myths, as a clew to origins, 195 ff.

Nabathæans, an Arabic tribe, 263.
Nabonidos, neo-Babylonian king, 154; worshipped Shamash at Agade, 215.
Nabu, god of Borsippa, 210; a Semitic god, 211; said to be son of Ea, 212.
Nâila, a Meccan goddess, spouse of Isâf, 133.
Nairs, 40, 59 ff.; Nair polyandry, 61, 63 ff.; relation to Thibetan, 69 ff.
Nakhla, valley southwest of Mecca, seat of Al-Uzza worship, 236.
Nana, a name of Ishtar at Kish, 181 ff.; etymology of, 182; goddess of Erim, 185; a Semitic goddess, 186 ff.; of Khallabi, 199, 260 ff.; applied to Ishtar at Erech, 256 ff.
Naphtali, a Hebrew clan, 273.
Naram-Sin, king of Agade, 153; date of, 156, 159; called "god," 168, 199.
Nasamones, a branch of Berber Hamites, 117.
Nasr, Arabic vulture god, 36.
Nebuchadnezzar I, king of Babylon, cir. 1130 B.C., 154, 219.
Nebuchadnezzar II, king of Babylon, 604-562 B.C., 154; repaired temple of Ishtar at Erech, 257.
Nejd, a region in central Arabia, 4.
Nergal, god of Kutu or Kutha, 215; later, god of underworld, 216; origin of, 216 ff.; a Sumerian god, 217; worship in Palestine, Phœnicia, and Athens, 217, n. 2.
Nestle, E., 284.
Neubaur, A., 230.
Neumahr, Melchior, 18.
Nidaba, the grain god of Gishgalla, 218.
Ninâ, goddess of the city Ninâ, 185; a Semitic goddess, 187 ff.; cult of 188 ff.; picture of, 189; daughter of Ea, 195.
Ninâ, one of the districts of Shirpurla, 185; a Semitic settlement, 192; colony of Eridu, 198, 200.
Ninagidkhadu, a name of Ishtar of Erech, 256.
Nineveh, capital city of Assyria, 261; name written by same ideogram as Ninâ, 187, 261; a Semitic town, 222; Ishtar goddess of, 261.
Ningirsu, god of Girsu, 185; husband of Bau, 191; origin of, 191 ff.; "king" and "warrior" of Enlil, 191, n. 7, 196, 202; connected with Tammuz, 193; developed Ishtar, 193 ff.; became a sun god, 194.
Ningishzida, deity developed from Bau-Ishtar, 190; coördinate with Tammuz, 264.
Ninib, another name for Ningirsu, q.v.
Ninkharsag, originally an Ishtar, 186.
Ninlil, spouse of Enlil, 203.
Ninmar, a goddess, daughter of Ninâ, 188.
Nippur, one of the oldest Babylonian cities, 162; first held hegemony in Babylonia, 163; antiquity of, 202; Sumerian foundation, 204; some Semitic elements, 204 ff.

Nöldeke, Theodor, 3, 6, 22, 44, 53, 88, 227, 278.
Nowack, Wilhelm, 85, 93, 99, 115, 238, 296.
Numerals, Hamitic and Semitic alike, 9; the decimal system, 170; Sumerian system sexagesimal, *ibid.*
Nusku, Assyrian fire god, origin uncertain, 232, n. 2.

Oannes, Berossos's name for Ea, 196.
Oasis, centre of Arabian life, 33, 39; Arabian life bound up in, 71; prototype of Eden, 96, n.; sacred tracts, 112; in North Africa, 117; significance of, in Semitic religion, 179 ff.
Odyssey, 249.
Oehler, G. F., 283.
Oman, women of, 44, 57.
Oppert, Jules, 158, 210, 225.
Osiris, water god of Egypt, 116.
Ovid, 242.
Ox, symbol of Sin, significance of, 201.

Palestine, physical features of, 144; produce of, 145; conquest of, by Semites, 146.
Palgrave, William Gifford, 6, 17, 44, 47, 57, 74, 75, 77.
Palm, date, cultivated in Arabian oases, 33, 39; extent in prehistoric time, 75; in Arabia, 75, n. 4; names of, in Semitic languages, 76; primitive name, *ibid.*; importance to Arabian and primitive Semitic life, 77 ff.; cultivation of, 78; sexes of, recognized, *ibid.*; gives name to a sacred place, 79, 126 ff.; connected by Semites with knowledge of human sexuality, 79, 91; sacred in Arabia, 88; Israel, 89 ff., Bab., 90 ff., 159 ff.; artificial fertilization of, 91, 161 ff.; significance of, in Gen., 92 ff.; tree of knowledge and life, 93 ff.; Arabic poem on, 95; etymology of Ishtar connected with, 104 ff.; in Egypt, 117, 118; at basis of Hamito-Semitic culture, 119; picture of, in Babylonian writing, 160; necessity made oasis countries earliest seat of its culture, 162; a palm orchard in Babylonia, *ibid.*; palm in Semitic religion, 179 ff.; sacred palm at Eridu, 197; at Nakhla, 236; among the Kenites, 285; at Sinai,
ibid.; a totem in a Judahite clan, 286; connection with Yahwe, 286 ff.
Palmyra, an oasis 150 miles northeast of Damascus, 232; Al-Lat and Shamash worshipped there, 234 ff.
Paphos, seat of worship of Ashtart in Cyprus, 249 ff.
Passover, a festival, 108 ff.; nomadic festival, 109; festival of Yahwe, 281 ff.
Paulitschke, Philipp, 21, 55.
Pausanias, 250, 253, 266, 267, 313, 314, 315, 316, 317.
Payne, Edward John, 14, 39, 157, 162, 172, 173, 175, 176, 177.
Peake, Arthur S., 141.
Peiser, F. E., 46, 53, 219, 311.
Perrot and Chipiez, 173.
Persians, Semitic influence on, 310 ff.
Peru, civilization and religion of, 175 ff.
Peschel, Oscar, 12, 13, 16.
Petermann, A., 75, 79, 98, 161, 171.
Peters, John P., 156, 199, 204, 292.
Petra, capital of Edom, seat of the worship of Al-Lat, 233 ff.
Petrie, W. M. Flinders, 274.
Philistines, origin of, uncertain, 231, n. 6.
Philo of Byblos (Gebal), 37, 150, 231.
Philostorgius, 99.
Phœnicia, beginnings of its religion, 149; goddesses in, 243 ff.
Piepenbring, Charles, 281, 284, 291.
Pietschmann, Richard, 93, 112, 245.
Pinches, T. G., 184.
Pindar, 314.
Pithecanthropus erectus, 13.
Pliny, 239.
Polyandry, 30, 39 ff.; not universal, 40 ff.; theory of, 52 ff.; did Semites practise? 59 ff.; in India, *ibid.*; in Thibet, *ibid.*; among Britons, 60; in many parts of the world, *ibid.*; causes of, *ibid.*; Semitic, 62 ff.; combined with polygamy, 63; Thibetan displaces Nair, 65 ff., 69 ff.; began before Semitic dispersion, 68; imposed restraints on men, 72; not found in lowest social developments, 72 ff.; among Hamites, 74, 115 ff.; among Nasamones, 117; effects of Semitic, 322.
Polybius, 253, 266.
Polygamy, 40 ff.; mingled with polyandry, 61 ff.; among the rich in agricultural countries, 171 ff.

Prescott, William, 175, 176, 177.
Prestwich, Joseph, 156.
Price, Ira M., 164, 185, 186, 188.
Pronouns of Hamitic and Semitic alike, 9.
Ptolemy, Claudius, 32.

Qa'aba, sanctuary of Allah at Mecca, 132 ff.; originally a heathen shrine, *ibid.*; Al-Uzza worshipped at, 235 ff.
Qazwini, an Arabic writer, 78.
Quatrefages de Bréau, Jean A. de, 13, 14.

Races, origin of white, 15 ff.; divisions of, 16; Mediterranean, 18.
Radau, Hugo, 157, 158, 160, 161, 163, 166, 167, 168, 169, 180, 181, 182, 184, 186, 187, 188, 189, 192, 197, 198, 199, 200, 202, 205, 211, 213, 214, 217, 220, 225, 229, 251, 256.
Ramman, temple of, in Ashur, 222; in prehistoric time, 226; extent of his worship, 224; worshipped by Anu-banini, etc., 225; member of second triad, *ibid.*; name means "thunderer," 226; a god of fertility, 228; a transformed Ishtar, 229; an ox, 228, n. 7.
Ramsay, William M., 312, 313, 314.
Ratzel, Friedrich, 12, 24, 25.
Rawlinson, George, 156.
Reclus, Elie, 40, 59, 61, 124, 125.
Reinisch, Leo, 48, 55, 100.
Reisner, George A., 31, 106, 157, 158, 165, 205, 228, 246.
Renan, Ernst, 321.
Reubenites, 271; in Egypt, 272.
Réville, Albert, 148, 173, 174, 177.
Rhea, a Phrygian goddess, same as Attis, 313.
Rhodes, Ashtart worship in, 252.
Ribeiro, a geologist, 14.
Richter, Max Ohnefalse, 87, 252.
Ridpath, John Clark, 13, 15, 25.
Ripley, William Z., 7, 16, 17, 18, 19, 20.
Ritter, Carl, 78.
Robertson, T., 275, 292.
Robinson, George L., 152.
Rogers, Robert W., 156, 163, 192, 199, 202, 217, 220.
Rome, mother goddess in, 178; Ashtart worship in, 253.
Rouvier, Jules, 230.

Sabæa, economic condition of, 124; kingdom of, succeeded Ma'in, *ibid.*; probably had a precursor in north Arabia, 125.
Sacy, S. de, 79.
Sahara, once submerged, 18.
Saho language, 10.
Sale, George, 39.
Salkhad, a seat of the worship of Al-Lat, 233.
Samura, name of a tree at Nakhla, 236.
Sargon, king of Agade, 153; conquered Amorites, 146; father of Naram-Sin, 155; deified, 168; worshipped Shamash and Ishtar, 213.
Sarpanit, goddess of Babylon, spouse of Marduk, 207; name derived from sun, 209; a reflection of Marduk, 210.
Sarzec, Ernest de, 160, 180, 183, 184, 186, 187, 188, 189, 190, 191, 192, 193, 198, 207, 210, 211, 214, 218, 220, 260, 261.
Sayce, A. H., 4, 24, 102, 106, 118, 196, 197, 209, 211, 228, 232, 283.
Schaff, Philip, 317.
Scheil, V., 156, 181, 183, 184, 196, 201, 310.
Schmidt, Nathaniel, 8, 25, 272.
Schrader, Eb., 5, 28, 29, 43, 90, 102, 106, 146, 168, 214, 229, 230, 284, 285.
Schultz, H., 284.
Schürer, Emile, 318.
Schwally, Friedrich, 95, 121.
Semiramis in myth of Dekerto-Atargatis, 243.
Semites, theories of cradle land, 1 ff.; relation of language to Hamitic, 9 ff.; said to belong to black race, 16; evidence insecure, 17; one stock with Hamites, 20; home in North Africa, 21; why entered Arabia, 27, 119; racial characteristics, 28; clans, 30 ff.; totemistic, 35 ff.; economic purpose of clans, 38 ff.; family, 39 ff.; sexual propensities of, 41 ff.; *beena* marriage of, 55; polyandry of, 61 ff.; passed savagery when separated from Hamites, 73; knew date-palm, 75, n. 4; early religious conceptions, 81; sanctuaries, sacrifices, etc., 106; gathered in oases for date harvest, 111; driven to Arabia by crowding of African oases, 119; mixture of religion of, with foreign, 147 ff.; influenced Babylonian syllabary, 168,

n. 1; goddesses of, 179 ff.; at Shirpurla, Lulubi, Kish, Guti, and Agade, 186, n. 1; influence on civilization, ch. viii; both evil and good, 309 ff.; good predominates, 322.

Sennacherib, first to mention Ishtar of Arbela, 262.

Sergi, G., 8, 16, 17, 18, 20, 26, 117, 270, 312, 313.

Serpent, nature of, in Eden, 93, 96 ff.

Sex, perception of, represented as fruit of tree of knowledge, 94; what Semites attributed to knowledge of, 102; connection with moral advancement, 107; and religious feeling, 307 ff., 321 ff.

Shalmeneser II, king of Assyria, 154; called Hadad, "Bir," 227.

Shamash, god of Agade and Larsa, 212; worshipped at Agade by Sargon, 213; antiquity of, 213 ff.; originally a goddess, probably Sumerian, 214.

Shamashshumukin, Semitic idiom in Sumerian prayer of, 165.

Shams, sun goddess, a survival of the mother goddess in south Arabia, 129 ff.

Shamsu-iluna, Babylonian king, built a fortress to Ramman, 225.

Sharastani, Mohammed, 99.

Shidlamtæa, an epithet of Nergal, 215.

Shirpurla, temple taxes of, 158; dates received at, 159; city of old Babylonia, 162; held hegemony at dawn of history, 163; religion of, 184 ff.; districts of, 185; three districts Semitic, 185; language spoken at, 186 ff.; name written without determinative, 260 ff.

Sicily, Ashtart worship in, 252 ff.

Sidon, religion of, 150 ff.; Ashtart worship in, 243 ff.

Simeon, a tribe, 271.

Sin, a god, father of Mana, 199; god of Ur, *ibid.*; a transformed Ishtar, 200; identified with moon, 202; son of Enlil, *ibid.*; member of the second triad, *ibid.*; worshipped by the Guti, 217.

Sin-gamil, a king of Ur who repaired temple of Nergal, 216.

Sippar, another name of Agade, 212; Khallabi near, 260.

Skipwith, Mr., 283.

Smend, Rudolf, 140, 284.

Smith, George, 92, 197, 239, 241, 261, 262.

Smith, George Adam, 121, 139, 145, 156, 230, 238.

Smith, Henry Preserved, 89, 132, 275.

Smith, I. G., 317.

Smith, W. Robertson, 7, 29, 30, 31, 32, 35, 36, 39, 41, 51, 52, 54, 55, 57, 59, 63, 64, 65, 66, 68, 70, 76, 81, 86, 87, 88, 89, 92, 100, 101, 104, 105, 106, 107, 108, 109, 112, 114, 123, 127, 132, 133, 136, 138, 148, 152, 234, 235, 237, 251, 254, 255, 265, 267, 279, 281, 283, 287, 289, 291, 312.

Social organization, ch. ii; effect on religious conceptions, 82; transformed in Arabia by time of Mohammed, 123.

Socin, Albert, 140.

Somali language, 10.

Somalis, Somaliland, 8, 20, 24, 25, 48, 55.

Sozomen, 99.

Spencer, Herbert, 40, 53, 59, 60, 63, 66, 72.

Spiegelberg, Wilhelm, 283.

Sprenger, A., 4, 24, 44, 138.

Springs, sacred among the Semites, 92 ff.

Stade, B., 95, 121, 147, 238, 270, 275, 279, 284, 296.

Starbuck, J. M., 107.

Starcke, C. N., 40, 49, 51, 53, 59, 60, 66, 67.

Steindorf, G., 10, 247.

Steurnagle, Carl, 251.

Strabo, 42, 64, 101, 115, 123, 210, 250, 253, 313, 314, 315.

Strack, Hermann L., 275.

Strassmaier, J. N., 46, 106, 226, 260.

Stumme, H., 19.

Suess, Ed., 13, 18.

Sumerians, problem of, 164 ff.; arguments of the Halévy school, 164 ff.; counter arguments, 165 ff.; solution, 167 ff.; inventors of cuneiform writing, 167; analogy of El-Amarna letters, 167 ff.; religious argument, 168; pictorial evidence, 170; numerical system, 170 ff.; goddesses of, 180 ff.; Sumir said to be original form of Girsu, 192, n. 1; Sumerian kingdom at Nippur, 204.

Sumula-ilu, Babylonian king, witness to the early worship of Marduk, 209.

Surippak, a city mentioned in Babylonian deluge story, 259.
Suti or Guti, 37; their religion, 217 ff.

Tabari, At-, 88.
Tabernacles, feast of, 108; descended from old Semitic date festival, 111, 288 ff.
Tacitus, 250, 251, 252, 266.
Taif, south of Mecca, seat of worship of Al-Lat, 233.
Tâlab Riyâm, a south Arabian god, developed from Athtar, 129.
Tallquist, K. L., 158, 159.
Tamesheq language, 10.
Tammuz, general features of his worship, 85 ff.; various relations to Ishtar, 85; connected with vegetation, 85 ff., 86 ff., 112 ff.; origin of wailing for, 86, 92 ff., 114 ff.; festival of, originally a fast before date harvest, 112, 289; connected with Bau-Ishtar, 190; with Ningirsu, 193; bewailed at Erech, 258; survivals of, 263 ff.; nature of, 264 ff.; called in Phœnicia Eshmun and Adon, 265 ff.; connected with caravan clans, 268; in Yahwe worship, 289 ff.
Tanith, name of Semitic goddess in North Africa, 148, 150, 263; meaning and etymology of name, 253, n. 6; mother goddess, 254; same as Dido, 254 ff.; "face of Baal," 150, 254.
Tarkhu, Hittite god, held by Jensen to be original of Atargatis, 240.
Tashmit, consort and reflection of Nabu, 212.
Tell-Ibrahim, modern name of Kutha, 215.
Telloh, modern name of Shirpurla, 183.
Tertullian, 255.
Teutonic pantheon, 178.
Thatcher, Oliver, 318.
Theodulus, son of Nilus, 237.
Thibetan polyandry, 61, 63 ff.; in Yemen, *ibid.;* relation to Nair, 69 ff.
Thomas, Richard H., 82.
Threshold, sacredness of, 101 ff.
Tiele, C. P., 163, 168, 222, 223, 275.
Tiglath-pileser I, king of Assyria, 154; called Ramman, god of "west country," 226; mentioned Aramæans, 271.

Tigris, overflow of, 156.
Totem, a clan shibboleth, 33 ff.; proofs of, 35 ff.; among Hebrews, 36 ff.; neighboring tribes, *ibid.;* break up of, 63; trees as, 87; at Erech, 268.
Toy, C. H., 36, 86, 91, 95, 113, 282, 295.
Tree worship, 87 ff.; in Abyssinia, 89; in Palestine, 89 ff.; significance of, in Eden, 93–97; at Eridu, 197.
Trumbull, H. Clay, 101, 282.
Tylor, E. B., 91.
Tyre, religion of, 149 ff.; worship of Ashtart in, 244; wealth of, 300.

Umu, a name of Ishtar at Erech, 256.
Ur, city of Babylonia, 162; its dynasty, 157; its temple taxes, 158; its god, Sin, 199; held a prehistoric hegemony, 199, 256.
Ur-Bau, Patesi of Shirpurla, 153; worshipped Nana of Erim, 186; Ninâ, 188; Ea, 198; Dumuzizuab, 211; meaning of his name, 251, n. 2.
Ur-Enlil, an old Babylonian king, 204, n. 1.
Ur-Gur, king of Ur, 153, 202; repaired temple of Shamash at Larsa, 212, 256.
Urkagina, king of Ur, 153; worshipped Bau, 189, 194.
Ur-Nina, king of Shirpurla, 153; worshipped Ninâ, 188; Bau, 189; meaning of his name, 251, n. 2.
Ur-Ninib, king of Isin, 256.
Uruazagga, one of the districts of Shirpurla, 185; a Semitic settlement, 192.
Uruk, ancient name of Erech, 256.
Urzaguddu, king of Kish, 203.

Venus, Latin name of Ashtart, 249.
Virgil, 253, 255.
Vlock, W., 3, 28.
Vogüe, Comte de, 232, 233, 234, 239.

Wadd, a Minæan god, 130 ff.; name derived from root "to love," 131 ff.; developed from mother goddess, *ibid.;* consort of Athirat, 247.
Waitz, Theodor, 60.
Wallace, Alfred Russell, 15, 18, 26, 74.
Ward, Wm. Hayes, 184, 189, 194, 210.
Weber, Ferdinand, 281.
Weber, Otto, 124, 125, 130, 272.
Weeks, feast of, 108; not primitive,

GENERAL INDEX

112 ff.; adapted from Tammuz wailing preceding date festival, 113 ff.
Weissbach, F. H., 164, 168.
Wellhausen, Julius, 36, 53, 63, 68, 69, 72, 79, 88, 89, 101, 108, 109, 111, 112, 133, 134, 136, 147, 227, 233, 234, 235, 236, 237, 238, 270, 280, 281, 283, 292, 296.
Wells, sacred among Semites, 92 ff.
Wellsted, J. R., 57, 74, 75, 77, 78, 111, 285.
Westermarck, Edward, 40, 41, 49, 51, 53, 60, 66, 67.
Wheat, indigenous to Babylonia, and one of the first grains there cultivated, 157; references to it in literature, *ibid.*, n. 2.
White, H. A., 243.
White races, origin of, 15 ff.; divisions of, 16.
Whitney, J. D., 14.
Wiedemann, A., 8, 20, 26.
Wife, residence of, during marriage, 50 ff.; residence of husband in her tent or tribe, 54 ff.; subject to husband, 123.
Wildeboer, G., 272, 275.
Wilken, G. A., 39, 47, 48, 61, 63.
Wilkinson, John Gardner, 296.
Winckler, Hugo, 31, 64, 106, 109, 111, 113, 130, 162, 163, 181, 198, 199, 205, 209, 217, 227, 255, 270, 272, 274, 279, 286, 289, 296.
Winstanley, W., 49, 137.
Women, Semitic, beauty fades early, 42; of Oman, 44 ff.; lived in homes of brothers or uncles, 45 ff., 49 ff.; residence of during marriage, 50 ff.; exalted position of, 53; kept children with them, 54; not creatures of man, 56 ff.; in Babylonia, 57 ff.; position modified, 58 ff.; scarcity of, 62; liberty limited in Thibetan polyandry, 70; desert women lower order, 71; sacrifices of, in Adonis worship, 246.
Woodhouse, F. C., 317.
Wright, William, 5, 10, 24, 28, 29, 312.
Wüstenfeld, Ferdinand, 44, 235.
Wylde, Augustus B., 25, 49, 99, 136, 138.

Yaguth, Arabic lion god, 35.
Yahu-bidi, king of Hamath, 284, 285.
Yahumelek, king of Gebal, 122, 244.
Yahwe, origin of, ch. vii; a Kenite god, 272; supporters of this view, 275; name revealed at Horeb, 276; unknown to fathers, *ibid.*; home at Sinai, 277; storm god theory of Yahwe, 279; a transformed mother goddess, 280 ff., 287; etymology of name, 282 ff.; connected with palm, 286 ff.; Yahwe's passover, 287 ff.; connected with Ashtart and Tammuz, 289 ff.; spiritual possibilities of covenant with, 291, 301 ff.; became a Baal, 297 ff.; genesis of spiritual conception of, 302 ff.; connection of law with, 304 ff.
Yaqut (Jacut), 44, 63, 76, 234.
Ya'uq, Arabic horse god, 36.
Yeha, town in Abyssinia, 135 ff.
Yemen, economic condition of, 124.

Zebulon, an Israelitish clan, 271.
Zemzem, the sacred spring at Mecca, 133, 235, 236.
Zimmern, Heinrich, 10, 87, 103, 140, 165, 200, 214, 215, 260, 274.
Ziru-bani-ti, a folk etymology of the name Sarpanit, 209, n. 8.
Zohair, an Arabian poet, 52.
Zwemer, S. M., 48, 77, 78, 91, 95, 111, 124, 125, 132, 134, 159, 161.

INDEX OF SCRIPTURE REFERENCES

Genesis

Reference	Page
ii	93, 96
ii, 8	96
ii, 9	95
ii, 14	96
ii, 15	96
iii	23, 89, 93, 96
iii, 3	95
iii, 9	95
iii, 22	95
xii, 4	271
xii, 18	89
xiv, 5	142
xiv, 13	238
xvii	280
xvii, 10–12	99
xviii	140
xviii, 1	89
xix	140
xxiv	271, 278
xxiv, 2	281
xxiv, 9	281
xxv, 12 ff.	32
xxviii, 1–xxxii, 1	271, 278
xxviii, 22	290
xxxi, 43	54
xxxiv	100, 281
xxxv, 8	89
xxxvi	32
xxxviii	90, 286
xlvi, 17	31
xlvii, 29	281
xlviii, 5, 6	52
xlix, 5 ff.	272

Exodus

Reference	Page
ii, 16 ff.	280
iii, 1	280
iii, 13	276
iii, 14	283
iii, 15	276, 283
iv, 24, 25	99, 100, 280, 281
vi, 2	276
xii, 48	99, 280
xiii	279
xiv	279
xv, 27	90, 285
xviii, 12 ff.	272, 276
xix	279
xx	292
xxi, 12–14	138
xxiii, 16	288
xxxii, 2	296
xxxiv	109, 292
xxxiv, 18–20	110
xxxiv, 22 ff.	288

Leviticus

Reference	Page
xvi	305
xxiii, 34	288
xxiii, 40–43	288
xxv, 49	51

Numbers

Reference	Page
v, 11–21	305
x, 29 ff.	277
xxi, 27–30	142
xxi, 29	141
xxvi, 45	31
xxxii, 12	251

Deuteronomy

Reference	Page
i, 39	94
v	292
vii, 5	290
vii, 13	105, 282
xxiii, 17, 18	251
xxiv, 1–3	45
xxvi, 5	271
xxviii, 4, 18	282
xxxii, 17	87
xxxiii, 2	277
xxxiii, 29	249
xxxiv, 3	90, 285

INDEX OF SCRIPTURE REFERENCES

Joshua

	page
v, 3, 9	280
xiii, 21	238
xiii, 31	142
xv, 32	227, 228
xxiv, 14	276

Judges

i, 16	90, 277, 285, 288
ii, 13	246
iii, 7	247
iii, 13	90
iv, 5	89
iv, 11	277
iv, 17 ff.	277
v	57
v, 4 ff.	277
v, 24 ff.	277
vi, 11	89
vii, 25	36
x, 6	148, 246
xi, 40	289
xvi, 23	230
xx, 33	90
xx, 47	277
xxi, 13	227

1 Samuel

i	287
ii	288
vii, 4	246
xv, 6	277
xxvi, 19	297
xxx, 26 ff.	278
xxx, 29	278
xxxi, 4	280
xxxi, 9	242

2 Samuel

i, 20	280
v, 2 ff.	230
viii, 3	227

1 Kings

i	138
ii	138
viii, 9	295
viii, 10, 11	279
viii, 21	295
ix, 8	286
x, 1 ff.	124
xi, 7, 33	141
xii, 28	37, 298

	page
xv, 18–20	226
xviii, 19	247
xix	277
xx	226
xxi	300

2 Kings

iii, 4	140
v, 17	227, 299
v, 18	226
vi, 24	226
x, 15	277
xvii, 24–34	139, 147, 149, 203, 217, 297
xvii, 27, 28	299
xxii, 13	304
xxiii, 4	247, 291
xxiii, 13	151
xxiii, 14	290, 291

1 Chronicles

ii, 55	277, 278
vii, 31	31
x, 4	280

Job

xxxvii, 4	279
xxxviii, 1	279

Psalms

xviii	279
xviii, 10	91
xxix, 3 ff.	279
lxviii, 5 [4]	277
lxviii, 33	279
civ, 13, 14	279
cxlvii, 8, 16–18	279

Isaiah

i, 13–15	302, 304
v, 1–7	302
xix, 1	279
l, 1	45, 302
lxv, 11	249
lxvi, 17	36

Jeremiah

ii, 28	148
iii, 1 ff.	302
iii, 4	68
vii, 18	246
xi, 13	148
xxxv	277
xlviii, 7, 13, 46	141

INDEX OF SCRIPTURE REFERENCES

Ezekiel
	page
i	279
viii, 1	113
viii, 10	36
viii, 14	85, 246
xx	302
xxii, 11	52
xxvii	300
xxviii	300
xli, 18	90, 286

Hosea
ii	302
ii, 5	151, 297
ii, 8	298
ii, 12	151
iii, 4	290
iv, 13	89
iv, 15	298
vi, 6	304
ix, 10	144
ix, 15	298
xi, 1 ff.	306
xii, 11	298

Amos
iii, 2, 3	302
v, 4 ff.	298
v, 21 ff.	298, 304
v, 24, 25	302
vi, 13	238
vii, 14	145

Habakkuk
iii	279
iii, 1	277

Zechariah
	page
xii, 11	227

Luke
xv, 16	145

John
iv, 24	303
xvii, 23	107

Acts
xix	314

Romans
ii, 28 ff.	281
iii, 30	280

1 Corinthians
v, vi	317
x, 20	87
xiii	302

2 Peter
i, 21	307

1 John
i, 5	302
iv, 8, 16	302

Revelation
xxi	96
xxii, 1, 2	96

REFERENCES TO APOCRYPHA

Tobit
i, 5	37

Epistle of Jeremiah
42, 43	42, 210

1 Maccabees
v, 43	238
x, 83, 84	230
xi, 4	230

2 Maccabees
xii, 26	238

Ethiopic Enoch
x, 10	96
xxiv	89, 96, 286
xxv	96

Psalter of Solomon
xvii	96

REFERENCES TO QUR'AN

	PAGE		PAGE
ii, 140	132	xix, 23	89
iv	131	xix, 25	89
iv, 23	65	xxxiii, 48	46
iv, 26	64	liii	131
iv, 29	123	liii, 19	235
v, 2, 3	132	lxv, 1–6	46
v, 96–98	132	lxv, 6	50
vi, 100	36	cxii	131

www.ingramcontent.com/pod-product-compliance
Lightning Source LLC
Chambersburg PA
CBHW071227230426
43668CB00011B/1335